T0291353

# Artificial Intelligence, Engineering Systems and Sustainable Development

# Artificial Intelligence, Engineering Systems and Sustainable Development: Driving the UN SDGs

EDITED BY

**TULSI PAWAN FOWDUR**
*University of Mauritius, Mauritius*

**SATYADEV ROSUNEE**
*University of Mauritius, Mauritius*

**ROBERT T. F. AH KING**
*University of Mauritius, Mauritius*

**PRATIMA JEETAH**
*University of Mauritius, Mauritius*

AND

**MAHENDRA GOOROOCHURN**
*University of Mauritius, Mauritius*

United Kingdom – North America – Japan – India – Malaysia – China

Emerald Publishing Limited
Emerald Publishing, Floor 5, Northspring, 21-23 Wellington Street, Leeds LS1 4DL

First edition 2024

**Reprints and permissions service**
Contact: www.copyright.com

**British Library Cataloguing in Publication Data**
A catalogue record for this book is available from the British Library

ISBN: 978-1-83753-541-5 (Print)
ISBN: 978-1-83753-540-8 (Online)
ISBN: 978-1-83753-542-2 (Epub)

INVESTOR IN PEOPLE

# Contents

# List of Figures and Tables

**Chapter 10**

**Chapter 13**

**Chapter 14**

**Chapter 16**

**Chapter 17**

**Chapter 18**

# About the Editors

**Dr Tulsi Pawan Fowdur** received his BEng (Hons) degree in Electronic and Communication Engineering with first-class honours from the University of Mauritius in 2004. He was also the recipient of a Gold medal for having produced the best degree project at the Faculty of Engineering in 2004. In 2005, he obtained a full-time PhD scholarship from the Tertiary Education Commission of Mauritius and was awarded his PhD degree in Electrical and Electronic Engineering in 2010 by the University of Mauritius. He is also a Registered Chartered Engineer of the Engineering Council of the UK, Fellow of the Institute of Telecommunications Professionals of the UK and Senior Member of the IEEE. He joined the University of Mauritius as an academic in June 2009 and is presently an Associate Professor at the Department of Electrical and Electronic Engineering of the University of Mauritius. His research interests include mobile and wireless communications, multimedia communications, networking and security, telecommunications applications development, Internet of Things (IoT) and artificial intelligence (AI). He has published several papers in these areas and is actively involved in research supervision, reviewing of papers and also organising international conferences.

**Dr Satyadev Rosunee** is an Associate Professor of Applied Sustainability in the field of Textiles and Entrepreneurship at the University of Mauritius. Satyadev earned his PhD from the University of Manchester Institute of Science & Technology (UMIST, UK), Masters from Leeds University and a Bachelor of Technology degree in Textile Technology from Maharaja Sayajirao University, Baroda, India. Satyadev was Dean of the Faculty of Engineering from 2015 to 2018 and founding member of two departments namely: Department of Textile Technology (1990–2012) and Department of Applied Sustainability & Enterprise Development (2012–now). Satyadev has supervised nine PhDs, awarded by the University of Mauritius. He has published about 50 papers in peer-reviewed journals and conference proceedings. He is passionate about sustainability and entrepreneurship as drivers of innovation and social good.

**Prof Robert T. F. Ah King** holds BTech (Hons), MPhil and PhD degrees in Electrical and Electronic Engineering. He is a Professor by way of Personal Chair in Power Systems in the Department of Electrical and Electronic Engineering at the University of Mauritius. He is a Registered Professional Engineer in Mauritius and a Chartered Engineer, UK. His research interests include power systems, computational intelligence and optimisation. He is a member of the Institution of Engineers Mauritius, Institution of Engineering and Technology (IET), UK and Institute of Electrical and Electronics Engineers (IEEE), USA. Prof Ah King is the Chair of the IEEE Mauritius Section. He is a Technical Committee Member on Soft Computing of IEEE Systems, Man, and Cybernetics Society. He was the General Chair for ELECOM 2016, ELECOM 2018, ELECOM 2020 and ELECOM 2022 conferences. He has been on the Technical Programme Committees of several conferences and has served as reviewer for several leading journals.

**Dr Pratima Devi Jeetah** is an Associate Professor in the Chemical and Environmental Engineering Department of the University of Mauritius. She has a PhD degree in Bioprocess Engineering and a Master degree in Sustainable Energy Engineering from the Sweden University of KTH. She has a first-class Bachelor's degree in Chemical and Environmental Engineering and she is a gold medallist. Her research interest is in waste management/waste valorisation which particularly focuses on lignocellulosic waste conversion to bio-ethanol and on producing sustainable green functional products. She has worked on several EU/ACP/ERASMUS+ funded projects namely Small Developing Island Renewable Energy Knowledge and Technology Transfer Network (DIREKT); Lifelong Learning on Energy Access, Security and Efficiency Project (L3EAP), GEVALOR: ReSources Project, FESTII project (Formation et Enseignment Superieur pour la Transition energetique dans les territoires Insulaires at en Indianoceanie) and the EDU-ABCM project (Capacity Building on Student-Centered Energy Education in Cameroon, Ethiopia, Mauritius and Mozambique). She has also worked on numerous internally funded project namely from the UNDP, Mauritius Research and Innovation Council, Higher Education Commission and University of Mauritius funded research projects. She was the Head of the Department of Chemical and Environmental Engineering from February 2018 to February 2020. She has organised several international conferences on Energy, Environment and Climate change and workshops on eco-friendly bio material. She was also selected as one of the young emerging scientists to present her research works at the 2nd Commonwealth Chemistry Conference event in May 2023. She has published numerous scientific papers in impact factor journals. She has also published several book chapters and research papers in conference proceedings. Her publications can be viewed under the following Google Scholar link https://scholar.google.com/scholar?hl=en&as_sdt=0%2C5&q=pratima+jeetah&oq=pratima.

**Dr Mahendra Gooroochurn** works as a Senior Lecturer in the Mechanical and Production Engineering Department of the University of Mauritius. He is a Chartered Engineer registered with the Engineering Council of UK, an accredited green building design and construction professional registered with the USGBC, an Edge Expert registered with the International Finance Corporation (IFC) and a WELL accredited professional registered with the International Well Building Institute (IWBI). He holds the following professional engineering memberships: MIET, MIEEE and MASHRAE. He has industry experience as research manager and head of sustainability in the building services engineering sector and has research interests in sustainability in the built environment, circular design, circular economy and climate action, in which he acts as reviewer for several journal publishers and has published book chapters, journals and conference papers. He has been the Ellen McArthur Foundation Circular Economy Pioneer for Mauritius from the British Council Sub-Saharan Arts programme and the COP26/COP27 representative of Mauritius for the Association of Commonwealth Universities (ACU) Futures Climate Research Cohort. He has organised several IEEE conferences in multidisciplinary engineering disciplines and workshops and exhibitions on sustainable development and circular economy.

# List of Contributors

| | |
|---|---|
| *Robert T. F. Ah King* | University of Mauritius, Mauritius |
| *Noushra Shamreen Amode* | University of Mauritius, Mauritius |
| *Lavesh Babooram* | University of Mauritius, Mauritius |
| *Khim Hoong Chu* | Honeychem Research, New Zealand |
| *Yasser M Chuttur* | University of Mauritius, Mauritius |
| *Zaheer Doomah* | University of Mauritius, Mauritius |
| *Tulsi Pawan Fowdur* | University of Mauritius, Mauritius |
| *Mahendra Gooroochurn* | University of Mauritius, Mauritius |
| *Visham Hurbungs* | University of Mauritius, Mauritius |
| *Neetish Hurry* | International Economics Ltd, Mauritius |
| *Pratima Jeetah* | University of Mauritius, Mauritius |
| *Deejaysing Jogee* | University of Mauritius, Mauritius |
| *Khalid Adam Joomun* | University of Mauritius, Mauritius |
| *Naraindra Kistamah* | University of Mauritius, Mauritius |
| *Samiah Mohangee* | University of Mauritius, Mauritius |
| *Ackmez Mudhoo* | University of Mauritius, Mauritius |
| *Anshu Prakash Murdan* | University of Mauritius, Mauritius |
| *Manta Devi Nowbuth* | University of Mauritius, Mauritius |
| *Vishwamitra Oree* | University of Mauritius, Mauritius |
| *Virendra Proag* | University of Mauritius, Mauritius |
| *Jean-Luc Probst* | University of Toulouse III Paul Sabatier, France |
| *Arvinda Kumar Ragen* | University of Mauritius, Mauritius |
| *Bhimsen Rajkumarsingh* | University of Mauritius, Mauritius |
| *Ramful Raviduth* | University of Mauritius, Mauritius |
| *Satyadev Rosunee* | University of Mauritius, Mauritius |

| | |
|---|---|
| *Ashven Sanghan* | University of Mauritius, Mauritius |
| *Asish Seeboo* | University of Mauritius, Mauritius |
| *Danraz Seebun* | University of Mauritius, Mauritius |
| *Yashwantraj Seechurn* | University of Mauritius, Mauritius |
| *Gaurav Sharma* | Shenzhen University, China; Shoolini University & Glocal University, India |
| *Mika Sillanpää* | University of Johannesburg, South Africa; Aarhus University, Denmark; Zhejiang Rongsheng Environmental Protection Paper Co. LTD, China; Chandigarh University, India |
| *Geeta Somaroo* | University of Mauritius, Mauritius |
| *Riaan Stopforth* | University of KwaZulu-Natal, South Africa |
| *Dinesh Surroop* | University of Mauritius, Mauritius |
| *K Tahalooa* | Mini Factory Ltd, Mauritius |
| *Roshan Unmar* | University of Mauritius, Mauritius |

# Preface

In 2015, all member states of the United Nations adopted the 2030 Agenda for sustainable development. In view of ensuring peace and prosperity in the present and future, for all people and the planet, the 2030 agenda provides a very comprehensive shared blueprint. The agenda sets forward the creation of a global partnership between all developed and developing countries, having as core objective an urgent call for action to attain the 17 Sustainable Development Goals (SDGs). From climate action to good health and well-being, 17 high level themes and 169 targets have been identified and expected to be delivered by 2030, in the United Nations' Sustainable Development Goals (SDGs). It is important that measures to end poverty and other deprivations are taken along with strategies that lead to reduction in inequalities, enhanced health and education, and the promotion of economic growth, without neglecting actions for preserving our oceans, forests and tackling climate change in general.

Development in any country is impossible if, reliable and affordable energy, safe water and sanitation, as well as telecommunication facilities, are not easily accessible. These elements are indispensable for productive growth, healthy development and allow productive industrial growth through efficient and robust transportation systems. Engineering disciplines have a crucial responsibility of forming engineers who at the most basic level should be able to implement transportation, energy and telecommunications systems, as well undertake projects on safe water and sanitation. Hence, engineers have a major role to play to support the delivery of the SDGs. Integrated and intelligent engineering solutions which can deliver robust infrastructure, sustainable energy and access to the latest communication technology are indispensable to accomplish several of these SDGs. It is also vital to bridge the digital divide, where access to the internet is still a major obstacle in several parts of the world. In order to provide the means for cohesive solutions that can achieve sustainable development, engineers will have to employ state of the art disruptive technologies such as 5G,IoT, AI, cloud computing, blockchain and 3D printing among others.

AI and machine learning techniques are now widely used in all branches of engineering to build and optimise systems, solve intractable problems and also provide AI technology with new data inputs for interpretation. The combination of AI and engineering can indeed act as a real catalyst to achieve the UN SDGs.

The main purpose of this book, therefore, is to analyse different concepts and case studies in engineering disciplines such as Chemical, Civil, Electrical, Telecommunications and Mechanical Engineering with a view to demonstrate how engineering systems and processes can leverage the power of AI to drive the UN SDGs. Such a study is of paramount importance and will be a valuable source of information for researchers, engineers and policymakers to be able to better design and adopt AI-enabled techniques in different engineering areas with a view to catalyze the achievement of the UN SDGs.

# Acknowledgements

We would first like to thank all the authors for their invaluable contributions to this edited book. We are thankful to the reviewers of the book proposal for their constructive comments and suggestions to improve the book. We are also extremely grateful to the editors and the book production team of Emerald Publishing, in particular Miss Kirsty Woods, for their excellent advice and guidance throughout this book project. Finally, we would like to thank Professor Boopen Seetanah who helped us in establishing our first contact with the Emerald team.

Chapter 1

# Advances of Artificial Intelligence in Engineering

*Tulsi Pawan Fowdur, Satyadev Rosunee, Robert T. F. Ah King, Pratima Jeetah and Mahendra Gooroochurn*

University of Mauritius, Mauritius

## Abstract

In this chapter, a general introduction on artificial intelligence (AI) is given as well as an overview of the advances of AI in different engineering disciplines, including its effectiveness in driving the United Nations Sustainable Development Goals (UN SDGs). This chapter begins with some fundamental definitions and concepts on AI and machine learning (ML) followed by a classification of the different categories of ML algorithms. After that, a general overview of the impact which different engineering disciplines such as Civil, Chemical, Mechanical, Electrical and Telecommunications Engineering have on the UN SDGs is given. The application of AI and ML to enhance the processes in these different engineering disciplines is also briefly explained. This chapter concludes with a brief description of the UN SDGs and how AI can positively impact the attainment of these goals by the target year of 2030.

*Keywords*: AI; machine learning (ML); UN SDGs; sustainability; engineering; systems

## 1.1 Artificial Intelligence (AI)

AI refers to a subfield of computing whose aim is to equip computer systems, robotic systems or any engineering system with the ability to conduct certain tasks and exhibit reasoning faculties normally possessed by intelligent beings (Zicari, 2018). AI enables automation, manages complexity and scalability and leverages data from remote systems in real time. AI methodologies include machine learning (ML), deep learning (DL), optimisation theory, game theory and

Artificial Intelligence, Engineering Systems and Sustainable Development, 1–13
doi:10.1108/978-1-83753-540-820241001

meta-heuristics (Russell & Norvig, 2020). DL and ML are most commonly used in engineering systems (Fowdur et al., 2021).

### 1.1.1 Definition and Types of AI

The founding father of AI, Alan Turing, defines this discipline as: 'AI is the science and engineering of making intelligent machines, especially intelligent computer programs. It is usually defined as the science of making computers do things that require intelligence when done by humans' (Copeland, 2000; Deloitte, 2018). There are two main classifications of AI, namely AI based on capabilities and AI based on functionalities.

For the classification of AI based on capabilities, there are three main types of AI as follows:

a. *Artificial Narrow Intelligence (ANI)*: ANI is limited to perform only very specific tasks that it has been trained to perform, such as, playing chess, purchasing suggestions on e-commerce site, self-driving cars, speech recognition and image recognition (Rahman, 2020). Consequently, it is often known as weak AI. It is used in most actual systems, for example, IBM's Watson supercomputer and Apple Siriis.

b. *Artificial General Intelligence (AGI)*: AGI exhibits human-like understanding and learning capabilities such as sensory-perception, good motor, natural language, creative, complex problem solving and social skills (Goertzel & Pennachin, 2007). AGI systems are currently still being researched and are yet to be deployed in practice.

c. *Artificial Super Intelligence (ASI) or Strong AI*: AI at this level can surpass human intellect and execute any task with better cognitive qualities. ASI can think, reason, solve puzzles, make judgements, plan, learn and communicate autonomously (Yampolskiy, 2017).

For the classification of AI based on functionalities, there are four main types of AI as follows (Hintze, 2016; Khan, 2021).

Reactive Machines: These forms of AI are the most fundamental, doing a single job with a specified set of rules and without memory. Both the Deep Blue system from IBM and AlphaGo from Google are instances of reactive machines.

Limited Memory: It has a short-term memory capacity and can temporarily store prior events or facts. It acquires knowledge from past events and applies it by analysing events or information. One of the most impressive applications of Limited Memory systems is autonomous vehicles.

Theory of Mind: This AI should recognise human emotions, individuals, beliefs and interact socially. It has not yet been developed and several research are currently being conducted in this field.

Self-Awareness: This AI will have its own consciousness and exhibit extraordinary intelligence, common sense, sentiments and self-awareness. It will also be fully autonomous. This is only a hypothetical concept and a lot of research remains to be done before it is actually developed (Hintze, 2016; Khan, 2021).

### 1.1.2 Categories of ML Algorithms

ML is the process of learning through the automatic detection of meaningful patterns in data. ML is useful to solve issues having tremendous complexity and adaptability (Shalev-Shwartz & Ben-David, 2014). The mathematical models of ML algorithms are mainly derived from statistical concepts (Alpaydin, 2004).

The main categories of ML algorithms are shown in Table 1.1 and defined as follows (Fowdur et al., 2021; Russell & Norvig, 2020):

a. *Supervised Learning*: It employs labelled data to develop the learning model (training process), which can be used for a classification or regression analysis. The objective of classification analysis is to assign a category label to each sample input. Regression predicts continuous values using statistical characteristics.

b. *Unsupervised Learning*: It consists of clustering and dimensionality reduction to find hidden patterns and relevant features in unlabelled data. Clustering groups samples into distinct clusters based on similarity measures. A high-dimensional data space can be reduced to a lower dimensional one via dimensionality reduction, without sacrificing too much information.

c. *DL*: DL is a subset of ML that is designed to learn autonomously without human intervention. With minimal human input, DL algorithms may readily be applied to situations and deliver extremely accurate results, even beyond human performance (Goodfellow et al., 2016). DL algorithms require the same data collection step as shallow learning but they automate the feature selection process to combine the feature selection and regression steps (Sutton et al., 2018). Algorithms perform the feature extraction independently of human inputs.

d. *Shallow Learning*: Shallow learning algorithms include three main learning steps: data collection, manual feature selection and regression. The data are characterised by pre-defined features. The feature extraction is done manually and necessitates domain knowledge of the data.

e. *Reinforcement Learning* (RL): In RL, the learners are not given instructions on the actions to perform. They train themselves through random independent actions in their training environment and are rewarded for each correctly performed action. Eventually, they are transformed into intelligent systems, capable of identifying the actions leading to the maximum reward (Sutton et al., 2018).

f. *Ensemble Learning*: In ensemble learning, many trained learners collaborate to produce a single output in response to a given input. A mechanism such as averaging is then used to integrate the results from all of the learners to provide a single, more reliable result. The rationale is that a group of decision is better than a standalone decision (Zhang & Ma, 2012).

Table 1.1. Main Categories of Machine Learning (ML) Algorithms (Fowdur et al., 2021).

| Machine Learning (ML) | Unsupervised learning | Shallow learning | Clustering:<br>• K-Means (Jordan, 2021)<br>• Hierarchical<br>• Gaussian mixture |
| | | | Dimension Reduction:<br>• Principal component analysis<br>• Isometric Mapping |
| | | Deep learning | • Restricted Boltzmann machine (Fischer & Igel, 2012).<br>• Generalised additive model |
| | Supervised learning | Shallow learning | Classification:<br>• Naïve Bayes<br>• K-nearest neighbour<br><br>Regression (Beeharry et al., 2018):<br>• Simple linear<br>• Multiple linear<br>• Polynomial |
| | | Deep learning | • Multi-layered perceptron<br>• Convolutional neural network (Khan et al., 2018) |
| | Reinforcement learning (Sutton et al., 2018) | | • Q-learning<br>• SARSA |
| | Ensemble learning (Mienye & Sun, 2022) | | • Random forest<br>• Gradient boosting machine |

### *1.1.3 Advantages of AI and ML*

AI and ML provide several advantages as summarised below (Chowdhury & Sadek, 2012; Davenport et al., 2020; Ogigau-Neamtiu, 2021; Phillips-Wren & Jain, 2006; Wuest et al., 2016).

a. *Repetitive and hazardous task automation*
   By employing intelligent process automation, recurrent and dangerous tasks are assigned to automated systems, thus enhancing efficiency, precision and adaptability, and reducing the risks.
b. *Error reduction and continuous enhancement*
   With ML and AI, algorithms are used to take decisions based on pre-collected data. The algorithms' accuracy improves as the amount of data increases, leading to error reduction and continuous improvement.
c. *Automated and faster decision support*
   Augmented decision-making processes based on AI decision models use fuzzy systems and neural networks to assist in decision support tasks such as: organising received data, integrating and visualising data, prioritising and filtering event specific relevant data, designing an optimal response, assessing and quantifying risks.
d. *Complex problem solving*
   AI is allowing complex problems including the processing of multi-dimensional and multi-variety data, and several challenges such as weather forecasting, medical diagnosis and self-driving cars, to be addressed by employing sophisticated DL models.

## 1.2 Advances of AI in Electrical, Electronic and Telecommunications Engineering

Electrical and electronic engineers design, develop and test new generations of devices and equipment in their quest for innovation. With the advent of AI, the field of electrical and electronic engineering has been empowered with nature-based methodologies to improve our everyday life. AI acts as an enabler for SDG targets by supporting the provision of energy services to the population as well as low-carbon systems. In fact, AI allows technologies like electrical autonomous vehicles and smart appliances to use demand response in the electricity sector with benefits across SDG 7 on affordable and clean energy, SDG 11 on sustainable cities and communities and SDG 13 on climate action.

The progress made in ML and natural language processing has impacted on almost every industry and area of scientific research as well as in engineering. Electrical and electronic engineers use AI to optimise systems as well as provide new insights in the development of AI technology for better interpretation. A recent example is the emergence of fully autonomous vehicles. Moreover, harnessing AI's potential can enhance the performance of a system. AI can automatically detect errors or performance degradation so that engineers can address these issues before these become critical.

AI actually refers to a system that mimics the human mind for decision-making and problem solving. Research within electrical and electronic engineering in AI have evolved over the years and can be categorised into expert systems, fuzzy logic systems, ML, artificial neural networks (ANNs) and DL. For instance, the application of AI has been quite substantial in power systems with implementations in the operation and planning of the infrastructure of the generation, transmission, distribution and utilisation of electrical energy. For example, AI is used to forecast the output of solar and wind power generation based on weather conditions and thus meet the load demand. ML has also flourished in areas of signal processing. It has enabled signal modelling, pattern recognition and inference development. With lesser noise in their inputs, the performance of Internet of Things (IoT) devices and other AI-enabled systems has greatly improved.

Led by the mobile and 5G broadband services in the IoT era, the tele-communication industry has experienced rapid growth due to the adoption of AI. Based on traffic information by region and time zone, AI enables communications service providers to build self-optimising networks. Preventive maintenance is possible for operators by using data-driven insights to monitor the state of equipment and anticipate failure based on patterns. Support requests for installation, set up, troubleshooting and maintenance can be handled by virtual assistants for customer support. A form of business process automation technology based on AI known as Robotic Process Automation can improve efficiency of billing, data entry, workforce management and order fulfilment. AI's powerful analytical capabilities can be harnessed to prevent fraud. Through smart upselling and cross-selling of their services, telecommunication companies can improve their revenue and increase their number of subscribers.

## 1.3 Advances of AI in Mechanical Engineering

Mechanical Engineering, being one of the oldest engineering disciplines, is at the core of the economic development of every nation, covering a broad range of areas such as structural design and analysis, maintenance engineering, risk management, tribology and materials engineering, thermal and energy engineering among others. With such a breadth of application areas, Mechanical Engineering, and its modern specialisation in the form of Mechatronics to cover the increasingly vital interface with electrical/electronics, software and control engineering, offer valuable tools and techniques to promote the UN SDGs. Ranging from materials innovation to develop more durable and better performance components for the broad infrastructural, biomedical, transport and aerodynamics sectors to allowing the development of material recipes for keeping materials in the loop for a circular economy, Mechanical Engineering has taken prominence in the energy sector where the thermodynamics principles govern several industrial phenomena which can be optimised to achieve energy efficiency, as a direct aid in our combat against the severe challenge of climate change. Of prime bearing for Mechanical Engineering are the following SDGs: SDG 7: Affordable and Clean Energy, SDG 9: Industry, Innovation and Infrastructure, SDG 12: Responsible Consumption and Production and SDG 13: Climate Action.

Mechanical Engineering has been at the forefront of the industrial revolution with advances in robotics and automation paving the way for the different phases of this transformation, including the Fourth Industrial Revolution pertaining to the use of data to optimise processes and resource use through the application of AI techniques. The manufacturing industry has been at the heart of our society's economic and technological growth, with a clear shift over the recent decade from mass production to product customisation to suit customer preferences, where AI algorithms have been instrumental in mapping customer requirements from online survey data into engineering specifications. The increasingly smart dimension of product lines has been made possible through a re-invention of the manufacturing sector, both from the customer end to be able to respond quickly and adequately to their preferences and from the industry's innovation and sustainability perspective to achieve resource efficiency, risk reduction and safety protocols. The use of AI in crash tests is an example of the latter. The availability of sensor data to collect states from industrial processes has enabled the development of automated fault diagnosis and predictive maintenance protocols with significant benefits with higher precision and less downtime.

The techniques provided by AI such as K-means clustering, Support Vector Machines, Principal Component Analysis and DL have been central in the management of this explosion of multidimensional and cross-disciplinary datasets in the broad manufacturing sector. In this respect, Enterprise Resource Planning (ERP) platforms are now essential digital platforms for the manufacturing industry, heavily utilising these AI techniques in trend analysis, pattern recognition and decision-making. In specific mechanical engineering sectors such as robot control, machine vision, fracture mechanics, materials innovation and fluidics to name a few, the power of AI is being harnessed to both complement and overcome the challenges of conventional theoretical and analytical methods, while serving as a basis for continual improvement through reinforcement learning. Like other sectors, Mechanical Engineering is poised to undergo fundamental AI-based changes over the next decade, with further closer linkages to other engineering and non-engineering disciplines.

## 1.4 Advances of AI in Chemical, Environmental and Energy Engineering (CEEE)

CEEE is a branch of engineering that studies the fundamental principles of energy, material and momentum transformation and reaction in order to use energy and materials more effectively, profitably and safely in industries and in the society and has proven to be a potent instrument for finding thorough solutions to a variety of environmental issues. Along with safeguarding people from harmful environmental effects like pollution, CEEE also aims at improving environmental quality, improving waste management, recycling, public health and the control of air and water pollution. CEEE has been extensively applied to typical and emerging environmental technologies such as wastewater treatment, biofiltration, anaerobic digestion among others and to develop a low carbon economy with strategies that will help society become more resilient to dangers associated with climate change. Hence, the following SDGs are directly relevant to the field of CEEE, SDG 6: Clean Water & Sanitation, SDG 7: Affordable & Clean Energy, SDG 12: Responsible Consumption & Production and SDG 13: Climate Action.

In order to achieve high-performance *t*, accurate control, optimal planning and operation scheme with the aid of ubiquitous sensing, proactive understanding, big data and automated learning, it is crucial to integrate AI technology with the CEEE sector. AI has been extensively utilised in numerous CEEE applications, including modelling, chemical process optimisation, process control, fault detection and diagnostics. AI approaches are increasingly useful nowadays due to their ease of use, generality, resilience and adaptability. Other current advances in AI in the CEEE field are reinforcement learning, statistical ML and evolutionary computation that show promise for solving a variety of problems in the chemical industry related to oil and other chemical product characterisation, decision-making, environmental perception and autonomous intelligent control. AI can be applied in chemical engineering to improve the efficiency of chemical processes such as in the petrochemical production and refining industry. The efficiency and efficacy of chemical processes can be increased by using AI to evaluate data from these processes and find trends. Additionally, chemical manufacturing can be made safer and more effective with AI to forecast the behaviour of chemical systems and make decisions based on information obtained. For instance, DL, a well-liked AI approach, has proven to be successful in identifying operation modes, fault identification and risk assessments in the refining process. As for the application of AI in the field of energy engineering, it has been reported that it is possible to use a variety of IoT components, such as sensors for light, humidity, temperature, speed, passive infrared and proximity. It is also useful for controlling heating, ventilation and air conditioning (HVAC) systems for lower energy consumption. AI can also be used to manage the power grid, predict equipment problems and improve the efficiency of power plants. In the environmental engineering sector, AI may be used to forecast environmental threats and improve the efficiency of environmental systems like in water treatment facilities, to evaluate environmental system data and find patterns that can be exploited to increase the effectiveness and efficiency of these systems. Moreover, AI can be used to forecast the carbon dioxide emissions at the global level, as well as low-cost estimates of soot and NOx emissions from the combustion of solid fuels (Jadidi et al., 2020; Jena et al., 2021).

## 1.5 Advances of AI in Civil Engineering

Civil Engineering has played an important role in the making of our modern society by offering technical solutions to the design of resilient infrastructures in various contexts, and in recent times in the engineering of sustainable solutions. The built environment is a key sector of Civil Engineering, where humans are known to spend more than 90% of their time, and hence can influence our well-being, welfare and productivity through the design choices made. Indeed, it is no surprise that the building sector has received high emphasis in sustainability agenda of nations around the world, with the promulgation of building regulations and energy codes to provide regulatory frameworks, whereas voluntary sustainability frameworks such as BREEAM, LEED, Green Star and Edge have been formulated to drive the construction industry market towards more sustainable avenues in the form of more ecological materials, better energy and water performance both during construction and operation. Therefore, of direct relevance for the Civil Engineering discipline are SDG 3: Good health and well-being, SDG 9: Industry, Innovation and Infrastructure, SDG 11: Sustainable Cities and Communities and SDG 13: Climate Action.

Some of the applications of AI in Civil Engineering include:

- Project management to reduce downtimes and prediction for timely procurement, risk analysis, modelling in structural engineering (Blake et al., 2021).
- Building information modelling, building environmental modelling, climate modelling and weather forecasting, hydraulic and hydrological modelling, flood management by predicting usage of a building project and using weather prediction algorithms to retain or empty rainwater retention systems on site (Adilkhanova et al., 2023; Zhang et al., 2022, 2023).
- Building systems control and building physics modelling (Xiao & You, 2023).
- Operational management, e.g. solid waste management through prediction of type and amount of solid waste generated (Cheah et al., 2022).
- Identification and mitigation of risks, risk control can be achieved by identifying potential hazards in the construction process and implementing measures to reduce or eliminate them (Regona et al., 2022).

## 1.6 Advances of AI in Applied Sustainability and Enterprise Development

Sustainability caught the world's attention after the publication of the Brundtland Report in 1987. The report highlighted the 'unsustainability' of current social, environmental and economic systems. The pursuit of endless economic growth, resource exploitation and unbridled production and consumption is irreversibly damaging the planet earth, which is our only home. Applied Sustainability uses an interdisciplinary approach to seek practical, workable and frugal solutions to the environmental, technological and societal challenges of the present time. The quest for sustainability in different contexts (both industry and society), circular economy, sharing economy, societal well-being, social innovation, climate change, 'for-profit' and 'not-for-profit' entrepreneurship are the fields being empowered by Applied Sustainability.

The SDGs frequently targeted are: SDG 1: No Poverty, SDG 4: Quality Education, SDG 8: Decent work & Economic growth, SDG 9: Industry, Innovation & Infrastructure, SDG 12: Responsible Consumption and Production, SDG 13: Climate Action and SDG 17: Partnerships for the goals.

There is large scope for the application of AI tools and techniques within the framework of applied sustainability, mainly in the fields of product design and textile manufacturing, an important legacy industry in Mauritius. Pattern recognition, fuzzy logic, ANNs and evolutionary algorithms have been success-fully employed in those areas and have proved to be better solutions than con-ventional mathematical or statistical models due to the high degree of non-linearity in the characteristics of the raw materials, transformation pro-cesses and end-products involved. Beginners in applied sustainability are intro-duced to the principles of AI tools and their implementation through software such as Matlab. The textile industry in Mauritius has strategically implemented AI tools to improve productivity, enable myriad forms of value addition, avoid machine down time, optimise processes and resource utilisation, smarten pre-dictive maintenance, among other potential benefits (Rosunee, 2019). One com-mon example is the use of AI in the quality inspection of products using automatic detectors of defects with in-built pattern recognition capabilities.

In the context of ongoing research, an applied sustainability research group at the University of Mauritius has recently developed an ANN that predicts the open-area of single-layer woven fabrics with better accuracy than classical theo-retical models. The back-propagation feed-forward neural network works with six inputs, namely warp sett, weft sett, warp linear density, weft linear density, number of two consecutive wefts over which warp crosses and number of two consecutive warps over which weft crosses. The network architecture comprises a hidden layer made of four neurons with log-sigmoidal transfer function and an output layer with linear function. The outcome of this work has important applications where the open area of a fibrous mass is a key design parameter. In addition, ANNs are being used in the predictive modelling of air permeability, thermal conductivity, moisture–vapour transmission and mechanical properties of fibrous materials. Evolutionary algorithms are being used for optimisation of design parameters when engaging in product design and engineering.

## 1.7 UN SDGs and AI

Sustainable development has been defined in a number of ways. However, the most cited definition is from the Brundtland Report (1987): 'Sustainable devel-opment is development that meets the needs of the present without compromising the ability of future generations to meet their own needs'.

The 17 UN SDGs were adopted by the United Nations in 2015. The SDGs provide a fairly comprehensive global roadmap for the environmental, social and economic sustainability of the planet. It is important to highlight that the 17 SDGs are interconnected and strive towards building a better future, while achieving equality and sustainability for all. The SDGs particularly emphasise that no one should be left behind. The goals uphold amongst others industrial innovation, climate action, good health and well-being and quality education, human dignity, peace and prosperity for people and the planet, now and in the foreseeable future. The SDGs explicitly call on all governments and institutions to establish structures to solve sustainable development challenges, creating enabling opportunities for the younger generation in a wide array of areas.

The education system has an important role in raising awareness of the SDGs and in teaching skills and values that lead to more sustainable behaviour. Universities, through their education and influence, may contribute directly to the achievement of a whole range of SDGs. They educate the next generation of decision-makers who will have a critical impact on the future of the planet. In addition to educating the next generation of decision-makers, which is most likely the most important factor, universities also make an important contribution to achieving the SDGs through research, public engagement and specific university policy targeting SDGs.

In an attempt to accomplish the UN SDGs, AI has the potential to be a potent tool for a circular economy and more sustainable living. It has been suggested that the existing AI capabilities could assist in resolving issues related to all 17 UN SDGs, ultimately helping hundreds of millions of people in both developed and developing nations. With AI innovation, the following SDGs can be achieved: humans will be able to use massive amounts of data to harness AI innovation and achieve ground-breaking improvements in sectors like healthcare, agriculture, education and transportation. Additionally, we are witnessing how AI-enhanced computing enables doctors to reduce medical errors, boost crop yields, customise student training and identify researchers. In many different economic domains and circumstances, AI can be utilised to control environmental changes and repercussions. Some potential applications include the integration of AI into renewable distributed electricity grids, safer supply chains, environmental control and regulation, weather forecasting and a reduction in global greenhouse gas (GHG) emissions. The Nutrition Early Warning System (NEWS) uses big data and ML to identify areas that are particularly vulnerable to food shortages, droughts and floods, as well as to rising food prices and soil erosion.

# References

Adilkhanova, I., Santamouris, M., & Yun, G. Y. (2023). Coupling urban climate modeling and city-scale building energy simulations with the statistical analysis: Climate and energy implications of high albedo materials in Seoul. *Energy and Buildings*, 290, 113092. ISSN 0378-7788. https://doi.org/10.1016/j.enbuild.2023.113092

Alpaydin, E. (2004). *Introduction to machine learning*. MIT Press.

Beeharry, Y., Fowdur, T. P., & Soyjaudah, K. M. S. (2018). Regression analysis, introduction, theory and applications in telecommunications. Chapter 3. In *Conventional and fuzzy regression: Theory and engineering applications*. Nova Science Publishers. Environmental Science, Engineering and Technology. ISBN: 978-1-53613-798-9.

Blake, R. W., Mathew, R., George, A., & Papakostas, N. (2021). Impact of artificial intelligence on engineering: Past, present and future. *Procedia CIRP*, 104, 1728–1733, ISSN 2212-8271. https://doi.org/10.1016/j.procir.2021.11.291

Cheah, C. G., Chia, W. Y., Lai, S. F., Chew, K. W., Chia, S. R., & Show, P. L. (2022). Innovation designs of industry 4.0 based solid waste management:

Machinery and digital circular economy. *Environmental Research, 213*, 113619. ISSN 0013-9351. https://doi.org/10.1016/j.envres.2022.113619

Chowdhury, M., & Sadek, A. W. (2012). Advantages and limitations of artificial intelligence. *Artificial Intelligence Applications to Critical Transportation Issues, 6.* Transportation Research Circular E-C168. https://www.researchgate.net/publication/307928959_Advantages_and_Limitations_of_Artificial_Intelligence

Copeland, J. (2000). *What is artificial intelligence?* AlanTuring.net. http://www.alanturing.net/turing_archive/pages/Reference%20Articles/What%20is%20AI.html

Davenport, T., Guha, A., Grewal, D. & Bressgott, T. (2020). How artificial intelligence will change the future of marketing. *Journal of the Academy of Marketing Science 48*, 24–42. https://doi.org/10.1007/s11747-019-00696-0

Deloitte. (2018). *Artificial intelligence white paper.* delloite.com. https://www2.deloitte.com/content/dam/Deloitte/nl/Documents/deloitte-analytics/deloitte-nl-data-analytics-artificial-intelligence-whitepaper-eng.pdf

Fischer, A., & Igel, C. (2012). An introduction to restricted Boltzmann machines. In *Progress in pattern recognition, image analysis, computer vision, and applications. CIARP 2012* (Vol. 7441). Springer.

Fowdur, T. P., Babooram, L., Nazir Rosun, M. N. I., & Indoonundon, M. (2021, July). *Real-time cloud computing and machine learning applications.* Nova Science Publishers. 978-1-53619-813-3. Computer Science, Technology and Applications Book Series.

Goertzel, B., & Pennachin, C. (2007). *Artificial general intelligence* (1st ed.). Springer.

Goodfellow, I., Bengio, Y., & Courville, A. (2016). *Deep learning* (pp. 1–2). MIT Press.

Hintze, A. (2016). *Understanding the four types of artificial intelligence.* govtech.com. https://www.govtech.com/computing/understanding-the-four-types-of-artificial-intelligence.html

Jadidi, M., Kostic, S., Zimmer, L., & Dworkin, S. B. (2020). An artificial neural network for the low-cost prediction of soot emissions. *Energies, 13*, 4787.

Jena, P. R., Managi, S., & Majhi, B. (2021). Forecasting the CO2 emissions at the global level: A multilayer artificial neural network modelling. *Energies, 14*, 6336. [CrossRef].

Jordan, J. (2021). Grouping data points with k-means clustering). [Online]. https://www.jeremyjordan.me/grouping-data-points-with-k-means-clustering

Khan, H. (2021). *Types of AI | Different types of artificial intelligence systems.* https://fossguru.com/types-of-ai-different-types-of-artificial-intelligence-systems.9.50. https://www.researchgate.net/publication/355021812_Types_of_AI_Different_Types_of_Artificial_Intelligence_Systems_fossgurucomtypes-of-ai-different-types-of-artificial-intelligence-systems#fullTextFileContent

Khan, S., Rahmani, H., Shah, S., & Bennamoun, M. (2018). *A guide to convolutional neural networks for computer vision.* Morgan & Claypool. ISBN: 978-3-031-01821-3. https://link.springer.com/book/10.1007/978-3-031-01821-3

Mienye, D., & Sun, Y. (2022). A survey of ensemble learning: Concepts, algorithms, applications, and prospects. *IEEE Access, 10*, 99129–99149. https://doi.org/10.1109/ACCESS.2022.3207287

Ogigau-Neamtiu, F. (2021). The advantages of integrating artificial intelligence in business processes. *Journal of Defense Resources Management, 12*(1). (22)/2021.

Phillips-Wren, G., & Jain, L. (2006). Artificial intelligence for decision making. In *International Conference on Knowledge-Based and Intelligent Information and Engineering Systems* (Vol. 4252, pp. 531–536). KES 2006. Lecture Notes in Computer Science. https://doi.org/10.1007/11893004_69

Rahman, W. (2020). *AI and machine learning* (p. 11). SAGE Publications India Pvt Ltd.

Regona, M., Yigitcanlar, T., Xia, B., & Li, R. Y. M. (2022). Opportunities and adoption challenges of AI in the construction industry: A PRISMA review. *Journal of Open Innovation: Technology, Market, and Complexity, 8*(1), 45. ISSN 2199-8531. https://doi.org/10.3390/joitmc8010045

Rosunee, S. (2019). Leveraging artificial intelligence to foster innovation and inclusive growth in the textile value chain. In V. Midha & A. Mukhopadhyay (Eds.), *Recent trends in traditional and technical textiles*. Springer. ISBN 978-981-15-9994-1.

Russell, S. J., & Norvig, P. (2020). *Artificial intelligence – A modern approach* (4th ed.). Pearson Series in Artificial Intelligence. ISBN: 978-0134610993.

Shalev-Shwartz, S., & Ben-David, S. (2014). *Understanding machine learning*. Cambridge University Press.

Sutton, R., Bach, F., & Barto, A. (2018). *Reinforcement learning: An introduction* (2nd ed.). MIT Press. ISBN: 978-0-262-19398-6.

Wuest, T., Weimer, D., Irgens, C., & Klaus-Dieter, T. (2016). Machine learning in manufacturing: Advantages, challenges, and applications. *Production & Manufacturing Research, 4*(1). https://doi.org/10.1080/21693277.2016.1192517

Xiao, T., & You, F. (2023). Building thermal modeling and model predictive control with physically consistent deep learning for decarbonization and energy optimization. *Applied Energy, 342*, 121165. ISSN 0306-2619. https://doi.org/10.1016/j.apenergy.2023.121165

Yampolskiy, R. (2017). *Artificial super intelligence*. CRC Press.

Zhang, F., Chan, A. P. C., Darko, A., Chen, Z., & Li, D. (2022). Integrated applications of building information modeling and artificial intelligence techniques in the AEC/FM industry. *Automation in Construction, 139*, 104289. ISSN 0926-5805. https://doi.org/10.1016/j.autcon.2022.104289

Zhang, C., & Ma, Y. (2012). *Ensemble machine learning* (1st ed.). Springer US.

Zhang, L., Qin, H., Mao, J., Cao, X., & Fu, G. (2023). High temporal resolution urban flood prediction using attention-based LSTM models. *Journal of Hydrology, 620*(Part B), 129499. ISSN 0022-1694. https://doi.org/10.1016/j.jhydrol.2023.129499

Zicari, R. (2018). *Explorations in artificial intelligence and machine learning freebook*. CRC Press, Taylor and Francis Group. https://www.routledge.com/rsc/downloads/AI_FreeBook.pdf

Part 1

# Impact of AI-Enabled Chemical and Environmental Engineering Systems on UN SDGs

Chapter 2

# Adoption of Machine Learning for Sustainable Solid Waste Management

*Pratima Jeetah, Geeta Somaroo, Dinesh Surroop,*
*Arvinda Kumar Ragen and Noushra Shamreen Amode*

University of Mauritius, Mauritius

## Abstract

Currently, Mauritius is adopting landfilling as the main waste management method, which makes the waste sector the second biggest emitter of greenhouse gas (GHG) in the country. This presents a challenge for the island to attain its commitments to reduce its GHG emissions to 30% by 2030 to cater for SDG 13 (Climate Action). Moreover, issues like eyesores caused by littering and overflowing of bins and low recycling rates due to low levels of waste segregation are adding to the obstacles for Mauritius to attain other SDGs like SDG 11 (Make Cities & Human Settlements Inclusive, Safe, Resilient & Sustainable) and SDG 12 (Guarantee Sustainable Consumption & Production Patterns). Therefore, together with an optimisation of waste collection, transportation and sorting processes, it is important to establish a solid waste characterisation to determine more sustainable waste management options for Mauritius to divert waste from the landfill. However, traditional waste characterisation is time consuming and costly. Thus, this chapter consists of looking at the feasibility of adopting machine learning to forecast the solid waste characteristics and to improve the solid waste management processes as per the concept of smart waste management for the island of Mauritius in line with reducing the current challenges being faced to attain SDGs 11, 12 and 13.

*Keywords*: Solid waste characterisation; smart solutions; waste sector; waste collection; sustainable waste management; landfill

Artificial Intelligence, Engineering Systems and Sustainable Development, 17–28
Copyright © 2024 Pratima Jeetah, Geeta Somaroo, Dinesh Surroop, Arvinda Kumar Ragen and
Noushra Shamreen Amode
Published under exclusive licence by Emerald Publishing Limited
doi:10.1108/978-1-83753-540-820241002

## 2.1 Introduction

Due to the rising volumes of garbage being produced each year, solid waste management (SWM) poses a serious obstacle to the sustainable development of both emerging and established nations. Solid waste disposal at Mare Chicose landfill in Mauritius has increased overall by 20.9% during the last 10 years, totalling 1,373 tons of solid trash each day, which is shortening the landfill's lifespan (Statistics Mauritius, 2021). The economic expansion, population growth and higher standard of life are the key causes of this increase in garbage output, which is posing problems for Mauritius since its only sanitary landfill is reaching saturation. This is causing consternation for the policymakers since along with the challenge of lack of land space for a potential new landfill, they are faced with the trial to find sustainable ways to cater for the large amounts of solid wastes being generated (MOESWMCC, 2019). Also, littering and lack of timely waste collection due to overflowing of bins (Nancoo, 2020) leads to eyesores in the island and implies that some waste end up in the environment instead of at a controlled facility for waste management despite the efforts of the government to ensure maximum waste collection which lead to high transportation and collection costs (MOESWMCC, 2019). These challenges are related to target 11.6 of SDG 11, and more specifically to the indicator 11.6.1, which aims to measure the amount of municipal solid waste (MSW) which is collected and managed in controlled facilities in relation to overall amount of MSW generated (UN, 2023). The government must thus ensure that by 2030, the majority of MSW is managed in a controlled facility, taking into account that there might not be enough space in the existing landfill to accommodate the large amounts of waste projected to be generated in 2030.

Further, the solid waste sector is the second largest GHG emitter in Mauritius due to the landfilling method which causes methane generation (Statistics Mauritius, 2021). Thus, through the adoption of alternative waste management scenarios which focus on diversion of waste from landfilling, Mauritius might increase its ability to attain the goal set to reduce its total GHG emissions by 30% by 2030 in line with SDG 13, and more precisely indicator 13.2.2 of target 13.2, which measures the annual GHG emissions (UN, 2023).

To establish sustainable waste management strategies that would be compliant to the Mauritian context and to address the challenges to attain SDG targets 11.6 and 13.2, together with an optimisation of waste collection and transportation processes, national waste characterisation studies are needed to ascertain the composition of MSW. By diverting various waste streams from the single landfill, the waste management authorities as well as the government will be able to evaluate the potential for waste materials that can be recovered, find out the waste generation sources, design equipment for the processing of waste more easily, evaluate the chemical, physical as well as the thermal properties of the wastes and ensure compliance with regulations. However, waste characterisation is time consuming and costly. But, since waste composition keeps on evolving with time, it is important to have an up-to-date characterisation study to recognise the proper valorisation techniques for the diverse waste streams instead of opting for landfilling.

Another issue faced in the waste sector is low recycling rates, which demonstrates that Mauritius has mostly a linear economic system (MOESWMCC, 2019), hence presenting an obstacle for Mauritius to attain SDG 12, especially target 12.5 which is to significantly reduce the amount of waste generated via prevention, reduction, recycling and reuse (UN, 2023). To address this issue, the Ministry of Environment, Solid Waste Management and Climate Change (MOESWMCC) has proposed the erection of Civic Amenity Centres and Material Recovery Facilities (MRF) to increase waste sorting and recycling and to deploy educational campaigns related to sustainable waste management to encourage recycling. Two Civic Amenity Centres (CAC) are already operational in the island, but the MRFs have not yet materialised (MOESWMCC, 2022). However, in spite of the implementation of CACs, source-segregation rates are still very low since it will take time for the sensitisation campaigns related to waste sorting and recycling to become effective as it involves a change in mindset related to the throw-away culture (MCCI, 2022).

A means to tackle the aforementioned challenges might be through the utilisation of smart waste management methods. Modern solutions, through the use of smart devices and technologies, have already started to being deployed for rendering the task of SWM more efficient (Namoun et al., 2022). Smart waste management involves the adaptation of traditional waste management using technology and automation to reduce time and optimise resource use and to enhance productivity (Fayomi et al., 2021).

Some applications include, enabling the collection of large amounts of data which in turn allows the usage of artificial intelligence (AI) and machine learning (ML) to predict waste generation patterns (Namoun et al., 2022) and assisting in the identification of several types of waste, hence aiding in waste segregation (Cheema et al., 2022). Another example of a form of technology used includes the Internet of Things (IoT), which enables human to human and human to computer interactions through the use of sensors, systems of data acquisition, pre-processing and edge analytics and finally cloud analytics (Dhana et al., 2019). The system of IoT is applied to implement the concept of 'smart bins', which enables the tracking of locations of the bins and through the use of sensors, enable the relevant stakeholders to determine the extent to which the bins are filled through information exchange via the internet (Yadav et al., 2021) in order to help in making decisions related to waste collection to prevent overflowing of bins and potentially save fuel. IoT also enables temperature monitoring through thermal sensors (Dhana et al., 2019) which can be useful to ensure safety by sending alarms in case of emergencies like waste catching fire (IoT Solutions Group, n.d.). Other technologies used comprise of spatial systems like Geographic Information Systems (GIS) (Gutierrez et al., 2015) and Global Positioning System (GPS) (Hidalgo-Crespo et al., 2022) which assist in data collection based on the location and identification technologies like radio frequency identification (RFID) (Fayomi et al., 2021) which allows the measurement of the mass of the waste components together with the identification of each waste type in the bin during collection.

Nonetheless, such methods of smart waste management are still at their infancy stages (Namoun et al., 2022) and even if some of these methods have already been deployed in some regions of the world, further research is required to explore the level to which these can be implemented successfully, especially, in developing countries like Mauritius. Thus, this chapter explores the different types of smart technologies that can be applied and adopted in Mauritius to render the task of SWM more effective and sustainable, in line with the government's vision to make smart cities a reality in Mauritius and to divert waste from the landfill by focusing on waste recovery and recycling (MOESWMCC, 2022).

## 2.2 Smart Waste Management Technologies for Waste Characterisation

This section explores the different types of existing technologies that can be used in Mauritius for the purpose of making waste characterisation less time consuming and more cost-efficient.

A waste characterisation at national level can be undertaken for attaining different aims which include the evaluation of potential environmental impacts associated with the waste during disposal, for understanding types of stabilisation methods or treatment methods for the waste or for administrative purposes, to prevent errors in placement of wastes by authorities and landfill operators. During the waste characterisation process, essentially, representative samples of waste are taken and sorted into different groups (waste types) and various laboratory tests are conducted in order to determine the chemical and physical characteristics of the waste. This enables the determination of the different types of waste being generated (organic [food waste, yard waste], inorganic [plastic, paper, metals, glass, etc.], hazardous, non-hazardous together with the proportion of each type of waste being generated). Other useful information gathered during the process comprise of the moisture content, ash content and the calorific value of the waste, which can be deterministic to assess the recovery potential of waste and determine which techniques of waste management can be deployed to manage the waste in a sustainable manner.

The traditional method for national waste characterisation is time-consuming and requires extensive deployment of financial and human resources to manually sort the waste and perform laboratory analysis. To save on resource utilisation and optimise the waste characterisation process, several technologies can be employed (Namoun et al., 2022), such as, infrared spectroscopy, Xray, sonar techniques and computer vision to aid in the sorting stage (Tao et al., 2019).

Infrared spectroscopy can be employed to characterise waste in terms of their physico-chemical properties like elemental composition which can thereafter be linked to the calorific value of waste. This technique can also be utilised to distinguish between different types of waste and is particularly useful to differentiate between different types of plastics in commingled waste (Zheng et al., 2018). This is possible since infrared spectroscopy is based on the absorption of infrared light which depends on the type of molecular bonding (Tao et al., 2019). Tao et al. (2019) have used this technique in conjunction with ML to determine the heating value and elemental composition in terms of carbon, hydrogen and oxygen content of waste which demonstrated the feasibility of this methodology to characterise waste. However, one limitation is that it takes more time for the identification of dark-coloured plastics due to low signal to noise ratio (Zinchik et al., 2021).

X-ray and sonar techniques are also used for the purpose of waste identification, but are based on the physical characteristics of the waste as opposed to infrared spectroscopy which relies on the chemical characteristics of the waste. These techniques use a database which contains information about the different shapes of waste and during the characterisation process, several types of cameras are used to visualise the shapes of the waste in the commingled waste pile and the system matches the waste shape from the pile to the shapes stored in the database to identify and sort the different waste types. The drawback with these methods is that they are highly prone to errors since wastes of different types can have the same shape and has thus limited applications (Wang et al., 2019).

Another way to assist in waste characterisation through technology is by using ML, which is a branch of AI, to predict waste generation patterns as well as identification of waste characteristics. One such method is through the use of images as data to feed into a system of ML to enable the system to distinguish between different types of waste. Shaikh et al. (2020) used this method to differentiate between bio-degradable and non-biodegradable fractions in commingled waste. Shaikh et al. (2020) developed a mobile application through which an image of the waste can be taken and sent to a web server after which different algorithms analyse the data to generate an output on the type of waste contained in the image. To enable more advanced waste characterisation, ML coupled with other techniques like infrared spectroscopy can be employed which has been undertaken by Tao et al. (2019) as mentioned previously. Utilisation of ML for predicting patterns of waste generation which are useful in the development of waste management strategies can be done through models like Support Vector Machine (SVM), artificial neural network (ANN), random forest regression, gradient boost regression tree, adaptive neuro-fuzzy inference system (ANFIS) amongst others (Lu et al., 2022).

The drawback with ML is that a large amount of data still has to be collected initially to be fed into the system and a powerful system is required for data storage (Solla, 2022). This also implies that manpower is still required for gathering data to be fed into the system and human intervention is crucial at the development phase to define and interpret the data (Solla, 2022). The data fed into the system should be as accurate as possible, otherwise, the concept of 'garbage-in, garbage-out' which essentially implies that poor data quality will lead to poor output from the technology being used, is unavoidable. The environmental impacts associated with AI should also not be overlooked since training a modern neural network is highly carbon intensive (Dodge et al., 2022) and hence might make the achievement of SDG 13 more challenging.

For the case of Mauritius, the use of technologies for waste characterisation might require more in-depth investigation, through the development of specific algorithms based on the characteristics of the local waste management scenario. More modular and compact infrared systems which are generally less costly as compared to near infrared spectroscopy can be applied for large scale waste characterisation in Mauritius (Mallet et al., 2021), however, a cost analysis should be undertaken since the manual characterisation followed by laboratory analysis, albeit more time consuming, might prove to be less costly for the case of Mauritius. As far as the prediction of waste generation patterns using ML is concerned, it has been reported that the hardware associated with its use are costly and lack seamless integration (Namoun et al., 2022). Thus, for a developing nation like Mauritius, for the waste characterisation stage, the traditional method might prove more beneficial as compared to the use of smart technologies. However, to reach a deterministic conclusion, future in-depth studies into the feasibility of smart waste management techniques for the purpose of waste characterisation are required, taking into account their economic, environmental as well as social impacts for the case of Mauritius specifically.

## 2.3 Smart Waste Management Technologies for Waste Collection and Transport

The municipal waste collection process involves collecting the waste from the point of generation or from the point of disposal by waste generators. There are several types of waste collection techniques, namely, collection from community containers (bins located in specific places wherein people put their waste for being later collected by refuse collection vehicles at frequent intervals), block collection system (refuse trucks travelling a predetermined route at specific intervals emit an audio signal to alert people to bring their bins to the trucks whereby the waste collectors empty the waste and return the bins), kerbsite collection (people leave their filled waste containers at the side of the road for the waste collectors to collect on specific days and back door collection (people store their waste in their yards and the waste collectors enter the yards to empty the bins into the refuse trucks. In Mauritius, the kerbsite collection method is used together with collection from community containers. One of the challenges that Mauritius faces with regards to waste collection is the overflowing of bins (Nancoo, 2020) which brings about several environmental nuisances like odour generation together with being an eyesore.

The waste transportation process comprises of transporting the collected waste to transfer stations and/or final disposal sites or treatment plants for waste recovery. In developing nations like Mauritius, the waste transportation process is fuel intensive and costly. The MOESWMCC (2019) of Mauritius reports that annually, a total cost of about 1.5 billion Mauritian Rupees is incurred for waste collection, transfer and disposal out of which 1 billion Mauritian Rupees is for waste collection only, which is considered to be high.

The smart technologies that are useful for the waste collection and transport processes comprise mostly of spatial systems like GIS, GPS among others coupled with IoT and sensor technologies. GIS allows the localisation of GPS households which have been previously identified and then can attribute information related to the weight of waste to them (Hidalgo-Crespo et al., 2022). This technique enables the effective storage of geo-referenced data for retrieval, analysis and display via GIS based on specifications defined by the user. This allows for better planning for waste collection routes which can avoid the issues related to over-flowing of bins and can also help to save fuel by determining the shortest route to take to collect the waste (Cheema et al., 2022). The basic functioning of such a system includes attaching an ultrasonic level sensor to the bins which uses the internet to send these data to a server for storage and processing which includes the use of ML and algorithms to determine the optimum route for waste collection, the output is then sent to the waste collectors in visual form through devices like mobile phones so that the driver can take the shortest route to reach the waste bins (Dhana et al., 2019). Spatial systems like GPS fitted to the truck can be used to collect additional data for the determination of traffic flow that can be employed by the ML system to further optimise collection routes (Gutierrez et al., 2015). Studies on the deployment of such technologies show significant cost savings in Norway (Nasar et al., 2020) and fuel and time savings in Pakistan.

Thus, such technologies might prove to be beneficial for Mauritius to cater for the issues faced with regards to overflowing of bins and saving of transportation costs during the waste collection process, especially for community containers. To enable the proper deployment of such a system in Mauritius, the characteristics of the Mauritian society needs to be taken into account, for instance, the types of roads, the traffic and the locations and types of the community bins (Nasar et al., 2020).

## 2.4 Smart Waste Management Technologies for Waste Segregation and Recovery

Waste segregation involves the process of sorting waste into different fractions (organic, plastic, paper, metal, glass) for the purpose of waste recovery through recycling, composting or waste-to-energy.

There are existing technologies that are already being deployed for waste sorting. One such technology is infrared as discussed earlier in the waste char-acterisation section. For waste sorting, infrared is more suitable since only sep-aration based on waste type is required. As previously mentioned, the challenge with the use of infrared is that its use is limited with dark coloured materials (Zinchik et al., 2021) and to address this constraint, the infrared detector can be coupled with an X-ray fluorescence detector to identify halogens like Chlorine and Bromine or with hyperspectral imaging spectroscopy to identify the entire shape of an item (Lange, 2021). During large-scale waste segregation at MRFs, infrared detectors allow efficient and cost-effective sorting of plastic waste for the purpose of recycling and enable fewer transportation requirements as compared to source segregation.

Another waste sorting technology which involves ML consists of the use of digital watermarks on recyclable products. These watermarks comprise of codes that can be detected by camera devices on high-speed sorting lines (Lange, 2021). This can also enable consumers to use their smartphones to scan the watermark to have access to waste sorting and recycling information (for example, material type, in which colour of waste bin it should go amongst other information) and can hence prevent improper sorting of waste, which avoids waste contamination and hence makes waste recycling more efficient.

For Mauritius, the adoption of automated systems for waste sorting for recovery purposes might prove to be efficient in line with a vision for more sustainable waste management to divert waste from the landfill to attain SDGs 11, 12 and 13. Matter-of-factly, the Government of Mauritius, with financial help from the Agence Française de Développement, has undertaken the development of a Strategy and Action Plan for a novel Solid Waste Management and Resource Recovery System since 2017 (Saran, 2019). The proposed strategic action plan consists of setting up of two preliminary projects in the Western and Southern part of Mauritius which aim at launching the new system for SWM for the island. The projects will comprise of an MRF for sorting of waste which may also have a composting plant that will use only organic and yard wastes, a Sorting Unit, which will provide a platform to receive recyclables and a CAC which will cater for household wastes namely hazardous household wastes, waste oil, construction and demolition wastes as well as bulky wastes (MOESWMCC, 2019). Integration of technologies like infrared on the waste sorting lines during the pilot phase might be beneficial to provide an insight on its applicability in Mauritius and might also save resources in the long run by avoiding the deployment of human resources who will require training to sort the waste adequately.

To make waste segregation and thereafter waste recovery more effective, other forms of technologies through mobile applications can also be deployed. For instance, in Mauritius, there is an existing online platform named 'YESNO SOLUTIONS' which allows people to locate the nearest bins dedicated for the collection of recyclables (YESNO SOLUTIONS, 2023). A study conducted in Mauritius with regards to mobile applications to locate the closest recycling bins has demonstrated that this technology enhances recycling activities of its users. However, this study also showed that such technologies are more likely to be adopted by people aged between 25 and 46, with very few users among the elderly and adolescents (Jankee, 2021). This highlights one major drawback of using new technologies that involve the waste generators, which is some waste generators might lack the skills required to use these tools or might not have access to such tools.

To engage more young children in recycling, the Mauritian start-up Panda & Wolf Holdings has developed a mobile game named 'Eco-Warriors'. This game, which aims to educate children about recycling and sorting of waste, has obtained the patronage of the UNESCO (Jackson, 2020). Such tools can be useful to sensitise young children on sustainable waste management issues to aid in changing the throw-away culture and hence provide a step towards the achievement of SDG 12. However, similar to the mobile applications that locate nearest recycling bins, the issue of accessibility arises, especially for children who are at the lower end of the social ladder and may not have the luxury of owning a smartphone.

## 2.5 Schematic Representation of Smart Waste Technologies

Fig. 2.1 summarises some of the smart waste technologies and techniques that could be applied for Mauritius for waste characterisation and the different waste management stages.

## 2.6 Conclusion

This chapter provided an insight on the different types of technologies that can be deployed for the purpose of smart waste management, focusing on waste characterisation, collection and transport and finally waste sorting and recovery in an attempt to suggest the feasibility of employing such modern solutions for a developing nation like Mauritius.

It could be noted that several technologies exist for the purpose of waste characterisation, however, most of these are still at their infancy stage and require more in-depth research to enable accurate deployment to ensure that most of the existing limitations are curbed. A potential technology that can be applied for large scale waste characterisation in Mauritius might be modular and compact infrared systems. It was also found that ML for waste characterisation and for

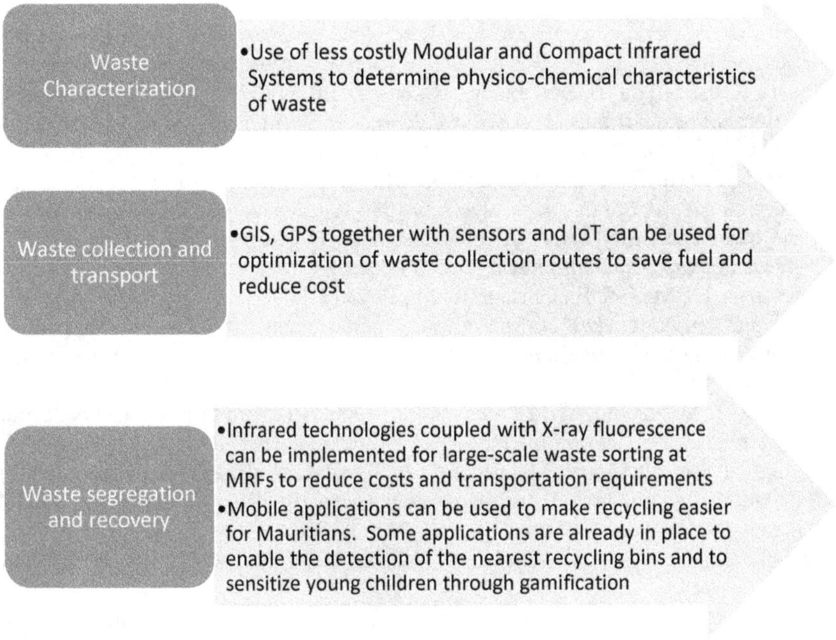

| Waste Characterization | • Use of less costly Modular and Compact Infrared Systems to determine physico-chemical characteristics of waste |
| --- | --- |
| Waste collection and transport | • GIS, GPS together with sensors and IoT can be used for optimization of waste collection routes to save fuel and reduce cost |
| Waste segregation and recovery | • Infrared technologies coupled with X-ray fluorescence can be implemented for large-scale waste sorting at MRFs to reduce costs and transportation requirements<br>• Mobile applications can be used to make recycling easier for Mauritians. Some applications are already in place to enable the detection of the nearest recycling bins and to sensitize young children through gamification |

Fig. 2.1.   Potential Applications of Smart Waste Management Techniques and Technologies.

determination of waste generation patterns requires large amounts of good quality data to be fed into the system in order to obtain accurate outputs and adequate infrastructure is needed to store the large amounts of data which together with being costly can also be carbon-intensive, especially for a developing country like Mauritius, hence defeating the purpose of using smart waste technologies to attain SDG 13. It has also demonstrated that, for waste management, like waste collection, transport, sorting and recovery, ML and other smart technologies have a strong potential to be beneficial for Mauritius. For waste collection and transport, adoption of spatial systems and IoT might enable Mauritius to reduce logistics-related costs and to prevent overflowing of refuse cans, which are some of the challenges that the island faces with regards to waste management. In view of waste sorting and recovery, it was found that a prospective utilisation of automated systems that employ infrared technology could be undertaken in the pilot MRF that the government plans to implement to attain SDGs 11 and 12. Moreover, locally devised mobile applications and online platforms are already being deployed to help Mauritians deposit their recyclables in the nearest recycling bin, and waste sensitisation for young children is being made possible through gamification on mobile phones in line with SDG 12.

## References

Cheema, S. M., Hannan, A., & Pires, I. M. (2022). Smart waste management and classification systems using cutting edge approach. *Sustainability*, *14*, 10226.

Dhana, S. K., Janani, B., Reenadevi, R., & Rajesh, R. (2019). Garbage monitoring system using smart bins. *International Journal of Scientific & Technology Research*, *8*(11).

Dodge, J., Prewitt, T., tachet Des Combes, R., odmark, E., Schwartz, R., Stubell, E., Luccioni, A. S., Smith, N. A., DeCario, N., & Buchanan, W. (2022). Measuring the carbon intensity of AI in cloud instances. In *ACM Conference on Fairness, Accountability, and Transparency (ACM FAccT)*.

Fayomi, G. U., Mini, S. E., Chisom, C. M., Fayomi, O. S. I., Udoye, N. E., Agboola, O., & Oomole, D. (2021). Smart waste management for smart city: Impact on industrialization. *IOP Conference Series: Earth and Environmental Science*, *655*, 012040.

Gutierrez, J. M., Jensen, M., Henius, M., & Riaz, T. (2015). Smart waste collection system based on location intelligence. *Procedia Computer Science*, *61*, 120–127.

Hidalgo-Crespo, J., Álvarez-Mendoza, C. I., Soto, M., & Amaya-Rivas, J. L. (2022). Quantification and mapping of domestic plastic waste using GIS/GPS approach at the city of Guayaquil. *Procedia CIRP*, *105*, 86–91.

IoT Solutions Group. (n.d.). What is the IoT? [online]. https://www.iotsg.co.uk/about/?cookies=allow

Jackson, T. (2020). *Mauritian startup aims to encourage recycling with UNESCO-backed eco-game*. [online]. https://disrupt-africa.com/2020/01/13/mauritian-startup-aims-to-encourage-recycling-with-unesco-backed-eco-game/

Jankee, K. (2021). Enhancement of polyethylene terephthalate bottles recycling in Mauritius through the creation of a mobile application. *European Journal of Sustainable Development, 10*(3), 27.

Lange, J.-P. (2021). Managing plastic waste—Sorting, recycling, disposal, and product redesign. *ACS Sustainable Chemistry & Engineering, 9*(47), 15722–15738.

Lu, W., Huo, W., Gulina, H., & Pan, C. (2022). Development of machine learning multi-city model for municipal solid waste generation prediction. *Frontiers of Environmental Science & Engineering, 16*(9).

Mallet, A., Pérémé, M., Awhangbo, L., Charnier, C., Roger, J. M., Steyer, J. P., Latrille, É, & Bendoula, R. (2021). Fast at-line characterization of solid organic waste: Comparing analytical performance of different compact near infrared spectroscopic systems with different measurement configurations. *Waste Management, 126*, 664–673.

MCCI. (2022). *The MCCI roadmap for a waste plastic free Mauritius.*

MOESWMCC. (2019). *La Gestion Des Dechets.*

MOESWMCC. (2022). *Strategy and action plan on resource recovery and recycling.*

Namoun, A., Tufail, A., Khan, M. Y., Alrehaili, A., Syed, T. A., & BenRhouma, O. (2022). Solid waste generation and disposal using machine learning approaches: A survey of solutions and challenges. *Sustainability, 14*, 13578.

Nancoo, H. (2020). *Pays sous les ordures: le service de voirie doit reprendre ses droits.* [online]. https://lexpress.mu/article/367692/pays-sous-ordures-service-voirie-doit-reprendre-droits

Nasar, W., Karlsen, A. T., Hameed, I. A., & Dwivedi, S. (2020). An optimized IoT-based waste collection and transportation solution: A case study of a Norwegian municipality. In *Conference: 3rd International Conference on Intelligent Technologies and Applications INTAP 2020, At: Gjøvik, Norway.*

Saran, T. P. (2019). *Waste disposal: Bold decisions necessary.* [online]. http://www.mauritiustimes.com/mt/waste-disposal-bold-decisions-necessary-2/

Shaikh, F., Kazi, N., Khan, F., & Thakur, Z. (2020). *IEEE 2020 Second International Conference on Inventive Research in Computing Applications (ICIRCA)- Waste Profiling and Analysis using Machine Learning* (pp. 488–492).

Solla, D. G. (2022). *Advanced waste classification with machine learning.* [online]. https://towardsdatascience.com/advanced-waste-classification-with-machine-learning-6445bff1304f

Statistics Mauritius. (2021). [online]. https://statsmauritius.govmu.org/Documents/Statistics/ESI/2022/EI1667/Env_Stats_Yr21_%20280722.pdf

Tao, J., Liang, R., Li, J., Yan, B., Chen, G., Cheng, Z., Li, W., Lin, F., & Hou, L. (2019). Fast characterization of biomass and waste by infrared spectra and machine learning models. *Journal of Hazardous Materials, 387.*

UN. (2023). *Make the SDGs a reality.* [online]. https://sdgs.un.org/#goal_section

Wang, Z., Peng, B., Huang, Y., & Sun, G. (2019). Classification for plastic bottles recycling based on image recognition. *Waste Management (Tucson, Arizona), 88,* 170–181.

Yadav, H., Umang, S., & Kumar, G. (2021). *Analysing challenges to smart waste management for a sustainable circular economy in developing countries: A fuzzy DEMATEL study.* Smart and Sustainable Built Environment.

YESNO SOLUTIONS. (2023). [online]. https://www.yesnosolutions.org/

Zheng, Y., Bai, J., Xu, J., Li, X., & Zhang, A. (2018). A discrimination model in waste plastics sorting using NIR hyperspectral imaging system. *Waste Management*, *72*, 87–98.

Zinchik, S., Jiang, S., Friis, S., Long, F., Høgstedt, L., Zavala, V. M., & Bar-Ziv, E. (2021). Accurate characterization of mixed plastic waste using machine learning and fast infrared spectroscopy. *ACS Sustainable Chemistry & Engineering*, *9*(42), 14143–14151.

Chapter 3

# Smart Fertilizer Application in Agricultural Land for Sustainable Crop Production and Consumption

*Robert T. F. Ah King, Bhimsen Rajkumarsingh, Pratima Jeetah, Geeta Somaroo and Deejaysing Jogee*

University of Mauritius, Mauritius

## Abstract

There is an urgent need to develop climate-smart agrosystems capable of mitigating climate change and adapting to its effects. Conventional agricultural practices prevail in Mauritius, whereby synthetic chemical fertilizers, pesticides and insecticides are used. It should be noted that Mauritius remains a net-food importing developing country of staple food such as cereals and products, roots and tubers, pulses, oil crops, vegetables, fruits and meat (FAO, 2011). In Mauritius, the agricultural sector faces extreme weather conditions like drought or heavy rainfall. Moreover, to increase the crop yields, farmers tend to use 2.5 times the prescribed amount of fertilizers in their fields. These excess fertilizers are washed away during heavy rainfall and contaminate lakes and river waters. By using smart irrigation and fertilization system, a better management of soil water reserves for improved agricultural production can be implemented. Soil Nitrogen, Phosphorus and Potassium (NPK) content, humidity, pH, conductivity and moisture data can be monitored through the cloud platform. The data will be processed at the level of the cloud and an appropriate mix of NPK and irrigation will be used to optimise the growth of the crops. Machine learning algorithms will be used for the control of the land drainage, fertilization and irrigation systems and real time data will be available through a mobile application for the whole system. This will contribute towards the Sustainable Development Goals (SDGs): 2 (Zero Hunger), 11 (Sustainable cities and communities), 12 (Responsible consumption and production) and 15 (Life on Land). With this project, the yield of crops will be boosted, thus reducing the hunger rate

Artificial Intelligence, Engineering Systems and Sustainable Development, 29–41
Copyright © 2024 Robert T. F. Ah King, Bhimsen Rajkumarsingh, Pratima Jeetah, Geeta Somaroo and Deejaysing Jogee
Published under exclusive licence by Emerald Publishing Limited
doi:10.1108/978-1-83753-540-820241003

(SDG 2). On top of that, this will encourage farmers to collect the waters and reduce fertilizer consumption thereafter sustaining the quality of the soil on which they are cultivating the crops, thereby increasing their yields (SDG 15).

*Keywords*: Smart; fertilization; irrigation; drainage; land; agriculture

## 3.1 Introduction

The demand for food is increasing as the world's population grows and as people's diets change. Crop yields are steadily declining, making it difficult for food supply to keep up with the demand. Agriculture's acute vulnerability as a result of climate change exacerbates this. As a result, adopting climate-smart agrosystems is more vital than ever, as it provides the following benefits: (i) increase in productivity so as to improve nutrition security and increase income through the production of more and better food, (ii) increased resiliency in order to reduce the likelihood of drought, pests, illnesses and other climate-related hazards and shocks and (iii) decrease in emissions per kilogram of food produced while avoiding agricultural deforestation, and finding ways to absorb carbon from the atmosphere (The World Bank Group, 2021).

In Mauritius, about 90% of land under cultivation is dedicated to sugarcane cultivation (52,387 ha), while the remaining land is devoted to food crops (8,137 ha) and tea cultivation (574 ha) (MOAIAFS, 2016). Vegetable cultivation represents about 17% of the agricultural sector in the Mauritian Gross Domestic Product (GDP) (MOAIAFS, 2020). The food crop production is mainly governed by small farmers covering a wide range of crops including potatoes, onion, tomatoes, chillies, leafy vegetables, garlic, ginger, crucifers and cucurbits, which are cultivated for commercialisation. Conventional agricultural practices prevail in Mauritius, whereby synthetic chemical fertilizers, pesticides and insecticides are used. It should be noted that Mauritius remains a net-food importing developing country of staple food such as cereals and products, roots and tubers, pulses, oil crops, vegetables, fruits and meat (FAO, 2011). The soils of Mauritius have been categorised as zonal, intrazonal and azonal. Low Humic Latosol, Humic Latosol, Humic Ferruginous Latosol, Latosolic Reddish Prairie and Latosolic Brown Forest soils are the most important five zonal soil groups covering approximately 70% of the total land area of Mauritius (Cheong et al., 2009). All these soils are derived from the weathering of basaltic rock and are differentiated by the rainfall regime as well as by their age.

In Mauritius, the agricultural sector faces extreme weather conditions like drought or heavy rainfall. Moreover, to increase the crop yields, farmers tend to use 2.5 times the prescribed amount of fertilizers in their fields. These excess fertilizers are washed away during heavy rainfall and contaminate lakes and rivers. For instance, excessive nitrate contamination in urban waterways was observed in the preliminary findings of an IAEA-supported study using isotopic techniques (Viegas, 2019). Soil moisture due to rainfall determines how fast a crop will grow from seed, including when it will be ready for harvesting. A good balance of soil water drainage and proper irrigation can lead to faster-growing plants, which can cut down on germination time and the length between seeding and harvest. Also, each year 6,000 farmers are hit by losses because of storm-related flooding in Mauritius (Africa Times, 2018). The reason being that there are no proper water drainage systems in the farmlands. Besides, in Mauritius, high fertilizer prices and increased frequency of rain floods and scarcity of water have provided an opportunity to recycle land drainage water for irrigation purposes. These problems can be solved by implementing an effective management of soil groundwater for enhanced agricultural productivity through the use of smart drainage, irrigation and fertilization systems. The soil quality can thereafter be tested to monitor the effectiveness of the smart system. This will thus lead to a reduction in the amount of fertilizer used and water demand during drought for agricultural land. A water collection system that could be put in place will also contain some minerals/nutrients. Thus, this chapter considers the use of smart drainage, irrigation and fertilizer application on agricultural lands in view of: (i) alleviating water demand for agricultural land, (ii) reducing the over-utilisation of fertilizer, (iii) preventing contamination of lakes and rivers and (iv) improving crop production in line with the Sustainable Development Goals (SDGs) 2, 11, 12 and 15.

## 3.2 Background Theory

Soil serves not only as a reservoir of water and nutrients for plants but also acts as a universal sink for pollutants (Kokkoris et al., 2019). Industrialisation and urbanisation have led to an increase in anthropogenic activities such as seepage from landfill, discharge of industrial waste, percolation of contaminated water and excess application of pesticides, herbicides and fertilizers. Heavy metals are present in the earth's environment and are metalloids having densities greater than 5 $g/cm^3$ (Ahemad, 2019). The main anthropogenic sources of heavy metal contamination in soil are from industrialisation, urbanisation and intensified agricultural activities (Bakshi et al., 2018). Heavy metals are persistent in the environment and are harmful to human health and natural resources (Ali et al., 2013) and due to their toxicity, they are considered as hazardous compounds. Although some heavy metal ions are vital nutrients for plant metabolism, if in high concentrations, they become toxic (Koller & Saleh, 2018). Heavy metals affect the soil biota which can result in bioaccumulation and soil degradation. In addition, they can affect vital microbial processes leading to a decrease in the number and activity of soil microorganisms. Heavy metals also inhibit the physiological metabolism of plants and pose several health risks as they do not have any biological role. Thus, heavy metals can disrupt the normal functioning of vital organs and glands such as the brain, heart, lungs, kidneys, bone and liver. According to UNEP (2020), soil pollution decreases the soil quality and affects at least 3.2 billion people (40% of the world's population). Moreover, the intensive application of fertilizers by farmers to fix soil nutrient shortages leads to heavy metals contamination.

### 3.2.1 Biotic and Abiotic Factors

The nutrients and moisture required for plant growth are present in soil. Soil should contain enough water to support microbiological activity. According to a study by Aliarab et al. (2020), Platycladus orientalis seedlings can withstand drought conditions as long as there is 25% soil moisture available. Unfortunately, the growth and quality of seedlings were hampered by a decrease in soil moisture. Organic matter improves the soil's chemical, physical and microbiological characteristics, aiding plant uptake and root elongation. Yet, excessive or insufficient soil moisture prevents plants from growing normally (Hsiao & Jackson, 1999). The root will no longer be able to absorb nutrients and moisture if there is an inadequate oxygen supply caused by an abundance of moisture. In addition, dry conditions lead to water stress, which can reduce leaf area and seed production as well as result in abscission of leaves. In nurseries, fertilizer application is frequently utilised to increase plant production and development. Among the necessary nutritional elements, nitrogen is required in the highest concentrations, and its availability and internal concentration have an impact on how biomass is distributed between roots and shoots (Bown et al., 2010). Leaching of basic cations like Ca, Mg, K and Na also regulates the pH of soil. The correct pH of soil also ensures effective nutrient recycling as well as enhances microbial activity for the elimination of hazardous compounds in the soil environment.

Over the past 200 years, agricultural intensification has also contributed to a significant rise of drained pastures and arable land globally. According to Gramlich et al. (2018), installing land drains has an impact on a landscape's water balance as well as its susceptibility to erosion, nutrient cycling, the transport of plant protection products (PPPs) and greenhouse gas emissions. A timely and sufficient water supply to crops is necessary for the sustainable production of food for the expanding global population. The rootzone's surplus water is harmful to crop growth and yield even if a suitable water supply is required for crop production. Inadequate land drainage and the resulting salinisation pose serious risks to the long-term viability of irrigated agriculture because they reduce crop growth and output. On poorly drained agricultural soils, an appropriate drainage is required to enable optimal aeration in the rootzone. Surface drainage, subsurface drainage, mole drainage, tile drainage, vertical drainage and biodrainage are a few examples of drainage systems (Singh, 2018). Using subsurface pipe and vertical well drainage techniques has been demonstrated to increase the value of saline-alkaline soil (Heng et al., 2022).

### 3.2.2 Smart Agricultural Systems

Even farmers with indigenous knowledge find it challenging to make wise judgements on crop health monitoring in the age of climate change, which ultimately results in crop failure and a decline in crop yield (Kishan Das Menon et al., 2021). Floods in Chennai in 2015 and its aftermath emphasise the importance of precision agriculture practices, including irrigation system automation (Arvindan & Keerthika, 2016). With site-specific crop monitoring and management, smart farming is anticipated to increase efficiency and sustainability. It conserves resources, money and time (Shukla et al., 2022). By utilising various machine learning (ML) techniques, Internet of Things (IoT) technology also aids in the collection of data regarding environmental factors like temperature, humidity, pH and rainfall to improve crop yield (Kishan Das Menon et al., 2021). The IoT-enabled automated initiatives are not only more affordable but also more effective. A remote control system for an automated irrigation system built on an Arduino board has been presented (Arvindan & Keerthika, 2016). In order to study the growth behaviour of the Moringa plant in diverse subtropical climatic circumstances, an IoT-based automated monitoring project for Moringa plants has been created (Shukla et al., 2022). It has been suggested to use a wireless sensor network to track agricultural conditions and upload sensor data to the cloud (Saha et al., 2022). To increase production, this method aids in collecting precise feedback about crop conditions based on sensor data. Tremblay et al. (2010) developed a fuzzy inference system (FIS) for N-fertilizers use. A software-defined control system with cloud computing was developed to control fertilization and irrigation levels for orchards in the United States. Convolution Neural Network was used to analyse and control the soil nutrients (Thorat et al., 2023).

## 3.3 Potential of Nanotechnology and Biotechnology in Developing Smart Fertilizers

Nanotechnology and biotechnology have immense potential for the development of smart fertilizers that can boost plant growth, increase agricultural output and lessen the environmental effect of agriculture (Chakraborty et al., 2023). By regulating the delivery of nutrients, nanoparticles can be utilised in the creation of intelligent fertilizers. For instance, encapsulated nanoparticles can be tailored to release nutrients over a longer period based on the plant's requirements, leading in a more effective use of fertilizers and a reduction in nutrient loss. In addition, nanoparticles can improve the solubility and availability of nutrients, enabling plants to absorb them more efficiently (Al-Juthery et al., 2021). Biotechnology can be utilised to create smart fertilizers that can be adjusted to individual plants or crops. This can be accomplished through the use of genetically modified microbes that boost nutrient uptake or through the creation of plants that manufacture their own fertilizers. Biotechnology can also be utilised to generate biofertilizers, which are microorganisms that can build symbiotic relationships with plants and assist them in acquiring soil nutrients (Venugopalan et al., 2022). Combining nanotechnology and biotechnology can result in the creation of even more sophisticated smart fertilizers. For instance, nanoparticles can be coated with specific biological molecules that can target particular plant tissues, resulting in improved nutrient absorption. Instead, nanoparticles can be loaded with bioactive substances that assist plants in defending themselves from pests and illnesses. Overall, nanotechnology and biotechnology have immense promise for the development of intelligent fertilizers (Skrzypczak et al., 2021). These technologies can lessen the environmental effect of agriculture, increase crop yields and contribute to a more sustainable food supply. Prior to their broad implementation, safety and environmental impacts of these technologies must be thoroughly evaluated. Studies have shown that the use of smart fertilizers can lead to significant improvements in crop yield and resource use efficiency compared to traditional fertilizer application methods (Javaid et al., 2022). In a study published in the Journal of Chemosphere, researchers compared the performance of smart fertilizers which use nanotechnology to control nutrient release with traditional fertilizers on cereals, oilseeds and pulses crop yields. The results showed that the use of smart fertilizers led to 10–30% increase in yield compared to traditional fertilizers. This suggests that smart fertilizers can enhance crop yield while reducing resource use, leading to more sustainable and efficient agriculture. Another study using a Zn NP-based nanofertilizer compared the performance of smart fertilizers which use biotechnology to enhance nutrient uptake with traditional fertilizers. The results showed that the use of smart fertilizers led to a 38% increase in yield compared to traditional fertilizers on Pennisetum Americanum (Moghaddasi et al., 2017). This suggests that smart fertilizers can enhance crop yield while reducing resource use, leading to more sustainable and efficient agriculture. Overall, these studies suggest that smart fertilizers have the potential to enhance crop yield and resource use efficiency compared to traditional fertilizers. However, further research is needed to fully understand the potential benefits and risks of these technologies.

## 3.4 Implementation of Smart Irrigation, Fertilization and Drainage System

The leaching of nutrients and heavy metals from the soil profile could be assessed for various scenarios such as: (i) Soil only, (ii) Soil and Chemical Fertilizers and (iii) Soil and Compost. A dataset on the evolution of soil Nitrogen, Phosphorus and Potassium (NPK), humidity, pH, electrical conductivity and water holding capacity throughout the crop growth period should thus be collected, monitored and analysed. Furthermore, it is also important to study the root system as well as the uptake of heavy metals by the crops in order to implement a smart agricultural system. Artificial intelligence (AI) could hence be used to monitor drainage water, nutrient recycling, fertilization levels and irrigation frequency in order to achieve optimum plant growth. The development of a smart mobile phone application will consequently capture real-time data for the whole system and solar energy will be utilised to power the smart system.

A block diagram of the system is shown in Fig. 3.1. The monitoring of soil NPK, humidity, pH, conductivity and moisture data are possible with the use of sensors and a cloud platform. To maximise the growth of the crops, the data is processed at the cloud level and a suitable NPK and irrigation mix is applied. The land drainage, fertilization and irrigation systems are controlled by ML algorithms, and a mobile application will provide real-time data for the entire system. Solar energy powers the entire system.

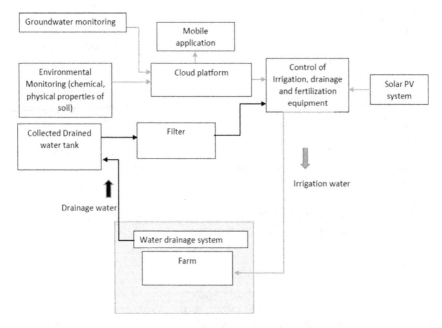

Fig. 3.1.   Block Flow Diagram of the Proposed Smart Irrigation,
Fertilization and Drainage System.

The description is given below:

- *Monitoring of soil properties: soil conductivity, moisture, humidity and pH*
  Soil properties and crop health can be monitored using sensors and ML algorithms. Temperature, soil nutrient levels (NPK), soil conductivity, sunlight intensity, moisture content, humidity and pH sensors can be used to monitor the physical and chemical properties of the soil and the information will be sent to a cloud platform for processing (Chettri, 2022). Expert systems and Artificial Neural Networks were combined by Song and He (2005) to predict nutrient level in crops. A startup group (InCeres) in Brazil developed an application based on soil application and nutrient uptake to predict soil fertility and quality (Ali, 2022).
- *Monitoring of groundwater level using ultrasonic sensors*
  Ultrasonic sensors can be placed in a vertical well to measure the level of groundwater. The transducer at the well's top generates an ultrasonic wave, which is transmitted via the well to the bottom of the well and reflected at the well's surface inside the well. The strength and duration of the reflected ultrasonic wave are used to measure the level of groundwater.
- *Drainage water reserve tank*
  The drainage water collected in the vertical well can thereafter be pumped out and stored in a tank.

- *Cloud platform*
  The cloud platform will collect and analyse the chemical and physical properties of soil and groundwater level and will automatically control irrigation, drainage and fertilization of the plants.
- *Control of irrigation, drainage and fertilization equipment*
  A control system will analyse the NPK content of the filtered underground water and mix it with NPK nutrients so as to optimise the crop growth according to the models developed in the various scenarios.
- *ML algorithms*
  Decision Tree, K Nearest Neighbour, Linear Regression model, Neural Network, Naïve Bayes and Support Vector Machine can be investigated as the ML algorithms.
- *PV system*
  A Photovoltaic system with battery storage can be used to supply energy for powering the pumps and the control system.

## 3.5 Case Studies

Many farmers have already experienced significant benefits from smart fertilization and irrigation and technologies (Khedwal et al., 2023). Some of the successful implementation of smart fertilization application has been enumerated in this section. For example, the vineyards of California are among the most water-intensive crops and confront the challenge of a growing water shortage. As a result, vineyard owners are turning to intelligent irrigation technology to optimise water usage and increase crop yield. E. & J. Gallo Winery, which has implemented a sophisticated irrigation system across its vineyards, is one such example (US Geological Survey, n.d.). The implementation of smart irrigation technology has resulted in several benefits including reducing water use by 20–30% based on regional requirements, efficient water management through seasonal balance, development of better irrigation schedules, improved grape quality leading to higher wine quality, increased revenue due to higher grape quality, less trimming of excess leaf canopies from over-irrigation, reduced irrigation costs through water and energy conservation and using current year's data to plan next year's water allocation. Moreover, the Indian farmers are utilising smart fertilization technology to decrease fertilizer use and increase crop yield, with one example being the Nutrient Expert System (NES) developed by the International Rice Research Institute (IRRI). The NES employs crop and soil data to determine the precise amount of fertilizer needed for optimum crop growth, allowing farmers to decrease fertilizer usage by as much as 30% for cost savings and reduced environmental impact (International Rice Research Institute, n. d.). In North America for instance, the NutriSolution 360 programme utilises satellite imagery, soil sampling and weather data to create a customised fertilization plan for each field. This programme has helped farmers to achieve up to 9% increase in crop yield while reducing fertilizer usage by 20% (US Geological Survey, n.d.). In Kenya, a programme called M-farm is used. It provides farmers with soil analysis results via their mobile, enabling them to make informed decisions about fertilizer usage. The programme has helped farmers in Kenya to increase the crop yields by up to 60% (Khedwal et al., 2023). Thus, smart fertilization and irrigation have proven to be highly successful in optimising use of fertilizers in agriculture to improve productivity in different regions.

## 3.6 Challenges and Limitations

This chapter has elaborated on the practices and technologies of climate-smart agriculture that can increase productivity, support farmers' adaptation to climate change and reduce levels of greenhouse gases. However, there exist several barriers that can affect climate-smart agriculture practices and technologies. Up to now, there are no existing policies and actions to remove these barriers in most African countries. It is, therefore, important to have a good understanding of what these barriers are and how they impinge on the adoption of climate-smart agriculture practices. Table 3.1 gives a brief overview of some of these barriers.

Table 3.1. Technological, Regulatory, Financial, Ethical Barriers and Risks.

| Technological Barriers | Regulatory Barriers | Financial Barriers | Ethical Concerns | Risks |
|---|---|---|---|---|
| Irregular internet connection in rural regions | Network and communication interruptions, hacking of accumulated farming data and host properties (Thilakarathne et al., 2021) | High cost of investments in increased use of chemicals, water and organic fertilizers | Farmers' willingness, engagement, attitude and knowledge | Droughts, humidity, rain and unstable climate conditions |
| Intensive data management and processing on a daily or weekly basis for farmers | Water tariffs and reduced fuel subsidies (IFAD, 2019) | Limited credit and finance (Barnard et al., 2015) | Paradigm shift from traditional farming to precision farming | Change in growing seasons |
| Reliability and scalability | Poor physical and social infrastructure (Barnard et al., 2015) | Limited access to appropriate farm equipment and tools (Barnard et al., 2015) | Gender inequalities especially in Africa (Barnard et al., 2015) | Pests and fungi |

## 3.7 Conclusion

This chapter elaborates on a better management of soil water reserves for increased agricultural production through the employment of a smart drainage, irrigation and fertilization system. In this respect, the proposed smart system will help in implementing a land drainage pipe system, a fertilizer control system, a smart drainage, nutrient recycling and fertilization and irrigation system in order to improve the performance of plant growth for different soil types in the Mauritian context. A drainage system will be created to capture extra water that percolates into the soil during heavy rains and reuse this water for irrigation. Also, the nutrients in the water that has been conserved will eventually help the farm in optimising in fertilizer utilisation. The right combination of NPK and irrigation will be employed to improve the growth of the crops. A cloud platform will monitor soil NPK, humidity, pH, conductivity and moisture data. Solar photovoltaic modules will be used to power the system, making it environmentally friendly.

Thus, the proposed concept will be beneficial to the society as it will contribute to a reduction in the water demand for agricultural land owing to the water collection system that will be put in place, a reduction in the amount of fertilizer used by farmers, reduced prices of agricultural products and prevention of lake and river water contamination due to leaching and carrying away of excess fertilizers during heavy rainfall. The smart agricultural system being outlined in this chapter is in line with the following SDGs: 2 (Zero Hunger), 11 (Sustainable cities and communities), 12 (Responsible consumption and production) and 15 (Life on Land). With the help of the smart irrigation, drainage and fertilization system, the yield of crops will be boosted thus reducing the hunger rate (SDG 2). This system will also support neighbourhood agro-businesses while keeping people employed and circulating money back into the community with the improved yields and promoting responsible consumption and production practices within the community (SDGs 11 and 12). Moreover, the system will encourage farmers to collect the waters and reduce fertilizer consumption which will sustain the quality of the soil on which they are cultivating the crops, hence increasing yields (SDG 15).

## References

Africa Times. (2018). https://africatimes.com/2018/01/26/mauritius-to-support-farmers-hard-hit-by-cyclone-flooding/

Ahemad, M. (2019). Remediation of metalliferous soils through the heavy metal resistant plant growth promoting bacteria: Paradigms and prospects. *Arabian Journal of Chemistry*, *12*(7), 1365–1377. https://www.sciencedirect.com/science/article/pii/S1878535214002688

Al-Juthery, H. W. A., Lahmod, N. R., & Al-Taee, R. A. H. G. (2021). Intelligent, nano-fertilizers: A new technology for improvement nutrient use efficiency (article review). In *IOP conference series: Earth and environmental science*.

Ali, O. (2022). *Artificial intelligence (AI) in soil quality monitoring*. Editorial Feature, AZO Robotics. https://www.azorobotics.com/Article.aspx?ArticleID=482

Aliarab, A., Vazifekhah, E. O., & Sadati, S. E. (2020). Effect of soil moisture content and nitrogen fertilizer on survival, growth and some physiological characteristics of Platycladus orientalis seedlings. *Journal of Forest Science, 66*(12), 511–523.

Ali, H., Khan, E., & Sajad, M. A. (2013). Phytoremediation of heavy metals—Concepts and applications. *Chemosphere, 91*(7), 869–881.

Arvindan, A. N., & Keerthika, D. (2016). Experimental investigation of remote control via Android smart phone of arduino-based automated irrigation system using moisture sensor. In *2016 3rd International Conference on Electrical Energy Systems (ICEES)* (pp. 168–175). IEEE. https://doi.org/10.1109/ICEES.2016.7510636

Bakshi, S., Banik, C., & He, Z. (2018). The impact of heavy metal contamination on soil health. [online]. ResearchGate. (researchgate.net).

Barnard, J., Manyire, H., Tambi, E., & Bangali, S. (2015). Barriers to scaling up/out climate smart agriculture and strategies to enhance adoption in Africa. https://www.nepad.org/file-download/download/public/16071

Bown, H. E., Watt, M. S., Clinton, P. W., & Mason, E. G. (2010). Influence of ammonium and nitrate supply on growth, dry matter partitioning, N uptake and photosynthetic capacity of Pinusradiata seedlings. *Trees, 24*(6), 1097–1107. In Razaq, M., Zhang, P., & Salahuddin, H.-L. S. (2017). Influence of nitrogen and phosphorous on the growth and root morphology of Acer mono.

Chakraborty, R., Mukhopadhyay, A., Paul, S., Sarkar, S., & Mukhopadhyay, R. (2023). Nanocomposite-based smart fertilizers: A boon to agricultural and environmental sustainability. *The Science of the Total Environment, 863*, 160859. https://doi.org/10.1016/j.scitotenv.2022.160859

Cheong, N., Laval, R., Kwong, K., & Du-preez, C. (2009). Effects of sugar cane (Saccharum hybrid sp.) cropping on soil acidity and exchangeable base status in Mauritius. *South African Journal of Plant and Soil, 26*, 9–17. doi:10.1080/02571862.2009.10639926

Chettri, B. (2022). *Automatic crop and soil monitoring using artificial intelligence. Animal feed.* Technical Articles, Engormix. https://en.engormix.com/feed-machinery/articles/automatic-crop-soil-monitoring-t51768.htm

FAO. (2011). Global food losses and food waste – Extent, causes and prevention. http://www.fao.org/3/a-i2697e.pdf

Gramlich, A., Stoll, S., Stamm, C., Walter, T., & Prasuhn, V. (2018). Effects of artificial land drainage on hydrology, nutrient and pesticide fluxes from agricultural fields – A review. *Agriculture, Ecosystems & Environment, 266*, 84–99. ISSN 0167-8809. https://doi.org/10.1016/j.agee.2018.04.005

Heng, T., Xin-Lin, H., Li-Li, Y., Xu, X., & Feng, Y. (2022). Mechanism of Saline–Alkali land improvement using subsurface pipe and vertical well drainage measures and its response to agricultural soil ecosystem. *Environmental Pollution, 293*, 118583. ISSN 0269-7491. https://doi.org/10.1016/j.envpol.2021.118583

Hsiao, T. C., & Jackson, R. B. (1999). Interactive effects of water stress and elevated $CO_2$ on growth, photosynthesis, and water-use efficiency. In *Carbon dioxide and environmental stress* (pp. 3–31). Academic Press. In Lee, E. U., Han, Y.S., Lee, S. I., Cho, K. T., Park, J. H. & You, Y. H. (2017). Effect of nutrient and moisture on the growth and reproduction of Epilobium hirsutum L., an endangered plant. *Journal of Ecology and Environment.* https://doi.org/10.1186/s41610-017-0054-z

IFAD. (2019). Opportunities, challenges and limitations of climate-smart agriculture - The case of Egypt. https://www.ifad.org/nl/web/latest/-/story/opportunities-challenges-and-limitations-of-climate-smart-agriculture-the-case-of-egypt

Javaid, M., Haleem, A., Singh, R. P., & Suman, R. (2022). Enhancing smart farming through the applications of Agriculture 4.0 technologies. *International Journal of Intelligent Networks*, *3*, 150–164.

Khedwal, R. S., Chaudhary, A., & Sindhu, V. K. (2023). *Challenges and technological interventions in rice–wheat system for resilient food–water–energy–environment nexus in North-western Indo-Gangetic Plains: A review.* Cereal Research Communications. https://doi.org/10.1007/s42976-023-00355-9

Kishan Das Menon, H., Mishra, D., & Deepa, D. (2021). Automation and integration of growth monitoring in plants (with disease prediction) and crop prediction. *Materials Today: Proceedings*, *43*(Part 6), 3922–3927. ISSN 2214-7853. https://doi.org/10.1016/j.matpr.2021.01.973

Kokkoris, V., Massas, I., Polemis, E., Koutrotsios, G., & Zervakis, G. (2019). Accumulation of heavy metals by wild edible mushrooms with respect to soil substrates in the Athens metropolitan area (Greece). *The Science of the Total Environment*, *685*, 280–296.

Koller, M., & Saleh, H. (2018). Introductory chapter: Introducing heavy metals. https://www.intechopen.com/books/heavy-metals/introductory-chapter-introducing-heavy-metals

Ministry of Agro-Industry and Food Security (MOAIAFS). (2016). Strategic plan (2016–2020) for the food crop, livestock and forestry sectors [online]. https://agriculture.govmu.org/Documents/Report/Book%20Final.pdf. Accessed on 24th August 2020.

Ministry of Agro-Industry and Food Security (MOAIAFS). (2020). Smart Agriculture Project to promote Mauritius' agro-ecological transition. (http://www.govmu.org/English/News/Pages/Smart-Agriculture-Project-to-promote-Mauritius%E2%80%99-agro-ecological-transition-.aspx)

Moghaddasi, S., Fotovat, A., Khoshgoftarmanesh, A. H., Karimzadeh, F., Khazaei, H. R., & Khorassani, R. (2017). Bioavailability of coated and uncoated ZnO nanoparticles to cucumber in soil with or without organic matter. *Ecotoxicology and Environmental Safety*, *144*, 543–551.

Saha, H. N., Roy, R., Chakraborty, M., & Sarkar, C. (2022). Chapter 20 – A crop-monitoring system using wireless sensor networking. In A. Abraham, S. Dash, J. J. P. C. Rodrigues, B. Acharya, & S. K. Pani (Eds.), *Intelligent data-centric systems, AI, edge and IoT-based smart agriculture* (pp. 345–359). Academic Press. ISBN 9780128236949. https://doi.org/10.1016/B978-0-12-823694-9.00003-7

Shukla, V. K., Nair, R. S., & Khan, F. (2022). Chapter 13 – Smart irrigation-based behavioral study of Moringa plant for growth monitoring in subtropical desert climatic condition. In A. Abraham, S. Dash, J. J. P. C. Rodrigues, B. Acharya, & S. K. Pani (Eds.), *Intelligent data-centric systems, AI, edge and IoT-based smart agriculture* (pp. 227–240). Academic Press. ISBN 9780128236949. https://doi.org/10.1016/B978-0-12-823694-9.00023-2

Singh, J. (2018). Salinization of agricultural lands due to poor drainage: A viewpoint. *Ecological Indicators*, *95*(Part 1), 127–130. ISSN 1470-160X. https://doi.org/10.1016/j.ecolind.2018.07.037

Skrzypczak, D., Mikula, K., Izydorczyk, G., Taf, R., Gersz, A., Witek-Krowiak, A., & Chojnacka, K. (2021). Smart fertilizers-toward implementation in practice. In *Smart agrochemicals for sustainable agriculture* (pp. 81–102).

Song, H., & He, Y. (2005). Crop nutrition diagnosis expert system based on artificial neural networks. In *Third International Conference on Information Technology and Applications.*

The World Bank Group. (2021). *Needed: A climate-smart-food-system that can feed 10 billion.* https://www.worldbank.org/en/news/feature/2021/09/22/needed-a-climate-smart-food-system-that-can-feed-10-billion

Thilakarathne, N., Yassin, H., Abu Bakar, M. S., & Abas, P. E. (2021). *Internet of Things in smart agriculture: Challenges, opportunities and future directions.* Conference Paper.

Thorat, T., Patle, B. K., & Kashyap, S. K. (2023). Intelligent insecticide and fertilizer recommendation system based on TPF-CNN for smart farming. *Smart Agricultural Technology, 3,* 100114. ISSN 2772-3755. https://doi.org/10.1016/j.atech.2022.100114

Tremblay, N., Bouroubi, M. Y., Panneton, B., Guillaume, S., Vigneault, P., & Belec, C. (2010). Development and validation of fuzzy logic inference to determine optimum rates of N for corn on the basis of field and crop features. *Precision Agriculture, 11,* 621–635.

UNEP. (2020). *Soil pollution is a risk to our health and food security.* https://www.unep.org/news-and-stories/story/soil-pollution-risk-our-health-and-food-security

US Geological Survey. (n.d.). E. & J. Gallo: Improving irrigation technology and grape quality. Fort Collins Science Center. https://www.usgs.gov/centers/fort-collins-science-center/science/e-and-j-gallo-improving-irrigation-technology-and-grape

Venugopalan, V. K., Nath, R., & Sarath, S. C. (2022). Smart fertilizers–A way ahead for sustainable agriculture. *Journal of Plant Nutrition.*

Viegas, L. (2019). Isotopes help trace the origin of urban water pollution in Mauritius (Chinese Edition). *IAEA Bulletin (Online), 60*(1), 14–15.

# Chapter 4

# Predicting Household Plastic Level Consumption Using Machine Learning and Artificial Intelligence (AI)

*Pratima Jeetah[a], Yasser M Chuttur[a], Neetish Hurry[b], K Tahalooa[c] and Danraz Seebun[a]*

[a]University of Mauritius, Mauritius
[b]International Economics Ltd, Mauritius
[c]Mini Factory Ltd, Mauritius

## Abstract

Mauritius is a Small Island Development State (SIDS) with limited resources, and it has been witnessed that many containers used for storing household and industrial products are made from plastic. When discarded as waste, those plastic containers pose a serious environmental and economic challenge for Mauritius. Moreover, landfill space is getting increasingly scarce, and plastic waste is contaminating both land and water. Therefore, it is of the utmost necessity to develop solutions for Mauritius' plastic wastes. Due to its abundance and accessibility, plastic waste is a promising material for recycling and energy production. One potential solution is the use of machine learning and artificial intelligence (AI) to predict household plastic consumption, allowing policymakers to design effective strategies and initiatives to reduce plastic waste. Such information is a critical component to be able to efficiently plan for the collection and routing of trucks when collecting recyclable plastics. The development of new strategies for the recycling of plastic waste and development of new industry can address the import and export potential of the country to achieve self-sustainability as well as contribute to reduction in plastic pollution and amount of waste landfilled. These plastics can thereafter be used effectively for recycling and for the making of 3D printing filaments which fall under the SDGs 9 (Industry, Innovation and Infrastructure) and 12 (Responsible consumption and production).

Artificial Intelligence, Engineering Systems and Sustainable Development, 43–53
Copyright © 2024 Pratima Jeetah, Yasser M Chuttur, Neetish Hurry, K Tahalooa and Danraz Seebun
Published under exclusive licence by Emerald Publishing Limited
doi:10.1108/978-1-83753-540-820241004

*Keywords*: Plastic waste; household level; machine learning; waste management; AI predicting tools; recycling

## 4.1 Introduction

The global fight to reduce plastic trash is one of the most rapidly expanding environmental concerns in history. However, it has been insufficient to make a difference in the rising volume of wasted plastic that ends up in the oceans. It has been reported that during the next decade, plastic waste that will enter rivers and eventually the seas will exceed 22 million tonnes and perhaps 58 million tonnes per year. While plastics use has generated several benefits for society in numerous industries and has recently been critical in the global pandemic for the manufacture of protective equipment, its increasing wide-spreading has also caused untold damage to the natural environment as well as societies. Plastic pollution amplifies numerous risks including flooding and contamination from plastic litter filling up and blocking sewers, environmental and health risks brought by emissions of toxic pollutants resulting from inadequately regulated incineration/combustion plants as well as global emissions caused by fossil fuel feedstocks used for virgin plastic production. Additionally, the longevity of plastics and its accumulation constitute a substantial threat to the natural environment due to the material's tremendously slow-paced decomposition rate over hundreds, even thousands of years, allowing fragmentation into microplastics and nanoplastics. The United Nations has identified this issue as a critical priority and included it in its Sustainable Development Goals (SDGs). One of the targets set by the United Nations under SDG 12 is to reduce the amount of waste generated per capita, including through prevention, reduction, recycling and reuse (UNEP, 2022). To achieve this target, countries and organisations need to have a better understanding of the factors that influence plastic waste generation, and they can use artificial intelligence (AI) to help predict household plastic waste. AI is an umbrella term for a set of technologies that enable machines to learn from data, identify patterns and make decisions without explicit human intervention. In recent years, AI has gained widespread popularity due to its potential to solve complex problems, including those related to the environment. By using AI to analyse data on plastic waste generation, organisations and governments can gain insights into the factors that drive waste production, such as demographics, income, consumption patterns and waste management practices.

## 4.2 Background Theory

With the rising concern about the damaging effects of plastic in the environment, numerous countries introduced measures aiming at reducing plastic usage around the world. Governments and businesses are reacting to the situation. Around 127 nations have passed laws prohibiting the use if 13 single-use plastic bags, and many more have enacted laws prohibiting the use of single-use plastics in general. Some governments have imposed taxes or waste-disposal levies on single-use plastics, as well as Extended Producer Responsibility (EPR) standards, recycling targets, packaging regulations and bans on the importation of plastic trash. Regional and international efforts to prevent plastic pollution are also underway, with a particular focus on the effects on the marine environment. In Europe, for instance, the European Union introduced a Single-Use Plastics Directive in 2019, a legislation and a holistic group of measures targeting reductions in plastic leakage on the land and in the marine environment.

As part of the Mauritian government's initiative to make Mauritius a plastic-free country, regulation was passed in on the prohibition on importation, production, ownership, sale, supply and use of many non-biodegradable single-use plastic products in 2020. It can be noted that low-density poly-ethylene (LDPE), high-density polyethylene (HDPE) and polyethylene tere-phthalate (PET) polymers are the most common types of plastics in the household waste stream. In 2016, just 6.25% of all waste produced in the country was recycled, compared to 44.3% of household waste recycled in the United Kingdom in 2015 (L'Express, 2019). Consequently, these plastic wastes can be recycled so as to prevent it from ending up in the environment. In order to facilitate plastic recycling, it is important to get data on the level of consumption which can be achieved through machine learning.

## 4.3 Using Machine Leaning and AI to Determine the Level of Household Plastic Consumption

Some recent research on predicting household plastic consumption using machine learning and AI has already been carried out by Adefemi et al. (2021), Tadesse et al. (2021), Adewale et al. (2020), Goh, Tan, et al. (2019) and Pratiwi et al. (2019). Those studies demonstrate that machine learning and AI have the potential to predict household plastic consumption. The next step will be for policymakers to use these predictions to design effective strategies and initiatives to reduce plastic waste. For example, if the model predicts that households in a particular area consume a large amount of single-use plastic, policymakers can design a campaign to encourage households to switch to reusable alternatives and devise a separate collection strategy to promote recycling of the household plastics that cannot be reused. The most appropriate way for collecting and separating plastic waste is through source segregation. However, this requires a huge logistic to be put in place with respect to the separation, collection and transportation. The existing waste management system in Mauritius does not include waste segregation at source. Hence, with the use of machine learning to predict the level of plastic waste at household level, a proper recycling framework can be devised.

Machine algorithms have already been successfully applied in many different areas such as in energy consumption prediction, predictive maintenance, sales forecasting, disease spread forecasting, traffic forecast, etc. (Goh, Tan, et al., 2019). The general steps that can be taken to develop a predictive model for household plastic consumption are shown in Fig. 4.1.

(1) *Data Collection*: The first step is to gather data on household plastic con-sumption. These data can be obtained from a variety of sources, including surveys, public records and data from waste management companies.

Fig. 4.1.   Steps for Predicting Household Plastic Usage Using
Machine Learning.

(2) *Data Preparation and preprocessing*: The next step is to prepare the data for
   analysis. This involves cleaning the data, removing duplicates and formatting
   it in a way that is suitable for analysis.
(3) *Feature Engineering/selection*: The next step is to identify relevant features
   that can be used to predict household plastic consumption. Features can
   include demographic data such as age, income and location, as well as
   behavioural data such as shopping habits and waste disposal practices.
(4) *Model development/selection*: After the features have been identified, a
   machine learning algorithm can be selected or developed to predict household plastic consumption. There are several machine learning techniques that
   can be used, including regression analysis, decision trees (DTs) and neural
   networks. The choice of algorithm will depend on the characteristics of the
   dataset, the available computational resources and the desired level of
   accuracy. Some of the commonly used machine learning algorithms for
   predicting household plastic usage include regression analysis, DTs, Random
   Forest (RF), neural networks and Support Vector Machines (SVMs). Brief
   explanation about each machine learning algorithm and the corresponding
   observed impact on the society in various countries are given further.

*Regression Analysis*: Regression analysis is a statistical technique used to
predict the relationship between a dependent variable and one or more independent variables. It can be used to predict household plastic usage based on
various demographic and behavioural factors. One of the key benefits of regression analysis is that it allows researchers to control for confounding variables that
might otherwise obscure the relationship between plastic consumption and other
factors, such as income or demographic characteristics. For example, a study by
Zhang et al. (2021) found that education and income were both significant predictors of plastic consumption, but only after controlling for other factors such as
household size and location. Another important application of regression analysis
is the ability to estimate the impact of policy interventions on plastic consumption. For instance, following a study conducted using regression analysis to
estimate the effect of a plastic bag fee on household plastic consumption in South
Korea, it was found that the fee led to a significant reduction in plastic bag use.
   In another work, Lee et al. (2019) aimed to analyse the effect of income, age
and household composition on plastic waste generation using multiple regression
analysis. The study sought to identify the socioeconomic factors that influence the
amount of plastic waste generated by households. The findings revealed that
income, age and household size were all significant predictors of plastic waste

generation, highlighting the importance of addressing these factors in efforts to reduce plastic waste. Additionally, Limbu et al. (2021) conducted a study to examine the factors influencing plastic waste generation in Nepal using binary logistic regression analysis. The study aimed to identify the factors that contribute to plastic waste generation in Nepal and to provide insights for policy interventions to address the problem. The study found that education, income and location were significant predictors of plastic waste generation, suggesting that policy interventions should focus on increasing awareness and providing incentives for waste reduction.

Furthermore, Zaman et al. (2020) evaluated the impact of a plastic bag tax on plastic consumption in Bangladesh using regression analysis. The study aimed to assess the effectiveness of a policy intervention in reducing plastic waste by imposing a tax on plastic bags. The findings revealed that the plastic bag tax had a significant positive effect on reducing plastic consumption, indicating that policy interventions can be effective in reducing plastic waste in low-income countries. Overall, the use of regression analysis has helped to shed light on the complex factors that influence household plastic consumption and identify effective policy interventions for reducing plastic waste.

*DTs*: DTs are a type of algorithm that uses a tree-like model of decisions and their possible consequences. They can be used to predict household plastic usage by dividing the data into smaller subsets based on the values of various features and predicting the outcome based on the subset in which the data point falls. Research has shown that DTs can be effective in predicting household plastic consumption. For instance, in a study by Prakash and Bhatia (2019), DTs were used to analyse household plastic waste generation patterns in urban India. The study found that DTs could accurately predict plastic waste generation based on demographic and socioeconomic factors.

DTs have also been applied in predicting household plastic recycling behaviour. In a study by Kwon and Kim (2020), DTs were used to identify the factors influencing plastic recycling behaviour among households in Korea. The study found that income, age and environmental attitudes were significant predictors of recycling behaviour. Other studies have also demonstrated the effectiveness of DTs in predicting household plastic consumption patterns. For instance, a study by Bhatia et al. (2017) used DTs to analyse household plastic waste generation in urban India, while a study by Thiemann et al. (2020) used DTs to predict household plastic packaging waste in Germany.

*RFs*: RFs are an ensemble learning method that combines multiple DTs to improve accuracy and avoid overfitting. They can be used to predict household plastic usage by creating several DTs and averaging their predictions. In Malaysia, RF was found to be the most accurate algorithm for predicting plastic waste generation in households compared to other machine learning algorithms (Kuan et al., 2020). In China, the algorithm was used to predict household plastic waste based on demographic, economic and behavioural factors (Li et al., 2019). The study found that the algorithm could accurately predict plastic waste generation and identify factors that influence plastic waste generation.

In the United Kingdom, RF was used to predict plastic waste generation in households and found to be accurate based on socioeconomic factors (Chauhan et al., 2019). In the United States, the algorithm was used to predict plastic waste generation based on the type of plastic used and the demographic characteristics of the household (Kaza et al., 2018). In Turkey, the algorithm was used to predict household plastic waste generation based on household income and demographic characteristics (Kilinc et al., 2018).

*Networks*: Neural networks are a type of machine learning algorithm inspired by the structure and function of the human brain. They can be used to predict household plastic usage by learning complex relationships between features and predicting the outcome based on those relationships. For instance, in a study by Yildirim and Alp (2021), neural networks were used to predict household plastic consumption patterns in Turkey. The study found that neural networks could accurately predict plastic consumption based on demographic and socioeconomic factors.

Similarly, in a study by Belhadji and Amrouche (2021), neural networks were used to predict household plastic waste generation in Algeria. The study found that neural networks outperformed traditional statistical methods in predicting plastic waste generation. Neural networks have also been applied in predicting household plastic recycling behaviour. In a study by Akbarpour Shirazi et al. (2021), neural networks were used to identify the factors influencing plastic recycling behaviour among households in Iran. The study found that neural networks could accurately predict recycling behaviour based on demographic and socioeconomic factors.

*Support Vector Machines (SVMs)*: SVMs are a type of machine learning algorithm that can be used for both classification and regression tasks. They can be used to predict household plastic usage by identifying a hyperplane that separates the data into two or more classes. For instance, in a study by Börekçi et al. (2019), SVM was used to predict household plastic waste generation in Turkey. The study found that SVM could accurately predict plastic waste generation based on demographic and socioeconomic factors. Similarly, in a study by Gao et al. (2019), SVM was used to predict household plastic waste generation in China. The study found that SVM could accurately predict plastic waste generation based on demographic and socioeconomic factors. SVM has also been applied in predicting household plastic recycling behaviour. In a study by Haque et al. (2020), SVM was used to predict plastic recycling behaviour among households in Bangladesh. The study found that SVM could accurately predict recycling behaviour based on demographic and socioeconomic factors. Other studies have also demonstrated the effectiveness of SVM in predicting household plastic consumption patterns.

(5) *Model Training and Validation*: Once the model has been developed, it must be trained and validated to ensure that it is accurate and reliable. This involves testing the model against a validation dataset to determine its predictive power.

(6) *Optimise Model*: The model parameters must then be optimised to improve its performance on the validation set.

(7) *Evaluate Model*: Once optimised, the model's performance must be evaluated on a holdout test set to estimate how well it is likely to perform on new, unseen data.

(8) *Deploy Model*: Finally, the trained model can be deployed in a production environment to make predictions on new data.

## 4.4 Recent Advancements in the Application of AI Tools in Waste Management

The Fourth Industrial Revolution, or simply Industry 4.0, emerged in 2011, as an initiative under the German government. In recent years, there have been significant advancements in the application of AI tools in waste management, with the potential to revolutionise the way waste is managed, sorted and recycled. Here are some examples of recent advancements in the application of AI tools in waste management:

*Robotic Waste Sorting:* Robotics can be used for automating the sorting of waste, improving efficiency and accuracy. A study by Zhang et al. (2021) used a robotic sorting system to separate different types of waste, and achieved an accuracy rate of 98.2%.

*Computer Vision:* Computer vision technology can be used to identify and sort waste in real-time. A study by Goh, Chan, et al. (2019) developed a computer vision system that can sort plastic waste based on its type, colour and transparency.

*Predictive Analytics:* Machine learning algorithms can be used to predict waste generation patterns, allowing waste management organisations to optimise waste collection routes and schedules. A study by Ooi et al. (2021) developed a predictive model to forecast daily waste generation in a residential area, and achieved an accuracy rate of over 90%.

*Smart Bins:* AI-powered sensors can be installed in waste bins to monitor the fill level and optimise waste collection routes. This helps to reduce collection costs and improve waste management efficiency. A study by Al-Amin et al. (2020) used a smart bin monitoring system in Malaysia and found that it reduced the number of collection trips and improved waste collection efficiency.

*Recycling*: AI tools can be used to improve recycling processes by identifying recyclable materials and improving sorting accuracy. A study by Li et al. (2021) developed a machine learning model to classify different types of plastic waste, achieving an accuracy rate of 94.5%.

Overall, the application of AI tools in waste management has the potential to significantly improve the efficiency and sustainability of waste management operations, reducing the amount of waste sent to landfills and promoting the circular economy.

## 4.5 Overview of Different AI Techniques for Segregation, Storage and Treatment of Plastic Waste

AI techniques have gained significant importance in predicting the performance of various methods used for segregation, storage and treatment of plastic waste. Machine learning algorithms such as Support Vector Machines (SVMs), RF, DT and artificial neural network (ANN) have been widely used in predicting the performance of plastic waste management methods. SVM has been used in predicting the amount of plastic waste produced, while RF has been used to predict the amount of plastic waste recycled (Alam, Khan, et al., 2021). DT has been used in predicting the plastic waste segregation process, and ANN has been used in predicting the performance of different treatment methods such as pyrolysis and gasification.

Although these AI techniques have shown promising results, their effectiveness is limited by several factors. Firstly, the accuracy of the prediction models is dependent on the quality and quantity of the data used to train the models. Secondly, the models may not consider all the variables that can affect the performance of plastic waste management methods. Thirdly, the models may not be able to capture the complexities and uncertainties associated with plastic waste management.

Several studies have compared the performance of different AI techniques when it comes to plastic waste management. For instance, Namoun et al. (2022) compared the performance of four AI techniques, namely ANNss, DTs, k-nearest neighbours and support vector machines, for predicting the quantity of plastic waste generated in households. They found that the ANN had the best performance in terms of prediction accuracy, followed by the DT, k-nearest neighbours and support vector machines.

Similarly, Ramkumar et al. (2020) compared the performance of three AI techniques, namely ANNs, DTs and RFs, for predicting the amount of plastic waste generated by a city. They found that the ANN had the best performance in terms of prediction accuracy, followed by the RF and DT.

On the other hand, Shao et al. (2019) compared the performance of two AI techniques, namely ANNs and support vector machines, for predicting the quantity and composition of plastic waste in households. They found that the support vector machine had a higher prediction accuracy than the ANN.

Another study by Alam, Islam, et al. (2021) compared the performance of three AI techniques, namely ANNs, DTs and support vector machines, for predicting the amount of plastic waste generated by households. They found that the ANN had the best performance in terms of prediction accuracy, followed by the support vector machine and DT.

Overall, it appears that ANNs tend to have the best performance in predicting the generation and composition of plastic waste, followed by DTs, support vector machines and k-nearest neighbours. However, the specific performance of these techniques may vary depending on the dataset, the specific problem being addressed and other factors.

## 4.6 Use of AI in Predicting Household Plastic Level Consumption, in View of Supporting the UN SDGs

The application of AI in predicting household plastic waste can support the UN SDG by providing policymakers with insights into the factors that influence waste generation and help them develop targeted policies and interventions to reduce waste. For example, AI can help governments identify areas with high levels of plastic waste generation and develop recycling programmes or educational campaigns to promote waste reduction. Similarly, AI can help organisations develop sustainable packaging solutions that take into account the demographics and consumption patterns of different households.

## 4.7 Conclusion

It has been found that the major fraction of the 76,000 tons of plastic waste produced every year in Mauritius consists of LDPE, HDPE and PET polymers which are the most common types of plastics in the household waste stream, recycling of the plastics can be a good alternative. Thus, machine learning algorithms are perfect for predicting the types and amount of household plastic generation which can thereafter be collected for upcycling or recycling. The use of AI in predicting household plastic waste has the potential to support the UN SDG by providing insights into the factors that drive waste generation and help policymakers develop targeted policies and interventions to reduce waste. By using AI to analyse data from various sources, governments and organisations can gain a better understanding of the complex factors that influence plastic waste generation and develop evidence-based strategies to address this critical environmental issue. However, it is important to address the challenges associated with the use of AI, including data privacy and standardisation, to ensure that AI is used responsibly and ethically to promote sustainable development. Despite the potential benefits of AI in predicting household plastic waste, there are also some challenges that need to be addressed. One of the main challenges is the lack of standardised data on plastic waste generation, which makes it difficult to compare data across different regions and countries. Additionally, there are concerns about data privacy and the ethical implications of using AI to analyse personal information.

## References

Adefemi, O., Adebiyi, A. A., & Akanbi, T. O. (2021). Predicting household plastic recycling behaviour using machine learning: A comparative study. *Journal of Cleaner Production, 278*, 123721.

Adewale, A. P., Zahedi, A., & Mahmood, N. Z. (2020). A machine learning approach for household plastic waste prediction in developing countries. *Journal of Environmental Management, 257*, 110024.

Akbarpour Shirazi, M., Farsi, M., & Vahdati Khaki, J. (2021). Predicting household plastic waste recycling behavior using neural networks: A case study of Tehran. *Journal of Cleaner Production, 315,* 128278.

Al-Amin, A. Q., Ahsan, A., Rahman, A., & Uddin, M. S. (2020). Smart bin monitoring system for smart city solid waste management. *Sustainability, 12*(13), 5387.

Alam, M. S., Islam, M. R., Ahmed, S., & Hasan, M. R. (2021). Prediction of household plastic waste generation using artificial intelligence-based techniques. *Journal of Cleaner Production, 312,* 127828.

Alam, M. N., Khan, M. M. A., Ali, M. H., Mamun, M. A. A., & Kabir, M. R. (2021). A Support Vector Machine (SVM) based plastic waste classification. *Journal of Cleaner Production, 319,* 128596.

Belhadji, A., & Amrouche, N. (2021). Modeling the generation of household plastic waste in Algeria: Comparison between statistical and neural networks models. *Waste Management, 123,* 1–11.

Bhatia, R., van der Horst, D., & Visschers, V. H. (2017). Household plastic waste generation in urban India: A study from Mumbai. *Environmental Science and Pollution Research, 24*(1), 902–912.

Börekçi, C., Altınay, M., & Kahraman, C. (2019). A new hybrid model for forecasting municipal plastic waste generation: SVM and fuzzy time series. *Journal of Cleaner Production, 231,* 1123–1133.

Chauhan, A., Kumar, A., Yadav, S. K., & Sharma, A. (2019). Household plastic waste prediction using machine learning: A case study of the United Kingdom. *Journal of Cleaner Production, 233,* 639–652.

Gao, X., Zhong, S., Liu, Y., Wang, L., & Shi, X. (2019). Modeling and forecasting household plastic waste generation in China using support vector machine. *Journal of Cleaner Production, 219,* 569–576.

Goh, K. H., Chan, L. W., & Lim, C. P. (2019). Plastic waste classification using machine learning. *Journal of Visual Communication and Image Representation, 59,* 24–31.

Goh, T., Tan, C. K., & Lai, S. K. (2019). Predicting plastic consumption in households: A neural network-based approach. In *2019 IEEE International Conference on Big Data (Big Data)* (pp. 4684–4687). IEEE.

Haque, M. M., Shams, S., & Azad, M. A. K. (2020). An evaluation of plastic recycling behavior among urban households in Bangladesh: An application of support vector machine. *Environmental Science and Pollution Research, 27*(19), 23435–23447.

Kaza, S., Yao, L. C., Bhada-Tata, P., & Van Woerden, F. (2018). *What a waste 2.0: A global snapshot of solid waste management to 2050.* World Bank Group.

Kilinc, E., Ilgin, M. A., & Vatansever, N. (2018). A novel method to predict household plastic waste generation using regression models and machine learning algorithms. *Journal of Cleaner Production, 172,* 1311–1320.

Kuan, Y. Y., Lim, C. Y., & Ng, K. M. (2020). Machine learning approaches for predicting plastic waste generation in Malaysia. *Journal of Environmental Management, 267,* 110585.

Kwon, O. Y., & Kim, H. (2020). Identifying the factors affecting household recycling behavior using decision tree analysis. *Journal of Cleaner Production, 267,* 122007.

Lee, S. J., Kim, S. S., & Kim, Y. (2019). Analysis of factors affecting household plastic waste generation using multiple regression analysis. *Journal of Material Cycles and Waste Management, 21*(2), 422–433.

L'Express. (2019). Recycling-what-happens-our-recyclable-waste. https://lexpress.mu/article/358730/recycling-what-happens-our-recyclable-waste

Limbu, T. K., Khadka, M. B., & Pradhananga, R. B. (2021). Factors influencing plastic waste generation in Nepal: A binary logistic regression analysis. *Environmental Science and Pollution Research, 28*(15), 18502–18512.

Li, C., Song, Y., Zhang, M., Wang, F., & Huang, Q. (2021). Development of a deep learning model for plastic waste classification. *Waste Management, 128*, 439–447.

Li, M., Yan, L., Liu, Q., Zhang, Y., & Wang, J. (2019). Exploring factors affecting household plastic waste generation using random forest algorithm: A case study of Shanghai, China. *Resources, Conservation and Recycling, 147*, 99–107.

Namoun, A., Tufail, A., Khan, M. Y., Alrehaili, A., Syed, T. A., & BenRhouma, O. (2022). Solid waste generation and disposal using machine learning approaches: A survey of solutions and challenges. *Sustainability, 14*, 13578.

Ooi, H. X., Tan, Y. C., & Ho, C. S. (2021). A predictive analytics model for solid waste generation forecasting in high-rise residential buildings. *Journal of Cleaner Production, 312*, 127879.

Prakash, M., & Bhatia, R. (2019). Prediction of household plastic waste generation in urban India using decision trees. *Environmental Science and Pollution Research, 26*(22), 22126–22136.

Pratiwi, A. E., Kusumastuti, R. D., & Mawardi, I. (2019). Predicting household plastic waste generation using socio-economic and demographic data: A case study of West Java Province, Indonesia. *Sustainability, 11*(14), 3853.

Ramkumar, T., Kumar, N. R., & Rani, M. D. (2020). Prediction of plastic waste generation in an Indian city using artificial intelligence techniques. *Sustainable Cities and Society, 63*, 102485.

Shao, S., Chen, X., & Chen, X. (2019). Modeling the quantity and composition of household plastic waste using artificial intelligence algorithms: A case study of Hangzhou, China. *Resources, Conservation and Recycling, 148*, 122–129.

Tadesse, G., Belbo, H., & Iakovou, E. (2021). Machine learning-based forecasting of household plastic waste generation and composition. *Journal of Environmental Management, 281*, 111914.

Thiemann, C., Thöns, S., & Teuteberg, F. (2020). Predicting household packaging waste from purchase data using decision trees. *Resources, Conservation and Recycling, 161*, 104964.

The United Nations Environment Program. (2022). Annual report 2022. https://www.unep.org/resources/annual-report-2022

Yildirim, E., & Alp, E. (2021). Predicting household plastic waste using artificial neural networks: A case study of Istanbul, Turkey. *Waste Management, 126*, 371–380.

Zaman, A., Ali, Q., & Hossain, M. A. (2020). Assessing the impact of plastic bag tax on plastic consumption in Bangladesh: A regression analysis. *Environmental Science and Pollution Research, 27*(9), 9325–9332.

Zhang, B., Chen, L., Liu, Y., & Chen, X. (2021). Estimating household plastic consumption in China: An analysis based on a double-hurdle model. *Waste Management, 125*, 1–8.

Chapter 5

# Ant Colony, Bee Colony and Elephant Herd Optimisations for Estimating Aqueous-Phase Adsorption Model Parameters

*Ackmez Mudhoo*[a]*, Gaurav Sharma*[b]*, Khim Hoong Chu*[c] *and Mika Sillanpää*[d]

[a]University of Mauritius, Mauritius
[b]Shenzhen University, China; Shoolini University & Glocal University, India
[c]Honeychem Research, New Zealand
[d]University of Johannesburg, South Africa; Aarhus University, Denmark; Zhejiang Rongsheng Environmental Protection Paper Co. LTD, China; Chandigarh University, India

## Abstract

Adsorption parameters (e.g. Langmuir constant, mass transfer coefficient and Thomas rate constant) are involved in the design of aqueous-media adsorption treatment units. However, the classic approach to estimating such parameters is perceived to be imprecise. Herein, the essential features and performances of the ant colony, bee colony and elephant herd optimisation approaches are introduced to the experimental chemist and chemical engineer engaged in adsorption research for aqueous systems. Key research and development directions, believed to harness these algorithms for real-scale water treatment (which falls within the wide-ranging coverage of the Sustainable Development Goal 6 (SDG 6) 'Clean Water and Sanitation for All'), are also proposed. The ant colony, bee colony and elephant herd optimisations have higher precision and accuracy, and are particularly efficient in finding the global optimum solution. It is hoped that the discussions can stimulate both the experimental chemist and chemical engineer to delineate the progress achieved so far and collaborate further to devise strategies for integrating these intelligent optimisations in the design and operation of real multicomponent multi-complexity adsorption systems for water purification.

Artificial Intelligence, Engineering Systems and Sustainable Development, 55–66
Copyright © 2024 Ackmez Mudhoo, Gaurav Sharma, Khim Hoong Chu and Mika Sillanpää
Published under exclusive licence by Emerald Publishing Limited
doi:10.1108/978-1-83753-540-820241005

*Keywords*: Adsorption; optimisation; ant colony; bee; elephant herd; model parameters

## 5.1 Introduction

Adsorption is an essential separation and purification process in chemical and environmental engineering. It has been immensely studied at laboratory scale in batch and column aqueous systems for myriad adsorbent, organic contaminant and inorganic pollutant combinations. Adsorption performance metrics hold validly at the laboratory-scale. However, adsorption behaviours are expected to be significantly in multicomponent multi-complexity real polluted water. 'Multicomponent' encompasses aqueous systems much likely to contain several pollutants, numerous non-pollutant species and materials, including the test adsorbent, which exhibit different adsorptive characteristics. 'Multi-complexity' refers to the chain of competing physicochemical (Yang et al., 2021) and biological (Huangfu et al., 2019) interactions amongst the several components in the real aqueous systems.

The elucidation of the *possible* adsorption mechanism based on adsorption isotherm model data is omnipresent when analysing laboratory-scale adsorption data. These models, mostly non-linear in mathematical structure, differ significantly in their margins of error (Benjelloun et al., 2021). They are categorised as one-parameter, two-parameter, three-parameter, four-parameter and five-parameter isotherms. Depending on the assumptions, they embody different adsorption equilibrium parameters. Adsorption isotherm and kinetic parameters are determined using the gradient and intercept of the best-fit regression line of the linear forms of non-linear models (Karri et al., 2020). Linearisation-based approaches distort adsorption isotherm and kinetic models. This induces misinterpretations of adsorption mechanisms (Karri et al., 2020), brings in oversimplification in understanding the true adsorption phenomena, causes estimation errors and induces statistical bias (González-López et al., 2021). For rate models used to describe adsorption kinetics (Syafiuddin et al., 2018), the rate constant, initial adsorption rate, intraparticle diffusivity (Luo & Crittenden, 2019), surface diffusion coefficient (Park et al., 2020) and mass transfer coefficient (Wang & Guo, 2020) are estimated to elucidate the mass transfer phenomena. For fixed bed adsorption, Yoon-Nelson, Bohart-Adams and Thomas models can be used to correlate empirical adsorption data of symmetrical breakthrough curves (Chu, 2020; Tovar-Gómez et al., 2013). However, these models cannot describe fixed bed adsorption having unsymmetrical breakthrough curves because of the inherent adsorption complexity (Tovar-Gómez et al., 2013).

Nature-inspired optimisation algorithms (hereinafter called 'NIOPAS') applied to aqueous adsorption systems are particularly *recent* and *limited*. Such optimisation algorithms are based on stochastic processes (Dehghani et al., 2021; Trojovský & Dehghani, 2022). In this chapter, the key characteristics and performances of the ant colony, bee colony and elephant herd optimisations incepted in aqueous bench scale adsorption analysis are compared with conventional approaches. These three swarm intelligence–based algorithms mimic the group behaviour of living organisms with good robustness (Jiang et al., 2021; Zhu et al., 2021). Other metaheuristics such as evolutionary algorithms (like Excel Solver's evolutionary algorithm) are not discussed here. Finally, we provide research directions which the experimental chemist and chemical engineer can consider *together* to integrate these intelligent optimisation algorithms in real-scale water treatment.

## 5.2 Adsorption Systems and Nature-Inspired Optimisation

Inaccurate adsorption model parameters can result in misrepresentations of the complex adsorption dynamics (Gopinath & Aravamudan, 2019; Tovar-Gómez et al., 2013). This weakness can then translate into an inadequate (even faulty) design and operation of adsorption systems. To bypass the plausibility of mis-interpreting the adsorption dynamics studied using linearisation, innovative NIOPAS have been used to determine adsorption constants. The ant colony (Ghazali et al., 2018; Jun et al., 2020; Karri et al., 2020; Khajeh et al., 2017; LotfiKatooli & Shahsavand, 2018), elephant herd (Aravamudan, 2021; Gopinath & Aravamudan, 2019; Gopinath et al., 2020) and bee colony (Ebrahimpoor et al., 2019; Ghaedi et al., 2015) optimisations are novel in the aqueous adsorption literature. We suggest the following example literature to the more avid reader: Nayar et al. (2021) and Dorigo and Stützle (2019) for ant colony, Hancer (2020) and Hakli and Kiran (2020) for bee colony and Aravamudan (2021), Gopinath and Aravamudan (2019) and Muthusamy et al. (2021) for elephant herd.

### 5.2.1 Ant Colony Optimisation (ACO)

ACO is a metaheuristic search algorithm which harnesses the approach of the shortest route-finding method (Jun et al., 2020; Karri et al., 2020). ACO mimics the manner in which real ants find a food source and reach it via the shortest route between their nest and that food source (Jun et al., 2020; Karri et al., 2020). Based on a communication mode determined by ant pheromonal deposits along ants' movement paths, their collective behaviour determines the optimal (i.e. shortest) nest-to-food source path and vice versa (Jun et al., 2020; Karri et al., 2020).

Recently, a hybrid inverse modelling-ACO approach that minimised the Pearson's Chi-square ($X^2$) and root means square error (RMSE) was applied to examine Cr(VI) adsorption efficacy by sugarcane-derived granular activated carbon (Karri et al., 2020). Optimal adsorption parameter predictions were realised which embodied a higher sensitivity of the non-linear characteristics of the adsorption isotherm models examined (Karri et al., 2020). The *variability* and *deviation* of model values predicted (q (Pred)) by this ACO-based approach and the linear transformed method (LTFM) versus the corresponding experimental equilibrium data (q (expt)) were examined using scatter plots (Karri et al., 2020). For the Freundlich adsorption isotherm model, the corresponding scatter plot indicated that the optimised model values obtained with the ACO-based approach closely agreed with the corresponding experimental data (Karri et al., 2020). For the non-linear Freundlich model, the $R^2$, $X^2$ and RMSE values obtained (best results) from the ACO-based method by minimising $X^2$ and RMSE were 0.991, 0.515 and

3.082, respectively (Karri et al., 2020). The $R^2$ values were less than 0.95 for the linearised form of the five adsorption isotherm models (Langmuir, Freundlich, Temkin, Dubinin-Radushkevich and Redlich-Peterson) used by Karri et al. (2020) for data fitting. Karri et al. (2020) eventually inferred that the ACO-based model predictions had yielded optimal parameters that better assimilated the sensitivity of the non-linear properties of the four adsorption isotherm models.

When assessing the adsorption behaviour of date palm leaves for crystal violet from aqueous media, a 'Memorised_ACO' method (which achieved both response surface methodology (RSM) modelling and process optimisation) resulted in a more accurate parameter prediction versus a stepwise-RSM with its shorter mathematical expression (Ghazali et al., 2018). The model derived from the stepwise-RSM approach in the Minitab software is depicted by Eq. (5.1) (Ghazali et al., 2018). The RSM model obtained by implementing the 'Memorised_ACO' approach is provided as Eq. (5.2) ($R^2 = 0.96$, $RMSE = 0.78$ and $F = 71.3$) (Ghazali et al., 2018). $x_1$ denotes pH, $x_2$ is for contact time (mins), $x_3$ denotes temperature (°C), $x_4$ is for the initial dye concentration (mg L$^{-1}$), $x_5$ denotes the amount of adsorbent (mg) and in Eq. (5.2), $y$ = % adsorption (Ghazali et al., 2018). There are significantly fewer terms in the ACO-RSM model, whose mathematical structure is thus generally more desirable (Ghazali et al., 2018). In one other study, an ACO approach applied for kinetic and isotherm model parameter predictions closely matched experimental values reporting methylene blue adsorption onto a peroxidase immobilised functionalised Buckypaper/polyvinyl alcohol membrane (Jun et al., 2020).

$$
\begin{aligned}
\text{Removal\% } or \text{ Adsorption\%} = {} & 86.7696 + 0.567458x_1 + 0.505708x_2 \\
& + 0.876792x_3 - 2.98254x_4 + 1.22696x_5 - 0.412602x_1^2 \\
& - 0.606477x_2^2 + 0.276023x_3^2 - 0.389977x_4^2 - 0.563227x_5^2 \\
& + 0.411438x_1x_2 - 0.341937x_1x_3 - 1.24294x_1x_4 \\
& + 1.24731x_1x_5 - 0.733188x_2x_3 + 0.903813x_2x_5 \\
& + 1.07144x_3x_4 + 0.649438x_3x_5 - 2.42506x_4x_5
\end{aligned}
$$

(Eq. 5.1)

$$
\begin{aligned}
y = {} & 78.85 - 1.37x_3 + 1.26x_1x_5 + 1.00x_2x_5 + 1.20x_3x_4 - 0.18x_1^2x_4 - 0.14x_2^2x_3 \\
& - 0.15x_4^2x_5 - 0.23x_5^2x_4
\end{aligned}
$$

(Eq. 5.2)

The ACO-based approach can also yield a reasonable suboptimal solution in a much shorter time (Ghazali et al., 2018). For example, an 'Ant Colony Molecular Simulation' (LotfiKatooli & Shahsavand, 2018) technique devised for predicting adsorption isotherm behaviour of various zeolitic adsorbents was simpler to implement. It consumed considerably less computational time to yield the same accuracy as a 'Grand Canonical Monte Carlo Molecular Simulation' (LotfiKatooli & Shahsavand, 2018) method. The outperformance of this ant colony algorithm-based method versus that of the random search-based Monte Carlo approach was attributed to its global optimisation feature that enabled strategically determining the optimal solution at every required condition (LotfiKatooli & Shahsavand, 2018).

### 5.2.2 Bee Colony Optimisation (BCO)

The bees-inspired optimisation algorithm is based on the ageing behaviour of honeybees in finding an optimum solution (Ghaedi et al., 2015). BCO has an edge over other methods in generating high-quality results within negligible processing times. There are very few applications of the BCO reported in the literature for aqueous adsorption systems. For example, the effects of adsorption process parameters on Eosin B adsorption by $Co_2O_3$ nanoparticles loaded on activated carbon were examined by multiple linear regression and artificial neural network (ANN) and were optimised using the bees algorithm (Ghaedi et al., 2015). The ANN model was better than the regression model for predicting Eosin B removal (Ghaedi et al., 2015).

An ANN-bees algorithm-based model and a D-optimal RSM approach were implemented to optimise five independent variables involved in acid red 27 dye sequestration from aqueous solutions by a polypyrrole/$SrFe_{12}O_{19}$/graphene oxide nanocomposite (Ebrahimpoor et al., 2019). The sequestration of the acid red 27 dye molecules by the nanocomposite adsorbent was modelled by the output parameter (percentage removal $R\%$) of a cost function (Eq. 5.3) as part of the ANN-bees algorithm-based approach (Ebrahimpoor et al., 2019). The input parameters are $v(1)$ for initial dye concentration (mg $L^{-1}$), $v(2)$ for adsorbent dosage (g), $v(3)$ for contact time (mins), $v(4)$ for pH and $v(5)$ for shaking rate (rpm). The $k$ and $\beta$ terms were defined as follows for the ANN's hidden (corresponding to subscript $1$ terms) and output (corresponding to the subscript $2$ terms) layers (Ebrahimpoor et al., 2019): $k_2$ = weight vector, $k_1$ = weight matrix, $\beta_2$ = scalar bias and $\beta_1$ = bias vector. The transfer function tanh in the hidden layer of the ANN is the hyperbolic tangent activation function, and the transfer function Pu in the output layer of the ANN is the purelin function (Ebrahimpoor et al., 2019). The two-factor interaction regression model developed by Ebrahimpoor et al. (2019) under the D-optimal RSM approach for computing $R\%$ is given in Eq. (5.4). The subscripted coded variables '$v$' in Eq. (5.4) are: $v_1$ is for initial dye concentration, $v_2$ is for adsorbent dosage, $v_3$ is for contact time, $v_4$ is for pH and $v_5$ is for shaking rate. The minimum cost function was $-3.244$ (iterations number = 20) and the corresponding $R\%$ = 99% under optimised conditions for the input parameters (initial dye concentration = 31 mg $L^{-1}$, adsorbent dosage = 62 mg, contact time = 60 min, pH of solution = 9.7, shaking rate = 271 rpm) (Ebrahimpoor et al., 2019). It was eventually inferred that the ANN-bees algorithm had outsmarted the D-optimal RSM by yielding 4% more dye removal (Ebrahimpoor et al., 2019).

$$R\% = \text{Pu}\left(k_2 \times \tanh(k_1 \times [v(1); v(2); v(3); v(4); v(5)] + \beta_1) + \beta_2\right) \qquad \text{(Eq. 5.3)}$$

$$
\begin{aligned}
R = &+73.45 + 2.79v_1 + 21.71v_2 - 2.85v_3 - 6.38v_4 - 3.29v_5 - 2.07v_1v_2 \\
&+ 13.05v_1v_4 - 3.70v_1v_5 + 6.47v_2v_3 + 8.57v_2v_4 + 3.56v_3v_4 + 10.30v_3v_5 \\
&- 1.45v_4v_5
\end{aligned}
\qquad \text{(Eq. 5.4)}
$$

### 5.2.3 Elephant Herd Optimisation (EHO)

The EHO approach is a novel soft computing method for parameter estimation (Aravamudan, 2021). It is derived from elephants' search for the optimum (largest) water source (waterhole) within the jungle based on their strong memory (Gopinath & Aravamudan, 2019). Detailed descriptions and discussions of an updated EHO algorithm applied to estimate homogeneous surface diffusion model parameters as part of batch adsorption kinetics data are provided in Aravamudan (2021) and Gopinath and Aravamudan (2019). This EHO method outsmarted the simulated annealing, Nelder–Mead simplex and genetic algorithms with its high precision and lesser computational effort (Aravamudan, 2021). Intraparticle diffusivity and mass transfer coefficient estimated by the EHO had, on average, about 52% and 63% smaller standard deviations, respectively, versus the other algorithms implemented in the analysis of adsorption data (Aravamudan, 2021).

## 5.3 Research Perspectives

The ACO, BCO and EHO optimisations have been applied to laboratory-scale systems. Hence, they still demand significant upgrading before being fully adequate for implementation in complex pilot-scale adsorption configurations. 'Complex', in a first instance, to emphasize the multicomponent character of the polluted water or wastewater. 'Complex' because of the process operations in actual wastewater treatment plants where batch, multiple-batch or continuous adsorption systems may be one or more of the unit operations (Ullah et al., 2020). Hence, the *breadth* and *depth* of fresh research probing the application of the ACO, BCO and/or EHO methods in parameter estimation defining batch and continuous fixed bed column-type *multicomponent* aqueous adsorption processes are *significant*.

'Multicomponent' because real water systems contain several competing species (Ambaye et al., 2021; Islam et al., 2020). Multicomponent adsorption is a significantly complex phenomenon because of interspecies competition for adsorption sites and due to the complex interactions among the adsorbent and several adsorbates (Pauletto et al., 2020; Yadav et al., 2021; Yettou et al., 2021). Modelling multicomponent adsorption processes is particularly difficult because of wide variations in adsorbent properties and adsorption operating conditions (contact time, pH, temperature, dosage and concentration (Yettou et al., 2021)). This modelling becomes more difficult because of the non-linearity of parameter variations (e.g. pH, temperature, concentration and time) (Pauletto et al., 2020). Interestingly, many multicomponent adsorption models are yet to be comprehensively applied using a NIOPAS-based approach.

Swarm intelligence–based algorithms are also relevant for solving optimisation problems in single-component adsorption systems. Some isotherm models used to fit single-component adsorption data contain multiple fitting parameters. Poorly chosen starting values can cause a conventional gradient-based optimisation method to never converge on a solution or converge to a local minimum (Chu et al., 2022). The problem of convergence to an unwanted local minimum is inherent to traditional gradient-based optimisation methods and is more likely to happen when the fitting algorithm has to determine multiple parameters (Chu et al., 2022). The three swarm intelligence–based optimisation methods discussed above provide an effective way to alleviate the issue of getting locked in a local minimum since they do not require the user to supply sensible starting values (Chu et al., 2022).

Despite the ACO's ability to constitute improved approaches for solving continuous problems, it has some limitations (Zhao et al., 2021). Zhao et al. (2021) indicated that the ACO's quality of the solution, its speed of convergence and its jumping out of local optimality were unsatisfactory. Interestingly, these limitations leave room for further enhancement of the ACO approach (Zhao et al., 2021). The BCO is endowed with a powerful global search capability (Hakli & Kiran, 2020). Yet, this global search capability can give rise to poor intensification of the obtained solutions and slow convergence (Hakli & Kiran, 2020). Ismaeel et al. (2019) and Muthusamy et al. (2021) have highlighted the EHO algorithm's insufficiency with respect to its lack of exploitation which causes slow convergence.

A next step may consist in exploring how one or more of ACO, BCO or EHO (or an enhanced version of either to improve convergence and precision [Elhosseini et al., 2019; Muthusamy et al., 2021; Ustun et al., 2022; Zhao et al., 2021]) can be effectively adapted in the design, process analysis and process optimisation of actual pilot-scale aqueous adsorption-based water treatment systems. Pilot-scale systems are complex. This complexity arises from size variation of the physical system, flow and flow regime variabilities, thermal, hydraulic and concentration gradients, degree of compactness (i.e. local porosity) of adsorbent(s) used, mechanical forces operating within the adsorption unit and hostile (acidic, alkaline, corrosive, toxic, too cold or too hot) characteristics of real wastewaters or other polluted waters. Hence, it will be interesting to assess the extent to which these complexities induce deviations from the more desirable adsorption behaviours observed at lower scales of operations.

## 5.4 Conclusion

We envisage that the application of NIOPAS selected for studying aqueous adsorption dynamics at larger scales *has huge research space and potential for expansion*. Such an expansion may be expected in the form of more comprehensive and efficient optimisation algorithms that integrate a robust representation of the dominant physical and chemical interactions of the adsorption phenomena across different multicomponent aqueous systems. More so, the integration of those dominant system-specific physicochemical phenomenological interactions will require performing in-depth global sensitivity analysis of different types of adsorption processes with respect to the various process parameters involved. Examples of these variables are pH, presence of different competing species, temperature, any possible chemical reactions among aqueous species, effects of mechanical stresses to which the adsorbate–adsorbent may be subject due to agitation and susceptibility of the adsorbent to be (bio)degraded. Thus, wide-ranging opportunities for collaboration among experimental chemists, chemical engineers and SCADA engineers open up in the application of NIOPAS for water remediation.

*The broader societal-engineering picture* – Many societies across the globe are faced with severe water pollution issues, some of which are highly disruptive and induce irreversible environmental health impacts (Madhav et al., 2020). For example, groundwater pollution by arsenic is a grim reality globally (Medunić et al., 2020) and fuels social vulnerability (Biswas et al., 2022). Research and development is continually underway to develop new adsorbents to 'super-accumulate' aqueous arsenic species (Dias & Fontes, 2020; Song et al., 2021). It is important to develop adsorption-based devices that remove micropollutants such as arsenic and xenobiotics from contaminated water. Thus, the design and process intensification of these devices should be conducted after the requisite global parametric optimisation has been applied to pilot-scale systems. NIOPAS such as the ACO, BCO and EHO are expected to have pivotal contributions in this sense. Eventually, the results of these studies can be echeloned in real-scale water treatment systems to produce cleaner and safer water.

## References

Ambaye, T. G., Vaccari, M., van Hullebusch, E. D., Amrane, A., & Rtimi, S. (2021). Mechanisms and adsorption capacities of biochar for the removal of organic and inorganic pollutants from industrial wastewater. *International Journal of Environmental Science and Technology*, *18*(10), 3273–3294. https://doi.org/10.1007/s13762-020-03060-w

Aravamudan, K. (2021). Soft computing optimization algorithms and their application in parameter estimation of a rigorous adsorption kinetics model. In *Soft computing techniques in solid waste and wastewater management* (pp. 145–169). Elsevier. https://doi.org/10.1016/B978-0-12-824463-0.00003-3

Benjelloun, M., Miyah, Y., Akdemir Evrendilek, G., Zerrouq, F., & Lairini, S. (2021). Recent advances in adsorption kinetic models: Their application to dye types. *Arabian Journal of Chemistry*, *14*(4), 103031. https://doi.org/10.1016/j.arabjc.2021.103031

Biswas, S., Sahoo, S., & Debsarkar, A. (2022). Social vulnerability of arsenic contaminated groundwater in the context of Ganga-Brahmaputra-Meghna basin: A critical review. In *Advances in geographic information science* (pp. 39–61). https://doi.org/10.1007/978-3-030-75197-5_3

Chu, K. H. (2020). Fitting the Gompertz equation to asymmetric breakthrough curves. *Journal of Environmental Chemical Engineering*, *8*(3), 103713. https://doi.org/10.1016/j.jece.2020.103713

Chu, K. H., Debord, J., Harel, M., & Bollinger, J.-C. (2022). Mirror, mirror on the wall, which is the fairest of them all? Comparing the Hill, Sips, Koble–Corrigan, and Liu adsorption isotherms. *Industrial & Engineering Chemistry Research*, *61*(19), 6781–6790. https://doi.org/10.1021/acs.iecr.2c00507

Dehghani, M., Hubálovský, Š., & Trojovský, P. (2021). Cat and mouse based optimizer: A new nature-inspired optimization algorithm. *Sensors, 21*(15), 5214. https://doi.org/10.3390/s21155214

Dias, A. C., & Fontes, M. P. F. (2020). Arsenic (V) removal from water using hydrotalcites as adsorbents: A critical review. *Applied Clay Science, 191*, 105615. https://doi.org/10.1016/j.clay.2020.105615

Dorigo, M., & Stützle, T. (2019). Ant colony optimization: Overview and recent advances. In *International series in operations research and management science* (pp. 311–351). https://doi.org/10.1007/978-3-319-91086-4_10

Ebrahimpoor, S., Kiarostami, V., Khosravi, M., Davallo, M., & Ghaedi, A. (2019). Bees metaheuristic algorithm with the aid of artificial neural networks for optimization of acid red 27 dye adsorption onto novel polypyrrole/SrFe$_{12}$O$_{19}$/graphene oxide nanocomposite. *Polymer Bulletin, 76*(12), 6529–6553. https://doi.org/10.1007/s00289-019-02700-7

Elhosseini, M. A., El Sehiemy, R. A., Rashwan, Y. I., & Gao, X. Z. (2019). On the performance improvement of elephant herding optimization algorithm. *Knowledge-Based Systems, 166*, 58–70. https://doi.org/10.1016/j.knosys.2018.12.012

Ghaedi, M., Ansari, A., Assefi Nejad, P., Ghaedi, A., Vafaei, A., & Habibi, M. H. (2015). Artificial neural network and bees algorithm for removal of Eosin B using cobalt oxide nanoparticle-activated carbon: Isotherm and kinetics study. *Environmental Progress & Sustainable Energy, 34*(1), 155–168. https://doi.org/10.1002/ep.11981

Ghazali, A., Shirani, M., Semnani, A., Zare-Shahabadi, V., & Nekoeinia, M. (2018). Optimization of crystal violet adsorption onto Date palm leaves as a potent biosorbent from aqueous solutions using response surface methodology and ant colony. *Journal of Environmental Chemical Engineering, 6*(4), 3942–3950. https://doi.org/10.1016/j.jece.2018.05.043

González-López, M. E., Laureano-Anzaldo, C. M., Pérez-Fonseca, A. A., Arellano, M., & Robledo-Ortíz, J. R. (2021). A critical overview of adsorption models linearization: Methodological and statistical inconsistencies. *Separation and Purification Reviews*, 1–15. https://doi.org/10.1080/15422119.2021.1951757

Gopinath, A., & Aravamudan, K. (2019). A novel, initial guess free optimization algorithm for estimating parameters of batch kinetics model used to simulate adsorption of pollutant molecules in aqueous streams. *Journal of Molecular Liquids, 275*, 510–522. https://doi.org/10.1016/j.molliq.2018.11.015

Gopinath, A., Retnam, B. G., Muthukkumaran, A., & Aravamudan, K. (2020). Swift, versatile and a rigorous kinetic model based artificial neural network surrogate for single and multicomponent batch adsorption processes. *Journal of Molecular Liquids, 297*, 111888. https://doi.org/10.1016/j.molliq.2019.111888

Hakli, H., & Kiran, M. S. (2020). An improved artificial bee colony algorithm for balancing local and global search behaviors in continuous optimization. *International Journal of Machine Learning and Cybernetics, 11*(9), 2051–2076. https://doi.org/10.1007/s13042-020-01094-7

Hancer, E. (2020). Artificial bee colony: Theory, literature review, and application in image segmentation. In *Studies in computational intelligence* (pp. 47–67). https://doi.org/10.1007/978-981-15-1362-6_3

Huangfu, X., Xu, Y., Liu, C., He, Q., Ma, J., Ma, C., & Huang, R. (2019). A review on the interactions between engineered nanoparticles with extracellular and intracellular polymeric substances from wastewater treatment aggregates. *Chemosphere, 219*, 766–783. https://doi.org/10.1016/j.chemosphere.2018.12.044

Islam, M. A., Morton, D. W., Johnson, B. B., & Angove, M. J. (2020). Adsorption of humic and fulvic acids onto a range of adsorbents in aqueous systems, and their effect on the adsorption of other species: A review. *Separation and Purification Technology, 247*, 116949. https://doi.org/10.1016/j.seppur.2020.116949

Ismaeel, A. A. K., Elshaarawy, I. A., Houssein, E. H., Ismail, F. H., & Hassanien, A. E. (2019). Enhanced elephant herding optimization for global optimization. *IEEE Access, 7*, 34738–34752. https://doi.org/10.1109/ACCESS.2019.2904679

Jiang, H., Liu, T., He, P., Ding, Y., & Chen, Q. (2021). Rapid measurement of fatty acid content during flour storage using a color-sensitive gas sensor array: Comparing the effects of swarm intelligence optimization algorithms on sensor features. *Food Chemistry, 338*, 127828. https://doi.org/10.1016/j.foodchem.2020.127828

Jun, L. Y., Karri, R. R., Mubarak, N. M., Yon, L. S., Bing, C. H., Khalid, M., Jagadish, P., & Abdullah, E. C. (2020). Modelling of methylene blue adsorption using peroxidase immobilized functionalized Buckypaper/polyvinyl alcohol membrane via ant colony optimization. *Environmental Pollution, 259*, 113940. https://doi.org/10.1016/j.envpol.2020.113940

Karri, R. R., Sahu, J. N., & Meikap, B. C. (2020). Improving efficacy of Cr (VI) adsorption process on sustainable adsorbent derived from waste biomass (sugarcane bagasse) with help of ant colony optimization. *Industrial Crops and Products, 143*, 111927. https://doi.org/10.1016/j.indcrop.2019.111927

Khajeh, M., Pourkarami, A., Arefnejad, E., Bohlooli, M., Khatibi, A., Ghaffari-Moghaddam, M., & Zareian-Jahromi, S. (2017). Application of chitosan-zinc oxide nanoparticles for lead extraction from water samples by combining ant colony optimization with artificial neural network. *Journal of Applied Spectroscopy, 84*(4), 716–724. https://doi.org/10.1007/s10812-017-0535-y

LotfiKatooli, L., & Shahsavand, A. (2018). An innovative approach for molecular simulation of nanostructured adsorption isotherms via the ant colony method. *Journal of Physical Chemistry C, 122*(10), 5710–5720. https://doi.org/10.1021/acs.jpcc.7b09476

Luo, J., & Crittenden, J. C. (2019). Nanomaterial adsorbent design: From bench scale tests to engineering design. *Environmental Science & Technology, 53*(18), 10537–10538. https://doi.org/10.1021/acs.est.9b04371

Madhav, S., Ahamad, A., Singh, A. K., Kushawaha, J., Chauhan, J. S., Sharma, S., & Singh, P. (2020). *Water pollutants: Sources and impact on the environment and human health* (pp. 43–62). https://doi.org/10.1007/978-981-15-0671-0_4

Medunić, G., Fiket, Ž., & Ivanić, M. (2020). Arsenic contamination status in Europe, Australia, and other parts of the world. In *Arsenic in drinking water and food* (pp. 183–233). Springer Singapore. https://doi.org/10.1007/978-981-13-8587-2_6

Muthusamy, H., Ravindran, S., Yaacob, S., & Polat, K. (2021). An improved elephant herding optimization using sine–cosine mechanism and opposition based learning for global optimization problems. *Expert Systems with Applications, 172*, 114607. https://doi.org/10.1016/j.eswa.2021.114607

Nayar, N., Gautam, S., Singh, P., & Mehta, G. (2021). Ant colony optimization: A review of literature and application in feature selection. In *Lecture notes in networks and systems* (pp. 285–297). https://doi.org/10.1007/978-981-33-4305-4_22

Park, M., Wu, S., Lopez, I. J., Chang, J. Y., Karanfil, T., & Snyder, S. A. (2020). Adsorption of perfluoroalkyl substances (PFAS) in groundwater by granular activated carbons: Roles of hydrophobicity of PFAS and carbon characteristics. *Water Research, 170*, 115364. https://doi.org/10.1016/j.watres.2019.115364

Pauletto, P. S., Dotto, G. L., & Salau, N. P. G. (2020). Optimal artificial neural network design for simultaneous modeling of multicomponent adsorption. *Journal of Molecular Liquids, 320*, 114418. https://doi.org/10.1016/j.molliq.2020.114418

Song, X., Wang, Y., Zhou, L., Luo, X., & Liu, J. (2021). Halloysite nanotubes stabilized polyurethane foam carbon coupled with iron oxide for high-efficient and fast treatment of arsenic(III/V) wastewater. *Chemical Engineering Research and Design, 165*, 298–307. https://doi.org/10.1016/j.cherd.2020.11.001

Syafiuddin, A., Salmiati, S., Jonbi, J., & Fulazzaky, M. A. (2018). Application of the kinetic and isotherm models for better understanding of the behaviors of silver nanoparticles adsorption onto different adsorbents. *Journal of Environmental Management, 218*, 59–70. https://doi.org/10.1016/j.jenvman.2018.03.066

Tovar-Gómez, R., Moreno-Virgen, M. R., Dena-Aguilar, J. A., Hernández-Montoya, V., Bonilla-Petriciolet, A., & Montes-Morán, M. A. (2013). Modeling of fixed-bed adsorption of fluoride on bone char using a hybrid neural network approach. *Chemical Engineering Journal, 228*, 1098–1109. https://doi.org/10.1016/j.cej.2013.05.080

Trojovský, P., & Dehghani, M. (2022). Pelican optimization algorithm: A novel nature-inspired algorithm for engineering applications. *Sensors, 22*(3), 855. https://doi.org/10.3390/s22030855

Ullah, A., Hussain, S., Wasim, A., & Jahanzaib, M. (2020). Development of a decision support system for the selection of wastewater treatment technologies. *Science of the Total Environment, 731*, 139158. https://doi.org/10.1016/j.scitotenv.2020.139158

Ustun, D., Toktas, A., Erkan, U., & Akdagli, A. (2022). Modified artificial bee colony algorithm with differential evolution to enhance precision and convergence performance. *Expert Systems with Applications, 198*, 116930. https://doi.org/10.1016/j.eswa.2022.116930

Wang, J., & Guo, X. (2020). Adsorption kinetic models: Physical meanings, applications, and solving methods. *Journal of Hazardous Materials, 390*, 122156. https://doi.org/10.1016/j.jhazmat.2020.122156

Yadav, A., Bagotia, N., Sharma, A. K., & Kumar, S. (2021). Simultaneous adsorptive removal of conventional and emerging contaminants in multi-component systems for wastewater remediation: A critical review. *Science of the Total Environment, 799*, 149500. https://doi.org/10.1016/j.scitotenv.2021.149500

Yang, Z., Gu, Y., Yuan, B., Tian, Y., Shang, J., Tsang, D. C. W., Liu, M., Gan, L., Mao, S., & Li, L. (2021). Thio-groups decorated covalent triazine frameworks for selective mercury removal. *Journal of Hazardous Materials, 403*, 123702. https://doi.org/10.1016/j.jhazmat.2020.123702

Yettou, A., Laidi, M., El Bey, A., Hanini, S., Hentabli, M., Khaldi, O., & Abderrahim, M. (2021). Ternary multicomponent adsorption modelling using ANN, LS-SVR, and SVR approach – Case study. *Kemija u Industriji, 9–10*, 509–518. https://doi.org/10.15255/KUI.2020.071

Zhao, D., Liu, L., Yu, F., Heidari, A. A., Wang, M., Oliva, D., Muhammad, K., & Chen, H. (2021). Ant colony optimization with horizontal and vertical crossover search: Fundamental visions for multi-threshold image segmentation. *Expert Systems with Applications, 167*, 114122. https://doi.org/10.1016/j.eswa.2020.114122

Zhu, H., Wang, Y., Ma, Z., & Li, X. (2021). A comparative study of swarm intelligence algorithms for UCAV path-planning problems. *Mathematics, 9*(2), 171. https://doi.org/10.3390/math9020171

Part 2

# Impact of AI-Enabled Civil Engineering Systems on UN SDGs

Chapter 6

# Artificial Intelligence–Based Clean Water and Sanitation Monitoring

*Deejaysing Jogee[a], Manta Devi Nowbuth[a], Virendra Proag[a] and Jean-Luc Probst[b]*

[a]University of Mauritius, Mauritius
[b]University of Toulouse III Paul Sabatier, France

## Abstract

It is now well-established that good water quality is associated with economic prosperity, reduced incidence on public health and the good functioning of the various ecosystems found in our environment. Water contamination is mostly related to both diffused (agricultural lands and geologic rock degradations) and point sources of pollution. Mauritius has many water resources which depend solely on precipitation for their replenishment. Water parameters which are of relevance include total dissolved solids (TDS), temperature, pH, electrical conductivity, turbidity, dissolved oxygen, dissolved and particulate organic carbon and major cations and anions. The traditional methods of analysis for these parameters are mostly using electrical and optical methods (probes and sensors in the field), while chemical titrations, Flame AAS and High-Performance Liquid Chromatography techniques are carried out in the laboratory. Image Classification techniques using neural networks can also be used to detect the presence of contaminants in water. In addition to basic water quality parameters, the field sensors range have been extended to cover important major ions and can now be integrated with Artificial Intelligence (AI)-based models for the prediction of variations in water quality to better protect human health and the environment, reduce operation costs of water and wastewater treatment plant unit processes.

*Keywords*: Artificial Intelligence (AI); water sector; water quality; image classification; neural networks; contaminants

Artificial Intelligence, Engineering Systems and Sustainable Development, 69–80
doi:10.1108/978-1-83753-540-820241006

## 6.1 Introduction

Rising population growth, improvement in lifestyle, increasing economic development and consequently, increasing water demands are all putting a lot of
pressure on the limited water resources. In addition to increasing water demands,
water resources are also impacted by land-use activities, seawater intrusion,
unsafe disposal of industrial wastewater, leachates from uncontrolled disposal of
solid wastes and stormwater from the urban environment. Climate change adds to
the challenges with torrential rainfall resulting from major losses to the sea and
drought events resulting from inadequate water, where storage facilities are weak.
It is now duly recognised that the past water management models, which involved
harnessing water, treating it, distributing and disposing of the wastewater, are no
longer a sustainable model for water resources. More than ever, the need for
developing sustainable water resources and using water more judiciously is getting
recognition by all water users. Past studies (Narayana Rao et al., 2023; Tarpani &
Azapagic, 2023) have highlighted a number of ways to use water more wisely,
minimise wastage, minimise losses, promote water demand management techniques and promote reuse of treated wastewater. While each of these approaches
will bring about much benefit, the challenges associated with losses and hence
wastages are very high. This situation is particularly so because of the structure of
the urban system where utilities are connected to a central system, and failure of
one part of the system often cause disturbances in others. One of the most
promising technologies in the world today is artificial intelligence (AI), which is
the ability of machines to act intelligently by making decisions to react to new
inputs without even being programmed to do so (Baum et al., 2021). Support
Vector Machine (SVM) is a machine learning (ML) algorithm that can be used to
solve complex regression, classification and outlier detection problems (Kanade,
2022). Fig. 6.1 shows how SVM can be used to perform optimal data

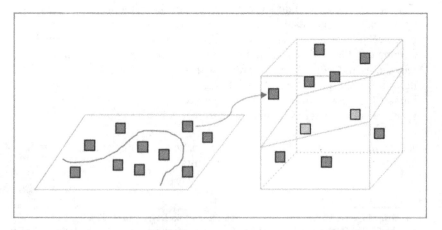

Fig. 6.1.   Artificial Intelligence (AI) Can be Used for Data
Classification. *Source:* Adapted From Kindson The Genius (2018).

transformations by identifying the hyperplane that perfectly segregate the data points based on pre-defined classes. SVM has been used in the prediction and classification of water quality of rivers and watersheds (Abobakr Yahya et al., 2019; Tan et al., 2012; Veeramsetty et al., 2022).

Compared to computer programs which generate outputs according to a set of clear instructions, AI-based models must be trained to learn input–output relationships in order to predict output data values or to create new data. AI in the water and sanitation sectors helps to make informed decisions regarding complex systems by offering the potential to predict water quality and minimise losses. Satellite image classification techniques have also been used for the early detection of contaminated surface waters and the identification of pollution sources (Mukonza & Chiang, 2022; Wang et al., 2022). This chapter focuses on the latest developments encompassing the application of AI-based techniques in the water sector, mainly water treatment, wastewater treatment and water quality monitoring.

## 6.2 AI and the Water Sector

The water infrastructure in any country serves these three main purposes: provides water for health and hygiene, provides water for economic development and ensures an infrastructure that will perform during harsh environmental conditions while maintaining water safety. When one part of this complex system fails, this is normally accompanied by severe disruptions. This complex system is now supported by AI and this process is expected to continue evolving over time, as AI is already proving itself as an effective water management tool (Hightide Technologies, 2023; Hill, 2018).

In the water and wastewater distribution networks, connections to remote sensors are enabling companies identify the presence and causes of losses and take remedial actions rather than reacting to disturbances. The applications of the artificial neural networks (ANN) have been one of the most successful model-free methods for Water Distribution Network (WDN) analysis and management (Mosetlhe et al., 2018). Hydraulic models based on genetic algorithm (GA) using data regarding discharge and pressure at various nodes of a WDN is enabling water companies to identify losses in the system (Desai & Rajapara, 2022). This study noted that the number of leakages obtained by GA in the network are reduced to 73% from the actual leakage calculations. A combination of supervised ML techniques such as SVM, Logistic Regression and ANN have been used to position sensors for minimising losses in water distribution networks (Gupta, 2017; Joseph et al., 2022; Kammoun et al., 2022).

Another sector, where AI is receiving much interest, is the management of stormwater drainage systems. These systems are subject to blockage by large debris, which hinder their smooth operation and hence cause many problems. The complexity of urban systems is making storm network systems very difficult to manage (Azari & Tabesh, 2022; Bednar, 2019). Real-time control systems, a form of AI, are becoming popular in stormwater management systems. An automated system with smart gates, as part of the CENTAUR system, is being used to divert flood waters where necessary to improve the management of flood waters (Smartcity, 2019).

Apart from these large sectors, where AI is becoming a strong working and management tool, there are several other sectors where AI is supporting the water sector, and already, we are noting some applications of AI in Mauritius.

## 6.3 AI and Water Quality

In the water quality sector, AI has shown particular strength in assessing the contaminant levels, and temporal and spatial variations of pollutants affecting water quality (Rajaee et al., 2020; Tung & Yaseen, 2020). In a study on AI and water quality, adaptive neuro-fuzzy inference system (ANFIS) algorithm was developed to estimate water quality index (WQI). Hmoud Al-Adhaileh and Waselallah Alsaade (2021) used K-nearest neighbours and Feed-Forward Neural Network (FFNN) to classify water quality. An accuracy of 100% was obtained using FFNN for water quality classification (WQC), while the ANFIS model accurately predicted WQI. In another study, the ANN models, namely long short-term memory (LSTM) deep learning algorithm and nonlinear autoregressive neural network (NARNET), were used together with three ML algorithms, namely, Naive Bayes, SVM and K-nearest neighbour (K-NN), for water quality forecasting. The highest accuracy (97.01%) was achieved for the WQC prediction by SVM algorithm, while the NARNET model better predicted WQI values when compared to LSTM algorithm (Aldhyani et al., 2020).

AI is extensively being applied to the field of water quality through image processing and pattern detection. Clean Water AI is an Internet of Things (IoT) device that categorises and detects harmful particles and dangerous bacteria (Keysight Technologies, 2023). It is based on the convolutional neural network (a class of deep, feed-forward ANN), mostly used to analyse visual imagery. The process involves first training the system with existing data and then correlating visual images with water quality indicators. IoT devices are being used to constantly monitor the water quality in water bodies to ensure that no permanent harm is induced in water bodies (IBM, 2018). A new algorithm (the 'meta-learning' method) capable of analysing data directly from satellite sensors, which allows environmental, coastal zone and industry managers, to monitor issues such as possible toxicity in shellfish and finfish, as well as harmful algal blooms (HABs), was developed by the University of Sterling (Science Daily, 2021). Horak et al. (2015) used the methods of colour-space transformation and analysis, combined with motion analysis in an image processing stage, to monitor water quality.

Earth observation in the form of satellite imageries taken at different points in time and over space is proving to be a useful tool to conduct impact analysis of climate change and detection of contaminated surface waters. The normalised different water index (NDWI) (EOS Data Analytics, 2023) uses near infrared and green bands of remote sensing images to differentiate water bodies from dry land.

Martinez et al. (2009) were able to observe a robust link between surface water reflectance and suspended sediment concentration at the river surface. A Medium Resolution Imaging Spectrometer (MERIS) algorithm was used by Gons et al. (2002) to retrieve moderate to high concentrations of Chlorophyll *a* in very different water bodies. Ferdous et al. (2019) demonstrated how Landsat 8 OLI could be applied to detect the TDS level in coastal surface waters. On the other hand, Karnawat and Patil (2016) proposed image processing as a new technique for the determination of turbidity using a high-definition camera to capture different water sample images having different turbidities.

## 6.4 AI in Water Treatment

Flood events cause drastic changes in the chemical and physical composition of surface waters and represent major challenges for water treatment plants. High levels of turbidity are caused by suspended sediments in water that result in the clogging of filters and eventual shutdown of other unit processes in treatment plants, thus disrupting the supply of potable water for domestic use for several days or even weeks. Real-time monitoring of certain physico-chemical parameters can help enormously in controlling the quality of incoming surface waters feeding water treatment plant and prevent damage to expensive equipment. Raj et al. (2020) developed a low-cost real-time water eminence computing structure for the monitoring of pH, turbidity and temperature of water by making use of water recognition sensors. According to the authors, the system can be upgraded by integrating algorithms to discover irregularities in water quality. Other authors have devised similar experimental setups (Daigavane & Gaikwad, 2017; Gokulanathan et al., 2019; Hakimi & Jamil, 2021; Hong et al., 2021; Pasika & Gandla, 2020; Singh et al., 2022; Taru & Karwankar, 2017) using Arduino circuit boards, sensors, microcontrollers, WI-FI connectivity, mobile applications, IoT and ML for the real-time monitoring of basic water parameters.

Data loggers and telemetry systems have been in use for a long period of time, particularly for sites with difficult access and for sites where more regular and frequent data are required. With time, software has been developed to automate both the collection and the analysis of such data, and this has given rise to different types of observatories (Bluedot Observatory, 2018; Texas Water Observatory, 2023). Here data collected through telemetry and sensor systems are analysed automatically, and regularly summaries are displayed on dash-boards, to enable more informed decision-making. Data loggers combined with automated data interpretation software have given rise to Smart Water Networks (Waterworld, 2017), which include a combination of GIS, CIS and SCADA systems to support water distribution networks.

Particle size determination of various materials is very important in many fields of civil and environmental engineering. Particle size analysis is used for quality control in water and wastewater treatment. The particle size distribution of sands used in filter beds for the treatment of water for domestic purposes is very important for the effective removal of suspended flocculated materials. The effects of the height of the beds and the size of particles have been assessed by Esfilar et al. (2023) to determine the critical porosity of an optimised triple-bed sand filter. Particle size of the bedding material affects directly the permeability and porosity of the substrate that influences the filter's performance and turbidity removal efficiency. The specific area, also related to the particle size distribution, affects the degradation and removal of phytotoxins in filter sands used for drinking water treatment (Mrkajic et al., 2021). Traditionally, particle size distribution of coarse and fine materials is determined using a set of stacked sieves arranged in the order of increasing aperture size with the sample placed on the topmost sieve having the largest mesh size. Fernlund (1998) compared the actual hand measured size and form, traditional sieve results and image analysis results of each particle in the samples. It was observed that the sieving method is highly influenced by the particle form and does not provide a measure of the size of the individual particles, while image analysis techniques gave highly accurate values of the axial dimensions defined for each individual particle. Much progress has been made since the past decades in developing vision or optical systems for the determination of particle size distribution using laser light scattering and diffraction techniques. For example, the Plateforme d'Analyses Physico-Chimiques (PAPC) of the University of Toulouse uses a HORIBA LA950-V2 laser scattering particle size analyser for sediment samples. The high performance LA950-V2 uses a laser beam to analyse particle sizes from 10 nm to 3 mm at a high accuracy of $\pm 0.6\%$ suitable for quality control and research and development. On the other hand, Microtrac MRB (2023) have a range of latest technologies comprising of dynamic image analysis (DIA), static image analysis, static laser light scattering (SLS, also known as laser diffraction) and dynamic light scattering (DLS) instruments for particle size analysis as alternatives to the traditional hand sieving method. These instruments can be integrated with AI-based techniques to optimise unit processes in water treatment plants for increased efficiency. AI techniques have been used to optimise selected unit processes in water treatment and desalination plants and provide practical solutions to water pollution and water scarcity (Alam et al., 2022). Particle size information during the flocculation processes allow operators to better control the quality of water produced by selecting the most optimal treatment parameters (Zielina, 2017). Membrane integrity tools having high sensitivities and accuracies are now being developed for the water industry (Lousada-Ferreira et al., 2016). The implementation of AI in water treatment plants will reduce operating cost and optimise use of chemicals. However, poor reproducibility, the availability and selection of data and lack of evidence in practical applications have hindered its implementation in real water treatment plants (Alam et al., 2022).

## 6.5 AI in Wastewater Treatment

Because fresh water is becoming a precious resource, more emphasis is now being placed on the use of treated wastewater as a viable water source. The treatment of wastewater depends very much on various unit treatment phases, particularly the removal of flocculated sludge material from sedimentation tanks and other important contaminants. Kaminski et al. (1997) investigated the removal efficiency of various particle size groups, with and without addition of flocculant, among different type of filters. Small particles in the range of 5–10 μm without chemical aids were poorly removed, while filtration with flocculant was found to be more sensitive to filtration conditions. Furthermore, the lower rate filters were less sensitive to particle size than higher rate filters. Variations in the composition of wastewaters coupled with uncertainties and variations in wastewater treatment systems lead to fluctuations in the resulting effluent water quality, operating costs and environmental risk of the receiving water bodies (Zhao et al., 2020). Suchetana et al. (2019) created a performance-based modelling approach using Hidden Markov Models and multinomial logistic regression that identified prominent climatic factors (precipitation and temperature), seasonality, total inorganic nitrogen (TIN) and total ammonia nitrogen (TAN) levels of effluent in previous weeks to correctly predict TIN levels in the effluent. Aeration of wastewater is an important step in the treatment process for digestion of organic matter by aerobic bacteria. Two novel applications of AI methods, namely, the M5 model tree and the evolutionary polynomial regression (EPR), to evaluate the aeration efficiency over stepped weir were investigated by Sattar et al. (2019). The EPR model was found to provide only one equation for each regime evaluated and performs better when compared to existing equations derived from regressive methods. The quality of the treated effluent depends on the membrane technology and the membrane filtration steps to comply with reuse or discharge limits (Lousada-Ferreira et al., 2016). After reviewing the AI-based models used in the treatment of wastewater from various sources, Kamali et al. (2021) found that all the models adequately predicted the performance of membrane bioreactor (MBR) technologies to recover clean water from polluted waters. However, more research and refinements are needed for the AI-based techniques to better predict the process performances in the case of high strength and highly polluted effluents. Schmitt et al. (2018) used ANN to predict transmembrane pressure and fouling occurrence in an anoxic-aerobic membrane bioreactor. It is also possible to evaluate particle growth, regrowth and membrane integrity in MBR permeate by counting the particles with mathematical data interpretation techniques. VisioRock is another integrated vision technology (now under the trade name RockSense 3DTM (Metso Outotec, 2023)) which has the ability to measure the particle size distribution of solids on a conveyor belt, determine the texture and colour separately for each size class and differentiate between minerals and size distribution for different type of particles. It can also seamlessly combine image analysis algorithms with AI tools such as neural networks or phenomenological process models, fuzzy logic and expert systems (Guyot et al., 2004). Useful applications of vision technologies that use a combination of powerful image analysis and AI could be the recovery of ores from the grit usually collected from the primary treatment stages of wastewaters.

## 6.6 Conclusion

Access to safe drinking water and basic sanitation is the major concern of the modern world which makes these two components high on the United Nations Sustainable Development Goals (SDGs) agenda (Resolution, 2015). Sachs et al. (2019) proposed six SDGs Transformations that describe major changes required in the organisation of political, societal and economic activities that would transform institutions, technologies, resource use and social relations in order to achieve key SDG outcomes. To ensure the sustainable management and availability of water and sanitation for all, Transformation 6 calls for the capture of the benefits from the recent digital revolution, namely AI and associated digital technologies, to achieve the key outcomes of the SDGs. AI is reshaping the water sector as AI has the potential to improve water management for meeting the SDGs aims, safe drinking water and basic sanitation for all.

## References

Abobakr Yahya, A. S., Ahmed, A. N., Binti Othman, F., Ibrahim, R. K., Afan, H. A., El-Shafie, A., Fai, C. M., Hossain, M. S., Ehteram, M., & Elshafie, A. (2019). Water quality prediction model-based support vector machine model for ungauged river catchment under dual scenarios. *Water, 11*(6), 1231.

Alam, G., Ihsanullah, I., Naushad, M., & Sillanpää, M. (2022). Applications of artificial intelligence in water treatment for optimization and automation of adsorption processes: Recent advances and prospects. *Chemical Engineering Journal, 427*, 130011.

Aldhyani, T. H., Al-Yaari, M., Alkahtani, H., & Maashi, M. (2020). Water quality prediction using artificial intelligence algorithms. *Applied Bionics and Biomechanics*. https://doi.org/10.1155/2020/6659314

Azari, B., & Tabesh, M. (2022). Urban storm water drainage system optimization using a sustainability index and LID/BMPs. *Sustainable Cities and Society, 76*, 103500. https://doi.org/10.1016/j.scs.2021.103500.124670

Baum, Z. J., Yu, X., Ayala, P. Y., Zhao, Y., Watkins, S. P., & Zhou, Q. (2021). Artificial intelligence in chemistry: Current trends and future directions. *Journal of Chemical Information and Modeling, 61*(7), 3197–3212.

Bednar, E. (2019). *Artificial intelligence of stormwater operations.* The University of Akron.

Blue dot Observatory. (2018). *Bluedot water observatory.* https://www.blue-dot-observatory.com/aboutwaterobservatory

Daigavane, V. V., & Gaikwad, M. A. (2017). Water quality monitoring system based on IoT. *Advances in Wireless and Mobile Communications, 10*(5), 1107–1116.

Desai, S., & Rajapara, G. (2022). Leakage optimization of water distribution network using artificial intelligence. In C. M. Rao, K. C. Patra, D. Jhajharia, & S. Kumari (Eds.), *Advanced modelling and innovations in water resources engineering. Lecture notes in civil engineering* (Vol. 176). Springer. https://doi.org/10.1007/978-981-16-4629-4_19

EOS Data Analytics. (2023). Index Stack (NDVI, NDWI, NDSI). https://eos.com/make-an-analysis/index-stack/

Esfilar, R., Moezi, A., Variji, M. A., & Rezaei, M. (2023). Optimization and technical paramctric assessment of a novel triple media rapid sand filter: The effect of height of beds and size of particles. *Chemical Engineering Research and Design, 190,* 745–758.

Ferdous, J., Rahman, M. T. U., & Ghosh, S. K. (2019). Detection of total dissolved solids from Landsat 8 OLI image in coastal Bangladesh. In *The Proceedings of the International Conference on Climate Change* (Vol. 3(1), pp. 35–44).

Fernlund, J. M. (1998). The effect of particle form on sieve analysis: A test by image analysis. *Engineering Geology, 50*(1–2), 111–124.

Gokulanathan, S., Manivasagam, P., Prabu, N., & Venkatesh, T. (2019). A GSM based water quality monitoring system using Arduino. *Shanlax International Journal of Arts, Science and Humanities, 6*(4), 22–26.

Gons, H. J., Rijkeboer, M., & Ruddick, K. G. (2002). A chlorophyll-retrieval algorithm for satellite imagery (Medium Resolution Imaging Spectrometer) of inland and coastal waters. *Journal of Plankton Research, 24*(9), 947–951.

Gupta, G. (2017). *Monitoring water distribution network using machine learning.* Graduate thesis, KTH Royal Institute of Technology School of Electrical Engineering. https://www.diva-portal.org/smash/get/diva2:1177842/FULLTEXT01.pdf

Guyot, O., Monredon, T., LaRosa, D., & Broussaud, A. (2004). VisioRock, an integrated vision technology for advanced control of comminution circuits. *Minerals Engineering, 17*(11–12), 1227–1235.

Hakimi, I. M., & Jamil, Z. (2021). Development of water quality monitoring device using arduino UNO. In *IOP conference series: Materials science and engineering* (Vol. 1144, No. 1, p. 012064). IOP Publishing.

Hightide Technologies. (2023). *How is artificial intelligence changing the water industry?* https://htt.io/resources/how-is-artificial-intelligence-changing-the-water-industry/

Hill, T. (2018). *How artificial intelligence is reshaping the water sector. Water finance and management.* https://waterfm.com/artificial-intelligence-reshaping-water-sector/

Hmoud Al-Adhaileh, M., & Waselallah Alsaade, F. (2021). Modelling and prediction of water quality by using artificial intelligence. *Sustainability, 13*(8), 4259. https://doi.org/10.3390/su13084259

Hong, W. J., Shamsuddin, N., Abas, E., Apong, R. A., Masri, Z., Suhaimi, H., Gödeke, S. H., & Noh, M. N. A. (2021). Water quality monitoring with arduino based sensors. *Environments, 8*(1), 6.

Horak, K., Klecka, J., & Richter, M. (2015). Water quality assessment by image processing. In *2015 38th International Conference on Telecommunications and Signal Processing (TSP)* (pp. 577–581). IEEE.

IBM. (2018). *AI and IoT technology help boost water quality in China.* https://www.ibm.com/blogs/client-voices/ai-and-iot-help-boost-water-quality-in-china/

Joseph, K., Sharma, A. K., & van Staden, R. (2022). Development of an intelligent urban water network system. *Water, 14*(9), 1320. https://doi.org/10.3390/w14091320

Kamali, M., Appels, L., Yu, X., Aminabhavi, T. M., & Dewil, R. (2021). Artificial intelligence as a sustainable tool in wastewater treatment using membrane bioreactors. *Chemical Engineering Journal, 417,* 128070.

Kaminski, I., Vescan, N., & Adin, A. (1997). Particle size distribution and wastewater filter performance. *Water Science and Technology, 36*(4), 217–224.

Kammoun, M., Kammoun, A., & Abid, M. (2022). Leak detection methods in water distribution networks: A comparative survey on artificial intelligence applications. *Journal of Pipeline Systems Engineering and Practice, 13*(3), 04022024. https://ascelibrary.org/doi/10.1061/%28ASCE%29PS.1949-1204.0000646

Kanade, V. (2022). *What is a support vector machine? Working, types, and examples.* Big Data. https://www.spiceworks.com/tech/big-data/articles/what-is-support-vector-machine/

Karnawat, V., & Patil, S. L. (2016). Turbidity detection using image processing. In *2016 International Conference on Computing, Communication and Automation (ICCCA)* (pp. 1086–1089). IEEE.

Keysight Technologies. (2023). *Clean water AI: Water quality monitoring using AI.* https://www.iotchallengekeysight.com/2019/entries/smart-water/143-0514-005430-clean-water-ai-water-quality-monitoring-using-ai

Kindson The Genius. (2018). Introduction to support vector machine (SVM). *The Genius Blog.* https://kindsonthegenius.com/blog/introduction-to-support-vector-machine-svm/

Lousada-Ferreira, M., Van Lier, J. B., & Van Der Graaf, J. H. J. M. (2016). Particle counting as surrogate measurement of membrane integrity loss and assessment tool for particle growth and regrowth in the permeate of membrane bioreactors. *Separation and Purification Technology, 161*, 16–24.

Martinez, J. M., Guyot, J. L., Filizola, N., & Sondag, F. (2009). Increase in suspended sediment discharge of the Amazon River assessed by monitoring network and satellite data. *Catena, 79*(3), 257–264.

Metso Outotec. (2023). RockSenseTM-Enabling optimization through sense. https://www.mogroup.com/portfolio/rocksense/

Microtrac MRB. (2023). *Particle Size Analysis for fluid and dry materials.* Microtrac Retsch GmbH. https://www.microtrac.com/knowledge/particle-size-analysis/

Mosetlhe, T., Hamam, Y., Du, S., & Alayli, Y. (2018). Artificial neural networks in water distribution systems: A literature synopsis. In *2018 International Conference on Intelligent and Innovative Computing Applications (ICONIC)* (pp. 1–5). IEEE. https://doi.org/10.1109/ICONIC.2018.8601090

Mrkajic, N. S., Hama, J. R., Strobel, B. W., Hansen, H. C. B., Rasmussen, L. H., Pedersen, A. K., Christensen, S. C. B., & Hedegaard, M. J. (2021). Removal of phytotoxins in filter sand used for drinking water treatment. *Water Research, 205*, 117610.

Mukonza, S. S., & Chiang, J. L. (2022). Satellite sensors as an emerging technique for monitoring macro-and microplastics in aquatic ecosystems. *Water Emerging Contaminants & Nanoplastics, 1*(4), 17.

Narayana Rao, R., Prasad, D. D., & Murali Krishna, K. V. S. G. (2023). Chapter 7 – Do's and don'ts of wastewater treatment, their reuse, and future directions. In D. Pal & A. Kumar (Eds.), *Antimicrobial resistance in wastewater and human health* (pp. 131–152). Academic Press. ISBN 9780323961240. https://doi.org/10.1016/B978-0-323-96124-0.00004-0

Pasika, S., & Gandla, S. T. (2020). Smart water quality monitoring system with cost-effective using IoT. *Heliyon, 6*(7), e04096.

Rajaee, T., Khani, S., & Ravansalar, M. (2020). Artificial intelligence-based single and hybrid models for prediction of water quality in rivers: A review. *Chemometrics and Intelligent Laboratory Systems, 200*, 103978. https://doi.org/10.1016/j.chemolab.2020.103978

Raj, S. B., Prasad, P. H., Prasath, S., & Moorthy, A. (2020). *Water quality monitoring system using Arduino. Special issues on computer applications.* SSRG International Journals. ISSN 2393-9141. https://www.internationaljournalssrg.org/uploads/specialissuepdf/SCA-2020/2020/OTHERS/P138.pdf

Resolution, G. A. (2015). Transforming our world: The 2030 Agenda for Sustainable Development. UN Doc. A/RES/70/1 (September 25, 2015).

Sachs, J. D., Schmidt-Traub, G., Mazzucato, M., Messner, D., Nakicenovic, N., & Rockström, J. (2019). Six transformations to achieve the sustainable development goals. *Nature Sustainability, 2*(9), 805–814.

Sattar, A. A., Elhakeem, M., Rezaie-Balf, M., Gharabaghi, B., & Bonakdari, H. (2019). Artificial intelligence models for prediction of the aeration efficiency of the stepped weir. *Flow Measurement and Instrumentation, 65*, 78–89.

Schmitt, F., Banu, R., Yeom, I. T., & Do, K. U. (2018). Development of artificial neural networks to predict membrane fouling in an anoxic-aerobic membrane bioreactor treating domestic wastewater. *Biochemical Engineering Journal, 133*, 47–58.

Science Daily. (2021). *Artificial intelligence to monitor water quality more effectively.* https://www.sciencedaily.com/releases/2021/05/210504112514.htm

Singh, S., Rai, S., Singh, P., & Mishra, V. K. (2022). Real-time water quality monitoring of River Ganga (India) using internet of things. *Ecological Informatics, 71*, 101770.

Smartcity. (2019). *3 ways AI is helping solve water crisis beneath the smart cities.* Smartcity Press. https://smartcity.press/water-crisis-solutions-with-ai/

Suchetana, B., Rajagopalan, B., & Silverstein, J. (2019). Investigating regime shifts and the factors controlling total inorganic nitrogen concentrations in treated wastewater using non-homogeneous hidden Markov and multinomial logistic regression models. *Science of the Total Environment, 646*, 625–633.

Tan, G., Yan, J., Gao, C., & Yang, S. (2012). Prediction of water quality time series data based on least squares support vector machine. *Procedia Engineering, 31*, 1194–1199.

Tarpani, R. R. Z., & Azapagic, A. (2023). Life cycle sustainability assessment of advanced treatment techniques for urban wastewater reuse and sewage sludge resource recovery. *Science of the Total Environment, 869*, 161771. ISSN 0048-9697. https://doi.org/10.1016/j.scitotenv.2023.161771

Taru, Y. K., and Karwankar, A. (2017). Water monitoring system using arduino with labview. In *2017 International Conference on Computing Methodologies and Communication (ICCMC)* (pp. 416–419). IEEE.

Texas Water Observatory. (2023). *Texas water observatory.* http://two.tamu.edu/

Tung, T. M., & Yaseen, Z. M. (2020). A survey on river water quality modelling using artificial intelligence models: 2000–2020. *Journal of Hydrology, 585*, 124670. https://doi.org/10.1016/j.jhydrol.2020.124670

Veeramsetty, V., Shadamaki, N., Pinninti, R., Mohnot, A., & Ashish, G. (2022). Water quality classification using support vector machine. *AIP Conference Proceedings, 2418*(1), 040022. AIP Publishing LLC.

Wang, Y., He, X., Bai, Y., Tan, Y., Zhu, B., Wang, D., Ou, M., Gong, F., Zhu, Q., & Huang, H. (2022). Automatic detection of suspected sewage discharge from coastal outfalls based on Sentinel-2 imagery. *Science of the Total Environment, 853,* 158374.
Waterworld. (2017). *Smart water networks: It's only "smart" if you have better outcomes.* https://www.waterworld.com/home/article/16189502/smart-water-networks-its-only-smart-if-you-have-better-outcomes
Zhao, L., Dai, T., Qiao, Z., Sun, P., Hao, J., & Yang, Y. (2020). Application of artificial intelligence to wastewater treatment: A bibliometric analysis and systematic review of technology, economy, management, and wastewater reuse. *Process Safety and Environmental Protection, 133,* 169–182.
Zielina, M. (2017). Monitoring of the processes in water treatment plant. Congress Sub-themes. iwra.org. https://iwra.org/member/congress/resource/abs778_article.pdf

Chapter 7

# Achieving SDG Targets in the Land Transport Sector Using Intelligent Transportation Systems

*Zaheer Doomah, Asish Seeboo and Tulsi Pawan Fowdur*

University of Mauritius, Mauritius

## Abstract

This chapter provides an overview of the potential use of Intelligent Transport Systems (ITS) and associated artificial intelligence (AI) techniques in the land transport sector in an attempt to achieve related United Nations Sustainable Development Goals (SDGs) targets. ITS applications that have now been extensively tested worldwide and have become part of the everyday transport toolkit available to practitioners have been discussed. AI techniques applied successfully in specific ITS applications such as automatic traffic control systems, real-time image processing, automatic incident detection, safety management, road condition assessment, asset management and traffic enforcement systems have been identified. These methods have helped to provide traffic engineers and transport planners with novel ways to improve safety, mobility, accessibility and efficiency in the sector and thus move closer to achieving the various SDG targets pertaining to transportation.

*Keywords*: SDGs; intelligent transportation; safety management; traffic engineering; emergency systems; optimisation

## 7.1 Introduction

Transportation has since aeons been the cornerstone of thriving societies by providing a mechanism for the exchange of goods in commercial activities and movement of people for work, leisure or defence purposes (Hoel et al., 2011). Although the transport systems have vastly improved over centuries, the sector is currently faced with defining challenges due to the ever-increasing demand associated with rapid

Artificial Intelligence, Engineering Systems and Sustainable Development, 81–93
Copyright © 2024 Zaheer Doomah, Asish Seeboo and Tulsi Pawan Fowdur
Published under exclusive licence by Emerald Publishing Limited
doi:10.1108/978-1-83753-540-820241007

urbanisation with a recent forecast by the International Transport Forum (ITF, 2021) predicting a two-fold increase in the total passenger-kilometres and freight demand worldwide by the year 2050. As a result, transportation professionals, apart from dealing with the intricate infrastructure systems, are also being tasked with resolving issues of growing complexity such as congestion, traffic crashes, poor system reliability, environmental pollution and energy inefficiencies (Sadek, 2007). A study on congestion related costs (CEBR, 2014) in the United Kingdom, France, Germany and the United States predicted that congestion costs are likely to increase in these economies by almost 50% between 2013 and 2030 to reach a total of $4.4 trillion. Moreover, transport is the primary cause of air pollution in urban areas, accounting for almost 25% of greenhouse gas emissions in Europe (European Commission, n.d.) while approximately 1.3 million people are losing their lives annually as a result of road crashes (WHO, 2018). These figures show that significant efforts are needed to move towards greater sustainability, with ambitious targets being set such as decarbonising the transport sector to reduce greenhouse gas emissions and vision zero to reduce road fatalities.

These efforts are essential to achieve the Sustainable Development Goals (SDGs) and targets as set out in the 2030 Agenda for Sustainable Development. Sustainable transport has been defined by the United Nations Secretary-General High-level Advisory Group on Sustainable Transport (2016) as the safe, affordable, accessible, efficient and resilient system for the movement of people and goods and has been earmarked as a major catalyst to sustainable development. Several SDG targets are directly and indirectly related to sustainable transport as shown in Fig. 7.1, indicating the crosscutting role of transport.

The path towards achieving the SDG targets has been severely hindered by the multiple crises suffered during the past years, with very slow progress made (United Nations, 2022), showing that rapid and innovative action needs to be taken to remedy the situation.

## 7.2 Intelligent Transportation Systems for Sustainability

Information technology (IT) has already helped in transforming various aspects of society and its use through Intelligent Transport Systems (ITS) represents one of the most cost-effective tools towards an optimised greener transport system. ITS have evolved significantly over the past decades and now encompass a broad spectrum of technologies and applications that work in an integrated manner to improve the efficiency of the system. Traditional applications of ITS include real-time traveller information, network monitoring, vehicle navigation and collision avoidance technologies, automatic tolling and congestion pricing systems, adaptive traffic signal control and vehicle-to-vehicle and vehicle-to-infrastructure communication (Ezell, 2010). The recent development of various technologies such as artificial intelligence (AI), 5G technology, big data, cloud computing, Internet of Things (IoT), digital twins and GIS spatial analysis have however led to the emergence of new ITS technologies such as Cooperative Intelligent Transport Systems (C-ITS), Connected and Autonomous Vehicles

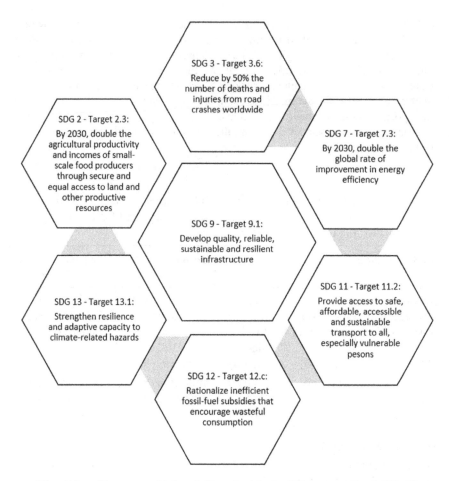

Fig. 7.1.    Transport-Related Sustainable Development Goal (SDG)
Targets.

(CAVs) and Mobility as a Service (MaaS) (Transport Scotland, 2017). These have
the potential to provide solutions to the complex issues in the transportation
system by empowering the actors in the industry – commuters, operators, and
service providers – with actionable information for quicker and proactive decision-making.

AI methods used in transport are multifold and their successful applications in
complex situations have been well documented by researchers: Artificial Neural
Networks (ANNs) have been utilised in road and public transport planning for
detection of incidents and prediction of traffic conditions, computational algorithms such as Ant Colony Optimisation (ACO) and Bee Colony Optimisation

(BCO) are used for optimised design of urban networks and Fuzzy Logic Model (FLM) has been applied to identify shortest routes in various traffic scenarios (Rusul et al., 2019). AI applications can, therefore, be used to bring significant improvements in the transport sector in the fields of traffic management, transportation safety, public transport, asset management and maintenance operations. Table 7.1 summarises the main AI techniques used in intelligent transportation management applications.

The section 7.3 discusses the techniques relevant to the AI applications in the transportation system.

Table 7.1. Intelligent Transport System (ITS) Applications and Artificial Intelligence (AI) Techniques in the Transport Sector and Sustainable Development Goals (SDG) Impact.

| ITS Applications | AI Techniques | Impacts on SDG Target |
|---|---|---|
| **Intelligent traffic management and control system** (Abduljabbar et al., 2019; Ait Ouallane et al., 2022; Teodorović, 2008) | Artificial Neural Network (ANN), Fuzzy Logic Model (FLM), genetic algorithms, swarm intelligence algorithms | SDG targets 2.3, 3.6, 7.3, 9.1 and 12.c |
| **Safety management and emergency systems** (Abduljabbar et al., 2019; Karthikeyan & Usha, 2022; Matveev et al., 2020) | ANN, machine learning (ML) and deep learning models | SDG target 3.6, 9.1, 11.2 and 13.1 |
| **Advanced public transportation management systems** (Abduljabbar et al., 2019; Chondrodima et al., 2022) | Particle swarm optimisation, ANN, ant colony optimisation (ACO) | SDG target 7.3, 9.1, 11.2 and 12.c |
| **Road network condition management** (Ranyal et al., 2022; Vyas et al., 2022) | Knowledge based systems, FLM, genetic algorithms, neural network, data mining, case based reasoning | SDG target 2.3, 3.6, 9.1, 11.2 and 13.1 |
| **Assessments and safety inspections** (Natali et al., 2023; Veres & Moussa, 2019) | | SDG target 3.6, 9.1 and 13.1 |
| **Transport network maintenance and budget optimisation** (Kobbacy, 2012) | | SDG target 9.1 and 12.c |

## 7.3 Intelligent Traffic Management and Control Systems

Mobility is of prime importance to people, especially the elderly and vulnerable population, and it helps to ensure high quality of life and economic prosperity. However, with the growing demand in the transport sector, conditions are rarely conducive to high mobility. Traditional transport infrastructure comprising physical elements for travel and associated control systems often suffer from heavy congestion, with the accompanying issues of environmental pollution, loss of productive time, increase in fuel consumption and vehicle operating costs.

The use of ITS has been widely implemented in the field of traffic management and control (Ait Ouallane et al., 2022) in an attempt to curb these issues and achieve SDG targets set in terms of greater accessibility, efficiency and sustainability. Areas of applications include:

i. Network and intersection management – maximising flow rate or minimise traffic delays along networks and at signalised junctions through optimised and dynamic traffic signal scheduling and ramp metring.
ii. Parking management – using of software applications and variable message signs to ensure efficient management of parking spaces and reduce cruising due to lack of parking space availability.
iii. Traffic law enforcement – Capturing and processing live events to tackle issues of speeding, red-light and parking violations and security problems by combining image capture with information filtering and network computing. Edge computing, deep learning and Convolutional Neural Network (CNN), which is capable of image classification and detection (Abduljabbar et al., 2019), can be applied to process images and provide the necessary reports.
iv. Road user charging systems – Collecting fees through electronic charging systems for use of specific transport corridors and types of vehicles which are more detrimental to the environment.

Various AI techniques have been used for the applications and include ANN, FLM and Genetic Algorithms (Olayode et al., 2020). Swarm intelligence algorithms based on the collective behaviour of groups in nature such as ants (ACO), bees (BCO) and birds (Particle Swarm Optimisation) have also shown promising impacts when used to solve complex vehicle routing and scheduling issues (Teodorović, 2008). Key benefits of the above in line with SDG targets include improving the operational performance of the transport system, increasing efficiency of transport operators, enhancing mobility, reducing environmental pollution and strengthening security.

## 7.4 Safety Management and Emergency Systems

Provision for the safe and secure movement of people and goods is of fundamental importance in high-quality transport systems. The current situation worldwide is however alarming, road injuries being one of the leading causes of death in lower- and upper-middle income countries. Moreover, climate-related events and natural hazards have the potential to wreak havoc in transport networks, causing severe disruptions and cutting off access to essential facilities and services. Making use of ITS can help to mitigate these issues and move closer towards the SDG targets of having safer and more resilient cities. ITS applications include:

i. Driver information and route guidance – providing timely information with dynamic/variable message signs to warn about specific events such as crashes, damaged road sections, speed limits and potential diversion routes to be taken.
ii. In-vehicle alert and crash avoidance systems – Giving real-time alerts to drivers on potential dangers using systems such as Sleepiness Warning System, Lane Keeping Assist System, Intelligent Night Vision System, Adaptive Front Lighting System and Pedestrian Detection System to enhance road safety and reduce the risk of collision.
iii. Integrated Accident Detection and Reporting Systems – Detecting and notifying crash events in real time and providing the information to rescue services, police stations and insurance companies for a better management of accidents.
iv. Emergency management – providing real-time information on the impact of climate-related events and natural hazards on traffic and transport infrastructure status through the use of Variable Message Signs, live traffic maps and other warning systems
v. Emergency Vehicle Warning – Alerting drivers of nearby emergency vehicles to enable the creation of free passage in advance and hence reducing time required to attend to people requiring care.

Matveev et al. (2020) have suggested the use of ANNs in the assessment of crashes and emergencies to determine the workforce and resources to be dedicated to minimise the impacts due to the incident. Deep learning models coupled with IoT have been successfully used for accident detection and initiation of rescue response (Pathik et al., 2022). ML algorithms can be used to detect climate-related events such as floods (Karthikeyan & Usha, 2022) to activate early warning mechanisms. Benefits from the AI-based systems in relation to SDG targets include making the transport system safer, reducing the time required for emergency responses and improving decision-making capabilities of drivers and emergency service providers during crisis.

## 7.5 Advanced Public Transport Management

Earlier transport policies used to focus on providing mobility for vehicles through greater speed and reduced delays, with little consideration given to vulnerable road users such as the elderly, pedestrians and people with disabilities. However, there has been a paradigm shift after the adoption of the UN SDGs with the focus now being on the provision of access to all people, improvement in quality of life and promotion of more social equity in transport. Better route planning, higher quality infrastructure, better information and greater access to mass transit are essential elements for ensuring sustainability in the transport sector. ITS applications include:

i. Real-time information for Public Transit Systems – providing live information on bus and rail routing and scheduling to travellers and information on delays and optimal travel mode selection.
ii. Real-time Operation Management – optimising the use of fleet and staff by analysing demand across networks, days and time and recommending most efficient options.
iii. Electronic Fare Payment – allowing travellers to pay fares through systems such as Smart Cards.
iv. Crowd Management – Improving travellers experience by better route planning and improved connections to manage crowds more efficiently at public transit stations especially during peak hours or special events.
v. Connected and Autonomous Vehicle Management – Analysing traffic and environmental conditions to determine actions of autonomous public transport vehicles.

The use of ANNs has proved successful in the optimisation of bus schedules (Ushakov et al., 2022) while Particle Swarm Optimisation has shown potential in accurately predicting the mobility of public transport vehicles and their arrival times (Chondrodima et al., 2022). ACO has been used for scheduling and vehicle routing (Teodorović, 2008), transit network design (Hu et al., 2001) and feeder-bus network design (Kuan et al., 2006). Deep neural networks such as CNNs coupled with real-time object detection systems such as YOLO have also been adopted for traffic light detection and recognition in autonomous vehicles (Yeh et al., 2021).

The benefits of implementing AI in public transport include improved passengers' experience through the development of safe, secure and comfortable travels with predictable timetables and delays as well as greater accessibility and mobility for all people.

## 7.6 Road Network Condition Management

Deterioration of roads happens over time and is directly linked to traffic flow, its intensity, varying weather conditions as well as movements within the underlying soil. Hence, implementation of a rigorous road inspection programme is crucial for an efficient and successful road management system. Globally, many road management authorities identify the defects/flaws visually by humans who need to do the inspection, while at the same time driving and documenting the data. This traditional method is costly and laborious. With the use of AI, this process can be significantly improved by the development of dependable prediction models for road conditions (Vyas et al., 2022).

AI-powered software used in this field needs to be trained in the first instance in order to be able to identify the defects or defective areas such as (i) potholes; (ii) edge defects; (iii) simple cracks; (iv) network cracking; and (v) weathering. AI-driven software learns from the annotated images and is trained to identify defects from the new data images. The training is completed and the system is ready for use only after its results have reached the level of an experienced human observer. Visual inspections by humans are now being replaced by the use of smartphones positioned on the windshield of the car, feeding data into the AI system.

Various AI systems exist for assessing the conditions of roads, namely RoadAI, RoadPlus, RoadMetrics and Road Asset Condition Assessment System (RACAS) among others. These systems are powerful and cost-effective, allowing road agencies to quickly gauge the current condition of road networks and to develop renewal/repair/maintenance strategies while at the same time preparing works programmes. These systems have been tested and are very practical, accurate, portable and affordable. Most of the systems are set up quickly with practically all being car mounted models having high-resolution cameras with precision GPS. Once the data is captured, the AI systems can be used for: (i) Defect Logging and Road Condition Assessment; (ii) Accurate Network Analysis and Modelling to Inform Forward Budgets; (iii) Develop Capital Renewal Works Programmes; (iv) Develop Targeted Maintenance Programmes to Optimise Budget Spend; (v) Collect Pre-Disaster Evidence of Road Condition; (vi) Investigate Road Complaints Without Leaving the Office; and (vii) Update Asset Management Plans and Long-Term Financial Plans.

Use of AI in asset management therefore offers many advantages: (i) road inventory is carried out by the system thus eliminating human errors and improving accuracy of asset tracking; (ii) significant cost and time savings are possible through automation; (iii) more effective monitoring of assets with less human intervention occurs in time; and (iv) the system allows for real-time visibility into the asset database enabling authorities to take appropriate decisions regarding allocation of resources.

## 7.7 Assessments and Safety Inspections

Integrity, safety and serviceability of road infrastructure such as bridges and viaducts are all assets that need lifelong guarantee, given the crucial role that each component plays in the transport system. Incidents such as the collapse of (i) the I-35 bridge in Minneapolis in 2007; (ii) the cable-stayed bridge in Genoa, Italy in 2018; (iii) the pedestrian bridge at Florida International University in 2018; and (iv) the steel single-arch bridge in Taiwan in 2019 have demonstrated that these events lead to high number of casualties (Mandirola et al., 2022). With time, the number of road users is on the rise, and forecasting of road traffic is crucial to determine the rate and degree of degradation of the road infrastructure. Supply forecasting utilises AI and ML techniques to forecast infrastructure performance as well as traffic demand, mode and destination choices (Veres & Moussa, 2019).

Utilisation of AI has also been adopted in the inspection and preventative maintenance of infrastructure such as bridges to identify potential problems due to wear and tear and suggest remedial measures (Natali et al., 2023). AI techniques include:

i. ANNs have been successfully applied to model road network (Ma et al., 2020a) while their coupling with deep learning has allowed prediction of vehicle fleet composition (Chen et al., 2021).
ii. Utilisation of robotics to undertake inspection in various types of environments, including those with high security risks in terms of personnel health. Computer vision-based approaches have been applied for the development of a traffic infrastructure inventory and its inspection with results clearly showing that semi-automated inspection is possible.
iii. Simulated annealing (SA) and Multi Attribute Decision-Making (MADM) have been commercially tested for the selection of optimal routes based on congestion levels, speed and other road parameters.

The benefits of implementing AI in the assessment and inspection of infrastructure include greater safety, better passengers' experience, greater accessibility and mobility at improved efficiency levels as well as building higher resilience in networks.

## 7.8 Optimisation of Network Maintenance and Budgets

Although agencies managing roadways worldwide are expected to invest around $900 billion per year, it is expected that this budget will be short of $180 billion yearly (Garemo et al., 2018). Road maintenance is crucial if agencies wish to (i) extend the lifespan of the road; (ii) reduce the vehicles operating costs; and (iii) enhance safety on the roads. However, road agencies have to face a number of issues, which include insufficient funds availability, shortage of skilled and experienced staff, inefficient use of the available resources and inadequate management. Authorities have to prepare a full list of assets (roads and its associated infrastructure) which require maintenance works before drawing a priority list based on perceived urgency as determined by the agencies. Various AI techniques have become popular for the optimisation of maintenance activities (Kobbacy, 2012) and include:

i. Knowledge-Based Systems (KBS) – The use of computer assisted Reliability Centred Maintenance (RCM) grounded on plant maintenance management system has been suggested by Gabbar et al. (2003).
ii. Case-Based Reasoning (CBR) – This technique utilises index schemes and similarity functions gained from past knowledge to solve new problems.
iii. Neural Networks (NNs) – These are commonly adopted to carry out modelling, statistical analysis and optimisation.

iv. Data Mining (DM) – This technique uses techniques such as ML and statistical methods to recognise patterns in data and create predictive models which allow to take decisions.

v. Fuzzy Logic (FL) – FL is an AI technique used with other AI techniques such as NNs and Genetic Algorithms to develop hybrid systems that can be used for maintenance applications.

The benefits of implementing these techniques include the formulation of a better maintenance management plan and greater budget optimisation that leads to the development of infrastructure, which is of higher quality, more reliable and sustainable.

## 7.9 Application of ITS to Achieve SDG Targets – Case Study of Mauritius

Transport systems are inherently complex, and AI has the potential to play a crucial role in providing and maintaining services that ever-increasing numbers of people depend upon every day, especially in Small Island Developing States (SIDS). Mauritius, being SIDS, faces social, environmental and economic challenges due to its small size, remoteness to other countries, limited resources and exposure to natural calamities and climate change (UNCTAD, 2014). Sustainable, resilient and inclusive land transport infrastructure is key to overcoming these challenges, but like other SIDS, this sector in Mauritius is also characterised by the issues of safety, efficiency, reliability and affordability (UNESCAP, 2016), with increasing traffic congestion, environmental pollution, poor public transport, road traffic crashes and degradation of road assets being major problems. Innovative solutions incorporating ITS can offer opportunities to overcome these challenges while also working towards achieving SDG targets in Mauritius. Potential avenues to explore in Mauritius include the use of ITS for:

(1) Traffic management and control – Utilisation of AI can assist to mitigate road traffic congestion and hence reduce environmental pollution, improve system efficiency and reliability and overall sustainability, thereby addressing SDG targets 9.1, 11.2 and 12.c.

(2) Road user safety – ITS through the deployment of in- and out-of-vehicle measures can help reduce the number of vehicle crashes and hence road-related deaths and serious injuries in Mauritius, addressing SDG targets 3.6 and 11.2.

(3) Public transport operations – AI-based applications can help to improve the services being provided by public transport companies in Mauritius and thus improve road users experience and satisfaction levels, leading to a shift towards public transport use. This can help to address SDG targets 9.1, 11.2 and 12.c.

(4) Road asset management – With its limited resources and vulnerability to climate related disasters, Mauritius needs to ensure that the land transport

assets are efficiently managed. Use of AI solutions can help agencies to maintain an updated inventory of the transport systems and take informed decisions with respect to maintenance activities and investment projects to ensure that the system is reliable and resilient, thereby addressing that SDG targets 9.1, 11.2 and 13.1.

## 7.10 Conclusion

Transport systems are inherently complex due to their interlinkages with other systems, vulnerability to climate-related events and uncertainty due to unforeseen events. With the digitisation of the transport infrastructure, AI will be playing a more crucial role in providing and maintaining essential daily services for the population. The application of AI techniques to several aspects of land transport systems has been discussed in this chapter. Various techniques have shown good potential in addressing the multiple challenges in the sector: (i) NNs are well-suited for optimising traffic control, safety management and road condition assessment; (ii) ML and deep learning models can be used to improve safety management, transport infrastructure assessment and maintenance; (iii) swarm intelligence algorithms have been applied successfully in traffic management and public transportation management; (iv) FLM can be adopted to enhance traffic control systems and road maintenance management; and (v) genetic algorithms have been utilised to improve traffic management and maintenance operations. To conclude, it is expected that the use of ITS will become more prevalent in the near future and will be an essential step in the quest to achieve the UN SDG targets and implement safer, more affordable, accessible, efficient and resilient transport.

## References

Abduljabbar, R., Dia, H., Liyanage, S., & Bagloee, S. A. (2019). Applications of artificial intelligence in transport: An overview. *Sustainability*, *11*(1), 189. https://doi.org/10.3390/su11010189

Ait Ouallane, A., Bakali, A., Bahnasse, A., Broumi, S., & Talea, M. (2022). Fusion of engineering insights and emerging trends: Intelligent urban traffic management system. *Information Fusion*, *88*, 218–248. https://doi.org/10.1016/j.inffus.2022.07.020

CEBR. (2014). *50% rise in gridlock costs by 2030*. CEBR. https://cebr.com/reports/the-future-economic-and-environmental-costs-of-gridlock/

Chen, C., Liu, B., Wan, S., Qiao, P., & Pei, Q. (2021). An edge traffic flow detection scheme based on deep learning in an intelligent transportation system. *IEEE Transactions on Intelligent Transport System*, *22*(3), 1840–1852. http://doi.org/10.1109/TITS.2020.3025687

Chondrodima, E., Georgiou, H., Pelekis, N., & Theodoridis, Y. (2022). Particle swarm optimization and RBF neural networks for public transport arrival time prediction using GTFS data. *International Journal of Information Management Data Insights*, *2*(2), 100086. https://doi.org/10.1016/j.jjimei.2022.100086

European Commission. (n.d.). *Climate action: Transport emissions.* https://climate.ec. europa.eu/eu-action/transport-emissions_en

Ezell, E. (2010). *Explaining international IT application leadership: Intelligent transportation systems.* The Information Technology and Innovation Foundation. https://itif.org/publications/2010/01/09/explaining-international-it-application-leadership-intelligent/

Gabbar, H., Yamashita, H., Suzuki, K., & Shimada, Y. (2003). Computer-aided RCM-based plant maintenance management system. *Robotics and Computer-Integrated Manufacturing, 19*(5), 449–458.

Garemo, N., Hjerpe, M., & Halleman, B. (2018). *A better road to the future – Improving the delivery of road infrastructure cross the world.* Mc Kinsey & Company. https://www.mckinsey.com/industries/travel-logistics-and-infrastructure/our-insights/improving-the-delivery-of-road-infrastructure-across-the-world

Hoel, L. A., Garber, N. J., & Sadek, A. W. (2011). *Transportation infrastructure engineering: A multimodal integration* (SI ed.). Cengage Learning.

Hu, J., Yang, Z., & Jian, F. (2001). Study on the optimization methods of transit network based on Ant Algorithm. In *IVEC2001. Proceedings of the IEEE International Vehicle Electronics Conference 2001.* IVEC 2001 (Cat. No.01EX522). https://doi.org/10.1109/ivec.2001.961756

ITF. (2021). *ITF transport outlook 2021.* OECD Publishing. https://doi.org/10.1787/16826a30-en

Karthikeyan, H., & Usha, G. (2022). Real-time DDoS flooding attack detection in intelligent transportation systems. *Computers & Electrical Engineering, 101,* 107995. https://doi.org/10.1016/j.compeleceng.2022.107995

Kobbacy, K. A. H. (2012). Application of artificial intelligence in maintenance modelling and management. *IFAC Proceedings Volumes, 45*(31), 54–59. https://doi.org/10.3182/20121122-2-ES-4026.00046

Kuan, S. N., Ong, H. L., & Ng, K. M. (2006). Solving the feeder bus network design problem by genetic algorithms and ant colony optimization. *Advances in Engineering Software, 37*(6), 351–359. https://doi.org/10.1016/j.advengsoft.2005.10.003

Ma, T., Antoniou, C., & Toledo, T. (2020a). Hybrid machine learning algorithm and statistical time series model for network-wide traffic forecast. *Transportation Research C, 111,* 352–372. http://doi.org/10.1016/j.trc.2019.12.022

Mandirola, M., Casarotti, C., Peloso, S., Lanese, I., Brunesi, E., & Senaldi, I. (2022). Use of UAS for damage inspection and assessment of bridge infrastructures. *International Journal of Disaster Risk Reduction, 72,* 102824. ISSN 2212-4209. https://doi.org/10.1016/j.ijdrr.2022.102824

Matveev, A., Maximov, A., & Bogdanova, E. (2020). Intelligent decision support system for transportation emergency response. *Transportation Research Procedia, 50,* 444–450. https://doi.org/10.1016/j.trpro.2020.10.058

Natali, A., Padalkar, M. G., Messina, V., Salvatore, W., Morerio, P., Bue, A. D., & Beltrán-González, C. (2023). Artificial Intelligence tools to predict the level of defectiveness of existing bridges. *Procedia Structural Integrity, 44,* 2020–2027. https://doi.org/10.1016/j.prostr.2023.01.258

Olayode, O. I., Tartibu, L. K., & Okwu, M. O. (2020). Application of artificial intelligence in traffic control system of non-autonomous vehicles at signalized road intersection. *Procedia CIRP, 91,* 194–200. https://doi.org/10.1016/j.procir.2020.02.167

Pathik, N., Gupta, R. K., Sahu, Y., Sharma, A., Masud, M., & Baz, M. (2022). AI enabled accident detection and alert system using IoT and deep learning for Smart cities. *Sustainability*, *14*(13), 7701. https://doi.org/10.3390/su14137701

Ranyal, E., Sadhu, A., & Jain, K. (2022). Road condition monitoring using Smart sensing and artificial intelligence: A review. *Sensors*, *22*(8), 3044. https://doi.org/10.3390/s22083044

Rusul, A., Hussein, D., Sohani, L. & Saeed, A. B. (2019). Applications of artificial intelligence in transport: An overview. *Sustainability*, *11*(1), 189. https://doi.org/10.3390/su11010189

Sadek, A. W. (2007). *Artificial intelligence applications in transportation*. Transportation research circular.

Teodorović, D. (2008). Swarm intelligence systems for transportation engineering: Principles and applications. *Transportation Research Part C: Emerging Technologies*, *16*(6), 651–667. https://doi.org/10.1016/j.trc.2008.03.002

Transport Scotland. (2017). *Future intelligent transport systems strategy*. https://www.transport.gov.scot/publication/future-intelligent-transport-systems-strategy/

United Nations. (2022). *The sustainable development Goals report 2022*. https://unstats.un.org/sdgs/report/2022/The-Sustainable-Development-Goals-Report-2022.pdf

United Nations Conference on Trade and Development. (2014). *Closing the distance – Partnerships for sustainable and resilient transport systems in SIDS*. https://unctad.org/publication/closing-distance-partnerships-sustainable-and-resilient-transport-systems-small-island

United Nations Economic and Social Commission for Asia and the Pacific – Ministerial Conference on Transport. (2016). *Transport connectivity for least developed countries, landlocked developing countries and small island developing state*. https://www.unescap.org/sites/default/files/pre-ods/MCT3_6E.pdf

United Nations Secretary-General High-level Advisory Group on Sustainable Transport. (2016). *Mobilizing sustainable transport for development: Analysis and policy recommendations*. https://sustainabledevelopment.un.org/content/documents/2375Mobilizing%20Sustainable%20Transport.pdf

Ushakov, D., Dudukalov, E., Shmatko, L., & Shatila, K. (2022). Artificial Intelligence as a factor of public transportations system development. *Transportation Research Procedia*, *63*, 2401–2408. https://doi.org/10.1016/j.trpro.2022.06.276

Veres, M., & Moussa, M. (2019). Deep learning for intelligent transportation systems: A survey of emerging trends. *IEEE Transactions on Intelligent Transportation Systems*, 1–17. https://doi.org/10.1109/TITS.2019.2929020

Vyas, V., Pratap Singh, A., & Anshuman. (2022). Modeling asphalt pavement condition using artificial neural networks. *Materials Today: Proceedings*. https://doi.org/10.1016/j.matpr.2022.05.050

World Health Organisation. (2018). *Global status report on road safety 2018*. https://www.who.int/publications/i/item/9789241565684

Yeh, T.-W., Lin, H.-Y., & Chang, C.-C. (2021). Traffic light and arrow signal recognition based on a unified network. *Applied Sciences*, *11*(17), 8066. https://doi.org/10.3390/app11178066

Part 3

# Impact of AI-Enabled Electrical Electronic and Telecommunications Engineering Systems on UN SDGs

Chapter 8

# Achieving Affordable and Clean Energy Through AI and 5G Powered Internet of Energy (IoE)

*Tulsi Pawan Fowdur and Ashven Sanghan*

University of Mauritius, Mauritius

## Abstract

Energy production and distribution is undergoing a revolutionary transition with the advent of disruptive technologies such as the Internet of Energy (IoE), 5G and artificial intelligence (AI). IoE essentially involves automating and enhancing the energy infrastructure: the power grid from grid operators to energy generators and distribution utilities. The IoE also relies on powerful connectivity networks such as 5G, big data analytics and AI to optimise its operation. By incorporating the technology that employs ubiquitous devices such as smartphones, tablets or smart electric vehicles, it will be possible to fully exploit the potential of IoE using 5G networks. 5G networks will provide high speed connections between devices such as drones, tractors and cloud networks, to transfer huge amounts of sensor data. Additionally, there are many sources of isolated data across the main energy production units (generation, transmission and distribution), and the data is increasing at phenomenal rates. By applying AI to these data, major improvements can be brought at each stage of the energy production chain. Tying renewable energy to the telecommunications sector and leveraging on the potential of data analytics is something which is gaining major attention among researchers and industry experts. This chapter therefore explores the combination of three of the most promising technologies i.e. IoE, 5G and AI for achieving affordable and clean energy, which is SDG 7 in the UN Sustainable Development Goals (SDGs).

*Keywords*: SDG 7; IoE; AI; 5G; energy management; smart grid; cybersecurity; automation

Artificial Intelligence, Engineering Systems and Sustainable Development, 97–108
Copyright © 2024 Tulsi Pawan Fowdur and Ashven Sanghan
Published under exclusive licence by Emerald Publishing Limited
doi:10.1108/978-1-83753-540-820241008

## 8.1 Introduction to Internet of Energy (IoE)

Climate change together with global emissions are considered to be high-priority topics in the present decade. The energy sector constantly needs to deal with the word sustainability from the early stage of energy production to the very end of consumption of energy. In the United States, there are around 7,700 power plants, and the network of high-voltage lines can be sum up to 707,000 miles (Energy, 2022). Consumers have to deal with losses up to $6 billion in a year due to waste and congestion. Furthermore, the insufficient usage of transmission lines contributes to an ineffective as well as wasteful power grid. Based on these statistics, it is very essential to develop an energy-saving system having the ability not only to decrease energy wastage but also provide an optimisation solution concerning the production and usage. The IoE can be an effective method of reducing waste, improving the stages namely generation, transmission and storage, and to utilise our power systems in the best possible manner.

IoE explicitly explains the automation and improvement that can be made in the energy architecture starting from the grid operators to power producers and distribution companies (Energy, 2022). The implementation of Internet of Things (IoT) technology inside energy systems in order to increase the overall performance of the whole architecture and at the same time causing a decrease in the production of energy waste summarises the concept of IoE. On the other hand, IoE applies the principle of one common communication network for linking the devices present in the energy power distribution architecture without considering how and where the processing of data is occurring (Mongay Batalla et al., 2022).

Associated with IoE, the IoT and smart grid technology provide a more efficient way of monitoring as well as delivering power by the power producers and distributors, respectively (Shahzad et al., 2020). Each part of the architecture communicates among themselves in such a way that the delivery of power from the start-up point, i.e. power generation, to the home premises is done effectively. The IoE incorporates an energy framework for the energy production and delivery by applying artificial intelligence (AI) at power plants as well as power delivery systems. IoE also deals with bringing an upgrade together with the automation of appliances and metering in one's home. Big data, the interchanging of large information based on energy, is also integrated in the concept of IoE. With the use of big data, real-time information can be obtained on the energy consumption trends allowing grid operators, energy generators and distribution companies to predict at which instant in time the rate of consumption will be the highest. By using these data, grid operators having the task to control and monitor the energy production and delivery can thus make necessary modifications to the energy supply (Energy, 2022).

The IoE can be considered as an upgrading feature in the smart grid for the analysis of the two-way flow of information on power and electricity (Mahmud et al., 2020). In the modern world, an increase in the number of people who are opting for smart homes together with smart devices has been noticed. With the IoE, these devices will obtain information about electricity prices. For instance, smart washing machines can be programmed to turn on when low prices in electricity are detected. Furthermore, the forecasting of energy consumption can be done for upcoming weather events by energy producers. Solar power levels can be predicted by utilities based on the capacity of the solar panel as well as the performance relative to that weather forecast (Energy, 2022).

Renewable energies are essential in the fight against greenhouse effect however they can be highly unreliable. However, with IoE, it is possible to make use of the free energy sources at a maximum rate. For example, on windy days, the excess energy can be stored or delivered to those wailing washing machine at lower fares. Power failures or surges can not only be identified more efficiently with the data provided by IoE but can also foresee maintenance issues. To summarise, the IoE can be a fascinating technology for monitoring energy usage in a more efficient manner. With the coming of interconnected smart grids, higher development in IoE is expected (Energy, 2022).

## 8.2 IoE Building Blocks

The building blocks of IoE are made up of four main components, namely the energy router, storage systems and materials, renewable resources and lastly plug-and-play with appliance integration as shown in Fig. 8.1.

The energy router consists of a power electronic transformer, an intelligent distributed control system and a communication unit (Wang et al., 2017). The router has the task to collect, process and send data associated to the grid. An improvement in the energy network in terms of reliability, efficiency and security is possible with the help of the router. Eventually, the optimisation of energy usage can happen by creating a balance between supply and demand among a huge number of distributed loads and sources (Hannan et al., 2018). The energy router can also make communication with other routers whenever the balancing of supply and demand occurs on a wider scale.

Storage systems and materials involve the concept of an Energy Storage System (ESS). The integration of ESS in IoE is expected to bring a positive upgrade in the efficiency, reliability and stability of the grid. ESS can also cause an

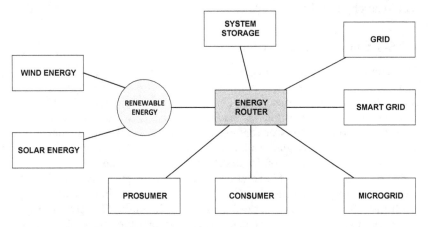

Fig. 8.1.    Internet of Energy (IoE) Building Blocks.

enhancement in the quality of power (Palizban & Kauhaniemi, 2016). Moreover, it should be able to provide a solution to problems concerning voltage fluctuation. Stress correlated to the grid can be significantly decreased with the involvement of a storage device. The latter will aim at storing energy for future usage, securing a smooth energy supply. The most commonly used storage devices are pumped hydro, flywheel, compressed air, fuel cells, batteries and super capacitors (Hannan et al., 2018).

The third building block of IoE is renewable sources of energy that are interconnected. Renewable resources in IoE ensure sustainable development, brings safer measures and most importantly a cleaner environment. The interconnection of two or more sources of renewable energies can be referred as Hybrid Energy Systems (HES) (Huang et al., 2017). The introduction of HES in IoE shall contribute to energy savings, reductions in pollution emission and creating a sustainable society with low carbon footprints. To integrate renewable resources, certain technologies such as power converter topologies together with control and modulation techniques are required to prevent problems including synchronisation and instability. Solar as well as wind, the commonly used renewable sources, are gaining great importance in the generation of electrical power and expected to facilitate IoE (Kafle et al., 2016).

The use of plug-and-play interface in IoE allows the connection between storage devices and renewable resources to be done in a much easier way (Nguyen et al., 2018). This scenario is similar to how a computer would instantly recognise a plug-and-play device like USB hardware and let it interface with the computer. Different types of interfaces (alternating current/direct current [AC/DC]) can be affiliated to the plug-and-play interface. This occurs since a microgrid can be of AC or DC type connecting to the interface of the plug-and-play. The interface also allows for an immediate identification when a generating or storage device makes a connection to the system. Whenever a renewable source plugs into the system for power donation, a generation request is sent to the energy router. The latter then checks the level of local power demand before granting access to the renewable source to start generating power. Hence, there is no room for an additional physical device (Kafle et al., 2016).

## 8.3 5G Communications for IoE

The main network requirements of IoE are identified as high flexibility, security, high capacity, radio coverage, power savings and cost savings (Mongay Batalla et al., 2022). Flexibility means the ability to adapt to changes (different traffic distributions and shorter latency budgets) in the network resources that are available in terms of flows or topology. A secure network for IoE refers to the confidentiality, integrity and availability of the system. High capacity deals with the increase in the number of devices the network can support.

5G technology can be the solution to the network requirements of the IoE. Broadly speaking, 5G means higher bit rates, increased link capacity, higher bandwidth efficiency and higher cell density. Furthermore, 5G networks shall be dealing with several security concerns: security architecture and policies, security strategies, security devices, wireless security and dangers of sensitive data related to IoE (Strielkowski et al., 2021).

One of the solutions that 5G can provide to the IoE network requirement is high flexibility. This feature is achievable with the introduction of network solutions based on virtualisation and software. The concept of virtualisation ensures that applications and services are separated, which provides the acceleration of newly implemented services on the network. With the addition of new services, the software solution leads to a reduction in cost and improvement to the network in terms of speed and easiness. Open Radio Access Network (RAN) can be used as the approach for the development of a flexible network.

Frequency bands used for 5G shall establish a seamless coverage over large areas. These bands shall meet the low frequency ranges requirements of energy supply operators in IoE, i.e. provide an increase in the coverage as well as the availability of communication networks. Certain frequency bands need to be reserved for IoE applications. For instance, to establish communication with vehicles, the automotive industry is looking for specific frequency bands. IoE will be created utilising 5G technology in those bands while concurrently utilising the licensed capacity that has been allotted, as in private networks (Trakadas et al., 2021).

With 5G, high capacity can be achieved by increasing the cell density with the usage of several microcells. Decreasing the size of cells causes a reduction in the number of users being served in a specific band but enhances the capacity per user. Greater exchange of traffic can be handled with the use of Device to Device (D2D) transmission (Mongay Batalla et al., 2022). This type of transmission results in the improvement of radio coverage and the power required to transmit the signal is lowered.

Another vital characteristic that 5G can provide to the IoE network requirement is high bit rates. The increase in bit rate is the result due to improvement in spectral efficiency. The latter is attained by using the principle of Multiple-Input Multiple-Output (MIMO) antennas (Yang, Yin, et al., 2019). This technique contributes to the increase in the wireless system's capacity, energy efficiency and reduction inter-user interference.

Moreover, 5G shall enhance the narrowband connectivity such as Narrowband-IoT (NB-IoT) (Gbadamosi et al., 2020). For instance, the low power consumption is expected with the development of techniques such as discontinuous reception and sleep mode. Other energy-saving mechanisms such as beamforming, new transmission systems and channel access management are being introduced with 5G networks.

Reduction in latency is another feature that 5G will be improving. Improvement in latency is very vital for applications with mission-critical status as in IoE (Strielkowski et al., 2021). 5G incorporates techniques that transfer time-sensitive components located at distant data centres to servers situated at the edge of the network. This technique shall cause improvement in the latency of data transmission.

## 8.4 AI and the IoE

AI can be employed in several IoE applications such as energy disaggregation, power voltage stability monitoring and cybersecurity as described in the subsections 8.4.1–8.4.4.

### 8.4.1 Energy Disaggregation

Energy disaggregation consists of gathering usage patterns of appliances by breaking down data from a single home sensor. Analysis of multiple of energy 'signatures' must be made so that the pattern of usage can be found. Through this analysis, prediction can be made to find suspicious consumption data due to manipulation of devices, malfunctioning metres, thefts and others (SparkCognition, 2019).

Chae et al. (2016) provided a forecasting model for short-range energy usage of a building. The model was based on Artificial Neural Network (ANN) along with the Bayesian regularisation algorithm and had the goal to examine the effects of certain parameters such as training data, number of neurons, time delay on the model generality and capability. Based on the results, it was shown that the model with adaptive methods had the ability to forecast electricity consumption at every 15 minutes interval together with the daily peak electricity usage in a test scenario of a commercial building complex.

### 8.4.2 Power Voltage Instability Monitoring

Power grids are equipped with a phasor measurement unit for capturing electrical waveforms for the detection of minute instabilities that can spread through the system and subsequently cause the grid to collapse. Phasor measurement units (PMUs) normally generate 4GB of data per day, and these data are usually dynamic in nature. Due to these two concerns, the use of machine learning algorithms is essential for the identification of voltage instabilities (SparkCognition, 2019).

Due to the complexity of network associated with the coupling disturbances, the fault feature extraction is becoming more demanding in energy systems. Yang, Pang, et al. (2019) made use of a modified version of the Convolutional Neural Network (CNN), referred as the Spearman rank correlation based CNNs (SR-CNN) to deal with the problem of fault feature extraction. With the addition of the Spearman rank correlation image layer on the normal CNN, several time-based signals that are measured by the PMUs are translated into data images. Comparable to other traditional methods, the fault may be diagnosed more rapidly and precisely while being thoroughly retrieved from distinct fault characteristics.

### 8.4.3 Grid Maintenance

Sometimes, data pertaining to operations involving breakers go undetected until the appearance of major faults. The use of machine learning algorithms with features such as historical maintenance, kVa loading, ambient conditions and vegetation index is helpful in predicting failures before they occur (SparkCognition, 2019).

Wang et al. (2019) devised two maintenance frameworks based on AI algorithms. The algorithms used were K-medoids clustering algorithm and genetic algorithm which were not only extended but modified as well. The two suggested intelligent maintenance frameworks are contrasted with the conventional maintenance planning methodologies in a comparative study. Based on the simulation results, it was shown that the two proposed frameworks provide better efficiency than the traditional ones. The approaches employed by Wang et al. (2019) are a representation of the next generation automated maintenance systems for smart grids with large scale.

### 8.4.4 Cybersecurity

With the coming of new malwares such as Havex, BlackEnergy and Flame, there is a need to strengthen energy infrastructure. According to Kasperly Labs, there are at least 11 million specific virus strains together with the daily addition of 28,000 (SparkCognition, 2019).

Tobiyama et al. (2016) proposed a method to detect malware by examining the behaviour of processes in potentially infected terminals. An investigation based on the application of Deep Neural Networks to analyse malware processes was carried out by the authors. Recurrent Neural Networks (RNNs) was first trained to obtain features of process behaviour. Then Convolutional Neural Network was trained to carry out a classification upon feature images which were generated from the trained RNN.

Handa et al. (2019) identified that, intrusion detection system may fail to manage all types of attacks and this might trigger false alarms. The latter can be a significant cause to high economic risks. Machine learning such as support vector machine (SVM) can be used to distinguish between normal and malicious traffic. Hence, the efficiency of intrusion can be increased against malwares.

## 8.5 IoE Use Cases

Given the huge potential of IoE, it has undoubtedly found several major appliances as outlined in the following subsections 8.5.1–8.5.4.

### 8.5.1 IoE in Building Energy Management Systems (BEMS)

The use of IoE in BEMS contributes to the reduction of energy consumption of buildings. This is achieved by sharing information about energy demand and supply resulting in low emission of carbon dioxide gas (Wei & Li, 2011). Several projects such as Smart Energy Efficient Middleware for Public Spaces were launched for the introduction of IoE-based BEMS. For BEMS to function efficiently, they must be secure, reliable, scalable and cost-effective. IoE-based BEMs, which are reliable, are believed to attract attention of more consumers, and at the same time, there is insurance that SDG 7 can be promoted through it. The system should also ensure a high level of security due to the large storage of data. Moreover, the IoE-based BEMS need to be scalable in case the consumer has to add new applications, services and devices to the existing system. To guarantee the efficiency of BEMS, an equilibrium should be established between the different costs involved in the IoE-based BEMS and the emission of greenhouse gas (GHG) (Hannan et al., 2018).

### 8.5.2 IoE and Smart Grid

The association of renewable microgrids with the main grid is not an easy task due to the discontinuous nature of renewable resources (Rana, 2017). IoE consists of elements, namely smart sensors as well as actuators, that can detect and control the intermittent nature of the renewable microgrids. One of the aims of smart grid is to provide monitoring as well as controlling means through two-way communication between energy management system and grid at any time and any place. IoE can be the complementary element of the smart grid vision as it involves the usage of 5G and AI.

5G incorporates many vital features such as ultra-high data rate, network slicing, security, connectivity and network function virtualisation which can be beneficial to next-generation smart grid. For example, the next-generation smart grid's main industrial control services' link needs may be provided with ease by 5G network's ultra-low latency of 0.5ms and huge access of 100 million connections per square kilometre (Liu et al., 2021). The integration of AI and machine learning is essential to improving the electrical grid. Their efficiency addresses human error and creates an automated, reliable and autonomous system that can make decisions based on data as well as information from both present and past experiences (Esenogho et al., 2022).

### 8.5.3 IoE and Smart Transport/Electric Vehicle (EV)

Whenever smart transport is mentioned, the focus is shifted to electric mobility or EVs. The market of EVs is expected to increase in the future, causing the transformation of transportation and at the same time creating a collaboration between energy and transportation. Elvas and Ferreira (2021) highlighted that a major concern about this expansion is the electric vehicles charging. Ensuring EV users can easily find and use charging stations while on the road is crucial. EVs and smart grids are expected to constantly communicate with each other in a two-way flow of information. The application of IoE in smart transport where it shall involve the use of 5G and AI makes the system involving EVs more efficient. To handle the mobile networks and traffic related to EVs, 5G is expected to play a pivotal role. 5G communication standards that were put forward in 2019 improved mobile networks, widespread machine connectivity and ultra-reliable, low-latency communication (Wu et al., 2022). The adoption of EVs on a large scale depends on their viability, safety and dependability, all of which may be greatly enhanced by the use of AI (Ahmed et al., 2021). For example, AI has been used in EVs for range optimisation whereby energy efficiency is increased.

### 8.5.4 IoE and Industry

The application of IoE has further been extended in the sector of industrial energy. With the incorporation of the internet in the market of energy, many energy transactions are occurring through the online mode. This may result in several problems in the conventional energy trading system. Among the major concerns are scalability, cyber-attacks and insufficient processing effectiveness. Companies dealing with power supply cannot guarantee both privacy and security of the energy trading system when being combined with a decentralised platform. For this particular reason, IoE together with blockchain technology must be employed in such a way to provide a secured as well as effective energy trading system. In addition, optimisation of exchange of data and power in parallel with other transaction between industries and grids can be achieved through the means provided by IoE (Baidya & Nandi, 2021).

## 8.6 Conclusion

In this chapter, the concept of IoE, which is basically the automation and enhancement of the energy infrastructure, has been explained. The energy infrastructure includes the power grid from grid operators and energy generators and utilities concerned with the distribution process. Further discussions were made on the building blocks of IoE whereby the importance of each component was highlighted. The network requirements of IoE were also explored and focus has been laid on different areas where specific AI can be utilised for IoE applications. Applications of IoE such as BEMS, Smart Grid, Industry and Smart Transport were also identified. IoE is a technology that promotes the SDG 7 by laying emphasis on modern energy, which must be affordable, reliable and at the same time sustainable. By automating as well as enhancing the energy infrastructure, energy wastage is being reduced. With the integration of renewable sources to the grid, IoE further decreases GHG emissions and helps to cope with climate change. It can, therefore, be concluded that IoE is a promising technology with vital solutions to the problems related to energy. However, the implementation of IoE may involve challenges such as complex control of electricity flow and the irregularity of weather-dependent sources of renewable energy. IoE is a sophisticated network that consists of sensors, decentralised smart grids and other devices for managing and controlling purposes. The system complexity is increased with monitoring, controlling and real-time prediction of data. The changing trend of renewable energy together with the fluctuating nature of demands further increases the difficulty in establishing an effective and smart energy system. Recognising energy resources, understanding the IoE-based infrastructure and developing techniques to use sensors in industrial application are among the future research directions for IoE.

# References

Ahmed, M., Zheng, Y., Amine, A., Fathiannasab, H., & Chen, Z. (2021). The role of artificial intelligence in the mass adoption of electric vehicles. *Joule, 5*(9), 2296–2322. https://doi.org/10.1016/j.joule.2021.07.012

Baidya, S., & Nandi, C. (2021). Solar energy generation and internet of energy (IoE) challenges and purview [review of solar energy generation and internet of energy (IoE) challenges and purview]. In *Internet of energy handbook* (pp. 175–187). CRC Press.

Chae, Y. T., Horesh, R., Hwang, Y., & Lee, Y. M. (2016). Artificial neural network model for forecasting sub-hourly electricity usage in commercial buildings. *Energy and Buildings, 111*, 184–194. https://doi.org/10.1016/j.enbuild.2015.11.045

Elvas, L. B., & Ferreira, J. C. (2021). Intelligent transportation systems for electric vehicles. *Energies, 14*(17), 5550. https://doi.org/10.3390/en14175550

Energy, A. (2022). *The Internet of Energy (IOE) explained: A beginner's guide.* Amigo Energy. https://amigoenergy.com/blog/the-internet-of-energy-ioe-explained/

Energy, J. (2022). The internet of energy: What is it and why is it important? Just energy. https://justenergy.com/blog/internet-of-energy-what-is-it-why-important/

Esenogho, E., Djouani, K., & Kurien, A. (2022). Integrating artificial intelligence Internet of Things and 5G for next-generation smartgrid: A survey of trends challenges and prospect. *IEEE Access,* 1. https://doi.org/10.1109/access.2022.3140595

Gbadamosi, S. A., Hancke, G. P., & Abu-Mahfouz, A. M. (2020). Building upon NB-IoT networks: A roadmap towards 5G new radio networks. *IEEE Access,* 1. https://doi.org/10.1109/access.2020.3030653

Handa, A., Sharma, A., & Shukla, S. K. (2019). Machine learning in cybersecurity: A review. *WIREs Data Mining and Knowledge Discovery, 9*(4). https://doi.org/10.1002/widm.1306

Hannan, M. A., Faisal, M., Ker, P. J., Mun, L. H., Parvin, K., Mahlia, T. M. I., & Blaabjerg, F. (2018). A review of internet of energy based building energy management systems: Issues and recommendations. *IEEE Access, 6,* 38997–39014. https://doi.org/10.1109/access.2018.2852811

Huang, Z., Lu, Y., Wei, M., & Liu, J. (2017). Performance analysis of optimal designed hybrid energy systems for grid-connected nearly/net zero energy buildings. *Energy, 141,* 1795–1809. https://doi.org/10.1016/j.energy.2017.11.093

Kafle, Y. R., Mahmud, K., Morsalin, S., & Town, G. E. (2016). Towards an internet of energy. In *2016 IEEE International Conference on Power System Technology (POWERCON).* https://doi.org/10.1109/powercon.2016.7754036

Liu, R., Hai, X., Du, S., Zeng, L., Bai, J., & Liu, J. (2021). Application of 5G network slicing technology in smart grid. *IEEE Xplore.* https://doi.org/10.1109/ICBAIE52039.2021.9389979

Mahmud, K., Khan, B., Ravishankar, J., Ahmadi, A., & Siano, P. (2020). An internet of energy framework with distributed energy resources, prosumers and small-scale virtual power plants: An overview. *Renewable and Sustainable Energy Reviews, 127,* 109840. https://doi.org/10.1016/j.rser.2020.109840

Mongay Batalla, J., Moshin, M., Mavromoustakis, C. X., Wesołowski, K., Mastorakis, G., & Krzykowska-Piotrowska, K. (2022). On deploying the internet of energy with 5G open RAN technology including beamforming mechanism. *Energies, 15*(7), 2429. https://doi.org/10.3390/en15072429

Nguyen, V. T., Luan Vu, T., Le, N. T., & Min Jang, Y. (2018). An overview of Internet of Energy (IoE) based building energy management system. *IEEE Xplore.* https://doi.org/10.1109/ICTC.2018.8539513

Palizban, O., & Kauhaniemi, K. (2016). Energy storage systems in modern grids—Matrix of technologies and applications. *Journal of Energy Storage, 6,* 248–259. https://doi.org/10.1016/j.est.2016.02.001

Rana, M. (2017). Architecture of the internet of energy network: An application to smart grid communications. *IEEE Access, 5,* 4704–4710. https://doi.org/10.1109/access.2017.2683503

Shahzad, Y., Javed, H., Farman, H., Ahmad, J., Jan, B., & Zubair, M. (2020). Internet of Energy: Opportunities, applications, architectures and challenges in smart industries. *Computers & Electrical Engineering, 86,* 106739. https://doi.org/10.1016/j.compeleceng.2020.106739

SparkCognition. (2019). *AI & the Internet of Energy (IoE)* [White paper]. https://www.sparkcognition.com/web/eng/wp/the-internet-of-energy/

Strielkowski, W., Dvořák, M., Rovný, P., Tarkhanova, E., & Baburina, N. (2021). 5G wireless networks in the future renewable energy systems. *Frontiers in Energy Research, 9.* https://doi.org/10.3389/fenrg.2021.714803

Tobiyama, S., Yamaguchi, Y., Shimada, H., Ikuse, T., & Yagi, T. (2016). Malware detection with deep neural network using process behavior. In *2016 IEEE 40th Annual Computer Software and Applications Conference (COMPSAC).* https://doi.org/10.1109/compsac.2016.151

Trakadas, P., Sarakis, L., Giannopoulos, A., Spantideas, S., Capsalis, N., Gkonis, P., Karkazis, P., Rigazzi, G., Antonopoulos, A., Cambeiro, M. A., Gonzalez-Diaz, S., & Conceição, L. (2021). A cost-efficient 5G non-public network architectural approach: Key concepts and enablers, building blocks and potential use cases. *Sensors, 21*(16), 5578. https://doi.org/10.3390/s21165578

Wang, K., Li, H., Feng, Y., & Tian, G. (2017). Big data analytics for system stability evaluation strategy in the energy internet. *IEEE Transactions on Industrial Informatics, 13*(4), 1969–1978. https://doi.org/10.1109/TII.2017.2692775

Wang, W., Lou, B., Li, X., Lou, X., Jin, N., & Yan, K. (2019). *Intelligent maintenance frameworks of large-scale grid using genetic algorithm and K-medoids clustering methods.* World Wide Web. https://doi.org/10.1007/s11280-019-00705-w

Wei, C., & Li, Y. (2011). Design of energy consumption monitoring and energy-saving management system of intelligent building based on the Internet of Things. In *Proceedings International Conference on Electronics and Communication Control (ICECC),* September 2011 (pp. 3650–3652).

Wu, W., Zhang, Y., Chun, D., Song, Y., Qing, L., Chen, Y., & Li, P. (2022). Research on the operation modes of electric vehicles in association with a 5G real-time system of electric vehicle and traffic. *Energies, 15*(12), 4316. https://doi.org/10.3390/en15124316

Yang, D., Pang, Y., Zhou, B., & Li, K. (2019). Fault diagnosis for energy internet using correlation processing-based convolutional neural networks. *IEEE Transactions on Systems, Man, and Cybernetics: Systems, 49*(8), 1739–1748. https://doi.org/10.1109/tsmc.2019.2919940

Yang, S., Yin, D., Song, X., Dong, X., Manogaran, G., Mastorakis, G., Mavromoustakis, C. X., & Batalla, J. M. (2019). Security situation assessment for massive MIMO systems for 5G communications. *Future Generation Computer Systems, 98*, 25–34. https://doi.org/10.1016/j.future.2019.03.036

Chapter 9

# Leveraging the Power of Blockchain in Industry 4.0 and Intelligent Real-Time Systems for Achieving the SDGs

*Tulsi Pawan Fowdur, Visham Hurbungs and Lavesh Babooram*

University of Mauritius, Mauritius

## Abstract

Intelligent real-time systems are significantly impacting several of the UN Sustainable Development Goals (SDGs) by revolutionising processes in several areas such as Industry 4.0, smart cities, transportation, agriculture, renewable energy, climate change and other economic activities. Given that much of the work to achieve the SDGs relies on information and communication technology, cybersecurity has a potentially immense role to play towards achieving these outcomes. Moreover, cyberattacks have emerged as a new functional threat for interconnected, smart manufacturers and digital supply networks, employed in intelligent real-time systems for the Fourth Industrial Revolution. The effects of cyberattacks can be much more widespread than ever before due to the interconnected nature of Industry 4.0-driven operations. Blockchain can be really useful in such situations as it provides edge protection and allows authentication of the machine-to-machine and human–machine operations, stable data share, life cycle management, access control compliance of devices and self-sustaining operations. Moreover, blockchain can be applied for tracking and tracing transactions through devices, which are performed during the operation, as well as to encrypt and transmit data securely. It is vital to establish complete trust in a technology that is being adopted so that its full potential can be exploited. It is consequently critical that the organisational and information technology strategy fully integrates secure, vigilant and resilient cybersecurity strategies such as blockchain. This will ensure that cyber risks are properly managed in the age of Industry 4.0. This chapter, therefore, analyses the application of blockchain in intelligent real-time systems such as Industry 4.0 so that the opportunities these systems present for the SDGs can be exploited safely with minimum risks to society.

*Artificial Intelligence, Engineering Systems and Sustainable Development, 109–121*
Copyright © 2024 Tulsi Pawan Fowdur, Visham Hurbungs and Lavesh Babooram
Published under exclusive licence by Emerald Publishing Limited
doi:10.1108/978-1-83753-540-820241009

*Keywords*: Industry 4.0; real-time systems; IoT; AI; blockchain; cybersecurity; SDGs

## 9.1 Introduction

Intelligent real-time systems and Industry 4.0 are certainly making their presence
felt with regard to various UN Sustainable Development Goals (SDGs). However, the lack of proper cybersecurity can jeopardise the benefits reaped from
real-time systems. This is observed in SDG 7, which pertains to the accessibility of
economical and sustainable energy. The increasing reliance on automation and
self-operating systems also translates into the susceptibility of newly introduced
architectures, in the absence of adequate security measures. Smart cities equipped
with adaptable socioeconomic, organisational and financial frameworks bring
improved resilience and longevity to cities and communities. With risks such as
vulnerable hardware, cyber warfare, unreliable internet bandwidth and dependability on applications, the skyrocketing digitalisation of modern cities and
communities is inevitably followed by the increasing need to coat architectures
with layers of security (Morgus, 2018).

The last decade witnessed the upheaval of the industrial oasis, known as
Industry 4.0. With the highlights being increased efficiency, lower costs and higher
incomes, Industry 4.0 necessitates smooth links between devices and refined
connection methods. Thanks to the integration of cutting-edge technologies like
the Internet of Things (IoT) and artificial intelligence (AI), modern industrial
infrastructure has established the groundwork for ideal smart factory systems,
where data-driven interconnectivity occurs between machines and people. Edge
sensor data are critical for overseeing the production process, anticipating
downtime and identifying machinery irregularities. However, if the data fails to
meet security protocols, it can incapacitate all data-related operations, crippling
the entire industrial oasis. Recent security flaws reported by the Guardian and
ABC confirm US and Australian concerns about cyber spying by other nations
seeking to acquire industrial copyright materials through intelligence-gathering
schemes. Amidst the COVID-19 pandemic that has swept the globe, Webber has
borne witness to approximately 50 cyberattacks, solely in Australia, since January
2020. The report reveals that the majority of these attacks were aimed at
large-scale industries like Bunnings, Alinta Energy and Toyota, including the
theft of confidential health records. As a result, security has become a crucial
concern across all aspects of Industry 4.0. However, current industrial security
reinforcement strategies typically rely on a trusted third party, such as a cloud or
certificate service provider, and are focused on server-side mechanisms (Rahman
et al., 2022).

Blockchain has set the foundation for overseeing the security of Industry 4.0,
given its undisputable features such as immutability, pseudo-anonymity and
traceability. Among the most recent and inspiring research, a consortium blockchain (CBC)-based strategy was suggested to safeguard Industry 4.0 (Rahman
et al., 2021). To address the requirements for both intrusion and privacy

measures for smart contracts in IoT networks, Alkadi et al. (2020) have come forward with a deep blockchain framework (DBF). Numerous publications have also presented a new approach to model sharing facilitated by blockchain, for enhancing the effectiveness of object detection with cross-domain adaptation for autonomous driving frameworks (Jiang et al., 2020). A distinct approach, known as authentication mechanism based on transfer learning empowered blockchain (ATLB), was investigated by Wang et al. (2021), where blockchain handles the data confidentiality of industrial transactions. Lin et al. (2021) also suggested a novel transfer learning-based, safe and reliable integration technique for Industry 4.0.

This chapter is further elaborated as follows. Section 9.2 provides the background theory on Industry 4.0 and blockchain technology. Section 9.3 describes a framework for the integration of blockchain in real-time systems and Industry 4.0. Section 9.4 gives an overview of some blockchain use cases in Industry 4.0 and its relevance to other applications which impact the UN SDGs. Section 9.5 concludes the chapter.

## 9.2 Background Theory

In this section, a description of the underlying concepts of Industry 4.0 and blockchain is given.

### 9.2.1 Industry 4.0

The Fourth Industrial Revolution, or simply Industry 4.0, emerged in 2011, as an initiative under the German government's technological agenda, to elevate cyber-physical systems (CPS) (Hompel et al., 2017; Vogel-Heuser & Hess, 2016) into Cyber-Physical Production Systems (CPPS) (Vogel-Heuser et al., 2012). One of the major connected initiatives of Industry 4.0 is SmartFactory (Zuehlke, 2010). The Industry 4.0 era involves production systems, encompassed as CPPS, which are empowered to make smart choices. This is leveraged by real-time communication and synchronisation between industrial equipment (Lu et al., 2020), leading to the smooth and dynamic large-scale manufacture of high-end customised items (Wang et al., 2016; Xu et al., 2021; Zhong et al., 2017).

Industry 4.0 revolves around the following key design concepts (Chakraborty & Mandal, 2022):

- Interoperability: As one of the most essential tenets, people, objects and machines must be able to come together to make up the IoT.
- Virtualisation: The idea of generating and mimicking the real world through the creation of a virtual copy in the form of CPSs is crucial. This thus allows the monitoring of surrounding areas.
- Decentralisation: The ability to function autonomously is the reason for integrating the future with CPSs, allowing for tailored goods and the rapid resolution of issues, thus nurturing a dynamic and adaptable manufacturing

ecosystem. In case of opposing ideas or failures to meet certain demands, the subject can simply be escalated to higher levels.

- Real-Time Capability: The capacity to transmit, process and interpret real-time data is essential for a smart factory, enabling innovative and on-the-go decision-making. An example is internal operations, such as equipment breakdowns in a manufacturing line.
- Service-Orientation: With a focus set on satisfying client demands, the Internet of Services must effectively bridge the gap between people and smart devices, allowing products to be developed based on client feedback.
- Modularity: One of the most important features of a smart factory is the fluidity to adapt to change. It usually takes a week for a company to evaluate the market and make operational adjustments based on those findings. Smart factories elevate themselves according to their ability to adapt dynamically to market and sessional shifts.

The main advantages of Industry 4.0 are as follows (Chakraborty & Mandal, 2022):

- Optimisation: The concept of self-optimisation is deeply rooted in smart devices, leading to completely uninterrupted manufacturing when a breakdown is identified. As an essential feature of high-priced industrial machinery, the industrial sector considerably benefits as a whole in the long run.
- Customisation: With personalisation requirements, a customer-centric industry has emerged, whereby swift and effortless delivery is the consumer's top priority, contributing to bridging the gap between consumers and suppliers. The communication process will be congestion-free due to the absence of middlemen, along with improved and shortened delivery time-frames and processes.
- Pushing Research: The development of several fields will be facilitated by accelerated research. When a new industry emerges, the required set of skills will be available to those who need training.

### 9.2.2 Blockchain Technology

Blockchain has seeped through the last recent years to become one of the most groundbreaking and revolutionary methods of providing decentralised trust, by eliminating the need for a trusted third party. Blockchain has been embraced by the self-operating and self-sustaining industries, given its undeniable features regarding the proper and secure management and storage of data. It is crystal clear that blockchain's major application in removing the requirement for any third entity is attested to, by the digital tokens used in the exchange and accessibility of virtual content and currencies between peer-to-peer users (Dinh et al., 2018). Smart contracts and cryptocurrency have paved the way to achieve data integrity and confidentiality (Tschorsch & Scheuermann, 2016). Blockchain technology may be used as a second layer for decentralised programme execution across several systems using a consensus mechanism (Kosba et al., 2016). This need for uncompromised data integrity is the reason why blockchain has taken massive involvement in the security realm, giving rise to applications like digital currencies and smart contracts (Bonneau et al., 2015). Blockchain technology is anticipated to develop and ease both accessibility and the management of inter-actions in a network of distributed independent peers. The same distributed architecture may be used to orchestrate the global state for general bytecode execution (Yeow et al., 2018). This encompassed the fragmentation of assets in the finance sphere, IoT in government services, as well as more decentralised applications.

Blockchain revolves around the concept of a ledger, bearing properties such as decentralisation. It is also public, distributed, shared among nodes and immu-table, alongside being protected by cryptographic hashing techniques. This ledger is a series of encrypted blocks of coordinated data, distributed over a peer-to-peer architecture, where the blocks are ordered by time. Thus, in a chain where the data are divided into blocks, each block is added to the preceding block. This tie made between blocks is governed by a hash. The blocks are then verified and approved via a distributed consensus method to ensure security, privacy and transparency in the chain.

Blockchain can be thought of as consecutively linked blocks that ultimately form the whole collection of transaction data. Every block, except for the first, is connected to its parent block. Since each block bears the hash of its parent block, any block can be located and accessed by tracing back through the chain. The first block is referred to as the genesis block. A block number is allocated to each block, which only includes legitimate transactions. Instead of storing these operations in plaintext, a Merkle tree is constructed using the hashes of individual transactions. The time sequence of the chain is guaranteed and maintained by a timestamp which is permanently associated with each transaction made (Arya et al., 2021).

Fig. 9.1 shows the phases involved in a blockchain-based transaction.

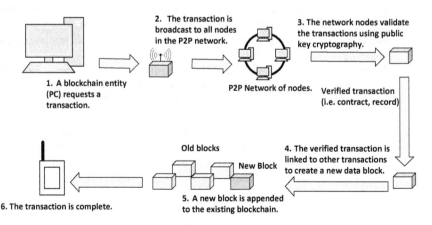

Fig. 9.1.   Blockchain-Enabled Transactions.

The main characteristics of blockchain are elaborated below (Arya et al., 2021):

(1) Decentralisation: Blockchain-based data are fragmented such that each node forming the blockchain possesses consistent data. Centralised data are authorised by a unified and trustworthy body. Such organisations operate effectively in most circumstances, but an increased number of middlemen cause the transaction cost to rise. For instance, in the financial sector, banks represent the centralised trusted authority where its involvement reduces the minimum realistic transaction cost. On the other hand, in a blockchain architecture, the presence of a central and trusted body is not required. This means that the total cost can be reduced when many transactions are made to purchase the same item. In addition, dividing the verification among numerous nodes takes the burden off the central server, which would otherwise have to coordinate and process these transactions.

(2) Persistency: Transactions in a blockchain are essentially recorded in blocks, resulting in a chronologically ordered, fragmented and distributed chain that the whole network adheres to. The blockchain ledger (BCL) is stored by each node, for recovery purposes in case of data loss. Resilience and reliability are simply achieved by storing data on various nodes such that any incomplete or falsified data can be easily identified.

(3) Anonymity: Banks keep the identification and sensitive data of their customers to authenticate operations, which then allows any transaction to be readily tracked. In the blockchain system, however, a user is allocated a wallet address, through which personal information and identity are masked. Numerous wallet addresses may also be used, in a system where no central authority holds the private data of a node. Transactions are openly validated, and miners cannot determine a wallet owner's identity. No central entity can request a user's sensitive records, adding further security.

(4) Transparency: The blockchain enables network visibility by providing decentralised and reliable transaction history. The importance of transparency cannot be overstated in the supply chain and logistics sector. By building a transparent structure, the blockchain network minimises the success of scams.

(5) Auditability: The user may quickly and easily check a transaction's legitimacy, thanks to the timestamp included in the blockchain network, resulting in better auditability through clearer and more easily traceable financial dealings.

(6) Time reduction: By having the same data on all nodes, blockchain speeds up the verification process. The mitigation of authentication at several checkpoints saves rounds of verification, settlement and approval. A single agreed-upon version saves time and processing power.

Additionally, when combined with AI, blockchain offers the following advantages (IBM, n.d.):

i. Authenticity: To overcome the challenges of explainable AI, blockchain's digital ledger may be used to gain an understanding of the AI's underlying structure and the data source it is pulling from. This increases faith in the reliability of data and, by extension, the suggestions provided by AI. By storing and including AI models on the blockchain, an audit trail is created, and by merging blockchain technology with AI, data protection is improved.

ii. Augmentation: AI can absorb, comprehend and correlate data at an unprecedented rate and depth, adding a new dimension of cognitive capacity to blockchain-based business networks. Blockchain goes hand in hand with AI, paving the way to more meaningful insights, better data consumption management and model sharing. This partnership also builds a credible and transparent data economy by enabling access to enormous amounts of data from inside and outside the business.

iii. Automation: When applied to multiparty enterprise applications, AI, automation and blockchain have the potential to improve efficiency, reduce manual steps and boost throughput. AI models integrated into smart contracts and implemented on a blockchain can provide suggestions such as recalling expired products, reordering, paying or purchasing stock based on predetermined thresholds and events, settling conflicts and choosing the most environmentally friendly shipping option, among other things.

## 9.3 Framework for Blockchain Integration in Industry 4.0 and Real-Time Systems

A typical generic framework for blockchain in industry 4.0 and real-time systems is shown in Fig. 9.2 (a). Edge sensor data are crucial for processes including process monitoring, predictive maintenance and locating irregularities in machinery. Rahman et al. (2021) presented a blockchain-based AI-enabled Advanced Persistent Threats (APT) detection system that safeguards Industrial IoT data against forgery, intending to protect edge IoT and server-side data communication paradigms and transmission methods, in a standard Industry 4.0 architecture. This was performed by adopting a reusable machine learning approach at the edge, to encrypt data before transmission. Additionally, storing APT detection and data exchanges in the BCL, as well as in the edge-compliant distributed hash table (DHT), guarantees improved functioning and effectiveness.

The suggested security mechanism has three stages:

(1) To begin with, the edge server is equipped with a deep transfer learning (DTL) model which is trained using two merged and precompiled datasets (Moustafa, 2019a, 2019b). On contact, the edge server queries for the presence of any APT within that data.

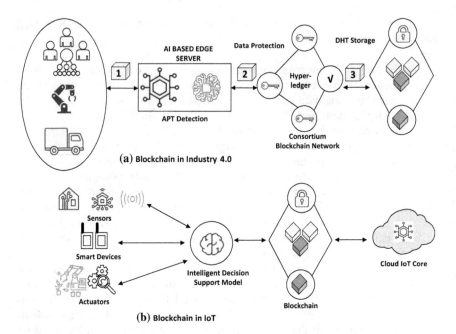

**Fig. 9.2.    Framework for Blockchain in Industry 4.0 and Real-Time Systems.**

(2) The linked DHT then receives both the detection history and sensor data. At this stage, it is imperative to determine whether any APTs were injected during data transmission across the network, before storing the items received. A blockchain consortium thus oversees the procedure and ensures that data are being exchanged only by registered and verified devices.

(3) Upon authentication, the BCL is updated with the latest data exchange, along with the APT detection state. The data are then stored in the DHT.

The suggested method by Rahman et al. (2021) employs the key characteristics of the DTL framework on top of the residual neural network (ResNet) model. The input variables include the generation of client data, in the order of a thousand transactions per second, after which parameters including throughput and latency are respectively calculated. Following a successful APT screening process at the edge, data are transmitted to the related DHT. Features such as identification, verification and acceptance of the IoT sensors are governed by the CBC. The irreversible ledger holds the sensor data and APT detection details. With the adoption of CBC, which increases the data transaction rate, this suggested model achieves a general accuracy of over 90%.

Fig. 9.2 (b) depicts an intelligent agricultural system which merges IoT and blockchain technology to create a trustworthy, safe and reliable decision system.

In light of improving plant health and production, this system is equipped with monitoring capabilities concerning the environment, together with crucial weather indicators including humidity, soil moisture, temperature and light intensity. Real-time field data are gathered by the system through installed sensors, followed by relevant event triggers such as preventive measures and decision-making. These judgements are made using intelligent fuzzy logic depending on input factors, to set off the transmission of alerts about watering needs to the user. Device-based transactions require recording and tracing through a decentralised ledger system like blockchain. These are executed during the process of the proposed Intelligent Climate and Watering Agriculture System (ICWAS). As a result, blockchain caters for the transaction by providing increased levels of security, and smooth availability and connection to the proposed system's many functionalities (Ting et al., 2022). Further examples of the application of blockchain in the IoT realm include energy monitoring systems (Swain et al., 2021), decentralised crowd sourcing mechanisms for predicting weather variables such as wind power (Shamsi & Cuffe, 2020), as well as supply chain management (Nirantar et al., 2022).

## 9.4 Blockchain Use Cases in Industry 4.0 and UN SDGs

The applications of blockchain specific to Industry 4.0 and targeting some of the UN SDGs are summarised as follows (Javaid et al., 2021):

i. Finance: Blockchain facilitates seamless currency exchange and supply transactions, while also fostering trust and speeding up multiparty transactions. Its influence extends beyond finance, and its adoption in other sectors owes much to its success in banking and payments. Blockchain and AI are transforming financial services by streamlining transactions involving multiple parties. For example, blockchain can accelerate loan procedures by enabling access to personal data and using automated procedures to evaluate applications. This results in faster closings, increased data trust and higher customer satisfaction, with a positive impact on SDG 8 (Zhang et al., 2020).

ii. Manufacturing data protection: In the context of Industry 4.0, blockchain's fundamental and core encryption techniques may be used to keep sensitive information secure. Data communicated over a public network are then protected from prying eyes. Blockchain offers many applications in the field of intellectual property, including evidence of copyright, registrations and clear rights, record-keeping, monitoring and control of licencing rights, establishing IP agreements and even administering the acquisition of privileges in the realm of Industry 4.0. These concepts positively affect SDGs 9 and 16 (Lu, 2019).

iii. Identifications of products and assemblies: Details for production and assembly verification are provided by blockchains. This could aid in identifying and addressing intricate and highly specific problems. Information about any goods, products, merchandise, machine parts and business delivery strategies is all readily available through blockchain. By gathering data at every level, interruptions and costs are greatly cut down in the present situation. The management of items and their assembly is thus ideal and fluid. This unquestionably advances SDG 9 (Zhu & Kouhizadeh, 2019).

iv. Supply chain: Some recent improvements significantly enhanced the way industrial organisations manage their supply chains. As blockchain technology progresses, the supply chain sector will look for practical means of ensuring transparency, traceability and effectiveness. The centralisation of Enterprise Resource Planning (ERP) systems gives Industry 4.0 businesses total control over their internal operations and empowers them to make long-term decisions for data-oriented businesses when coupled with real-time data updates. Blockchain and AI are revolutionising distribution networks across sectors and opening up new possibilities by digitising a mostly paper-based process, rendering the information trusted, verifiable and shared. For instance, a company may monitor data on carbon emissions at the component or product level, enhancing the precision and sophistication of decarbonisation activities (Mohamed & Al-Jaroodi, 2019).

v. Integration of system: Blockchain technology brings up additional opportunities for collaboration outside of a company's internal ecosystem by including partnerships, customers and supply chains via an organisation. Anyone may now be informed of the operation as it happens. Data may also be accessed by Industry 4.0, reducing the possibility of material being suppressed or misrepresented. At this point, the outcome market, which aims to revolutionise company paradigms and flourish to support bigger firms, is starting to take shape. This can have a positive impact on SDG 17 (Rathee et al., 2019).

## 9.5 Conclusion

Our society has undergone a complete metamorphosis as a result of the Fourth Industrial Revolution, which has also altered our mode of production and resulted in both a sustainable future and top-tier manufacturing methods. Industry 4.0 capabilities have lately been thought of as possibly advancing sustainable environmental decisions as they allow for better strategic planning between the organisational objective and the information technology used. Currently employed across many different industries, blockchain technology has been adopted by several governments to improve environmental durability and continuity. As a revolutionary technology, blockchain is reshaping information technology and symbolises a cultural shift in the way information is propagated. Businesses are scrambling to figure out how to leverage distributed ledger technology to reinvent operations, manufacturing and transaction management. Real-time data collecting and analytics for environmentally friendly or low-carbon manufacturing, tracking and archiving operations connected to pollution and environmental deterioration and novel methods of environmental responsibility are all outputs of blockchain technology. In this chapter, some fundamental concepts on blockchain as well as its integration in Industry 4.0 and real-time intelligent systems have been discussed, alongside the advantages that it brings to the UN SDGs through its integration in different applications and systems.

# References

Alkadi, O., Moustafa, N., Turnbull, B., & Choo, K.-K. R. (2020). A deep blockchain framework-enabled collaborative intrusion detection for protecting IoT and cloud networks. *IEEE Internet of Things Journal*, 8(12), 9463–9472. https://doi.org/10.1109/jiot.2020.2996590

Arya, J., Kumar, A., Singh, A. P., Mishra, T. K., & Chong, P. H. J. (2021). *Blockchain: Basics, applications, challenges and opportunities*. https://doi.org/10.13140/RG.2.2.33899.16160

Bonneau, J., Miller, A., Clark, J., Narayanan, A., Kroll, J. A., & Felten, E. W. (2015). SoK: Research perspectives and challenges for bitcoin and cryptocurrencies. In *2015 IEEE Symposium on Security and Privacy*. https://doi.org/10.1109/sp.2015.14

Chakraborty, A., & Mandal, N. (2022). Introduction of industry 4.0. *Turkish Online Journal of Qualitative Inquiry*, 12, 8342–8350.

Dinh, T. T. A., Liu, R., Zhang, M., Chen, G., Ooi, B. C., & Wang, J. (2018). Untangling blockchain: A data processing view of blockchain systems. *IEEE Transactions on Knowledge and Data Engineering*, 30(7), 1366–1385. https://doi.org/10.1109/tkde.2017.2781227

Hompel, M. T., Vogel-Heuser, B., & Bauernhansl, T. (2017). *Handbuch Industrie 4.0 Bd. 4 Allgemeine Grundlagen*. Berlin Springer Vieweg Proquest.

IBM. (n.d.). *Combined values of blockchain and AI*. IBM. https://www.ibm.com/topics/blockchain-ai

Javaid, M., Haleem, A., Pratap Singh, R., Khan, S., & Suman, R. (2021). Blockchain technology applications for Industry 4.0: A literature-based review. *Blockchain: Research and Applications*, 2(4), 100027. https://doi.org/10.1016/j.bcra.2021.100027

Jiang, X., Yu, F. R., Song, T., Ma, Z., Song, Y., & Zhu, D. (2020). Blockchain-enabled cross-domain object detection for autonomous driving: A model sharing approach. *IEEE Internet of Things Journal*, 7(5), 3681–3692. https://doi.org/10.1109/jiot.2020.2967788

Kosba, A., Miller, A., Shi, E., Wen, Z., & Papamanthou, C. (2016). Hawk: The blockchain model of cryptography and privacy-preserving smart contracts. In *2016 IEEE Symposium on Security and Privacy (SP)* (pp 839–858). https://doi.org/10.1109/sp.2016.55

Lin, H., Hu, J., Wang, X., Alhamid, M. F., & Piran, M. J. (2021). Toward secure data fusion in industrial IoT using transfer learning. *IEEE Transactions on Industrial Informatics*, 17(10), 7114–7122. https://doi.org/10.1109/tii.2020.3038780

Lu, Y. (2019). The blockchain: State-of-the-art and research challenges. *Journal of Industrial Information Integration*, 15, 80–90. https://doi.org/10.1016/j.jii.2019.04.002

Lu, Y., Xu, X., & Wang, L. (2020). Smart manufacturing process and system automation – A critical review of the standards and envisioned scenarios. *Journal of Manufacturing Systems*, 56, 312–325. https://doi.org/10.1016/j.jmsy.2020.06.010

Mohamed, N., & Al-Jaroodi, J. (2019, January 1). *Applying blockchain in Industry 4.0 applications*. IEEE Xplore. https://doi.org/10.1109/CCWC.2019.8666558

Morgus, R. (2018). *Securing digital dividends, mainstreaming cybersecurity in international development.* https://d1y8sb8igg2f8e.cloudfront.net/documents/Securing_Digital_Dividends_Gv2FUiZ.pdf

Moustafa, N. (2019a). *The Bot-IoT dataset.* IEEE Dataport. https://doi.org/10.21227/r7v2-x988

Moustafa, N. (2019b). *The TON_IoT dataset.* https://research.unsw.edu.au/projects/toniot-datasets

Nirantar, K., Karmakar, R., Hiremath, P., & Chaudhari, D. (2022). *Blockchain based supply chain management.* In *2022 3rd International Conference for Emerging Technology (INCET).* https://doi.org/10.1109/incet54531.2022.9824449

Rahman, Z., Khalil, I., Yi, X., & Atiquzzaman, M. (2021). Blockchain-based security framework for a critical Industry 4.0 cyber-physical system. *IEEE Communications Magazine, 59*(5), 128–134. https://doi.org/10.1109/mcom.001.2000679

Rahman, Z., Yi, X., & Khalil, I. (2022). Blockchain based AI-enabled Industry 4.0 CPS protection against advanced persistent threat. *IEEE Internet of Things Journal, 1.* https://doi.org/10.1109/jiot.2022.3147186

Rathee, G., Sharma, A., Kumar, R., & Iqbal, R. (2019). A secure communicating things network framework for industrial IoT using blockchain technology. *Ad Hoc Networks, 94,* 101933. https://doi.org/10.1016/j.adhoc.2019.101933

Shamsi, M., & Cuffe, P. (2020). Towards the use of blockchain prediction markets for forecasting wind power. In *2020 6th IEEE International Energy Conference (ENERGYCon).* https://doi.org/10.1109/energycon48941.2020.9236467

Swain, A., Swain, K. P., Samal, S. R., Pattnaik, S. K., Mishra, A., Das, J. K., Palai, G., & Bandopadhaya, S. (2021). Blockchain powered energy monitoring system. In *2021 19th OITS International Conference on Information Technology (OCIT).* https://doi.org/10.1109/ocit53463.2021.00038

Ting, L., Khan, M., Sharma, A., & Ansari, M. D. (2022). A secure framework for IoT-based smart climate agriculture system: Toward blockchain and edge computing. *Journal of Intelligent Systems, 31*(1), 221–236. https://doi.org/10.1515/jisys-2022-0012

Tschorsch, F., & Scheuermann, B. (2016). Bitcoin and beyond: A technical survey on decentralized digital currencies. *IEEE Communications Surveys & Tutorials, 18*(3), 2084–2123. https://doi.org/10.1109/comst.2016.2535718

Vogel-Heuser, B., Bayrak, G., & Frank, U. (2012). *Forschungsfragen in "Produktionsautomatisierung der Zukunft."* Diskussionspapier Für Die Acatech Projektgruppe "ProCPS – Production CPS.

Vogel-Heuser, B., & Hess, D. (2016). Guest editorial Industry 4.0 – Prerequisites and visions. *IEEE Transactions on Automation Science and Engineering, 13*(2), 411–413. https://doi.org/10.1109/tase.2016.2523639

Wang, S., Wan, J., Zhang, D., Li, D., & Zhang, C. (2016). Towards smart factory for industry 4.0: A self-organized multi-agent system with big data based feedback and coordination. *Computer Networks, 101,* 158–168. https://doi.org/10.1016/j.comnet.2015.12.017

Wang, X., Garg, S., Lin, H., Jalilpiran, M., Hu, J., & Hossain, M. S. (2021). Enabling secure authentication in industrial IoT with transfer learning empowered blockchain. *IEEE Transactions on Industrial Informatics, 17*(11), 7725–7733. https://doi.org/10.1109/tii.2021.3049405

Xu, X., Lu, Y., Vogel-Heuser, B., & Wang, L. (2021). Industry 4.0 and Industry 5.0—Inception, conception and perception. *Journal of Manufacturing Systems*, *61*, 530–535. https://doi.org/10.1016/j.jmsy.2021.10.006

Yeow, K., Gani, A., Ahmad, R. W., Rodrigues, J. J. P. C., & Ko, K. (2018). Decentralized consensus for edge-centric internet of things: A review, taxonomy, and research issues. *IEEE Access*, *6*, 1513–1524. https://doi.org/10.1109/access.2017.2779263

Zhang, L., Xie, Y., Zheng, Y., Xue, W., Zheng, X., & Xu, X. (2020). The challenges and countermeasures of blockchain in finance and economics. *Systems Research and Behavioral Science*, *37*(4), 691–698. https://doi.org/10.1002/sres.2710

Zhong, R. Y., Xu, X., Klotz, E., & Newman, S. T. (2017). Intelligent manufacturing in the context of Industry 4.0: A review. *Engineering*, *3*(5), 616–630. https://doi.org/10.1016/j.eng.2017.05.015

Zhu, Q., & Kouhizadeh, M. (2019). Blockchain technology, supply chain information, and strategic product deletion management. *IEEE Engineering Management Review*, *47*(1), 36–44. https://doi.org/10.1109/emr.2019.2898178

Zuehlke, D. (2010). SmartFactory—Towards a factory-of-things. *Annual Reviews in Control*, *34*(1), 129–138. https://doi.org/10.1016/j.arcontrol.2010.02.008

Chapter 10

# A Reliability-Based Two Stage Phasor Measurement Unit (PMU) Placement Optimisation Model Using Mathematical- and Nature-Based Evolutionary Algorithms

*Robert T. F. Ah King and Samiah Mohangee*

University of Mauritius, Mauritius

## Abstract

To operate with high efficiency and minimise the risks of power failures, power systems require careful monitoring. The availability of real-time data is crucial for assessing the performance of the grid and assisting operators in gauging the present security of the grid. Traditional supervisory control and data acquisition (SCADA)-based systems actually employed provides steady-state measurement values which are the calculation premise of State Estimation. More often, however, the power grid operates under dynamic state and SCADA measurements can lead to erroneous and inaccurate calculation results. The introduction of the phasor measurement unit (PMU) which provides real-time synchronised voltage and current phasors with very high accuracy is universally recognised as an important aspect of delivering a secure and sustainable power system. PMUs are a relatively new technology and because of their high procurement and installation costs, it is imperative to develop appropriate methodologies to determine the minimum number of PMUs as well as their strategic placements to guarantee full observability of a power system. Thus, the problem of the optimal PMU placement (OPP) is formulated as an optimisation problem subject to various constraints to minimise the number of PMUs while ensuring complete observability of the grid. In this chapter, integer linear programming (ILP), genetic algorithm (GA) and non-linear programming (NLP) constrained models of the OPP problem are presented. A new methodology is proposed to incorporate several constraints using the NLP. The optimisation methods have been written in Matlab software and verified on the standard Institute of Electrical

Artificial Intelligence, Engineering Systems and Sustainable Development, 123–143
Copyright © 2024 Robert T. F. Ah King and Samiah Mohangee
Published under exclusive licence by Emerald Publishing Limited
doi:10.1108/978-1-83753-540-820241010

and Electronics Engineers (IEEE) 14-bus test system to authenticate their effectiveness. This chapter targets United Nations Sustainable Development Goal 7.

*Keywords*: Phasor measurement unit; optimisation; power systems; integer linear programming; genetic algorithm; non-linear programming

## 10.1 Introduction

Supervisory control and data acquisition (SCADA) systems allow the supervision of the power grid based upon steady-state load flow analysis. They provide unsynchronised measurements of bus voltage magnitudes and current injections as well as active and reactive power flows. Because of the low data scan rate (2–4 samples/cycle), SCADA systems cannot detect small disturbances of the order of sub seconds. Consequently, corrective measures cannot be undertaken in time (Zambrano et al., 2011). Further, SCADA systems cannot track and monitor rapidly-occurring transients which, if left undetected, can lead to a complete collapse of the entire power grid and catastrophic blackouts. A pertinent case is the cascaded blackout which occurred on 14 August 2003 in the United States and Canada due to the breakdown of a coal-fired generating station. An investigation carried out reported that a lack of access to real-time data was the main cause of the blackout and, had there been better monitoring systems, the disaster could have been duly avoided (Blackout, 2003).

These shortcomings can be overcome with the installation of phasor measurement units (PMUs), which provide time-synchronised measurements of the voltage and current waveforms by using timing signals from the global positioning system (GPS). PMUs can sample 50/60 Hz waveforms at a rate of up to 60 samples/cycle and are a crucial element of wide area monitoring systems (WAMSs) for monitoring, protection and control (Singh et al., 2011).

A power grid is deemed to be completely observable if the state variables, that is, the voltage phasors, of all buses are known. Implementing PMUs at each bus in a substation would allow direct measurement of current and voltage phasors but the high installation costs of PMUs and communication channels restrict their placement across the grid. The US Department of Energy estimates the average overall cost per PMU for procurement, installation and commissioning to range from $40,000 to $180,000 (US Department of Energy, 2014). Besides, because a PMU can measure the voltage phasor of the bus at which it is connected as well as the current phasors of all branches emerging from the PMU-connected bus, it is neither vital nor economical to place PMUs at each bus in a substation. One considerable challenge faced by planning engineers lies in the careful selection of the most optimal PMU locations to ensure robust observability of the power grid. This calls for reliable techniques to address the issue of optimal PMU placement (OPP).

Johnson and Moger (2021) have presented the progress achieved until then in the field of optimal placement of PMUs. The characteristics of problem formulations and shortcomings of methods and constraints considered have been discussed. Yuvaraju and Thangavel (2022) presented the optimal PMU placement technique by considering the WAMS data traffic index and installation cost index with complete system observability. Optimal PMU positions were obtained using the teaching learning-based optimisation technique. Further reduction in the PMU number was obtained by considering zero injection bus (ZIB) case which resulted in a reduction in installation cost. Okendo et al. (2021) considered Depth-First method, mixed-integer linear programming (MILP) and artificial bee colony (ABC) algorithm. The optimal solution with highest system observability redundancy index (SORI) with exclusion of ZIB was obtained by ABC algorithm. In order to minimise the installed number of PMUs and maximise the measurement redundancy of the network, Baba et al. (2020) have proposed a new symmetry approach of multiple objectives for the optimum placement of PMU problem. By reducing and excluding pure transit node, their technique resulted in placement set in which only the strategic, significant and the most desirable buses are selected without considering ZIBs.

The endeavour of this chapter is to design PMU placement optimisation algorithms to ensure that a network is fully observable with a minimal set of PMUs, usually less than the number of buses in the system, under different constraints. In the second stage process, reliability is maximised using the same number of PMUs obtained initially. The proposed methodology considers two conventional methods, namely, integer linear programming (ILP) and non-linear programming (NLP), and, one nature-based evolutionary algorithm, genetic algorithm (GA).

Five different constraints which are considered are:

(1)  Strict observability (no conventional measurements),
(2)  N-1 contingency criterion (single PMU failure),
(3)  Inclusion of ZIBs,
(4)  Inclusion of ZIBs and N-1 contingency criterion,
(5)  Controlled islanding (CI).

For the PMU placements found, the SORI is calculated to show the measurement redundancy level. The first four cases aim at providing optimal PMU placements for State Estimation. CI is designed to disconnect an affected area of the power system in case of disturbances or faults in a bid to kerb the possibility of power outages and blackouts. Benchmark Institute of Electrical and Electronics Engineers (IEEE) 14-bus test system is used to test the accuracy and validity of the proposed methods and results are compared with published works.

Vulnerable people have the right for universal access to affordable, reliable and modern energy services as per Sustainable Development Goal (SDG) 7 in order to meet diverse basic services, such as access to drinking water and sanitation, health care, education, information and adequate and safe housing with important contribution to reducing poverty in all its dimensions. In our modern world, almost everything is powered by electricity which makes it an essential commodity. Optimal PMU placement enables the reduction in implementation cost to ensure reliable operation of distribution systems. It forms an integral part of the power utility infrastructure to ensure access to affordable, reliable, sustainable and modern energy for all.

## 10.2 Optimal PMU Placement Formulation

### 10.2.1 PMU Placement Rules

A bus is described as observable if its voltage can be directly or indirectly measured. The three PMU placement rules developed based upon the fundamental laws of branch current and node voltage are detailed (Rahman & Zobaa, 2016).

Observability Rule 1: A PMU installed at a bus measures the voltage phasor of the bus and all incident branch currents. This is referred to as 'direct measurements'.

Observability Rule 2: If the voltage and current phasors at one end of a branch are known, the voltage phasor at the other end can be determined by applying Ohm's law. This is referred to as 'pseudo measurements'.

Observability Rule 3: If the voltage phasors at both ends of a branch are known, the branch current can be determined by applying Ohm's law. This is also referred to as 'pseudo measurements'.

### 10.2.2 Zero-Injection Bus (ZIB)

A ZIB is a bus with no load or generator and no current is injected into the system at a ZIB. According to Kirchoff's current law (KCL), the sum of flows on all branch currents associated with a ZIB is zero (Rahman & Zobaa, 2016). Accounting for ZIBs can considerably reduce the number of PMUs required to achieve full observability.

#### 10.2.2.1 PMU Placement Rules in the Presence of ZIBs

The measurements derived from the three ZIB rules detailed below are known as 'extended measurements'. More details can be found in Mousavian and Feizollahi (2015).

ZIB Rule 1: If there is a ZIB whose incident current phasors are known except one, KCL can be used to calculate the unknown current phasor.

ZIB Rule 2: The voltage phasor of a ZIB can be determined, provided that the voltage phasors of all adjacent buses to the ZIB are known.

ZIB Rule 3: The voltage phasors of a group of adjacent ZIBs can be determined, provided that the voltage phasors of all adjacent buses to the ZIBs are known.

### 10.2.3 Bus Observability Index (BOI) and SORI

To rank PMU placement solutions accordingly, two indices are proposed to assess the quality of the optimisation, BOI and SORI (Dua et al., 2008).

The BOI for bus $i$ ($\beta_i$) indicates the number of PMUs which are able to observe bus $i$. The maximum BOI is limited to the maximum connectivity ($\eta_i$) of bus $i$ plus one.

$$\beta_i = \eta_i + 1 \tag{10.1}$$

For an $N$-bus system, SORI ($\gamma$) is defined as the sum of all $N$ BOIs for all of the buses of the system.

$$\gamma = \sum_{i=1}^{N} \beta_i \tag{10.2}$$

### 10.2.4 Assumptions

(1) All PMUs installed in the network have the same cost, irrespective of the number of incident branches to a bus.
(2) A PMU installed at a bus has a sufficient number of channels to measure the bus voltage phasor as well as all incident branch currents.

### 10.2.5 Formulation of the Proposed Methodology for ILP and GA

#### 10.2.5.1 Objective Function Formulation
For an $N$-bus system, the objective function of the OPP problem is formulated as:

$$\text{Minimise } \sum_{i=1}^{N} x_i \tag{10.3}$$

The OPP problem being discrete in nature, $x_i$ represents the binary decision variable given as:

$$x_i = \{1, \text{if a PMU is installed at bus } i \; 0, \text{otherwise} \tag{10.4}$$

#### 10.2.5.2 Case 1: Strict Observability (No Conventional Measurements)

Observability is the only constraint and is formulated as:

$$[F]_{N \times 1} = [A]_{N \times N} [X]_{N \times 1} \geq [B]_{N \times 1} \tag{10.5}$$

where,
$[F]$ is a $N \times 1$ vector containing all the observability functions.
$[A]$ is a $N \times N$ binary connectivity matrix with entries defined as shown in Eq. (10.6).

$$a_{ij} = \{1, if\ i = j \quad 1, if\ i\ and\ j\ are\ connected\ 0, otherwise \qquad (10.6)$$

$[X]$ is a $N \times 1$ binary decision variable vector with entries defined as shown in Eq. (10.7).

$$[X] = [x_1\ x_2\ x_3 \ldots x_N]^T \qquad (10.7)$$

$[B]$ is a $N \times 1$ column vector whose entries are all ones as shown in Eq. (10.8).

$$[B] = [1\ 1\ 1 \ldots 1]^T_{1 \times N} \qquad (10.8)$$

The *i*th array of $[F]$ is given in Eq. (10.9).

$$f_i = \sum_{j=1}^{N} a_{ij}x_i \geq 1, \forall i \in \qquad (10.9)$$

where,
  $f_i$ is the linear observability function of bus $i$.
  $\mathfrak{J}$ is the set of buses.

### 10.2.5.3 Case 2: N-1 Contingency (Single PMU Outage)
Eq. (10.5) is modified to establish the modified constraint for ensuring full observability in the case of N-1 contingency as shown:

$$[F]_{N \times 1} = [A]_{N \times N}\ [X]_{N \times 1} \geq 2 \times [B]_{N \times 1} \qquad (10.10)$$

### 10.2.5.4 Case 3: Inclusion of ZIBs
To model ZIB buses, some existing constraints from Case 1 must be removed and new constraints must be formed based upon ZIB Rules 1–3 detailed in Section 10.2.2.1. The approach to ZIB modelling consists of purposely allowing for the existence of unobservable buses. The ZIB and its connected buses are defined as a set of ZIB (SOZIB and its adjacent buses). Combining the three ZIB rules, it is deduced that, for each SOZIB in a network, one bus can be deliberately made unobservable if all the other buses in the SOZIB are being observed by at least one PMU. For buses not belonging to SOZIBs, the constraints in Eq. (10.5) are maintained. The new constraints to incorporate ZIBs in the problem are formulated as:

$$f_{injt,i} = f_i + \sum_{j \in adj_i} f_j \geq m - 1 \qquad (10.11)$$

where,
  $f_{injt,i}$ is the linear joint observability function of $ZIB_i$.
  $m$ is the total number of buses in $SOZIB_i$.
  $adj_i$ is the set of buses adjacent to $ZIB_i$.
  $\sum_{j \in adj_i} f_j$ is the sum of the linear observability functions of all the adjacent buses $j$
to $ZIB_i$.

The location of ZIB and radial bus for IEEE 14-bus system for which the proposed methodology has been applied are ZIB location: bus 7; Radial bus location: bus 8.

For illustration, the ZIB modelling for the IEEE 14-bus system is presented in Fig. 10.1.

Constraints for buses 4, 7, 8 and 9 are grouped together to form the linear joint observability function of $ZIB_7$, $f_{injt,7}$.

$$
\begin{aligned}
f_4 &= x_2 + x_3 + x_4 + x_5 + x_7 + x_9 \geq 1 \\
f_7 &= x_4 + x_7 + x_8 + x_9 \geq 1 \\
f_8 &= x_7 + x_8 \geq 1 \\
f_9 &= x_4 + x_7 + x_9 + x_{10} + x_{14} \geq 1 \\
&\downarrow \\
f_{injt,7} &= x_2 + x_3 + 3x_4 + x_5 + 4x_7 + 2x_8 + 3x_9 + x_{10} + x_{14} \geq 3
\end{aligned}
\tag{10.12}
$$

### 10.2.5.5 Case 4: Inclusion of ZIBs and N-1 Contingency Criterion

Eq. (10.11) is modified to establish the modified constraint for ensuring full observability in the case of N-1 contingency as shown:

$$
f_{injt,i} = f_i + \sum_{j \in \text{adj}_i} f_j \geq 2(m-1)
\tag{10.13}
$$

$f_{injt,7}$ for Case 4 is the same as in Eq. (10.12) with the exception that the right-hand side is changed to 6.

For buses with more than one ZIB, the same procedure is followed.

### 10.2.5.6 Pre-allocation of PMUs

Pre-allocation of PMUs is performed exceptionally in cases where the initial optimisation leads to unobservable buses. The flow chart is shown in Fig. 10.2.

### 10.2.5.7 Case 5: CI

The constraints for CI are formulated based upon the following equation:

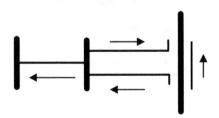

Fig. 10.1.    Part of the Institute of Electrical and Electronics Engineers (IEEE) 14-Bus System.

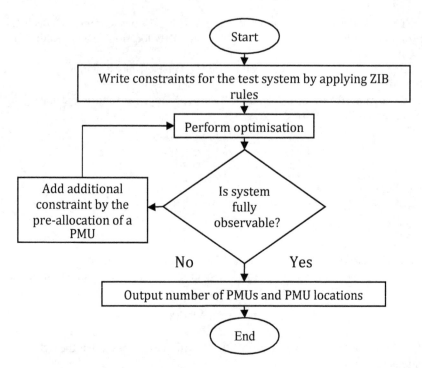

Fig. 10.2.    Flow Chart for the Pre-allocation of Phasor Measurement Units (PMUs).

$$[F^{CI}]_{N \times 1} = [A^{CI}]_{N \times N} [X]_{N \times 1} \geq [B]_{N \times 1} \qquad (10.14)$$

where,

$[F^{CI}]$ is a $N \times 1$ vector containing all the observability functions for CI.

$[A^{CI}]$ is a $N \times N$ binary connectivity matrix post-islanding with entries defined as shown in Eq. (10.15):

$$a_{ij}^{CI} = \{ 0 \text{2, if line } i - j \text{ is opened in the CI process } a_{ij}, \text{otherwise} \qquad (10.15)$$

The $i$th array of $[F^{CI}]$ is given as:

$$f_{CI,i} = \sum_{j=1}^{N} a_{ij}^{CI} x_i \geq 1, \forall i \in \qquad (10.16)$$

where,

$f_{CI,i}$ is the linear CI function of bus $i$.

Results of CI scheme performed in Nezam-Sarmadi et al. (2010) for the IEEE 14-bus system are used to devise the OPP problem to achieve full observability for both normal and post-islanding conditions. The results are shown in Table 10.1.

Table 10.1. Phasor Measurement Unit (PMU) Placements Found by Integer Linear Programming (ILP) and Genetic Algorithm (GA).

| Case | Optimal Number of PMUs | Most Optimal PMU Locations | Highest SORI | Similar or Exact Results |
|------|------|------|------|------|
| Case 1 | 4 | 2, 6, 7, 9 | 19 | ILP (Dua et al., 2008), BILP and GA (Theodorakatosa et al., 2014) |
| Case 2 | 9 | 2, 4, 5, 6, 7, 8, 9, 10, 13 | 39 | GA (Mousavian & Feizollahi, 2015), ILP (Nezam-Sarmadi et al., 2010) |
| Case 3 | 3 | 2, 6, 9 | 15 | ILP (Dua et al., 2008), BILP (Theodorakatosa et al., 2014) |
| Case 4 | 7 | 2, 4, 5, 6, 9, 10, 13 | 33 | GA (Mousavian & Feizollahi, 2015), ILP (Dua et al., 2008) |
| Case 5 | 5 | 4, 5, 6, 7, 9 | 25 | ILP (Huang et al., 2014) |

The CI scheme resulted in two islands with six buses in Island 1 (buses 1, 5, 6, 11, 12, 13) and eight buses in Island 2 (buses 2, 3, 4, 7, 8, 9, 10, 14). The opened lines were 1–2, 2–5, 4–5, 10–11, 13–14.

The constraints for Islands 1 and 2 for the IEEE 14-bus system are:

Island 1

$$f_{CI,1} = x_1 + x_5 \geq 1$$

$$f_{CI,5} = x_1 + x_5 + x_6 \geq 1$$

$$f_{CI,6} = x_5 + x_6 + x_{11} + x_{12} + x_{13} \geq 1$$

$$f_{CI,11} = x_6 + x_{11} \geq 1$$

$$f_{CI,12} = x_6 + x_{12} + x_{13} \geq 1$$

$$f_{CI,13} = x_6 + x_{12} + x_{13} \geq 1$$

Island 2

$$f_{CI,2} = x_2 + x_3 + x_4 \geq 1$$

$$f_{CI,3} = x_2 + x_3 + x_4 \geq 1$$

*(Continued)*

---

$$f_{CI,4} = x_2 + x_3 + x_4 + x_7 + x_9 \geq 1$$

$$f_{CI,7} = x_4 + x_7 + x_8 + x_9 \geq 1$$

$$f_{CI,8} = x_7 + x_8 \geq 1$$

$$f_{CI,9} = x_4 + x_7 + x_9 + x_{10} + x_{14} \geq 1$$

$$f_{CI,10} = x_9 + x_{10} \geq 1$$

$$f_{CI,14} = x_9 + x_{14} \geq 1 \tag{10.17}$$

---

### 10.2.5.8 Second-Stage PMU Placement

In the second stage, for each case, a new objective function is formulated and maximised subject to the existing constraints and an additional equality constraint which indicates that the number of PMUs should be restricted to the minimum number $\lambda$ as found in the first stage so to obtain the most reliable PMU placement. Eq. (10.18) shows the Objective Function and the additional constraint for Cases 1–4.

$$\text{Mazimise } [B]^T[A][X]$$
$$s.t.$$
$$\sum_{i=1}^{N} x_i = \lambda \tag{10.18}$$

For Case 5, $[A]$ is replaced by $[A^{CI}]$.

### 10.2.5.9 Parameters Used for GA

The parameters used for the GA in the simulations are LB = 0, UB = 1, $\text{Max}_{gen}$ = 150, $N_{pop}$ = 100, $p_c$ = 0.8, $p_m$ = 0.005.

## 10.2.6 Formulation of the Proposed Methodology for NLP

### 10.2.6.1 Objective Function Formulation

The OPP problem is formulated as a NLP model and is solved using the Sequential Quadratic Programming (SQP) algorithm. The quadratic objective function is formulated as:

$$\text{Minimise} \sum_{i=1}^{N} x_i^2 \tag{10.19}$$

$x_i$ represents the continuous decision variable and is defined on a bounded set as:

$$0 \leq x_i \leq 1 \tag{10.20}$$

**10.2.6.2 Case 1: Strict Observability (No Conventional Measurements)**
To enforce the continuous variables $x_i$ to be binary, the non-linear observability function, $g_i$, of bus $i$ is defined as:

$$g_i : (1 - x_i)\prod_{j\in \text{ad}_i}(1 - x_j) = 0, \forall i \in \tag{10.21}$$

where,
  $\text{ad}_i$ is the set of buses adjacent to bus $i$.
  The mathematical formulation poses no problem to converge to a local solution because all the $N$ equality constraints are twice-continuously differentiable. The feasible solution set of the OPP formulation is non-convex because it consists of non-linear equality constraints. Therefore, multiple solutions with the same number of PMUs can be found which correspond to distinct local minimisers (Theodorakatosa et al., 2015).

**10.2.6.3 Case 2: N-1 Contingency (Single PMU Outage)**
The optimal PMU set is split into two sets: primary set and backup set. The primary PMU set is obtained from Case 1 and to obtain the backup PMU set, all the terms $(1 - x_i)$ and $(1 - x_j)$ which are associated to the main PMU set are eliminated from the non-linear observability functions in Eq. (10.21) to avoid picking up the same bus appearing in the primary set. If one PMU fails, the backup PMU set will ensure full observability of the network.

**10.2.6.4 Case 3: Inclusion of ZIBs**
In the NLP modelling, inclusion of ZIBs in the problem is formulated as:

$$g_{injt,i} : g_i\prod_{j\in \text{adj}_i}g_j = 0 \tag{10.22}$$

where,
  $g_{injt,i}$ is the non-linear joint observability function of $\text{ZIB}_i$.
  $\prod_{j\in \text{adj}_i}g_j$ is the product of the non-linear observability functions of all the adjacent buses $j$ to $\text{ZIB}_i$.
  ZIB modelling for the IEEE 14-bus system is shown in Eqs. (10.23) and (10.24).

$$g_4 : (1 - x_2)(1 - x_3)(1 - x_4)(1 - x_5)(1 - x_7)(1 - x_9) = 0$$
$$g_7 : (1 - x_4)(1 - x_7)(1 - x_8)(1 - x_9) = 0$$
$$g_8 : (1 - x_7)(1 - x_8) = 0$$
$$g_9 : (1 - x_4)(1 - x_7)(1 - x_9)(1 - x_{10})(1 - x_{14}) = 0$$
$$\downarrow$$
$$g_{injt,7} : (1 - x_2)(1 - x_3)(1 - x_4)^3(1 - x_5)(1 - x_7)^4(1 - x_8)^2(1 - x_9)^3(1 - x_{10})(1 - x_{14}) = 0 \tag{10.23}$$

Higher order terms are neglected and Eq. (10.23) is simplified as:

$$g_{injt,7} : (1 - x_2)(1 - x_3)(1 - x_4)(1 - x_5)(1 - x_7)(1 - x_8)(1 - x_9)(1 - x_{10})(1 - x_{14}) = 0 \tag{10.24}$$

### 10.2.6.5 Case 4: Inclusion of ZIBs and N-1 Contingency Criterion
Similarly to Case 2, the primary PMU set is obtained from Case 3. To obtain the
backup PMU set, all the terms $(1 - x_i)$ and $(1 - x_j)$ which are associated to the
main PMU set are eliminated from the constraints established for Case 3.

### 10.2.6.6 Case 5: CI
The constraints to implement CI are formulated as:

$$g_{CI,i} : (1 - x_i)\prod_{j \in adjCI_i}(1 - x_j) = 0, \forall i \in \qquad (10.25)$$

where,

$g_{CI,i}$ is the non-linear CI function of bus $i$.
adjCI$_i$ is the set of buses adjacent to bus $i$ in the island in which bus $i$ is located.
The constraints for Islands 1 and 2 for the IEEE 14-bus system are:

Island 1
$$g_{CI,1} : (1 - x_1)(1 - x_5) = 0$$
$$g_{CI,5} : \left(1 - x_1\right)(1 - x_5)(1 - x_6) = 0$$
$$g_{CI,6} : \left(1 - x_5\right)(1 - x_6)(1 - x_{11})(1 - x_{12})(1 - x_{13}) = 0$$
$$g_{CI,11} : (1 - x_6)(1 - x_{11}) = 0$$
$$g_{CI,12} : \left(1 - x_6\right)(1 - x_{12})(1 - x_{13}) = 0$$
$$g_{CI,13} : \left(1 - x_6\right)(1 - x_{12})(1 - x_{13}) = 0$$

Island 2
$$g_{CI,2} : (1 - x_2)(1 - x_3)(1 - x_4) = 0$$
$$g_{CI,3} : (1 - x_2)(1 - x_3)(1 - x_4) = 0$$
$$g_{CI,4} : (1 - x_2)(1 - x_3)(1 - x_4)(1 - x_7)(1 - x_9) = 0$$
$$g_{CI,7} : (1 - x_4)(1 - x_7)(1 - x_8)(1 - x_9) = 0$$
$$g_{CI,8} : (1 - x_7)(1 - x_8) = 0$$
$$g_{CI,9} : (1 - x_4)(1 - x_7)(1 - x_9)(1 - x_{10})(1 - x_{14}) = 0$$
$$g_{CI,10} : (1 - x_9)(1 - x_{10}) = 0$$
$$g_{CI,14} : (1 - x_9)(1 - x_{14}) = 0 \qquad (10.26)$$

**10.2.6.7 Second-Stage PMU Placement**

Eq. (10.27) shows the objective function and the additional constraint for Cases 1–4.

$$\text{Maximise } \left( [B]^T [A] \right)^2 ([X])^2$$
$$\text{s.t.} \tag{10.27}$$
$$\sum_{i=1}^{N} x_i^2 = \lambda$$

For Case 5, $[A]$ is replaced by $[A^{CI}]$.

## *10.2.7 Flow Chart of the Proposed Approach to the OPP Problem*

Fig. 10.3 shows the procedure adopted for each of the 5 OPP cases considered.

## 10.3 Results

The OPP problem was implemented in *Matlab* and solved with MILP (*intlinprog*), NLP solver (*fmincon*) and GA (*ga*). The test system's information and single line diagram are available in Power Systems Test Case Archive (1999).

### *10.3.1 Results for ILP and GA*

Table 10.1 shows the results for linear programming and GA for Cases 1–4. The IEEE 14-bus system requires 4 PMUs to be placed at buses 2, 6, 7 and 9 with a maximum SORI value of 19. The number of PMUs increases from 4 to 9 when accounting for single PMU loss because each bus should be observed by a minimum of 2 PMUs. Inclusion of ZIBs results in only 3 necessary PMUs for full observability with the corresponding bus numbers 2, 6 and 9. Accounting for single PMU outage in the presence of ZIBs results in an increase in the number of PMUs from 3 to 7.

Case 5 pertains to CI for the IEEE 14-bus system. The proposed method results in 5 sufficient PMUs for the IEEE 14-bus system. The PMUs placed at buses 5 and 6 ensure complete observability of Island 1 and the PMUs at buses 4, 7 and 9 ensure full observability of Island 2.

Both optimisation methods successfully found the same global solutions for all the test systems.

### *10.3.2 GA Plot for Case 1 for the IEEE 14-Bus System*

Fig. 10.4a shows the plot of the best and mean fitness versus generation for case 1 for the IEEE 14-bus system. Fig. 10.4b is an example of the first stage process; the *Matlab* code for the GA has been simulated a total of 50 times to obtain the frequency of obtaining the optimal number of PMUs. Fig. 4c is the 3-D plot for the second stage process to visualise graphically the frequency of obtaining the most reliable PMU placement.

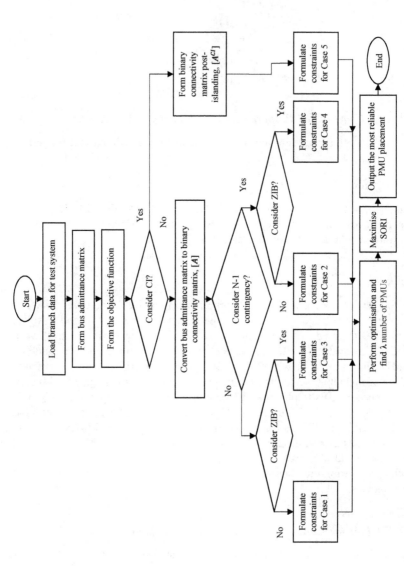

Fig. 10.3.    Flow Chart of the Proposed Approach to the Optimal PMU Placement (OPP) Problem.

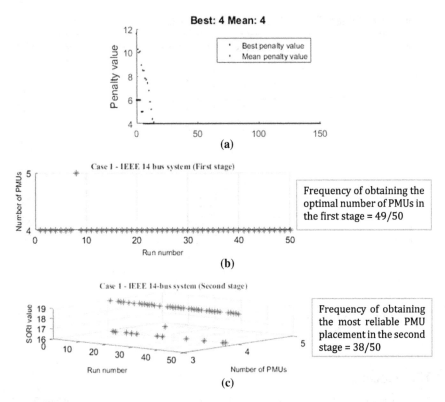

Fig. 10.4. (a) Plot of the Best and Mean Fitness Versus Generation (b) First Stage Plot (c) 3-D Plot of the Second Stage for Visualising the Number of Phasor Measurement Units (PMUs) and the System Observability Redundancy Index (SORI) Value.

### 10.3.3 Some Other PMU Placements With Smaller SORI Values Found by GA

GA was able to obtain other PMU placements with smaller SORI values. Table 10.2 shows some other PMU placements found by GA for all the five cases.

### 10.3.4 Results of NLP for IEEE 14-Bus System

Table 10.3 shows the results obtained by the NLP solver with the given starting VB point for the IEEE 14-bus system. Backup PMU placements for Cases 2 and 4 have been obtained by eliminating the buses that have been found for Cases 1 and 3, respectively, for PMU placement. Whenever necessary, the second stage

Table 10.2. Other Phasor Measurement Unit (PMU) Placements.

| Case | Optimal Number of PMUs | Most Optimal PMU Locations | SORI |
|------|------------------------|----------------------------|------|
| Case 1 | 4 | 2, 8, 10, 13 | 14 |
| | | 2, 7, 10, 13 | 16 |
| | | 2, 7, 11, 13 | 16 |
| | | 2, 6, 8, 9 | 17 |
| Case 2 | 9 | 1, 2, 3, 6, 7, 8, 9, 11, 13 | 34 |
| | | 1, 2, 4, 6, 7, 8, 9, 11, 13 | 37 |
| Case 3 | 3 | 2, 6, 9 | 15 |
| Case 4 | 7 | 1, 2, 4, 6, 9, 10, 13 | 31 |
| | | 1, 2, 4, 6, 9, 11, 13 | 31 |
| Case 5 | 5 | 3, 5, 6, 8, 9 | 20 |
| | | 2, 5, 6, 7, 9 | 24 |

process was performed to obtain the maximum SORI value. Similar results using BIP and GA were reported in Theodorakatosa et al. (2015).

## 10.4 Conclusion

The key focus of this chapter was to develop a reliability-based two-stage PMU placement optimisation model using mathematical and nature-based evolutionary algorithms. The proposed methodology obtains the optimal solution using simple network connectivity information about four standard IEEE test systems and while considering five cases with different constraints. The final solution obtained in the second stage PMU placement is sufficient to take care of full system observability and provides maximum reliability which is vital for state estimation. This concept of reliability of observability was possible because the OPP problem has multiple solutions. The OPP being discrete in nature, Linear Programming is an ideal optimisation technique but it results in only one PMU placement because it is a deterministic algorithm. GA provides multiple PMU placements with different SORI values and, hence, different reliabilities. The NLP model was also presented where various constrains were incorporated and tested on test systems of different sizes. It becomes particularly difficult to optimise power systems of large sizes using the NLP formulation. However, depending on the initial point, the optimisation model yields different PMU placements with the same minimum number of PMUs which can ensure full system observability. Optimal PMU placement enables the reduction in implementation cost to ensure reliable operation of distribution systems and forms an integral part of the power utility infrastructure for targeting UN SDG 7.

Table 10.3. Phasor Measurement Unit (PMU) Placements Found by Non-Linear Programming (NLP).

**Case 1**

| Initial Point | Optimal Number of PMUs | Most Optimal PMU Locations | SORI | Similar or Exact Results |
|---|---|---|---|---|
| *First Stage* | | | | |
| $x_0 = 0.6, i = 1 \ldots 14$ | 4 | 2, 8, 10, 13 | 14 | BIP and GA (Theodorakatosa et al., 2015) |
| $x_0 = \{0, 0.6, 0, 0.4, 0, 0.1, 0.8, 0, 0.7, 0, 0.1, 1, 0\}$ | | 2, 7, 10, 13 | 16 | |
| $x_0 = \{0, 0.6, 0, 0.4, 0.5, 0, 1, 0, 0.8, 0.1, 0.8, 0, 1, 0\}$ | | 2, 7, 11, 13 | 16 | |
| $x_0 = \{0, 1, 0, 1, 0, 1, 0.1, 0.9, 0, 0.5, 0, 0, 0.8, 0, 0.1, 1\}$ | | 2, 6, 8, 9 | 17 | |
| *Second Stage* | | | | |
| $x_0 = \{0, 0.6, 1, 0.9, 0, 0, 1, 0.8, 1, 0.7, 0, 0.1, 1, 0\}$ | 4 | 2, 6, 7, 9 | 19 | |

**Case 2**

| PMU Placement Number | Number of PMUs | Primary PMU Set | SORI | Initial Point | Number of PMUs | Backup PMU Set | SORI |
|---|---|---|---|---|---|---|---|
| 1 | 4 | 2, 8, 10, 13 | 14 | $x_0 = \{0, 0.6, 0, 0.4, 0, 0, 1, 0.8, 0, 0.7, 0, 0.1, 1, 0\}$ | 5 | 1, 3, 6, 7, 9 | 20 |

Table 10.3. Phasor Measurement Unit (*Continued*)

**Case 2**

| PMU Placement Number | Number of PMUs | Primary PMU Set | SORI | Initial Point | Number of PMUs | Backup PMU Set | SORI |
|---|---|---|---|---|---|---|---|
| 2 | | 2, 7, 10, 13 | 16 | $x_0 = \{1, 0.7, 1, 0.1, 1, 0, 0.3, 0.4, 0.8, 1, 0.8, 0.7, 1, 0\}$ | | 3, 5, 6, 8, 9 | 20 |
| 3 | | 2, 7, 11, 13 | 16 | $x_0 = \{0.9, 0.7, 0, 1, 0.7, 1, 0.1, 0.4, 1, 0.4, 0.7, 0, 1, 0\}$ | | 1, 4, 6, 8, 9 | 21 |
| 4 | | 2, 6, 8, 9 | 17 | $x_0 = \{0, 1, 0, 1, 0.9, 1, 0.5, 0.8, 0.7, 1, 0.9, 0.7, 0.9, 1\}$ | | 4, 5, 7, 10, 13 | 22 |
| 5 | | 2, 6, 7, 9 | 19 | $x_0 = \{0.8, 0.1, 0.8, 1, 0.9, 1, 0.2, 0.4, 0.7, 0.8, 0.1, 0.7, 0.9, 0.6\}$ | | 4, 5, 8, 10, 13 | 20 |

**Case 3**

| Initial Point | Optimal Number of PMUs | Most Optimal PMU Locations | SORI |
|---|---|---|---|
| *Second Stage* | | | |
| $x_0 = 0.4, i = 1 \ldots 14$ | 3 | 2, 6, 9 | 15 |

**Case 4**

| PMU Placement Number | Number of PMUs | Primary PMU Set | SORI | Initial Point | Number of PMUs | Backup PMU Set | SORI |
|---|---|---|---|---|---|---|---|

*First Stage*

| | | | | $x_0 = 0.99, i = 1 \ldots 14$ | | |
|---|---|---|---|---|---|---|
| 1 | 3 | 2, 6, 9 | 15 | | 4 | 1, 4, 10, 16 13 |

*Second Stage*

| | | | | $x_0 = 0.95, i = 1 \ldots 14$ | | |
|---|---|---|---|---|---|---|
| 2 | 3 | 2, 6, 9 | 15 | | 4 | 4, 5, 10, 18 13 |

## Case 5

| Initial Point | Optimal Number of PMUs | Most Optimal PMU Locations | SORI |
|---|---|---|---|
| *First Stage* | | | |
| $x_0 = 0.2, i = 1 \ldots 14$ | 5 | 1, 3, 6, 8, 9 | 18 |
| $x_0 = 0.9, i = 1 \ldots 14$ | | 3, 5, 6, 8, 9 | 20 |
| *Second Stage* | | | |
| $x_0 = 0.95, i = 1 \ldots 14$ | 5 | 4, 5, 6, 7, 9 | 25 |

# References

Baba, M., Nor, N. B. M., AmanSheikh, M., Irfan, M., & Tahir, M. (2020). A strategic and significant method for the optimal placement of phasor measurement unit for power system network. *Symmetry*, *12*, 1174. https://doi.org/10.3390/sym12071174

Blackout. (2003). *Final report on the August 14, 2003 Blackout in the United States and Canada: Causes and recommendations*. Department of Energy. (2018). [Online]. https://energy.gov/oe/downloads/blackout-2003-final-report-august-14-2003-blackout-united-states-and-canada-causes-and

Dua, D., Dambhare, S., Gajbhiye, R. K., & Soman, S. A. (2008). Optimal multistage scheduling of PMU placement: An ILP approach. *IEEE Transactions on Power Delivery*, *23*(4), 1812–1820.

Huang, L., Sun, Y., Xu, J., Gao, W., Zhang, J., & Wu, Z. (2014). Optimal PMU placement considering controlled islanding of power system. *IEEE Transactions on Power Systems*, *29*(2), 742–755.

Johnson, T., & Moger, T. (2021). A critical review of methods for optimal placement of phasor measurement units. *International Transactions on Electrical Energy Systems*, *31*(3). https://doi.org/10.1002/2050-7038.12698

Mousavian, S., & Feizollahi, M. J. (2015). An investment decision model for the optimal placement of phasor measurement units. *Expert Systems with Applications*, *42*(21), 7276–7284.

Nezam-Sarmadi, S. A., Nouri-Zadeh, S., Ranjbar, A. M., & Pishvaie, M. R. (2010). An islanding algorithm to restore a PMU installed power system. In *Power and Energy Engineering Conference (APPEEC)*, 2010 Asia-Pacific.

Okendo, E. O., Wekesa, C. W., & Saulo, M. J. (2021). Optimal placement of Phasor Measurement Unit considering System Observability Redundancy Index: Case study of the Kenya power transmission network. *Heliyon*, *7*(7). https://doi.org/10.1016/j.heliyon.2021.e07670

Power Systems Test Case Archive – UWEE. (1999). Power systems test case archive – UWEE. [online]. https://www2.ee.washington.edu/research/pstca/

Rahman, N. H. A., & Zobaa, A. F. (2016). Optimal PMU placement using topology transformation method in power systems. *Journal of Advanced Research*, *7*(5), 625–634.

Singh, B., Sharma, N. K., Tiwari, A. N., Verma, K. S., & Singh, S. N. (2011). Applications of phasor measurement units (PMUs) in electric power system networks incorporated with FACTS controllers. *International Journal of Enineering, Science and Technology*, *3*(3), 64–82.

Theodorakatosa, N. P., Manousakisa, N. M., & Koress, G. N. (2014, November). Optimal placement of PMUs in power systems using binary integer programming and genetic algorithm. In *MedPower* (pp. 2–5). IET.

Theodorakatosa, N. P., Manousakisa, N. M., & Koress, G. N. (2015). Optimal PMU placement using nonlinear programming. In *OPT-i An International Conference on Engineering and Applied Sciences Optimization*, 4–6 June 2014, Kos Island Greece, Greece. HAL.

US Department of Energy. (2014). Factors affecting PMU installation costs. https://www.smartgrid.gov/files/recovery_act/PMU-cost-study-final-10162014_1.pdf

Yuvaraju, V., & Thangavel, S. (2022). Optimal phasor measurement unit placement for power system observability using teaching–learning based optimization. *International Journal of Electrical Power & Energy Systems*, *137*, 107775. https://doi.org/10.1016/j.ijepes.2021.107775

Zambrano, A. A., Leon, M. A., & Rivas, E. (2011). Phasor measurement unit using GPRS wireless connectivity. In *2011 IEEE PES Conference on Innovative Smart Grid Technologies Latin America (ISGT LA)*, 19–21 October 2011, Medellin, Colombia (pp. 1–7). IEEE.

Chapter 11

# Quantitative Assessment of Models and Indices for Interior Thermal Comfort Taking Into Account the Effects of Solar Radiation and Wind

*Bhimsen Rajkumarsingh, Robert T. F. Ah King and Khalid Adam Joomun*

University of Mauritius, Mauritius

## Abstract

The performance of thermal comfort utilising machine learning and its accept-ability by students and other users at the Professor Sir Edouard Lim Fat Engi-neering Tower at the University of Mauritius are evaluated in this study. Students and building occupants were asked to fill out surveys on-site as data was gathered from sensors throughout the structure. The Thermal Sensation Vote (TSV) and other important data were collected through the surveys, including the effect of wind on thermal comfort. An adaptive model incorporating solar and wind effects was evaluated using multiple linear regression techniques and RStudio. Three models were used to evaluate thermal comfort, including the adaptive one. Numerous models were compared and evaluated in order to select the best one. It was found that the adaptive model (Model 1) was deemed to be the best model for its application. It was also found that Fanger's PMV/PPD (Model 2) was a very good approach to determining thermal comfort. Through thorough analysis, it was concluded that the range of air temperature and wind speed for thermal comfort was 25.830°C–28.0°C and 0.26 m/s to 0.42 m/s, respectively. In order for cities to remain secure, resilient and sustainable, it will be important to manage thermal comfort and reduce populations' exposure to heat stress (SDG 11). The achievement of income and productivity goals will be hampered if measures to protect populations from heat stress are not taken (SDG 8). Thermal regulation is also necessary for the provision of numerous health services (SDG 3).

Artificial Intelligence, Engineering Systems and Sustainable Development, 145–155
Copyright © 2024 Bhimsen Rajkumarsingh, Robert T. F. Ah King and Khalid Adam Joomun
Published under exclusive licence by Emerald Publishing Limited
doi:10.1108/978-1-83753-540-820241011

*Keywords*: Assessment; models; indices; thermal comfort; solar radiation; wind

## 11.1 Introduction

Thermal comfort is a crucial element of building design because people today spend most of their time indoors. Inside a building, many activities are performed, such as teaching a class full of students, relaxing, working, cooking, playing and working out. Thermal comfort is subsequently impacted by temperature rise, which is a result of these activities that generate heat. On the other hand, low temperatures may also prove to be a major factor. This is why having the right ambient temperature is imperative for one's thermal comfort. Any individual can have better physical and mental productivity in a thermally comfortable and convenient environment. According to the definition of thermal comfort, it is the mental state that conveys happiness with the thermal environment and is measured through subjective assessment (ASHRAE, 2013).

Throughout the years, there were numerous models that were developed in order to enhance and predict the comfort of occupants. Each of these models has their own particular approach and findings. In 1923, the effective temperature (ET) index (Ogunsote & Bogda, 2002) was developed followed by equivalent warmth (EW) (Bedford, 1936), operative temperature (OT) (ISO EN 7730, ASHRAE 55), equatorial comfort index (ECI) developed by Webb in 1959, resultant temperature, Wet bulb-globe temperature (Yaglou & Minaed, 1957), Apparent temperature (Heat index)-AT (Steadman, 1984), the wind chill temperature (WCT) developed by ASHRAE, 1997, wind chill equivalent temperature (WCET) (OFCM, 2003), Standard effective temperature (SET) (Gagge et al., 1986) and so on. In 1960, the Fanger's predicted mean vote (PMV) index (Fanger, 1970) was first introduced and is now commonly used by various researchers (Huo et al., 2023; Omidvar & Jungsoo, 2020; Park et al., 2021; Sirhan & Golan, 2021; Zheng et al., 2021).

On-site comfort testing was done in the hopes that it would show that the building's residents have good or at least acceptable living circumstances (Hu et al., 2022). In that study, in Chinese university classrooms, thermal comfort levels from ideal temperature ranges were measured using linear regression models. In a study (Silva et al., 2023), temperature, air speed, relative humidity, metabolic rate and clothing levels were employed on an adaptive comfort model to estimate the thermal comfort in a building situated in Portugal. In order to obtain the highest level of thermal comfort, Wang et al. (2023) used a supervised hybrid model that combines machine learning (ML) and genetic algorithms. It was found that the hybrid system can raise the threshold of thermal comfort.

This research focuses on the comfort of occupants in a building with the effect of wind. In order to provide an optimum analysis, a new adaptive model is developed that is able to determine and predict thermal comfort on a Thermal Sensation Vote (TSV) scale for a building. The model enables us to understand the different floor heights and its ambient conditions. The scale will range from −3 (very cold) to +3 (very hot) while 0 is comfortable. Upon further tests, this new model can be applicable for various buildings. The aim of this work was to do a quantitative analysis of the thermal comfort for each floor of a building using different existing thermal models and an adaptive thermal, one which incorporates both solar radiation and wind speed.

This chapter is organised as follows: Section 1 gives an introduction to the scope of this project and also explains the aim and objectives on how this project was carried out. Section 2 gives the different comfort indices that have been used in this project. The methodology part of this work is given in Section 3 and contains all the information about how the study was conducted. Section 4 explains in depth the derivation of the new adaptive model. Hence a comparison between the measured TSV value and the calculated ones are performed using MATLAB and RStudio. Correlations between operative temperature and wind speed with the measured TSV values are further discussed to provide ample justification. Furthermore, the different models are compared using different mathematical tools. Section 5 gives a conclusion to this chapter.

## 11.2 Background Theory on Comfort Indices

### 11.2.1 Adaptive Model (Model 1)

This model incorporates all the main environmental parameters that influence thermal comfort. It consists of humidity, air temperature, wind velocity and solar radiation. All these parameters are used to define a convenient model that satisfies the TSV values of the participants.

### 11.2.2 Fanger's PMV Model (Model 2)

By using a 7-point scale voting system from ASHRAE, Fanger carried out a test on a large group of people whereby their votes were recorded. Consequently, it was called the PMV and was defined as 'the difference between internal heat generation and heat loss to the actual environment for a person with skin temperature and sweat production at their comfort levels at their current activity level' by Fanger (1970). The Fanger's PMV model includes all the major parameters that are air temperature, mean radiant temperature, wind velocity and relative humidity as well as the insulation of cloth and the metabolic rate.

The results of the PMV are expressed on the 7-point ASHRAE scale of thermal sensation. In order for the surroundings to be considered comfortable, the PMV value should lie in the range of −0.5 to +0.5.

$$\text{PMV} = \left[0.303^{-0.0036M} + 0.028\right] \times \left[(M - W) - 3.05 \times 10^{-3}[5733 - 6.99(M - W) - p_a]\right.$$

$$- 0.42[(M - W) - 58.15] - 1.7 \times 10^{-5} \times M(5867 - p_a) - 0.0014 \times M(34 - t_a)$$

$$\left. - 3.96 \times 10^{-8} \times f_{cl}[(t_{cl} + 273)^4 - (t_{-}r + 273)^4)] - f_{cl} \times h_c(t_{cl} - t_a)\right] \tag{11.1}$$

$$t_{cl} = 35.7 - 0.028 \times (M - W) - I_{cl}$$
$$\times \left\{ 3.96 \times 10^{-8} \times f_{cl}\left[(t_{cl} + 273)^4 - (t_{-}r + 273)^4\right] + f_{cl} \times h_c(t_{cl} - t_a) \right\} \quad (11.2)$$

$$h_c = \begin{cases} 2.38|t_{cl} - t_a|^{0.25}, & 2.38|t_{cl} - t_a|^{0.25} > 12.1\sqrt{v_{ar}} \\ 12.1\sqrt{v_{ar}}, & 2.38|t_{cl} - t_a|^{0.25} < 12.1\sqrt{v_{ar}} \end{cases} \quad (11.3)$$

$$f_{cl} = \begin{cases} 1.00 + 1.290I_{cl}, & I_{cl} \leq 0.078\,(m^2K/W) \\ 1.05 + 0.645I_{cl}, & I_{cl} > 0.078\,(m^2K/W) \end{cases} \quad (11.4)$$

where:
   $M$: Metabolic rate (W/m²)
   $W$: Mechanical power (W/m²)
   $I_{cl}$: Clothing insulation (m²K/W)
   $t_a$: Air temperature (°C)
   $t_r$: Average radiant temperature (°C)
   $v_{ar}$: Relative Air speed (m/s)
   $p_a$: Partial water vapour pressure (Pa)
   $t_{cl}$: Clothing surface temperature (°C)
   $h_c$: Coefficient of heat transmission by convection (W/(m² K))
   $f_{cl}$: Clothing area factor

### 11.2.3 Predicted Percentage of Dissatisfied (PPD)

PPD can be derived from the PMV 7-point scale and they are related as follows. It follows a symmetric curve around the 0 value (Jadhav, 2018). For example, if the PMV value is ±0.5 then the PPD will be 10%. This concludes that 10% of the population is dissatisfied and the other 90% are satisfied.

$$PPD = 100 - 95 \times \exp\left(-0.03353 \times PMV^4 - 0.2179 \times PMV^2\right) \quad (11.5)$$

### 11.2.4 Tropical Summer Index (TSI) (Model 3)

This index was proposed by Sharma and Ali in 1986 and is mostly suitable for hot–dry and warm–humid regions. The experiment was conducted on 18 young males over 3 back-to-back summer seasons in India. Through multiple regression analysis and several observations, the equation below was deduced (Sharma & Ali, 1986).

$$TSI = 0.33T_w + 0.75T_g - 2\sqrt{V} \quad (11.6)$$

where $T_w$ is the wet bulb temperature (°C), $T_g$ is the globe temperature (°C), $V$ is the wind speed (m/s) and TSI is the Tropical Summer Index.

The TSI under a particular environment is defined as the air/globe temperature of motionless air at relative humidity of 50% that generates identical thermal comfort sensations. It incorporates the required environmental parameters such as wind speed, globe temperature, air temperature and humidity.

## 11.3 Methodology

For this research work, the location for the field measurement was conducted in an eight-storey building located at Reduit in the premises of University of Mauritius. The building has been inaugurated under the name of Professor Sir Edouard Lim Fat Engineering Tower. The building consists of several class-rooms, laboratories and offices. The building is usually closed during public holidays and Sundays and is only available to students during semester periods. The materials used are mainly plaster (13 mm) and concrete (200–375 mm).

### 11.3.1 Collection of Data From Sensors

In order to provide an extensive review of thermal comforts for different class-rooms, offices and labs, some sensors were already installed on each level of the building excluding the ground floor. Twelve Monnit wireless sensors including temperature, humidity, light, airflow detectors and one cellular gateway were used to collect environmental parameters. The sensor measuring parameters are namely:

On the first, fourth and eighth floor, the sensors were installed in all corners and the extra sensors were installed on the remaining floors.

Two extenders were implemented to provide wider coverage for the wireless sensors to the gateway. However, for this work, only data for temperature, humidity and light intensity were used. The airflow sensors were originally placed to detect if the air conditioners were on. In order to collect the wind speed data in the allocated rooms, an anemometer is being used. As for the globe temperature, a globe thermometer was used.

### 11.3.2 Survey

The experimental data were collected on 7/05/21 and the questionnaires were distributed to 50 students on each level on the Engineering Tower. The experiments were carried out in the time ranging from 12.00 p.m. to 16.10 p.m. The same gateway was used to capture the environmental variables (humidity, temperature, wind speed and solar radiation). The values for the solar intensities were recorded in units (Lux). It was converted to W/m$^2$ using a conversion formula (Singh, 2015).

The TSV values were collected through a set of questionnaires distributed to the students. Questions varied on how the participant felt to how they wanted to feel. Also, TSV values were collected based on the 7-point scale. It is to be noted that the participants had no control over cooling systems as the research was uncontrolled.

### 11.3.3 Software Tools

The RStudio and MATLAB applications are used to calculate linear and multiple linear regression. The RStudio was used to calculate the different regression analysis from the data collected. The analysis consisted of multiple linear, linear and Pearson correlation coefficients. MATLAB in particular is used to do several calculations and plotting of different models. Moreover, the Centre for built environment (CBE), a thermal comfort tool, is used to calculate the theoretical values for the PMV , PPD and thermal satisfaction. These values are used for the Fanger's model which is Model 2.

### 11.3.4 Data Processing

Also on the ground floor, two different scenarios were considered. The first scenario was an open environment and the second one was a closed environment. The only two parameters that varied between these scenarios were the wind speed and the air temperature. This was done in order to give a clearer understanding of how wind affects thermal comfort.

So as to prevent overloading of the gateway, the sensor's data were collected in the interval of 10 minutes. This was done so as to protect the gateway from crashing from an overcharging of data. Meaning that each minute in the 10-minute span was allocated to a specific sensor.

### 11.3.5 Validity of the Model

The validity of the model was performed through several indicators. In this case, Pearson correlation coefficient ($r$), $R$-squared value ($R^2$), Root mean square error (RMSE), Mean absolute error (MAE) and Mean absolute percentage error (MAPE) were used.

### 11.3.6 Performance Comparison

Models 1, 2 and 3 are compared with the measured TSV since all the values converge to a PMV or TSV scale.

## 11.4 Results

This section of the document consists of different comparison analysis of the 3 models.

### 11.4.1 Comparison Analysis Between TSV (Measured) and TSV (Calculated)

From Table 11.1, the $R^2$ for Model 1 approximates the measured TSV value by 98% whereas the $R^2$ for Model 2 approximates the measured TSV by 91%. Both $R^2$ show a strong linear relationship as they are both above 90%. However, the model which is closer to 100% is taken as the best model which is Model 1. This can be further supported with a very small $p$-value. The $p$-value for Model 1 is $1.953 \times 10^{-8}$ whereas the $p$-value for Model 2 is $1.51 \times 10^{-5}$. Both values are very small and are considered acceptable to reject the null hypothesis. The null

Table 11.1. Summary of Models 1 and 2.

|  | Model 1 | Model 2 |
|---|---|---|
| $R^2$ | 0.9814 | 0.9145 |
| $p$ value | $1.953 \times 10^{-8}$ | $1.51 \times 10^{-5}$ |
| SSE (sum of squared estimate errors) | 0.07131 | 0.2708 |
| RMSE | 0.09441 | 0.1840 |
| Pearson Correlation coefficient | 0.9918063 | 0.9563166 |
| MAE | 0.0790 | 0.205 |
| MAPE | 5.3621 | 24.75 |

hypothesis states that no statistical relationship and significance exists between the Model 1/2 and measured TSV. So, the smaller the value the better the model.

Moreover, the SSE which is a measure of discrepancy between the data and the models proves that Model 1 is optimum since it has a small value as compared to Model 2. Coupled with the above, the residuals for Model 1 is shown to be closer to the best fit line as compared to Model 1. This can be determined through the RMSE value which is smaller than Model 2. So, the smaller the value the least spread is the residuals error. The Pearson correlation coefficient for both models shows that they have a large positive correlation. However, Model 1 ($R = 0.991806$) shows the most significant value as it nearly approaches the perfect positive correlation region which is 1. The MAEs for Model 1 is significantly smaller than Model 2. This shows that there is a small difference between the predicted value and the measured one. Further, MAPE indicates that the forecast for Model 1 is much better than Model 2, since it shows a low MAPE of 5.36% and Model 2 shows a high MAPE of 24.75%.

From the comparison above, it is clear that Model 1 is the best model to use for thermal comfort. However, Model 2 is also a good thermal comfort forecasting tool since it complies well with the measured data set. So, it is nevertheless a reliable model for this research work.

### 11.4.2 Comparison Analysis Between Thermal Sensations of Models 1, 2 and 3

As given in Table 11.2, the different models above show their different conclusions they reached for thermal comfort. For comfort status, Model 3 uses comfortable as indicator, whereas Models 1 and 2 use neutral. So, they both have the same meaning.

On the ground floor for indoor environment, it can be seen that Models 1 and 2 show the same satisfaction as the measured data. However, Model 3 shows that the environment is comfortable. This can be explained as Model 3 uses a temperature range to converge to an answer whereas the first two models use a TSV/PMV scale which is the same. Moreover, considering the outdoor environment,

Table 11.2. Comparison of Models 1, 2 and 3.

| Floor Levels | Measured TSV | Calculated TSV (Model 1) | PMV (Model 2) | TSI (Model 3) |
|---|---|---|---|---|
| 0 | Slightly warm | Slightly warm | Slightly warm | Comfortable |
| 0(O.E) | Slightly cool | Slightly cool | Slightly cool | Slightly cool |
| 1 | Slightly warm | Slightly warm | Slightly warm | Comfortable |
| 2 | Neutral | Neutral | Neutral | Comfortable |
| 3 | Neutral | Neutral | Neutral | Comfortable |
| 4 | Neutral | Neutral | Neutral | Comfortable |
| 5 | Slightly warm | Slightly warm | Slightly warm | Comfortable |
| 6 | Neutral | Neutral | Neutral | Comfortable |
| 7 | Neutral | Neutral | Neutral | Comfortable |
| 8 | Slightly warm | Slightly warm | Slightly warm | Comfortable |

all the 3 models converge to the same conclusion as the measured one which is slightly cool. This can be explained due to low temperature and a significantly high outdoor air speed.

Considering the first to the eighth floor, Model 1 and 2 show a mutual agreement with the measured data. However, Model 3 is only different for the first, fifth and eighth floor. The Model 3 converges to a comfortable status whereas the measured TSV value shows a slight warm condition. This discrepancy is mainly due to the different approach Model 3 takes while the other two models take almost the same steps.

### 11.4.3 Thermal Comfort Analysis

This study gives an environment-specific range of acceptable or adequate temperatures and wind speeds. Also, the acceptance of thermal and wind speed is closely related to comfort zone. The slight distinction is that while comfort zone considers the complex interaction between environmental factors like air temperature, humidity, mean radiant temperature, wind speed and the human body, thermal adequacy is focused on the idea of acceptable temperatures that are derived from personal thermal responses in the field.

However, this field survey did not directly ask respondents about the appropriate temperatures and wind speed. Therefore, the temperature acceptability range is determined by showing only the temperature within the comfort range for this study ($-0.5 <$ TSV COMFORT $> +0.5$).

### 11.4.4 Acceptable Range of Temperature

Practical equality between each model can be analysed. Model 1 has the exact same comfort temperature as the measured data set with a temperature range between 25.77°C and 28°C. This is because Model 1 data is based solely on this study following a strong correlation relationship of 99%, this justifies their similarity. However, Model 2 has a very slight dissimilarity with a temperature range between 25.22°C and 27.75°C. According to Model 2, the comfort temperature for this study is found between 25.22°C and 27.75°C which is slightly smaller than the other 2 data sets. This can be explained as this model has different analytical techniques to determine thermal comfort.

Model 1 and Model 2 and the measured TSV all have the same index, i.e. TSV and PMV. That is why the thermal comfort range can be determined in the range of $-0.5$ to $0.5$. However, Model 3 has a different approach.

Model 3 already has a dedicated range for thermal comfort (25°C–30°C).

### 11.4.5 Acceptable Range of Wind Speed

Comparing different models with the same index, the acceptable range for comfortable wind speed can be determined. From the measured TSV data, 0.26 m/s to 0.42 m/s are observed to be the required wind speed for comfort. It can be seen that Model 1 is quite similar to the study. However, Model 2 differs very slightly as from its conclusion, the comfort range is from 0.28 m/s to 0.5 m/s. Since the Model 1 and 2 use different approaches, this slight dissimilarity can be explained.

## 11.5 Discussions and Conclusions

From the results above, each model has its own methods and analysis. Some use the same index while some have their own index. Model 1 has shown an accuracy of 98% to the real data. The new adaptive model provides a new variable to be considered in this study. This new variable is the floor height whereby the user can choose to input his/her height accordingly.

Model 2 also has shown very good compliance with 91% accuracy. Model 3 uses its own index for comfort. From the results above, on the ground, first, fifth and eighth floor it tends to underestimate the comfort status. It gives a comfortable status while it is perceived to be slightly warm. It is not a very accurate representation of the actual sensation. However, since it was originally based on the climate of India, it can be concluded that this model is suitable for very hot regions.

# References

ASHRAE. (1997). American society of heating, refrigerating and air conditioning engineers handbook fundamentals volume. Chap. 8. Thermal Comfort, 8.1–8.28.

ASHRAE. (2013). Standard 55 – Thermal environmental conditions for human occupancy. Am. Soc. Heating Refrig. Air-Conditioning Eng. Atlanta, USA.

ASHRAE. (2020). Standard 55 – Thermal environmental conditions for human occupancy. https://www.ashrae.org/technical-resources/bookstore/standard-55-thermal-environmental-conditions-for-human-occupancy

Bedford, T. (1936). *The warmth factor in comfort at work*. Rep. Industr. Hlth. Res. Bd. (No. 76), London.

Fanger, P. (1970). *Thermal Comfort: Analysis and Applications in Environmental Engineering*. Copenhagen: Danish Technical Press.

Gagge, A., Fobelets, A., & Berglund, P. (1986). A standard predictive index of human response to the thermal environment. *Transactions/American Society of Healing, Refrigerating and Air Conditioning Engineers*, *92*(2B), 709–731.

Hu, J., He, Y., Hao, X., Li, N., Su, Y., & Qu, H. (2022). Optimal temperature ranges considering gender differences in thermal comfort, work performance, and sick building syndrome: A winter field study in university classrooms. *Energy and Buildings*, *254*, 111554.

Huo, W., Cheng, Y., Jia, Y., & Guo, C. (2023). Research on the thermal comfort of passenger compartment based on the PMV/PPD. *International Journal of Thermal Sciences*, *184*, 107876. https://doi.org/10.1016/j.ijthermalsci.2022.107876

ISO 7730:2005. (2015). Ergonomics of the thermal environment—Analytical determination and interpretation of thermal comfort using calculation of the PMV and PPD indices and local thermal comfort criteria. https://www.iso.org/standard/39155.html

Jadhav. (2018). *Role of CFD in Evaluating Occupant Thermal Comfort*. https://www.linkedin.com/pulse/role-cfd-evaluating-occupant-thermal-comfort-sandip-jadhav

OFCM. (2003). *Report on Wind Chill Temperature and extreme heat indices: Evaluation and improvement projects*. FCM-R19-2003. U.S. Department of Commerce/National Oceanic and Atmospheric Administration, Office of the Federal Coordinator for Meteorological Services and Supporting Research.

Ogunsote, O. O., & Bogda, O. P. (2002). Comfort limits for the effective temperature index in the tropics. *Architectural Science Review*, *45*(2), 125–132.

Omidvar, A., & Jungsoo, K. (2020). Modification of sweat evaporative heat loss in the PMV/PPD model to improve thermal comfort prediction in warm climates. *Building and Environment*, *176*. https://doi.org/10.1016/j.buildenv.2020.106868

Park, J., Choi, H., Kim, D., & Kim, T. (2021). Development of novel PMV-based HVAC control strategies using a mean radiant temperature prediction model by machine learning in Kuwaiti climate. *Building and Environment*, *206*, 108357. https://doi.org/10.1016/j.buildenv.2021.108357

Sharma, M., & Ali, S. (1986). Tropical Summer Index – A study of thermal comfort of Indian subjects. *Building and Environment*, *21*, 11–24.

Silva, I., Mendonça, P., & Maia, C. (2023). Thermal comfort in the Modern Movement—Evaluating the winter behavior of a housing building in Porto, Portugal. *Energy Reports*, *9*(2), 569–575. https://doi.org/10.1016/j.egyr.2023.03.084

Singh, V. (2015). Lux and W/m2 relationship. https://physics.stackexchange.com/questions/135618/rm-lux-and-w-m2-relationship

Sirhan, N., & Golan, S. (2021). Efficient PMV computation for public environments with transient populations. *Energy and Buildings*, *231*, 110523. https://doi.org/10.1016/j.enbuild.2020.110523

Steadman, R. (1984). A universal scale of apparent temperature. *Journal of Applied Meteorology and Climatology*, *23*, 1674–1687. https://doi.org/10.1175/1520-0450(1984)023%3C1674:AUSOAT%3E2.0.CO;2

Wang, P., Hu, J., & Chen, W. (2023). A hybrid machine learning model to optimize thermal comfort and carbon emissions of large-space public buildings. *Journal of Cleaner Production*, *400*, 136538. https://doi.org/10.1016/j.jclepro.2023.136538

Webb, C. G. (1959). An analysis of some observations of thermal comfort in an equatorial climate. *British Journal of Industrial Medicine*, *16*(3), 297–310.

Yaglou, C. P., & Minaed, D. (1957). Control of heat casulaties at military training centers. *Archives of Industrial Health*, *16*(4), 302–316.

Zheng, Z., Zhang, Y., Mao, Y., Yang, Y., Fu, C., & Fang, Z. (2021). Analysis of SET* and PMV to evaluate thermal comfort in prefab construction site offices: Case study in South China. *Case Studies in Thermal Engineering*, *26*, 101137. https://doi.org/10.1016/j.csite.2021.101137

Chapter 12

# The Role of the Internet of Things for a More Sustainable Future

*Anshu Prakash Murdan and Vishwamitra Oree*

University of Mauritius, Mauritius

## Abstract

In this chapter, we investigate the role of the Internet of Things (IoT) for a more sustainable future. The IoT is an umbrella term that refers to an interrelated network of devices connected to the internet. It also encompasses the technology that enables communication between these devices as well as between the devices and the cloud. The emergence of low-cost microprocessors, sensors and actuators, as well as access to high bandwidth internet connectivity, has led to the massive adoption of IoT systems in everyday life. IoT systems include connected vehicles, connected homes, smart cities, smart buildings, precision agriculture, among others. During the last decade, they have been impacting human activities in an unprecedented way. In essence, IoT technology contributes to the improvement of citizens' quality of life and companies' competitiveness. In doing so, IoT is also contributing to achieve the Sustainable Development Goals (SDGs) that were adopted by the United Nations in 2015 as an urgent call to action by all countries to eradicate poverty, tackle climate change and ensure that no one is left behind by 2030. The World Economic Forum (WEF) recognises that IoT is undeniably one of the major facilitators for responsible digital transformation, and one of its reports revealed that 84% of IoT deployments are presently addressing, or can potentially address the SDGs. IoT is closely interlinked with other emerging technologies such as Artificial Intelligence (AI) and Cloud Computing, for the delivery of enhanced and value-added services. In recent years, there has been a push from the IoT research and industry community together with international stakeholders, for supporting the deployment and adoption of IoT and AI technologies to overcome some of the major challenges facing mankind in terms of protecting the environment, fostering sustainable development, improving safety and enhancing the agriculture supply chain, among others.

Artificial Intelligence, Engineering Systems and Sustainable Development, 157–168

Copyright © 2024 Anshu Prakash Murdan and Vishwamitra Oree

Published under exclusive licence by Emerald Publishing Limited

doi:10.1108/978-1-83753-540-820241012

*Keywords*: Internet of Things (IoT); Sustainable Development Goals (SDGs); smart cities; environmental monitoring; energy optimisation; IoT challenges

## 12.1 Introduction

The Internet of Things (IoT) refers to a network of interconnected physical objects, including buildings, vehicles and other devices equipped with sensors, software and network connectivity that enable them to gather and exchange data (Gartner, 2020). It has the potential to improve quality of life of citizens and the competitiveness of companies by enabling more efficient and effective operations, enhancing safety and security, providing personalised health care, improving transportation systems and creating smart cities (Atzori et al., 2010). IoT concepts involve the integration of various technologies, such as cloud computing, machine learning and artificial intelligence (AI), to enable these devices to communicate with each other and make intelligent decisions without human intervention. The goal of IoT is to create a seamless, interconnected network of devices that can provide valuable insights, automate processes and enhance the efficiency and effectiveness of various industries.

IoT can also play a key role in achieving the United Nations Sustainable Development Goals (SDGs) by assisting endeavours that address various global challenges, including climate change, poverty, hunger, health, education and sustainable cities. For example, IoT-enabled sensors can help monitor environmental factors such as air (Rastogi & Lohani, 2022) and water quality, leading to better public health outcomes (Garrido-Momparler & Peris, 2022), thereby supporting SDG 3 (Good Health and Well-being). IoT technology can also help optimise energy usage in buildings and homes (Imran et al., 2022), supporting SDG 7 (Affordable and Clean Energy). In agriculture, IoT technology can support SDG 2 (Zero Hunger) by enabling farmers to better monitor crops and soil conditions, leading to increased yields and reduced waste (Sarpal et al., 2022). IoT technology can also help improve access to education and healthcare in remote areas (Alshamrani, 2022), supporting SDG 4 (Quality Education) and SDG 10 (Reduced Inequalities). Furthermore, IoT technology can support the development of smart cities that are sustainable, efficient and inclusive (Beştepe & Yildirim, 2022), thus supporting SDG 11 (Sustainable Cities and Communities).

However, it is also important to highlight the challenges associated with integrating IoT technology for sustainability. They include issues related to data privacy and security, interoperability between different systems and devices and the cost of implementation (Karale, 2021). For instance, the massive amount of data produced by IoT devices can create privacy concerns, and ensuring that different devices can communicate with each other can be a challenge. Despite these challenges, the integration of IoT technology for sustainability presents many opportunities, such as the ability to optimise resource use and reduce waste, enhance environmental monitoring and management and develop new business models that drive sustainability.

## 12.2 IoT and SDGs

IoT has the potential to contribute to all 17 SDGs by enabling more efficient and effective use of resources, reducing waste and emissions, and improving access to critical services. However, the ensuing subsections will focus on the SDGs where IoT can have the most significant impact. These include SDGs 2, 3, 10 and 11.

### *12.2.1 SDG 2 – Zero Hunger*

SDG 2 aims to end hunger, achieve food security and improved nutrition and promote sustainable agriculture. IoT can be a key in achieving this goal by enabling various applications that improve agriculture and food systems, leading to increased yields, reduced waste and improved food safety. The following applications illustrate ways in which IoT can contribute to SDG 2:

- Precision Agriculture: IoT technology can empower farmers optimise crop yields and reduce waste by enabling real-time monitoring of environmental factors such as soil moisture, temperature and humidity. IoT-enabled sensors can also monitor crop health, detect pests and diseases and enable targeted interventions such as irrigation and fertilisation (Prasanna Lakshmi et al., 2023).
- Livestock Management: IoT technology can assist livestock farmers monitor the health and well-being of their animals, enabling early detection and treatment of diseases. IoT-enabled sensors can also monitor feeding and drinking patterns, enabling more efficient use of resources and reducing waste (Iwasaki et al., 2019).
- Supply Chain Management: IoT technology can be used to optimise the supply chain management of food products, ensuring timely delivery and reducing waste. IoT-enabled sensors can monitor storage conditions, expiration dates and usage patterns, enabling more efficient and effective distribution (Tsang et al., 2022).
- Food Safety: IoT technology can help improve food safety by enabling real-time monitoring of food processing and transportation. IoT-enabled sensors can detect contamination and spoilage, enabling timely intervention and reducing the risk of foodborne illnesses (Mantravadi & Srai, 2023).
- Sustainable Agriculture: IoT technology can enable farmers adopt sustainable agriculture practices, leading to reduced greenhouse gas emissions, improved soil health and increased biodiversity. IoT-enabled sensors can monitor carbon sequestration, water usage and pesticide use, supporting farmers to make data-driven decisions that balance economic, social and environmental objectives (Pathmudi et al., 2023).

### 12.2.2 SDG 3 – Good Health and Well-Being

SDG 3 aims to ensure healthy lives and promote well-being for one and all. IoT can prove to be decisive in achieving this goal by enabling various applications that improve healthcare delivery, disease prevention and public health outcomes.

Some promising applications that illustrate ways in which IoT can contribute to SDG 3 are provided hereunder:

- Remote Monitoring: IoT-enabled medical devices can help healthcare providers monitor patients remotely, enabling them to provide timely and personalised care. For example, wearable devices such as fitness trackers and smartwatches can monitor vital signs detect abnormal activity patterns and alert users as well as healthcare providers in case of emergencies (Meena et al., 2023).
- Chronic Disease Management: IoT technology can help patients with chronic illnesses such as diabetes, heart disease and asthma better manage their conditions. IoT-enabled devices can provide real-time feedback on patients' health status, medication adherence and lifestyle choices, helping them make informed decisions about their health (Qin et al., 2022).
- Public Health Surveillance: IoT technology can contribute to monitor and control the spread of infectious diseases by enabling real-time monitoring of outbreaks, early detection of disease clusters and contact tracing (Ferreira et al., 2023). For example, IoT-enabled sensors can monitor environmental factors such as air and water quality, which can impact public health outcomes.
- Emergency Response: IoT technology can be instrumental in decreasing emergency response times and reducing fatalities in the event of disasters such as natural calamities, terrorist attacks and public health emergencies (Al-Nabhan et al., 2019). For example, IoT-enabled devices can provide real-time data on the location and status of victims, enabling emergency responders to prioritise and allocate resources effectively.

### 12.2.3 SDG 10 – Reduced Inequalities

SDG 10 aims to reduce inequality within and among countries, including inequalities in income, opportunities and access to basic services. IoT can substantially support this goal by enabling various applications that improve social and economic inclusion, promote accessibility and reduce disparities. Some ways in which IoT can contribute to SDG 10 are outlined below:

- Assistive Technologies: IoT technology can be used to enhance the quality of life for people with disabilities and elderly people by facilitating assistive technologies that promote accessibility, mobility and independence. IoT-enabled devices such as smart prosthetics, wearable sensors and smart homes can provide real-time support and personalised care (Luperto et al., 2023).

- Healthcare: IoT technology can be instrumental in progressing healthcare outcomes by enabling remote patient monitoring, personalised care and preventive interventions. IoT-enabled devices such as wearable sensors, smart medical devices and telemedicine systems can provide real-time health data, support chronic disease management and allow early detection and treatment of illnesses (Aceto et al., 2018).
- Financial Inclusion: IoT technology can help improve financial inclusion by enabling access to financial services and resources, including banking, loans and insurance (Bhat et al., 2023). IoT-enabled devices such as mobile phones, smart cards and biometric identification systems can provide access to financial services, facilitate secure transactions and support economic empowerment.

### 12.2.4 SDG 11 – Sustainable Cities and Communities

SDG 11 aims to create sustainable, resilient and inclusive cities and communities that enhance the quality of life for all residents. IoT can provide substantive support in attaining this goal by assisting in various applications that improve urban planning, resource management and citizen engagement. The following key use cases to demonstrate how IoT can help achieve SDG 11:

- Smart City Planning: IoT technology can be applied to create smart cities that are more sustainable, efficient and livable (Kaginalkar et al., 2021). IoT-enabled devices such as sensors, cameras and drones can provide real-time data on traffic flow, air quality and energy use, enabling more informed and effective urban planning and management.
- Energy and Resource Management: IoT technology can help enhance the efficiency and sustainability of energy and resource management in cities. IoT-enabled devices such as smart metres, water sensors and waste management systems can provide more accurate monitoring and control of energy and resource use, reducing waste and improving resource efficiency (Manikanda Kumaran et al., 2023).
- Transportation: IoT technology can help improve transportation systems in cities, reducing congestion, improving safety and curtailing emissions. IoT-enabled devices such as smart traffic lights, connected vehicles and parking sensors can promote more efficient use of transportation resources, improving accessibility and reducing travel times (Lv & Shang, 2023).
- Citizen Engagement: IoT technology can help advance citizen engagement in urban planning and decision-making. IoT-enabled devices such as social media platforms, mobile apps and public participation platforms can support more inclusive and transparent decision-making processes, empowering citizens to participate in shaping their communities (El-Haddadeh et al., 2019).

## 12.3 Synergy Between IoT and AI

IoT and AI are two transformative technologies that can revolutionise development globally and spur accomplishments in the SDGs. IoT technology enables the collection of vast amounts of data from connected devices, while AI technology can analyse these data to provide valuable insights and support intelligent decision-making. The synergy between IoT and AI can help unlock new opportunities for sustainability across multiple sectors and applications. There are numerous fields in which the benefits of IoT and AI can be collectively leveraged to promote sustainability and a few of them are detailed below:

- Energy Efficiency: IoT-enabled sensors and devices can collect real-time data on energy use, while AI algorithms can process these data to identify patterns and optimise energy consumption. This can help reduce waste, lower energy costs and promote sustainable energy use. For instance, a complete system integrating building information modelling, machine learning as well as the non-dominated sorting genetic algorithm-II (NSGA II) was proposed to look into the impact of energy consumption factors and come up with an optimal design (Hosamo et al., 2022).
- Smart Agriculture: IoT-enabled sensor networks are typically utilised to gather data on soil moisture, temperature and other environmental factors, while AI algorithms analyse the data to provide insights into crop health, water usage and other factors that affect agricultural productivity (Vij et al., 2020). Real-time analytics further assist farmers in taking corrective action to optimise farm productivity, reduce waste and promote sustainable land use. In addition to this, Unmanned Aerial Vehicle (UAV) sensing systems as well as AI perception algorithms are increasingly being applied in precision agriculture (PA) applications (Su et al., 2023).
- Intelligent Transportation: IoT-enabled sensor networks are currently used to accumulate real-time data on traffic flow, vehicle performance and other factors. These data are analysed by AI algorithms to optimise transportation networks, reduce congestion and improve safety (Shatnawi et al., 2020).
- Smart Buildings: IoT-enabled sensors and devices can capture real-time data on energy use, occupancy and other factors, while AI algorithms can make data-driven decisions and logic choices to boost building performance, kerb energy costs and enhance occupant comfort (Zheng et al., 2016). Embedding AI in IoT in such applications will promote sustainable building design and operation.
- Environmental Monitoring: IoT-enabled sensors and devices can assemble real-time data on environmental factors such as water quality, air quality and weather patterns, while AI algorithms can analyse these data to provide insights into environmental health and sustainability (Al-Sharafi et al., 2023). The integrated IoT/AI systems will foster more effective environmental management and conservation.

## 12.4 Case Studies

Smart Water Management: The city of Barcelona implemented a smart water management system using IoT technology to reduce water wastage and improve efficiency. The system includes sensors installed in water pipes, which provide real-time information on water flow and quality. Subsequently, the collected real-time data are analysed and processed by powerful AI algorithms to optimise water distribution, detect leaks and reduce water consumption. As a result, the city was able to save around 25% of water consumption and reduce carbon emissions (Utility Magazine, 2021).

Smart Energy Management: A commercial building in Amsterdam called the Edge uses IoT technology to manage energy consumption efficiently. The building has an advanced building management system that uses IoT sensors and data analytics to monitor and control the lighting, heating and ventilation systems. The system adjusts the temperature and lighting based on the occupancy of the building, reducing energy consumption by up to 70% and achieving a Platinum rating for energy efficiency (Bloomberg Businessweek, 2015).

Waste Management: Waste management is a critical issue in cities around the world, and IoT technology is being used to address this challenge. In Santander, Spain, sensors are installed in waste bins to monitor the fill level and optimise waste collection. The data collected is used to optimise collection routes, reduce fuel consumption and carbon emissions and improve the efficiency of waste collection (Smart Cities Council, 2018).

Smart Transportation: IoT technology is being used in transportation to optimise traffic flow, reduce emissions and improve road safety. In Amsterdam, a smart traffic management system uses IoT sensors to monitor traffic flow and adjust traffic signals to reduce congestion and improve safety. The system has reduced travel time by up to 10%, reduced $CO_2$ emissions by 15% and reduced accidents by 40% (Westermo, 2023).

## 12.5 Challenges and Opportunities

The integration of IoT technology in achieving sustainability comes with both challenges and opportunities. One of the main challenges relates to the cost of implementing IoT systems, which may require significant upfront investments. In addition, the complexity of IoT systems can also present challenges, as these systems often involve multiple components and require advanced technical expertise to design and implement.

Another challenge refers to data privacy and security, as IoT systems collect and transmit large amounts of data that can be sensitive and confidential. This requires careful consideration of privacy and security measures to protect these data and prevent unauthorised access.

The need for reliable and resilient wireless connectivity represents another critical challenge. The success of IoT depends on the ability of devices to communicate with each other seamlessly and in real time. This requires a robust and reliable wireless network that can support the large volume of data generated by IoT devices. Additionally, IoT devices are often located in remote or challenging environments, such as underground or underwater, where traditional wireless networks may not be available or may not be reliable. Therefore, there is a need for innovative solutions that can provide reliable and resilient wireless connectivity to IoT devices, such as low-power, wide-area networks (LPWANs), satellite-based networks and mesh networks. These solutions must also be scalable and cost-effective to ensure the widespread adoption of IoT technology. By addressing the challenge of reliable and resilient wireless connectivity, IoT can achieve its full potential in improving sustainability across various industries.

Furthermore, as the number of connected devices increases, the management and coordination of these devices become increasingly challenging. IoT devices generate a massive volume of data, and managing these data and extracting meaningful insights require sophisticated tools and techniques. Moreover, IoT networks are complex, consisting of diverse devices with different capabilities, protocols and communication standards. The interoperability of these devices and systems is critical to the success of IoT technology, and achieving this requires extensive coordination and standardisation efforts. Additionally, the integration of multiple IoT platforms and technologies can lead to fragmentation and further complicate the management of large-scale IoT networks. To address these challenges, there is a need for robust and scalable IoT platforms and management systems that can handle the growing complexity of IoT networks. These platforms must provide comprehensive tools for managing IoT devices, data and security, as well as enable seamless integration with other systems and platforms. Additionally, there is a need for standardised protocols and communication standards to ensure interoperability and facilitate the management of large-scale IoT networks.

On the other hand, the integration of IoT technology in achieving sustainability presents many opportunities. One such opportunity is the ability to monitor and optimise resource usage, such as energy and water consumption, which can help organisations reduce costs and improve efficiency.

Another opportunity is the ability to collect and analyse data in real time, which can lead to better decision-making and enable organisations to respond quickly to changing conditions. For example, IoT sensors can monitor air quality in real time, allowing organisations to take immediate action to reduce emissions and improve air quality. Furthermore, IoT technology can enable new business models and revenue streams, such as the provision of pay-per-use services, which can kerb waste and encourage more sustainable consumption patterns.

## 12.6 Conclusion and Future Directions

IoT technology has made significant strides in recent years, with the increasing availability of low-cost sensors, wireless connectivity and cloud computing. These technological developments have spurred the deployment of large-scale IoT networks that can gather vast amounts of data from a wide range of sources, including environmental sensors, vehicles and buildings.

The potential applications of IoT technology in achieving sustainability are vast and diverse. IoT can be used to monitor and manage energy consumption in buildings, homes and industrial processes, optimise transportation systems to reduce emissions and monitor air and water quality to address environmental issues. It can also be used to enable precision agriculture, reduce waste, improve recycling and enhance supply chain management to promote ethical and sustainable practices.

However, several challenges need to be addressed to fully leverage the potential of IoT technology in achieving sustainability. These include data security and privacy concerns, the interoperability of IoT devices and systems, the need for reliable and resilient wireless connectivity and the complexity of managing large-scale IoT networks.

Despite these challenges, the opportunities associated with the integration of IoT technology in accelerating progress on the SDGs are vast. For example, a study conducted by the World Economic Forum estimated that IoT solutions could reduce global greenhouse gas emissions by up to 15% by 2030, which would be a significant contribution towards achieving the United Nations' SDGs.

Overall, IoT technology has the potential to revolutionise the way we approach sustainability challenges, but it requires careful planning and management to ensure that it is deployed in an ethical, equitable and sustainable manner.

As IoT technology and AI continue to evolve, there are several potential recommendations for future research and development to promote sustainability:

- Integration of Blockchain Technology: The integration of blockchain technology with IoT and AI can provide a secure and transparent platform for sharing data and enabling decentralised decision-making (Bothra et al., 2023). Blockchain can also help promote sustainability by enabling more efficient and transparent supply chain management, reducing waste and improving traceability.
- Interoperability and Standardisation: The development of interoperability standards and protocols can enable different IoT devices and AI systems to communicate and share data more seamlessly, promoting more efficient and effective sustainability outcomes (Martikkala et al., 2021).
- Ethics and Governance: The development of ethical and governance frameworks for IoT and AI can help ensure that these technologies are used in a responsible and sustainable manner. This includes addressing issues such as data privacy, bias and algorithmic accountability (Keshta, 2022).
- Collaborative Research and Development: The collaboration between academia, industry and government can promote more innovative and effective IoT and AI solutions for sustainability. This can include public–private partnerships, joint research initiatives, and knowledge-sharing platforms.
- Multi-disciplinary Approaches: The integration of multiple disciplines, such as engineering, social sciences and environmental sciences, can enable a more holistic and integrated approach to IoT and AI development for sustainability.

This can promote more effective solutions that consider the complex and interconnected nature of sustainability challenges.

# References

Aceto, G., Persico, V., & Pescapé, A. (2018). The role of information and communication technologies in healthcare: Taxonomies, perspectives, and challenges. *Journal of Network and Computer Applications, 107*, 125–154. https://doi.org/10.1016/J.JNCA.2018.02.008

Al-Nabhan, N., Al-Aboody, N., & Alim Al Islam, A. B. M. (2019). A hybrid IoT-based approach for emergency evacuation. *Computer Networks, 155*, 87–97. https://doi.org/10.1016/J.COMNET.2019.03.015

Al-Sharafi, M. A., Al-Emran, M., Arpaci, I., Iahad, N. A., AlQudah, A. A., Iranmanesh, M., & Al-Qaysi, N. (2023). Generation Z use of artificial intelligence products and its impact on environmental sustainability: A cross-cultural comparison. *Computers in Human Behavior, 143*, 107708. https://doi.org/10.1016/J.CHB.2023.107708

Alshamrani, M. (2022). IoT and artificial intelligence implementations for remote healthcare monitoring systems: A survey. *Journal of King Saud University – Computer and Information Sciences, 34*(8), 4687–4701. https://doi.org/10.1016/J.JKSUCI.2021.06.005

Atzori, L., Iera, A., & Morabito, G. (2010). The internet of things: A survey. *Computer Networks, 54*(15), 2787–2805. https://doi.org/10.1016/J.COMNET.2010.05.010

Beştepe, F., & Yildirim, S. Ö. (2022). Acceptance of IoT-based and sustainability-oriented smart city services: A mixed methods study. *Sustainable Cities and Society, 80*, 103794. https://doi.org/10.1016/J.SCS.2022.103794

Bhat, J. R., AlQahtani, S. A., & Nekovee, M. (2023). FinTech enablers, use cases, and role of future internet of things. *Journal of King Saud University – Computer and Information Sciences, 35*(1), 87–101. https://doi.org/10.1016/J.JKSUCI.2022.08.033

Bloomberg Businessweek. (2015). *The edge is the greenest, most intelligent building in the world.* https://www.bloomberg.com/features/2015-the-edge-the-worlds-greenest-building/

Bothra, P., Karmakar, R., Bhattacharya, S., & De, S. (2023). How can applications of blockchain and artificial intelligence improve performance of internet of things? – A survey. *Computer Networks, 224*, 109634. https://doi.org/10.1016/J.COMNET.2023.109634

El-Haddadeh, R., Weerakkody, V., Osmani, M., Thakker, D., & Kapoor, K. K. (2019). Examining citizens' perceived value of internet of things technologies in facilitating public sector services engagement. *Government Information Quarterly, 36*(2), 310–320. https://doi.org/10.1016/J.GIQ.2018.09.009

Ferreira, D. D., Santos, L. O., Alvarenga, T. A., Rodríguez, D. Z., Barbosa, B. H. G., Ferreira, A. C. B. H., dos Santos Alves, D. F., Carmona, E. V., Duran, E. C. M., & de Moraes Lopes, M. H. B. (2023). Applications of digital and smart technologies to control SARS-CoV-2 transmission, rapid diagnosis, and monitoring. *Omics Approaches and Technologies in COVID-19*, 405–425. https://doi.org/10.1016/B978-0-323-91794-0.00018-4

Garrido-Momparler, V., & Peris, M. (2022). Smart sensors in environmental/water quality monitoring using IoT and cloud services. *Trends in Environmental Analytical Chemistry*, *35*, e00173. https://doi.org/10.1016/J.TEAC.2022.E00173

Gartner. (2020). *Internet of things*. https://www.gartner.com/en/information-technology/glossary/internet-of-things

Hosamo, H. H., Tingstveit, M. S., Nielsen, H. K., Svennevig, P. R., & Svidt, K. (2022). Multiobjective optimization of building energy consumption and thermal comfort based on integrated BIM framework with machine learning-NSGA II. *Energy and Buildings*, *277*, 112479. https://doi.org/10.1016/J.ENBUILD.2022. 112479

Imran, Iqbal, N., & Kim, D. H. (2022). IoT task management mechanism based on predictive optimization for efficient energy consumption in smart residential buildings. *Energy and Buildings*, *257*, 111762. https://doi.org/10.1016/J.ENBUILD. 2021.111762

Iwasaki, W., Morita, N., & Nagata, M. P. B. (2019). IoT sensors for smart livestock management. In *Chemical, gas, and biosensors for internet of things and related applications* (pp. 207–221). https://doi.org/10.1016/B978-0-12-815409-0.00015-2

Kaginalkar, A., Kumar, S., Gargava, P., & Niyogi, D. (2021). Review of urban computing in air quality management as smart city service: An integrated IoT, AI, and cloud technology perspective. *Urban Climate*, *39*, 100972. https://doi.org/10. 1016/J.UCLIM.2021.100972

Karale, A. (2021). The challenges of IoT addressing security, Ethics, privacy, and laws. *Internet of Things*, *15*, 100420. https://doi.org/10.1016/J.IOT.2021.100420

Keshta, I. (2022). AI-driven IoT for smart health care: Security and privacy issues. *Informatics in Medicine Unlocked*, *30*, 100903. https://doi.org/10.1016/J.IMU.2022. 100903

Luperto, M., Monroy, J., Moreno, F. A., Lunardini, F., Renoux, J., Krpic, A., Galindo, C., Ferrante, S., Basilico, N., Gonzalez-Jimenez, J., & Borghese, N. A. (2023). Seeking at-home long-term autonomy of assistive mobile robots through the integration with an IoT-based monitoring system. *Robotics and Autonomous Systems*, *161*, 104346. https://doi.org/10.1016/J.ROBOT.2022.104346

Lv, Z., & Shang, W. (2023). Impacts of intelligent transportation systems on energy conservation and emission reduction of transport systems: A comprehensive review. *Green Technologies and Sustainability*, *1*(1), 100002. https://doi.org/10. 1016/J.GRETS.2022.100002

Manikanda Kumaran, K., Manivannan, R., Kalaiselvi, S., Anitha Elavarasi, S. (2023). An IoT based environment conscious green score meter towards smart sustainable cities. *Sustainable Computing: Informatics and Systems*, *37*, 100839. https://doi.org/10.1016/J.SUSCOM.2022.100839

Mantravadi, S., & Srai, J. S. (2023). How important are digital technologies for urban food security? A framework for supply chain integration using IoT. *Procedia Computer Science*, *217*, 1678–1687. https://doi.org/10.1016/J.PROCS.2022.12.368

Martikkala, A., Lobov, A., Lanz, M., & Ituarte, I. F. (2021). Towards the interoperability of IoT platforms: A case study for data collection and data storage. *IFAC-PapersOnLine*, *54*(1), 1138–1143. https://doi.org/10.1016/J.IFACOL.2021.08.134

Meena, J. S., Choi, S. B., Jung, S.-B., & Kim, J.-W. (2023). Electronic textiles: New age of wearable technology for healthcare and fitness solutions. *Materials Today Bio*, *19*, 100565. https://doi.org/10.1016/J.MTBIO.2023.100565

Pathmudi, V. R., Khatri, N., Kumar, S., Abdul-Qawy, A. S. H., & Vyas, A. K. (2023). A systematic review of IoT technologies and their constituents for smart and sustainable agriculture applications. *Scientific African, 19*, e01577. https://doi.org/10.1016/J.SCIAF.2023.E01577

Prasanna Lakshmi, G. S., Asha, P. N., Sandhya, G., Vivek Sharma, S., Shilpashree, S., & Subramanya, S. G. (2023). An intelligent IOT sensor coupled precision irrigation model for agriculture. *Measurement: Sensors, 25*, 100608. https://doi.org/10.1016/J.MEASEN.2022.100608

Qin, Y., Li, X., Wu, J., & Yu, K. (2022). A management method of chronic diseases in the elderly based on IoT security environment. *Computers & Electrical Engineering, 102*, 108188. https://doi.org/10.1016/J.COMPELECENG.2022.108188

Rastogi, K., & Lohani, D. (2022). Context-aware IoT-enabled framework to analyse and predict indoor air quality. *Intelligent Systems with Applications, 16*, 200132. https://doi.org/10.1016/J.ISWA.2022.200132

Sarpal, D., Sinha, R., Jha, M., & Padmini, T. N. (2022). AgriWealth: IoT based farming system. *Microprocessors and Microsystems, 89*, 104447. https://doi.org/10.1016/J.MICPRO.2022.104447

Shatnawi, N., Al-Omari, A. A., & Al-Qudah, H. (2020). Optimization of bus stops locations using GIS techniques and artificial intelligence. *Procedia Manufacturing, 44*, 52–59. https://doi.org/10.1016/J.PROMFG.2020.02.204

Smart Cities Council. (2018, October 9). *How Santander, Spain is using sensors to tackle waste.* https://www.smartcitiescouncil.com/article/how-santander-spain-using-sensors-tackle-waste

Su, J., Zhu, X., Li, S., & Chen, W. H. (2023). AI meets UAVs: A survey on AI empowered UAV perception systems for precision agriculture. *Neurocomputing, 518*, 242–270. https://doi.org/10.1016/J.NEUCOM.2022.11.020

Tsang, Y. P., Yang, T., Chen, Z. S., Wu, C. H., & Tan, K. H. (2022). How is extended reality bridging human and cyber-physical systems in the IoT-empowered logistics and supply chain management? *Internet of Things, 20*, 100623. https://doi.org/10.1016/J.IOT.2022.100623

Utility Magazine. (2021, September 23). *Success story: Embracing IoT & smart metering for a water resilient Barcelona – Utility Magazine.* https://utilitymagazine.com.au/success-story-suez-iot-barcelona/

Vij, A., Vijendra, S., Jain, A., Bajaj, S., Bassi, A., & Sharma, A. (2020). IoT and machine learning approaches for automation of farm irrigation system. *Procedia Computer Science, 167*, 1250–1257. https://doi.org/10.1016/J.PROCS.2020.03.440

Westermo. (2023). *Westermo networking technology connects smart traffic systems throughout Amsterdam.* https://www.westermo.com/about-us/success-stories/amsterdam-smart-traffic-system

Zheng, Z., Lixiongwang, & Hienwong, N. (2016). Intelligent control system integration and optimization for zero energy buildings to mitigate urban heat island. *Procedia Engineering, 169*, 100–107. https://doi.org/10.1016/J.PROENG.2016.10.012

Part 4

# Impact of AI-Enabled Mechanical and Mechatronics Engineering Systems on UN SDGs

Chapter 13

# Mechatronics Implementation of Passive Building Elements to Improve Thermal Comfort and Promote Energy Efficiency in Buildings

*Mahendra Gooroochurn*

University of Mauritius, Mauritius

## Abstract

The need to design buildings with due consideration for bioclimatic and passive design is central to promoting sustainability in the built environment from an energy perspective. Indeed, the energy and atmosphere considerations in building design, construction and operation have received the highest consideration in green building frameworks such as LEED and BREEAM to promote SDG 9: Industry, Innovation and Infrastructure and SDG 11: Sustainable Cities and Communities and contributing directly to support SDG 13: Climate Action. The research literature is rich of findings on the efficacy of passive measures in different climate contexts, but given that these measures are highly dependent on the prevailing weather conditions, which is constantly in evolution, disturbed by the climate change phenomenon, there is pressing need to be able to accurately predict such changes in the short (to the minute) and medium (to the hour and day) terms, where AI algorithms can be effectively applied. The dynamics of the weather patterns over seasons, but more crucially over a given season means that optimum response of building envelope elements, specifically through the passive elements, can be reaped if these passive measures can be adapted according to the ambient weather conditions. The use of representative mechatronics systems to intelligently control certain passive measures is presented, together with the potential use of artificial intelligence (AI) algorithms to capture the complex building physics involved to predict the expected effect of weather conditions on the indoor environmental conditions.

Artificial Intelligence, Engineering Systems and Sustainable Development, 171–182
Copyright © 2024 Mahendra Gooroochurn
Published under exclusive licence by Emerald Publishing Limited
doi:10.1108/978-1-83753-540-820241013

*Keywords*: Mechatronics; energy efficiency; thermal comfort; passive design; sustainability in built environment; climate change

## 13.1 Introduction

The energy performance of buildings is a determinant factor in the sustainability assessment of green building design and construction. The built environment is known to contribute massively to the global carbon emissions, with up to a 40% share, and hence takes an important place in the fight against climate change. This has been evidenced as a direct correlation between power demand and urbanisation, and in the face of climate change, with harsher summers and winters, significant rises in energy consumption to meet cooling or heating loads depending on the climate zone. In the tropical context of Mauritius, where a predominantly cooling requirement exists, the increased installation of air-conditioning equipment over the last decade is a clear sign of this unsustainable coupling between the built environment and the effect of climate change.

Green building rating systems such as LEED[1] and BREEAM[2] encourages an integrative design approach where passive and bioclimatic design is given due consideration as a preliminary step towards optimising the energy performance. Indeed, a lack of consideration of the influence of building orientation, fabric, glazing and layout on the dynamics of the underlying building physics can lead to poor indoor environmental quality originating from undue heat gains or losses, poor natural ventilation and lack of daylight penetration, with the result of having to rely on active energy systems yielding an unnecessarily high carbon footprint. On the other hand, a passive and bioclimatic design philosophy can go a long way to harnessing natural resources such as air, light and heat available at the project site itself, with passive building elements properly designed to provide the needed regulation to prevent them from deteriorating the indoor conditions.

The relationship between the prevailing weather and the indoor conditions, created by the complex interaction of the building envelope with the former, allows to formulate this phenomenon as a control problem where building elements can be designed to influence the interior state based on the recommendations for human comfort based on guidelines such as the ASHRAE-55 standard (ASHRAE, 2020). Once this first step is achieved, this chapter demonstrates through case studies on common passive measures considered in Mauritius to showcase how the energy performance can be further improved by modulating the influence of these passive elements based on the ambient and indoor conditions. The problem formulation is amenable to a mechatronics systems design philosophy with the control and software components benefitting from an artificial intelligence (AI) paradigm derived from modelling the complex building physics to enable prediction of the targeted indoor parameters. The objective of this chapter is to present the findings from literature on related research to show the

---

[1]https://www.usgbc.org/leed
[2]https://www.breeam.com/

importance of passive and bioclimatic design before further emphasising the appeal of adopting an automated regulation of these passive elements. The promise of deep learning through artificial neural networks as a prediction model for this task is a current active area of research.

This clearly sets the basis for the application of technological solutions from the fields of Internet of Things (IoT) sensing, AI, mechatronics system design and control to support the achievement of related SDGs, namely SDG 9: Industry, Innovation and Infrastructure, where the building stock becomes the driver for a sustainable building industry with development of associated technologies, SDG 11: Sustainable Cities and Communities where the built environment becomes the driver for mitigating and adapting the effects of climatic change by curtailing carbon emissions, if not achieving regenerative design through renewable energy systems, and hence contributing directly to support SDG 13: Climate Action.

## 13.2 Passive and Bioclimatic Design

A passive design methodology refers to the integration of architectural measures into the building design that permits to regulate the interaction of natural elements such as air, light and heat between the outdoor and indoor conditions. Therefore, the building fabric, glazing, orientation and layout are important considerations that can be used to control this interaction. Moreover, other building features such as windows, louvres, external shading devices such as overhangs, eaves, recesses and exterior shading devices such as awnings and shutters as well as interior shading devices such as blinds and curtains can be used to further affect this interaction. Since the design of these elements needs to be carried out in conjunction with the ambient weather condition, passive and bioclimatic design go hand in hand, and it has become common to use building simulation software to study the influence of design parameters Taleb (2014) and Lee and Won (2017).

Of primary concern to the issue of rising energy consumption in the face of warmer summers in Mauritius is heat regulation, where analysis of survey data has shown evidence of lack of consideration for passive design in residential buildings (Gooroochurn, 2022b). The heat regulation can be in terms of limiting heat gains for regions and/or periods of the year where there is a need for cooling as well as situations where heat gains are beneficial. However, passive measures cannot be ascertained to yield the desired indoor conditions during a whole year, lending to the need for a hybrid design where active systems are used during these instances. An interesting approach for integrating passive design measures into our modern vernacular architecture is by considering the underlying principles behind our traditional buildings as supported by the investigation by Tinker and Ghisi (2004) in Malaysia. Along the same line, the traditional creole houses in Mauritius can become the basis for passive design in their modern concrete counterparts.

As mentioned above, glazing is a key building element that influences the interior condition, admitting both light and heat. The Window-to-Wall Ratio

(WWR) has been particularly investigated in several studies with the view to prescribe suitable range of values for various climate zones (Alwetaishi, 2019; Su & Zhang, 2010). The solar heat gain coefficient (SHGC) and thermal conductance (U-value) are associated parameters that can be specified to determine the amount of heat gains through glazed as influenced by the type of glazing itself (high performance or normal glass) and number of layers (typically single, double or triple glazing). Cool building strategies through shading of building elements has been recommended for warm and hot climate zones, with the Estidama[3] rating system for the Middle East having a dedicated credit for this purpose. Ouedraogo et al. (2012) concluded that shading strategies was highly recommended for the hot and arid climate of Burkina Faso, reporting up to 40% reduction in cooling load through the use of curtains.

Another building element that can be a major source of heat gain is the roof due to its continuous exposure to direct solar radiation throughout the day, especially when the angle of incidence is at right angles with the roof surface, as determined by the angle of elevation of the sun and the slope of the roof. This becomes a primary concern for Mauritius under peak summer conditions when the elevation angle is 90° and with near zero sloped roofs. The excessive heats gains can be kept out by reflective and radiative strategies (Al-Obaidi et al., 2014), although being a permanent passive measure.

Nature-based solutions (NBS) in the form of planted trees and vegetation as roof and non-roof measures can be used to shield the roof Zahedi et al. (2023), Feitosa and Wilkinson (2018), and Jim and Tsang (2011), with promising results reported by Mungur et al. (2020) in Mauritius and Morau et al. (2012) for La Reunion and the wall fabric Gómez-Muñoz et al. (2010), Berry et al. (2013), and Morakiny et al. (2013) from the sun. The radiative effect caused by high thermal mass of building fabric can be addressed by use of air buoyancy to carry away the heat. Gooroochurn et al. (2020) studied a space-saving ventilated wall using double-sided hollow cavity blocks, for which up to 6°C drop in interior wall surface temperature was obtained. Another measure attracting interest from the research community, and already finding its way into the construction industry, is phase change material (PCM), with up to 9°C reduction in temperature recorded by Piselli et al. (2018), and further promising results obtained by Ji and Li (2023) and Hou et al. (2023).

Overall, the findings from literature clearly support a passive design paradigm, with variation in performance across climate zones and across seasons showing the potential to reap further benefits by adopting an adaptive control of the influence of these passive measures. As observed in Mauritius for central plateau regions like Curepipe, Floreal and Bois Cheri where there is enough variation in weather conditions across seasons to warrant a change in the heat transfer strategy, whereas coastal areas such as Port-Louis, Tamarin and Plaisance, despite having a predominantly cooling requirement year-round experiences the effect of micro-climates, and it is not uncommon to warrant cooling in winter and

---

[3]https://pages.dmt.gov.ae/en/Urban-Planning/Estidama-Program

heating in summer. In this scenario, coupled with the change in climate patterns fuelled by global warming, where regions with overly a high cooling degree day have shown a sizeable heating degree day and vice versa, it can be concluded that resilience against the effect of climate change can be built-in in construction projects through adaptive passive design measures.

## 13.3 Tropical Context of Mauritius and Limitation of Fixed Passive Measures

This section elaborates further on the climate context across Mauritius and local construction practices to provide the underlying knowledge needed to understand the need for passive design while also demonstrating the key limitations they can represent at certain periods of the year if not amenable to modulation. In general, Mauritius experiences high levels of humidity throughout the year, with a warm coastal region, and a central region at higher altitude with a generally higher humidity level and warm temperature during summer spanning from October to March and a cool regime during winter spanning from April to September.

The effect of climate change has had important changes in these weather regimes in recent years, with summer temperatures exceeding 35°C along coastal regions and winter temperatures as low as 8°C recorded in traditionally warmer regions of the island, clearly showing signs of a shift in climate. As confirmed by several past studies Baglivo et al. (2022) and Cabeza and Chàfer (2020), the longer term effects of climate change need to be factored in the response to be provided due to drastic consequences if the appropriate passive design measures are not integrated into the building architecture. The higher summer temperatures have pushed households and businesses to invest in air-conditioning equipment, typically split-units, which, despite using latest inverter technology, still represents a significant increase in electricity consumption, and leading to further carbon emissions given that the electricity mix is still at around 1 $kgCO_2$/kWh.

In general, the diurnal change in temperature does not undergo significant changes with around 10°C drop in temperature recorded between daytime and night-time at the University of Mauritius campus at Reduit. The cooler night temperature shows the potential to use night flushing to dissipate accumulated heat in the building structure and to cool down the operative air temperature, while providing oxygen-rich fresh air. However, the continued problem of thermal discomfort during night-time in summer, which has been the major reason behind residential property owners investing in air-conditioning units, especially along coastal regions, is due to a lack of a suitable building system to promote exchange between the outdoor and indoor air, lack of pressure gradient across the building envelope to promote cross-ventilation and restriction to open windows due to the coincidence of vector propagation during the summer season.

The solar angles captured in the solar chart for a given location is a vital factor to consider in the design of passive systems. The solar angles, namely elevation and azimuth, do not change dramatically across seasons in Mauritius, as the duration of days varies from around 11 hours to 14 hours and the elevation angle has a maximum value of 90° and a minimum value of around 45°.

### 13.3.1 Local Construction Practices

Over the decades, the construction culture has had a clear shift from corrugated iron sheet and wood constructions to concrete, mainly to provide resistance against cyclones. The common block used for residential projects is 150 mm wide blocks, whereas commercial constructions typically use the 200 mm dimension. These concrete blocks are hollow on one side, and provide a U-value of around 2.2 W/m²K when rendered on both sides using cement mortar. The slab thickness of houses is typically 150 mm, cast in situ with steel bar reinforcement, achieving a U-value of around 2 W/m²K. The slope of these roofs is typically 2% to provide for run-water drainage, and hence can be considered as flat roofs. Roofs in residential constructions are generally not waterproofed, hence become dark grey with soiling over time.

### 13.3.2 Limitations of Passive Design

Based on the climate regime prevailing around representative warm regions around the coast (yielding a general need for cooling throughout the year) and warm climate during summer and cool climate during winter for the central region, the following passive measures can be prescribed:

- Roof shading, green roof, cool roof, shading of glazed areas, either external or internal, tall trees with leaves throughout the year as a means to ward off direct solar radiation and to shade the wall, roof and glazing exclusively throughout the year. Although there is a general need to keep solar heat gains out of the interior spaces while allowing daylight to penetrate, as described above, the weather changes over days in a given season mean that the cooling and heating requirements will be different, hence relying on fixed passive measures such as cool roof and externa fins will restrict the ability to benefit from any beneficial heating during cold days.
- Roof shading and external shading, internal shading and the use of deciduous trees that shed leaves in winter. The use of cool roof is not recommended as this will limit heat gains in winter, although the other benefits of green roof such as roof protection, air purification, rainwater retention and outdoor liveable spaces may warrant its installation, and the heat gains can then be compensated through the glazed openings. In any case, all the measures need to be adjustable to cater for the general heating and cooling requirements across seasons, and also to cope with daily changes in the climate for a given season.

In general, it is clear that fixed passive measures do not provide the customisation needed to achieve optimum performance with respect to interior and prevailing weather conditions. The Mechatronics Implementation of Modulable Passive Building Elements section provides mechatronics system design guidelines for few passive measures and the associated AI methodology that can be adopted with identification of the input and output parameters.

## 13.4 Mechatronics Implementation of Modulable Passive Building Elements

Although the deciduous trees prescribed for winter for central regions provide the general flexibility needed to cope with differing heat requirements between seasons, it does not offer the precise flexibility needed due to dynamic changes in weather patterns within a given season. This section describes examples that can be considered to provide the absolute flexibility being targeted. The needed model to predict the influence of ambient climatic conditions on the building physics for the specific building design under consideration can be developed using a simulation approach based on the 3 × 3 array model discussed in Gooroochurn et al. (2021), using which the following flexible passive measures can be used to influence the interior conditions by controlling one or more of these automated passive measures to achieve desirable interior conditions as far as possible, which can be set using guidelines from ASHRAE-55 standard (ASHRAE, 2020).

### 13.4.1 Curtain Control

The ability to control the curtains for given orientation at a given point in time with respect to the known solar position gives the possibility to admit or block direct solar radiation, which, as per the study carried by Gooroochurn et al. (2021), is a major source of heat gains, hence can be effectively used to influence interior conditions. The targeted system, using suitable linear or rotary actuators, will allow retracting or extending the curtains in response to the current interior conditions, targeted interior conditions and the prevailing outside conditions as well as the trained building model developed for the specific construction in question.

### 13.4.2 External Shading Control

The external shading can achieve better heat regulation as compared to the curtain system described above using a similar control strategy for a glazing of a given orientation, although such systems require greater maintenance due to exposure to exterior conditions, are costlier and may also impede external views.

### *13.4.3 Roof Shading*

Roof shading can take different forms, but for it to be deployable as and when needed, a control strategy similar to the external shading needs to be employed, and hence limits the installation of fixed permanent structures such as roofed terraces, albeit such systems are controllable, but represent significant investment. On the other hand, using a simpler solar shade canvas membrane with a system allowing the latter to be rolled out and in can be a more cost effective retrofit and installation for the flat roofs in Mauritius, with the added advantage of providing ready disassembly during cyclonic conditions.

### *13.4.4 Roof Pooling*

Roof pooling is a measure reported in literature as a means to dissipate heat from roof surfaces with the benefit of providing the flexibility for reducing heat gains through the roof slab when water is flushed over the roof, and allowing heat gains when no water is allowed to flush or stand on the roof. The automated system can be implemented using a tank (of volume depending on the size of roof for allowing 5–10 cm of water depth over the roof) at ground level, a circulating pump with solenoid valves in the pipe network to allow the water to stand when needed. The control system will simply allow water to pool over the roof whenever there is need to reduce heat gains to the interior spaces.

### *13.4.5 Wind Catcher*

A wind catcher is a flap mounted on the side of a window opening, whose angle can be varied and hence used to increase the amount of air flow into the spaces, depending on the exterior wind speed and direction. This system can be controlled using a window-mounted air speed sensor and an exterior wind measurement device, providing the wind speed and direction. The desired indoor air flow can be set based on the parameters recommended by the ASHRAE-55 standard (ASHRAE, 2020). Through this measure, the air flow, and hence the air change per hour, can be adjusted inside a given space, which has the beneficial effect of providing fresh air to the interiors, dissipating heat and bringing the chill effect of moving air to the occupants.

### *13.4.6 Solar Chimney*

A glass-based solar chimney prototype with adjustable openings has been proposed in Gooroochurn (2022a) as illustrated in Fig. 13.1, which can operate in several models, namely cooling, heating and night flushing modes (See Table 13.1), the latter needing a circulating fan inside the body of the solar chimney. This system can be controlled using a Fuzzy Logic control system to decide which of the louvres to be opened to implement a given mode, based on time of the day, interior and exterior temperatures.

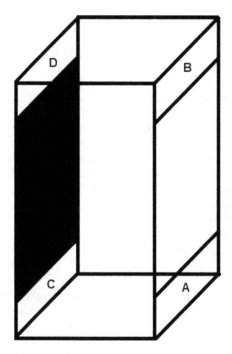

Fig. 13.1.   Glass-Based Solar Chimney (Gooroochurn, 2022a).

Table 13.1.  Operating Modes of Solar Chimney.

| Mode of Operation | Openings Opened | Openings Closed |
|---|---|---|
| Inactive | None or A and B | C and D |
| Cross-ventilation/cooling mode | B and C | A and D |
| Heating mode | A and D | B and C |
| Night-flushing mode | A and D | B and C |

## 13.5 Discussion and Conclusion

The huge body of literature supports the application of passive and bioclimatic design in buildings, without which it can be ascertained that any further measures such as active energy systems control and renewable energy integration are not fully sustainable options. Given that the built environment has very high environmental impacts through the carbon emissions linked to the energy requirements during operation, passive design is a quintessential paradigm that needs to be enforced in all buildings. This chapter has demonstrated the limitations in achieving further benefits as these same passive measures can thwart the ability to derive benefits from natural resources available at the project site, and at other times if they are designed to be fixed.

An AI-based control system can be developed using a simulation approach because it is not practical to develop a custom experimental model for each building typology. With the trained AI model able to predict the interior conditions, given a current set of internal and external conditions as well as predicted weather patterns, the passive elements such as roof shading, roof pooling, curtain or external fin systems can be designed using a mechatronics paradigm so that they can be appropriately controlled to decide on the influence of the passive measure on the building physics as far as heat gains or losses are concerned. Furthermore, adaptive passive measures in the form of wind catcher and solar chimney have been presented as means to regulate air flow through the interior spaces. Used in conjunction, heat transfer and air movement controls can go a long way to optimising the parameters of the interior conditions passively, hence minimising, if not eliminating, the need for active systems. In this respect, the ability to modulate the influence of the passive measures as opposed to fixed systems is a significant step towards promoting a proper indoor environmental quality sustainably.

The complex building physics can be addressed using AI techniques such as deep learning to capture the underlying processes involved, and in so doing serve as vital knowledge base for predictive control of the passive measures. Such a design paradigm will enable to make judicious decision at building design stage to achieve proper indoor conditions passively as far as possible and the implementation of low-cost mechatronics system solutions for automating the passive measures to cater for variations in ambient weather conditions on a daily or seasonal basis, and curtail the unsustainable drive of relying on active cooling and ventilation systems to meet thermal comfort and air quality needs in buildings in Mauritius. With the proven contribution of passive design in support of the sustainable development goals, application of AI-driven technological solutions to allow control of the influence of these passive measures will no doubt further support sustainable use of natural resources at the project site, a key circular design paradigm.

# References

Al-Obaidi, K. M., Ismail, M., & Rahman, A. M. A. (2014). Passive cooling techniques through reflective and radiative roofs in tropical houses in Southeast Asia: A literature review. *Frontiers of Architectural Research, 3*(3), 283–297.

Alwetaishi, M. (2019). Impact of glazing to wall ratio in various climatic regions: A case study. *Journal of King Saud University – Engineering Sciences, 31*(1), 6–18.

ANSI/ASHRAE 55. (2020). *Standard environmental conditions for human comfort conditions.*

Baglivo, C., Congedo, P. M., Murrone, G., & Lezzi, D. (2022). Long-term predictive energy analysis of a high-performance building in a mediterranean climate under climate change. *Energy, 238,* 121641. https://doi.org/10.1016/j.energy.2021.121641

Berry, R., Livesley, S. J., & Aye, L. (2013). Tree canopy shade impacts on solar irradiance received by building walls and their surface temperature. *Building and Environment, 69,* 91–100.

Cabeza, L. F., & Chàfer, M. (2020). Technological options and strategies towards zero energy buildings contributing to climate change mitigation: A systematic review. *Energy and Buildings, 219,* 110009. https://doi.org/10.1016/j.enbuild.2020.110009

Feitosa, R. C., & Wilkinson, S. J. (2018). Attenuating heat stress through green roof and green wall retrofit. *Building and Environment, 140,* 11–22.

Gómez-Muñoz, V., Porta-Gándara, M., & Fernández, J. (2010). Effect of tree shades in urban planning in hot-arid climatic regions. *Landscape and Urban Planning, 94*(3–4), 149–157.

Gooroochurn, M. (2022a). A hybrid glass-based solar chimney to promote cross-ventilation and night flushing, 2022 International Conference on Electrical. *Computer, Communications and Mechatronics Engineering (ICECCME), Maldives, Maldives, 2022,* 1–5. https://doi.org/10.1109/ICECCME55909.2022.9988027

Gooroochurn, M. (2022b). A new passive design analysis methodology and correlation to occupant perception. In *Fifth International Conference on Efficient Building Design, 2022, October 20–21,* American University of Beirut, Beirut, Lebanon.

Gooroochurn, M., Coret, J. Y., Brown NVenkannah, S., & Wright, A. J. (2021). Assessing the efficacy of passive measures for the tropical context of Mauritius through parametric simulations and in-situ measurement. In *CIBSE 2021 Technical Symposium* (pp. 13–14).

Gooroochurn, M., Shamachurn, H., Surnam, B. Y. R., & Cadersa, A. (2020). Experimental and simulation analysis of the performance of a low cost and space preserving ventilated façade for hot and humid climates. In *The Fourth International Conference on Efficient Building Design (ASHRAE),* November 2020, Beirut.

Hou, J., Liu, Z., Zhang, L., Zhang, T., Hou, C., & Fukuda, H. (2023). Parametric and economic analysis of incorporating phase change material (PCM) into exterior walls to reduce energy demand for traditional dwellings in northeast of Sichuan hills, China. *Applied Thermal Engineering, 223,* 119982. https://doi.org/10.1016/j.applthermaleng.2023.119982

Ji, R., & Li, X. (2023). Numerical analysis on the energy performance of the PCMs-integrated thermochromic coating building envelopes. *Building and Environment, 233*(2023), 110113. https://doi.org/10.1016/j.buildenv.2023.110113

Jim, C. Y., & Tsang, S. (2011). Ecological energetics of tropical intensive green roof. *Energy and Buildings, 43*(10), 2696–2704.

Lee, C., & Won, J. (2017). Analysis of combinations of glazing properties to improve economic efficiency of buildings. *Journal of Cleaner Production, 166,* 181–188.

Morakiny, T. E., Balogun, A. A., & Adegun, O. B. (2013). Comparing the effect of trees on thermal conditions of two typical urban buildings. *Urban Climate, 3,* 76–93.

Morau, D., Libelle, T., & Garde, F. (2012). Performance evaluation of green roof for thermal protection of buildings in reunion island. *Energy Procedia, 14,* 1008–1016.

Mungur, M., Poorun, Y., Juggurnath, D., Ruhomally, Y. B., Rughooputh, R., Dauhoo, M. Z., Khoodaruth, A., Shamachurn, H., Gooroochurn, M., Boodia, N., Chooneea, M., & Facknath, S. (2020). A numerical and experimental investigation of the effectiveness of green roofs in tropical environments: The case study of Mauritius in mid and late winter. *Energy, 202,* 117608.

Ouedraogo, B., Levermore, G., & Parkinson, J. (2012). Future energy demand for public buildings in the context of climate change for Burkina Faso. *Building and Environment, 49,* 270–282.

Piselli, C., Castaldo, V. L., & Pisello, A. L. (2018). How to enhance thermal energy storage effect of pcm in roofs with varying solar reflectance: Experimental and numerical assessment of a new roof system for passive cooling in different climate conditions. *Solar Energy, 192,* 106–119.

Su, X., & Zhang, X. (2010). Environmental performance optimization of window-to-wall ratio for different window type in hot summer and cold winter zone in China based on lifecycle assessment. *Energy and Buildings, 42*(2), 198–202.

Taleb, H. (2014). Using passive cooling strategies to improve thermal performance and reduce energy consumption of residential buildings in U.A.E. buildings. *Frontiers of Architectural Research, 3,* 154–165.

Tinker, J. A., & Ghisi, E. (2004). An evaluation of thermal comfort in typical modern low income housing in Malaysia. In *Thermal performance of exterior envelopes of whole buildings IX.*

Zahedi, R., Daneshgar, S., Farahani, O. N., & Aslani, A. (2023). Thermal analysis model of a building equipped with green roof and its energy optimization. *Nature-Based Solutions, 3,* 100053. https://doi.org/10.1016/j.nbsj.2023.100053

Chapter 14

# Demystifying Climate Change and Climate Action Through the Circular Homes Concept – An Educational Tool for Community Engagement

*Mahendra Gooroochurn*

University of Mauritius, Mauritius

## Abstract

Climate change has been identified as a pressing social, environmental and economical challenge that has been unequivocally linked to human activity through latest Intergovernmental Panel on Climate Change (IPCC) reports. It is here to stay with us for generations to come and is already causing severe tribulations across the world. As nations devise policies to mitigate to climate change to stay within the 1.5 degrees Celsius target and small island developing states (SIDS) like Mauritius and the developing world in general find means to adapt to its consequences, a core shortcoming highlighted is the lack of community engagement and grassroots action so that policies permeate to concrete action. Of prime importance for this to happen is raising awareness on the climate change phenomenon, which has so far been a topic deemed complex for the general public, hence creating systemic barriers for climate action. The use of artificial intelligence (AI) can play a significant role in designing such community outreach programmes based on outcomes reported in literature in the educational sector in support of Sustainable Development Goal (SDG) 4: Quality Education. There is growing interest for a green lifestyle in the world population, and this chapter shows how the home can be used as a basic building block for allowing each household to contribute to climate action, while offering an effective case study to raise awareness on climate change through practical examples and demonstration, in support for SDG 11: Sustainable Cities and Communities. Based on an energy-water-materials nexus, the circular home concept is a clear contribution to SDG 13: Climate Action, with huge potential to use AI

Artificial Intelligence, Engineering Systems and Sustainable Development, 183–194
Copyright © 2024 Mahendra Gooroochurn
Published under exclusive licence by Emerald Publishing Limited
doi:10.1108/978-1-83753-540-820241014

techniques and underpinning technologies to implement and optimise the efficacy of the proposed measures.

*Keywords*: Climate change; passive design; circular economy; community engagement; energy-water-materials nexus; codesign

## 14.1 Introduction

All nations of the world are preoccupied by the effect of climate change, such have been the dramatic consequences of natural calamities linked to climate change. Climate change adaptation and mitigation have to become a central component for the sustainable development of our world. Climate action provides opportunities for green job creation, technological innovation as well as social inclusion, character building and above all a genuine care for the natural ecosystems we are part of, crucial for our survival at the least, if not for our well-being. Debates on climate change have become a recurrent annual event through the organisation of the Conference of Parties (COPs), the latest one being COP27 at Sharm-El-Sheikh, Egypt to follow on its predecessor, COP26, which took place in Glasgow, UK. The latter was particularly marked by intense manifestation from climate activists, including our youth, generally demanding clear action plan for concrete actions to tackle climate change at its roots in communities beyond the policies and strategies contained in Nationally Determined Contributions (NDCs) for each country.

Abudu et al. (2022) remarked in a study for the Middle East and North African region, that there are important barriers for nations to live to the commitments stipulated in their NDCs, which raises questions on the methodology used to recommend those measures. In this respect, Vyas et al. (2022) stress on the need for a framework to track the implementation of NDCs showing the essence of community engagement for climate action. Dietzel (2022) further reported that the drive for climate action can be used to bring the needed systemic changes. Based on findings reported in literature with methodologies used for addressing climate change, it has become clear that unilateral governmental or federal effort tends not to permeate to the grassroots and hence does not have the intended outcome. Therefore, SDG17: Partnerships should be(come) part and parcel of any incentive for sustainable development, including climate action.

In the current state, although our world citizens are increasingly aware of the impacts of climate change given the dramatic changes in their livelihoods and observing those of their neighbours, Sutton and Tobin (2011) reported a general lack of knowledge on the climate change phenomenon, which leads to lack of clarity from the community perspective on what they should do to bring their share of contribution. Given that the specific priorities and course of action differ from country to country, and even within a country at state or district level, there is a pressing need for joint effort by public–private sectors with universities and research institutes bringing the scientific basis for the prioritisation of the measures, and working with non-governmental organisations (NGOs) and communities to cocreate and implement.

The study by Howard (2022) who looked at community engagement for climate action from a parent-led lens found that parents are highly concerned with the future of their children, which adds further merit to raising awareness and capacity building to make each community member a partner for climate action. The complexities of climate change are unfortunately not limited to the physical dimension only, but permeates to the psychological and mental states as well MacDonald et al. (2015), Majeed and Lee (2017), Vesely et al. (2021). On the positive side, Ballard et al. (2021) observed that climate action initiatives have been found to bring a heightened level of civic engagement skills, where our young generation has meaningful ideas and solutions to bring to the table at all levels of the climate change mitigation and adaptation process MacDonald et al. (2013). Moreover, Singh et al. (2022) recommend women empowerment as an effective means to develop climate resilience. Another key research finding essential to develop and dispense community dialogues on climate change is that individual responsibility towards climate change brings higher risk perception and apprehension, whereas group-based dialogues and incentives have the opposite, desired effect.

An important barrier in connecting people to climate initiatives has been the language used to communicate findings and recommended response from them. Without a proper, non-technical content, and clearly demonstrable outcomes through tried and tested outcomes, for example through real-world labs and prototypes, community engagement initiatives can be ineffective, whereas only attracting the interest of people for climate advocacy without clear guidelines on what they can do at their level does not reap maximum benefits from this crucial partnership. Therefore, a multi-lateral partnership from social sciences, media communication, engineering and other disciplines related to the specific intervention in question is crucial for success. Artificial intelligence (AI) tools can be useful in developing and monitoring the efficacy of such educational and training programmes.

One area with high potential for engaging with the community at large is the home, since everyone can relate to it in one form or another, and it pertains to the more general category of built environment, which has received strong interest in sustainability agendas of nations, and relates to several climate-linked disciplines such as materials, health, energy, water, biodiversity and transport Singh et al. (2021), Grafakos et al. (2020). The residential sector represents a high portion of the built environment, and using it as the basis to explain what is climate change, what are its impacts and what can be done at household level can be an interesting avenue for community engagement, which has been the approach taken in developing the circular home concept, based on an energy-water-materials nexus. A powerful means to achieve this is through passive and bioclimatic design, where AI can provide the needed customisation through modelling and prediction of the complex building physics each building typology has with respect to its location and prevailing climatic conditions. Indeed, as a consequence of climate change with harsher weather patterns, the indoor conditions are expected to deteriorate with respect to accepted limits. Renewable energy is certainly an avenue to reduce the carbon footprint of the built environment (Karnama (2019)), but energy efficiency should be the first priority for a sustainable solution as recommended by green building standards such as Building Research Establishment Environmental Assessment Methodology (BREEAM) and Leadership in Energy and Environmental Design (LEED).

The built environment has systematically been the cause of loss of biodiversity and permeable land areas, and logically has been a major contributor to climate change through carbon emissions, and the associated loss in carbon sinking capability due to deforestation and displacement of vegetated areas. However, nature-based solutions for the built environment can bring several synergies for energy and water management at site level. For example, trees can be used to provide shading to ward off unwanted heat gains through walls and glazed areas, whereas a green roof has numerous benefits, most notably as an attempt to replicate the natural hydrology displaced by the erection of infrastructures. As noted by Asdak et al. (2018), the occurrence of flooding and landslide has risen due to the effect of climate change through short-duration, high-intensity rainfall patterns, exacerbated by the increased run-off created by hard surfaces of the built environment. It is, therefore, crucial that the natural systems in place prior to construction be restored or enhanced as far as possible as a means to adapt to climate change.

Abass et al. (2022) investigated the problem of flooding in Ghana, and found that additional factors such as lack of building regulations or non-enforcement of same, inadequate drainage systems in place and poor solid waste management leading to clogging of natural pathways and drains are other culprits. The overarching role of community engagement for flood management has been highlighted by Puzyreva et al. (2022).

As mentioned above, inadequate management of solid waste can negatively impact the efficacy of other climate initiatives such as water management Bello et al. (2022), Abass et al. (2022). The emission of greenhouse gases (GHG) from landfill waste is among the main environmental impact. Sharma et al. (2021) recommended a circular economy (CE)-based paradigm for sustainable waste management (SWM), including the creation of green jobs to support the process by educating and training informal workers. The CE, with the three-pillar model proposed by the Ellen McArthur Foundation, has indeed been applied extensively to find solutions to climate change, and the circular homes concept has been devised based on this framework as described later.

AI techniques have been widely used in the sustainable management of waste, as reviewed by Lin et al. (2022). Cheah et al. (2022) used an Industry 4.0 approach to reduce, reuse and repurpose waste by using Radio Frequency Identification (RFID) and wireless communications technologies. Andeobu et al. (2022) developed an AI-based methodology for SWM in Australia. Sliusar et al. (2022) made use of drone technology at landfill sites to characterise the spatial and volumetric factors of waste, and in environmental impact assessment and compliance, for example, methane emissions.

## 14.2 CE and Climate Change

The CE framework developed by the Ellen McArthur Foundation (illustrated in Fig. 14.1) has become a widely applied and effective tool for climate action, and serves as an intuitive basis for community engagement, given the simplicity of the language used to lay down the three pillars: (1) Designing out waste and pollution, (2) keeping materials and products in the loop and (3) regenerate natural systems. The three pillars carry strong insights into sustainable development, which can be adapted to a specific problem area and context. The designing out waste and pollution and keeping materials and products in the loop pillars can be generally likened to the man-made, technical cycles, while the regenerate natural systems pillar pertains to natural cycles related to our ecosystem, of which human beings are part and parcel. The CE framework, therefore, encapsulates very well the solutions that can be considered for the climate change phenomenon as a reversal of the disruption of natural systems by anthropogenic activities.

These three pillars have been adapted as follows for the circular homes concept, and the same ideology serves to educate and train community members on climate change and climate action through their households:

Fig. 14.1.    Circular Economy (CE) Framework. *Source:* Ellen McArthur Foundation.

A. Keeping products and materials in use: this pillar can be interpreted in a unique way for the built environment, where sustainable use of natural resources at the building site are harnessed as far as possible to meet the needs of the occupants, while not allowing them to impoverish the indoor environmental quality of spaces. This pillar is, therefore, translated to the energy dimension of the circular home by applying passive design principles to showcase how the problem of thermal discomfort in homes is caused by climate change to allow the participants to devise low-cost solutions for their specific home layout and context, with little or no reliance on air-conditioning.

B. Design out waste and pollution: this pillar is used to raise awareness on the need to make sustainable use of the materials we encounter in our livelihoods to prevent the linear economy paradigm of take-make-waste. The range of possibilities in the form of sharing, reuse maintaining, upcycling, refurbishment and recycling is considered, for which segregation at source is a must. In the absence of current logistics for segregated collection of material streams in Mauritius, avenues for community partnerships with enterprises, recyclers, artists and craftsmen can be considered, whereas the organic waste stream can be readily composted at home or community level.

C. Regenerate natural systems: this pillar is used firstly to raise awareness of the climate change phenomenon as a cause of man-made activities due to disruption of natural mechanisms in place, with their own home as example, such as increased run-off caused by permeable surfaces, displacement of biodiversity to erect their homes and how their own homes can become reservoir of heat by the heat island effect. This pillar is then interpreted as a means to regenerate the hydrology of the plot of land, hence for the water dimension of the circular home.

As observed, the circular homes concept is kept simple with one dimension for each pillar, and within each dimension, only one measure. This is done on purpose based on the priority for Mauritius, namely to encourage passive design in homes to reverse the trend of air-conditioning, run-off management at local level and solid waste segregation at source. The circular homes concept can certainly be adapted for other contexts, and over time augmented to raise the level of homes, but in the current circumstances for Mauritius, being able to implement these three measures in our households will go a long way to leveraging climate action at household level to neighbourhood and national levels.

## 14.3 Circular Homes Concept and Adaptation to Mauritius

### 14.3.1 Energy Dimension

Although energy use takes several forms in a household, such as lighting, appliances and hot water generation, air-conditioning homes to achieve comfortable levels is rapidly becoming a prime concern for peak power demand during summer conditions, and becoming an unsustainable measure in our economy given the significant carbon emissions associated as well as refrigerant leakage risk.

The energy portion for air-conditioning can be as much as 60%, so simple passive measures need to be considered to regulate the heat gains into the interior spaces. Through the circular homes concept, members of the community are educated in non-technical language on the path of the sun, and its implications on heat gains through the roof and glazing areas, which allows them to understand the thermal perception in their homes and what they need to do to deal with the problem at source (passive design) instead of dealing with the effect (air-conditioning).

Of the several measures presented, roof shading using simple arrangements, that can cost as little as Rs 75/m$^2$ is a primary passive measure since previous research works (Gooroochurn et al., 2021) have shown the roof to be a major source of heat gains and radiative temperature. Use of tall trees around buildings to shade glazing in low elevation sun orientations such as the east and west is also an outcome from the exercise, while having a synergy with biodiversity promotion and also the water dimension. The importance of air movement, either natural, wind-driven or forced, low-power, ceiling fan-driven, is also stressed so that air quality and thermal comfort go hand in hand.

### 14.3.2 Water Dimension

Water use in our homes takes several forms, broadly categorised as potable and non-potable. The efficient use of potable water is certainly a sustainable measure through installation of water efficient fixtures as is the use of harvested rainwater to meet non-potable ends such as irrigation, toilet flushing and car washing. However, the measure prescribed under the water dimension stems from an understanding of how rainwater run-off is channelled at the home site, and from this knowledge, how the run-off can be percolated into the ground as opposed to the road drains or outright onto the road itself. As mentioned above, this dimension relates to the 'Regenerate natural systems' pillar since preconstruction, all rainwater would percolate into the ground, and the run-off is a consequence of the erection of the building, hence by ensuring the run-off percolates into the ground to replenish our underground aquifers, this pillar of the CE is being supported. Rainwater harvesting instead of percolating the water into the ground is an adjunct measure that can be considered in this dimension, although the volume of water generated from medium to heavy intensity rainfalls (10 m$^3$ for a 100 mm rainfall event for a 100 m$^2$ house) far exceeds the requirement for non-potable at a typical home, hence percolation into the ground through soak-aways and retention for slow discharge are crucial. The community members are also shown practically how an undesirable resource causing flooding can be given its due value by managing it through retention as harvested rainwater or percolation into the ground to fill our boreholes.

### 14.3.3 Materials Dimension

The materials dimension can be related to the various uses of materials over the life of a building, starting at the construction stage, through the operation and finally de-construction. The building sector has a high environmental impact when it comes to its materials needs, which has prompted the formulation of material ingredients declaration and associated impacts, typically assessed by a life cycle assessment exercise and when carried by a third-party resulting in the issuance of an Environmental Product Declaration (EPD). The choice of environmental-friendly materials at any stage of the building can be made through green product databases. The materials dimension of the circular home pertains to the management of solid waste generated during the running of the household given that of approximately 500,000 tons of solid waste sent to landfill annually in Mauritius, 80% comes from households. Therefore, being able to divert household waste from landfills and using them to produce functional and decorative items would represent a win-win situation with reduced expenditure on waste collection logistics, second-hand materials as ingredients, less stress on an already saturated landfill site in Mauritius and reduction of GHG emissions from the solid waste itself and the transportation logistics involved. The reason why these materials are rendered useless and categorised as waste is because they are commingled, including with organic waste, which makes recycling impossible. The possibilities for sustainable use of materials and preventing them from becoming waste can be unravelled from the butterfly diagram (illustrated in Fig. 14.2).

The emphasis of the materials dimension in the circular home is to achieve the minimum level of waste segregation at source to enable other measures such as recycling (which is the outermost loop in the butterfly diagram, hence the least preferred for a CE transformation), as well as consider other more desirable options for sustainable management of these unwanted or unneeded materials through sharing, maintaining, reuse and refurbishment found at the inner loops through community initiatives. Although door-to-door collection facilities do not provide separate collection of these segregated material streams at present, the circular homes prepare households for the future, but more importantly, opens up numerable opportunities for concerted community action such as artwork, crafts and even materials innovation for functional items, for which there is a growing repository of material recipes available online.

### 14.3.4 AI for Climate Solutions Based on Circular Homes Concept

As presented in the introduction part of this chapter, each of the dimensions of the circular home can benefit from AI techniques, including the community engagement exercise where the training can be developed and monitored using an AI framework. The energy dimension can utilise machine-learning algorithms to develop predictive models for the building physics of different building layouts, for which the datasets can be produced using simulation models. These predictive models can themselves be used to understand the factors influencing energy consumption as well as feed into control routines for any active energy systems. The water dimension can benefit from weather forecasts to decide the discharge schedule and rate from any retention system so as to make space for the next

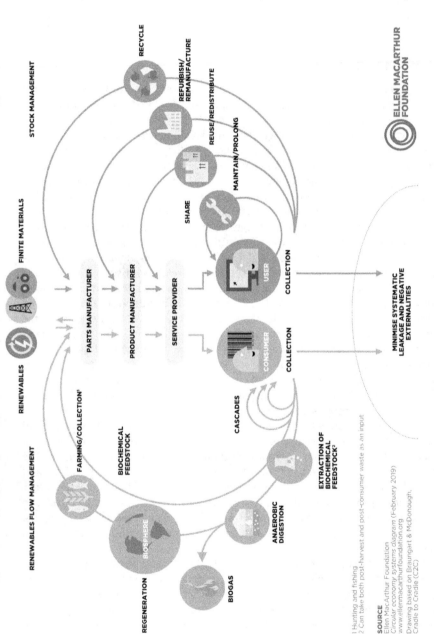

Fig. 14.2. Butterfly Diagram. *Source:* Ellen McArthur Foundation.

rainfall event. Finally, the materials dimension can benefit from AI algorithms to develop prediction model for solid waste generation for different localities to feed into SWM strategies.

## 14.4 Conclusion

The circular homes concept was developed to surmount several barriers reported in literature to promote community engagement for climate action so that concrete measures are implemented at grassroots while providing an effective basis to raise awareness on climate change. The circular home concept has already been run through community workshops, where participants from different backgrounds, including non-technical, have been able to apply the passive design principles to their home layouts and produce results that predict thermal perception, which correlated to what they actually perceive. With this understanding, each participant can understand the sources of overheating and prescribe suitable shading measures to regulate the heat gains, which combined with air circulation using ceiling fans will contribute to enhancing thermal comfort.

The major innovation of the circular home concept was the use of the home as a case study, enabling the population at large to relate with something they see and experience every day, and can access for any further information they need. For example, to understand the route of rainwater run-off from their roof and other hard surfaces at ground level, this aspect was not always evident to the participants, but through a survey of their homes, they were able to understand the issue. Finally, the materials dimension paves the way to achieve the minimum performance to enable circular use of materials. The circular homes concept provides a tangible system that can be implemented and practically demonstrated to citizens, which should be a requirement of projects involving community engagement. The proposed measures under the energy, water and materials categories can be implemented using low-cost products available on the market, and can be realised within a budget of MUR 10,000–15,000 (around USD 300–400), where a strong engagement from the community members is essential. The concept has been adapted to the Mauritian context based on priorities and research findings, hence can similarly be adapted to define what the energy, water and materials dimensions are aimed at achieving. In this respect, the academic and research community have an important role to play, as well as, in creating the communication media in a non-technical language to reach out to the community.

The three aspects considered in the circular home concept can benefit from AI techniques for developing predictive models that will enhance. The energy dimension, relying on using passive methods to regulate heat transfer and air movement principally, can benefit from a trained model able to capture the complex building physics involved between the interior and exterior of a building with the prevailing ambient weather parameters being an important factor. For the water dimension, weather forecasting using AI, specifically prediction of rainfall event and intensity can inform the retention or discharge of rainwater run-off stored in tanks. Finally, the materials dimension can be enhanced by developing trained AI models to predict the volume of each type of waste streams segregated at household level, aggregated at neighbourhood level to inform municipal collectors or recycling companies on the frequency of trips so that the transportation logistics are optimised.

# References

Abass, K., Dumedah, G., Frempong, F., Muntaka, A. S., Appiah, D. O., Garsonu, E. K., & Gyas, R. M. (2022). Rising incidence and risks of floods in urban Ghana: Is climate change to blame? *Cities, 121*, 103495. https://doi.org/10.1016/j.cities.2021.103495

Abudu, H., Wesseh, P. K., & Lin, B. (2022). Climate pledges versus commitment: Are policy actions of Middle-East and North African countries consistent with their emissions targets? *Advances in Climate Change Research.* https://doi.org/10.1016/j.accre.2022.06.004

Andeobu, L., Wibowo, S., & Grandhi, S. (2022). Artificial intelligence applications for sustainable solid waste management practices in Australia: A systematic review. *Science of the Total Environment, 834*, 155389. https://doi.org/10.1016/j.scitotenv.2022.155389

Asdak, C., Supian, S., & Subiyanto. (2018). Watershed management strategies for flood mitigation: A case study of Jakarta's flooding. *Weather and Climate Extremes, 21*, 117–122. https://doi.org/10.1016/j.wace.2018.08.002

Ballard, J., Borden, L., & Perkins, D. F. (2021). Program quality components related to youth civic engagement. *Children and Youth Services Review, 126*, 106022.

Bello, A. S., Al-Ghouti, M. A., & Abu-Dieyeh, M. H. (2022). Sustainable and long-term management of municipal solid waste: A review. *Bioresource Technology Reports, 18*, 101067. https://doi.org/10.1016/j.biteb.2022.101067

Cheah, C. G., Chia, W. Y., Lai, S. F., Chew, K. W., Chia, S. R., & Pau Loke Show, P. L. (2022). Innovation designs of industry 4.0 based solid waste management: Machinery and digital circular economy. *Environmental Research, 213*, 113619. ISSN 0013-9351. https://doi.org/10.1016/j.envres.2022.113619

Dietzel. (2022). Non-state climate change action: Hope for just response to climate change? *Environmental Science & Policy, 131*, 128–134. https://doi.org/10.1016/j.envsci.2022.01.023

Gooroochurn, M., Coret, J. Y., Brown, N., Venkannah, S., & Wright, A. J. (2021). Assessing the efficacy of passive measures for the tropical context of Mauritius through parametric simulations and in-situ measurement. In: *CIBSE 2021 technical symposium* (pp. 13–14). London.

Grafakos, S.,Viero, G., Reckien, D., Trigg, K., Viguie, V., Sudmant, A., Graves, C., Foley, A., Heidrich, O., Mirailles, J. M., Carter, J., Chang, L. H., Nador, C., Liseri, M., Chelleri, L., Orru, H., Orru, K., Aelenei, R., Bilska, A., ... Dawson, R. (2020). Integration of mitigation and adaptation in urban climate change action plans in Europe: A systematic assessment. *Renewable and Sustainable Energy Reviews, 121*, 109623. https://doi.org/10.1016/j.rser.2019.109623

Howard, L. (2022). When global problems come home: Engagement with climate change within the intersecting affective spaces of parenting and activism. *Emotion Space and Society*, *44*, 100894. https://doi.org/10.1016/j.emospa.2022.100894

Karnama. (2019). Energy X.0: Future of energy systems. *Results in Engineering*, *3*, 100029. https://doi.org/10.1016/j.rineng.2019.100029

Lin, K., Zhao, Y., Kuo, J., Deng, H., Cui, F., Zhang, Z., Zhang, M., Zhao, C., Gao, X., Zhou, T., & Wang, T. (2022). Toward smarter management and recovery of municipal solid waste: A critical review on deep learning approaches. *Journal of Cleaner Production*, *346*, 130943. https://doi.org/10.1016/j.jclepro.2022.130943

MacDonald, J. P., Harper, S. L., Willox, A. C., & Edge, V. L. (2013). Rigolet Inuit Community Government, a necessary voice: Climate change and lived experiences of youth in Rigolet, Nunatsiavut, Canada. *Global Environmental Change*, *23*(1), 360–371.

MacDonald, J. P., Willox, A. C., Ford, J. D., Shiwak, I., & Wood, M. (2015, September). IMHACC Team and Rigolet Inuit community government protective factors for mental health and well-being in a changing climate: Perspectives from Inuit youth in Nunatsiavut Labrador. *Social Science & Medicine*, *141*, 133–141.

Majeed, H., & Lee, J. (2017). The impact of climate change on youth depression and mental health. *The Lancet Planetary Health*, *1*(3), e94–e95.

Puzyreva, K., Henning, Z., Schelwald, R., Rassman, H., Borgnino, E., Beus, P., Casartelli, S., & Leon, D. (2022). Professionalization of community engagement in flood risk management: Insights from four European countries. *International Journal of Disaster Risk Reduction*, *71*, 102811. https://doi.org/10.1016/j.ijdrr.2022.102811

Sharma, H. B., Vanapalli, K. R., Samal, B., Cheela, V. R. S., Dubey, B. K., & Bhattacharya, J. (2021). Circular economy approach in solid waste management system to achieve UN-SDGs: Solutions for post-COVID recovery. *Science of the Total Environmental*, *800*. https://doi.org/10.1016/j.scitotenv.2021.149605

Singh, C., Madhavan, M., Arvind, J., & Bazaz, A. (2021). Climate change adaptation in Indian cities: A review of existing actions and spaces for triple wins 2021. *Urban Climate*, *36*, 100783. https://doi.org/10.1016/j.uclim.2021.100783

Singh, P., Tabe, T., & Martin, T. (2022). The role of women in community resilience to climate change: A case study of an Indigenous Fijian community. *Women's Studies International Forum*, *90*, 102550. https://doi.org/10.1016/j.wsif.2021.102550

Sliusar, N., Filkin, T., Huber-Humer, M., & Ritzkowski, M. (2022). Drone technology in municipal solid waste management and landfilling: A comprehensive review. *Waste Management*, *139*, 1–16. https://doi.org/10.1016/j.wasman.2021.12.006

Sutton, S. G., & Tobin, R. C. (2011). Constraints on community engagement with Great Barrier Reef climate change reduction and mitigation 2011. *Global Environmental Change*, *21*(3), 894–905. https://doi.org/10.1016/j.gloenvcha.2011.05.006

Vesely, S., Masson, T., Chokrai, P., Becker, A. M., Fritsche, I., Klöckner, C. A., Tiberio, L., Carrus, G., & Panno, A. (2021). Climate change action as a project of identity: Eight meta-analyses. *Global Environmental Change*, *70*, 102322.

Vyas, S., Khatri-Chhetri, A., Aggarwal, P., Thornton, P., & Campbell, B. M. (2022). Perspective: The gap between intent and climate action in agriculture Global. *Food Security*, *32*, 100612. https://doi.org/10.1016/j.gfs.2022.100612

Chapter 15

# Robotics and Automated Systems for Enabling an Industry 4.0 Transformation in Mauritius

*Mahendra Gooroochurn[a] and Riaan Stopforth[b]*

[a]University of Mauritius, Mauritius
[b]University of KwaZulu-Natal, South Africa

## Abstract

Industry 4.0 has been identified as a key cornerstone to modernise economies where man and machines complement each other seamlessly to achieve synergies in decision-making and productivity for contributing to SDG 8: Decent Work and Economic Growth and SDG 9: Industry, Innovation and Infrastructure. The integration of Industry 4.0 remains a challenge for the developing world, depending on their current status in the industrial revolution journey from its predecessors 1.0, 2.0 and 3.0. This chapter reviews reported findings in literature to highlight how robotics and automated systems can pave the way to implementing and applying the principles of Industry 4.0 for developing countries like Mauritius, where data collection, processing and analysis for decision-making and prediction are key components to be integrated or designed into industrial processes centred heavily on the use of artificial intelligence (AI) and machine learning techniques. Robotics has not yet found its way into the various industrial sectors in Mauritius, although it has been an important driver for Industry 4.0 across the world. The inherent barriers and transformations needed as well as the potential application scenarios are discussed.

*Keywords*: Robotics; automation; Industry 4.0; artificial intelligence; mechatronics; machine learning

Artificial Intelligence, Engineering Systems and Sustainable Development, 195–206
Copyright © 2024 Mahendra Gooroochurn and Riaan Stopforth
Published under exclusive licence by Emerald Publishing Limited
doi:10.1108/978-1-83753-540-820241015

## 15.1 Introduction

Industrial revolution has evolved over the years. The First Industrial Revolution consisted of the mechanical systems that were powered by steam, which started since 1784. Industrial infrastructures would use the pressure created by the steam to power the motion of pistons and turbines. Often pulley and belt systems from a single powered shaft would be used to power a factory of machinery. The Second Industrial Revolution consisted of electricity that would turn motors, which started in 1870 and would then in turn power the machines. The operation of the machines and factory environment would be of a similar fashion as with the First Industrial Revolution, by having the central shaft to be motorised, yet smaller motors are possible for the powering of individual machinery.

The Third Industrial Revolution introduced the use of power electronics with feedback sensory systems in the year 1969, allowing for the speed and position control of different actuators, to increase precision. The artificial intelligence (AI) techniques allowed for the prediction and accuracy of the processes implemented, therefore reducing error, and reducing a lot of physical labour to achieve the same results. The Fourth Industrial Revolution started in 2011, which was based on the Third Industrial Revolution, yet included the communication of devices through the internet. Devices are able to identify with the AI when repairs or services are to be implemented. Service centres can be contacted automatically by the machines and parts be ordered. Diagnostics of the machinery allows for management at different levels to be able to monitor the performance of systems. Different systems and machines can communicate with each other, allowing for the minimisation of delays in the transport and production of parts.[1] Industry 4.0 (I4.0) is widely considered as an important contributor to industrial innovation and sustainability based on its capabilities for resource optimisation through data-based prediction models and real-time decision-making by collecting data through sensor networks.

The unique advantages offered by automated systems, including robotic systems, have been well documented in literature whereby mass production at high quality is made possible along with job creation in the adjunct areas while offering competitive advantage to manufacturers. Bianco et al. (2023) further studied the contribution of Industry 4.0 in developing resilience in manufacturing companies to cope with the challenges of the COVID-19 pandemic and found a positive outcome through enhanced flexibility, reliability, robustness and responsiveness. The achievement of high levels of product quality in turn leads to customer satisfaction, which has been a key driver in embracing Industry 4.0 (Raval and Joshi, 2022). The ability for robotic systems to be adapted through the Reconfigurable Manufacturing Systems (RMS) paradigm gives flexibility to cope with market and product changes. This explains the pathways to Industrial 4.0 taken by leading nations such as the United States, the United Kingdom, Germany and Japan. The integration of robotic and automated systems is, therefore, providing a strong impetus for an Industry 4.0 transformation as confirmed by the study of Bilgen (2021), and developing countries need to find

---

[1]https://www.weforum.org/agenda/2016/01/the-fourth-industrial-revolution-what-it-means-and-how-to-respond/

means to overcome the barriers to their penetration in their industrial processes, with the lack of skilled resources identified as an impediment (Emma-Ikata and Doyle-Kent, 2022).

Azamfirei et al. (2023) concluded that beyond the technological challenges of robotic application in the Zero-Defect Manufacturing philosophy, people and process-oriented challenges are predominant barriers in the five global Swedish manufacturing companies considered. The potential for application of the Industry 4.0 framework cuts across several sectors, including the crucial food sector where underlying technologies such as AI, robotics and Internet of Things (IoT) have been found to be enablers for developing a sustainable and resilient food supply chain in support of several Sustainable Development Goals (SDGs) (SDG 1: No Poverty, SDG 2: Zero Hunger, SDG 3: Good Health and WellBeing and SDG 12: Responsible Consumption and Production) (Hassoun et al., 2022). Molinaro and Orzes (2022) investigate the application of underexploited technologies such as robotics, blockchain and augmented reality in the wood sector, from sustainable forest management and raw materials production to the fabrication of finished products.

The design of robotic systems is a highly multidisciplinary approach and well captured by the field of Mechatronics through its synergy of the mechanical, electrical and electronic and computer engineering disciplines, and as highlighted by Stopforth et al. (2016), this poses a challenge for engineers specialised in these individual areas to apply the underlying principles in a holistic manner, with collaborative efforts recommended between institutions. As highlighted by Garg et al. (2023), this complexity for choosing a suitable robotic system for a given application across the scale of enterprises is further increased by the different and advanced specifications of systems on the market, for which a fuzzy logic-based approach is proposed to guide in the selection.

The application of robotics provides the added advantage of long hours of operation and avoidance of repeated stress injuries in workers as well as preventing contact with hazardous environments, where the principles of machine learning (ML) through the Industry 4.0 framework has increased the functionality of such solutions (Javaid et al., 2021). For example, Cheng et al. (2023) report the use of robotic arms for automatic sampling of vehicle exhaust, hence avoiding human contact with emissions. Ghosh et al. (2020) discussed the current application of robotic manipulators in tele-operated mode in nuclear industry, yet posing high physical load on the operators, for which a framework to enhance the interaction with the system is proposed at various levels of complexities.

ML is not only used in decision-making processes of an enterprise but as highlighted by Escobar-Naranjo et al. (2023), an ML approach can be used as part of the design and control of the system itself, for example, for trajectory optimisation of robotic systems in obstacle avoidance. Vaisi (2022) reports the use of heuristic and meta-heuristic methods for solving robotic application problems. Benahmed et al. (2023) emphasise on the criticality of having rigorous and precise maintenance of aircraft and highlight the financial and scheduling issues that can crop up if not done properly. A robotic system is proposed for upkeep of the aircraft interior space, using machine vision and AI techniques for waste identification and collection, specifically a convolutional neural network. The lack of flexibility provided by conventional pre-programmed robotic systems is highlighted by D'Avella et al. (2023), which poses a problem in unstructured environments. The authors proposed an AI-based system using smart technologies for a jewellery loading mechanism on a production line using custom end effector, required sensors and actuators and a vision pipeline system for detecting features on the pieces to inform the picking and hooking phase of the process. An accuracy of 95% was achieved with a targeted 8s cycle time. Furthermore, Bhagwan and Evans (2023) proposed an Industry 4.0 approach to the energy crisis by increasing energy efficiency and productivity through well-informed, data-driven methods.

The possibility to integrate the virtual environment in the design of robotic and automated system opens the door for yet another emerging area of mechatronics systems design, one being the creation of digital twins to model a physical entity in a software environment (Mazumder et al., 2023). Vlădăreanu et al. (2020) discuss the development of the various components of a digital twin for a high frequency hardening robot, which again symbolises the highly multidisciplinarity of this application area. Another wide area of application from a virtual perspective is robotic process automation (RPA), which involves automation of organisational and business processes. Given the vast amount of historical datasets available over the years in companies, AI techniques become attractive avenues for automated extraction, recognition, classification, prediction and optimisation of processes. Specifically, artificial neural networks, text mining and natural language processing techniques are reported to be key AI methods used for RPA (Ribeiro et al., 2021). Gradim and Teixeira (2022) present the application of RPA for automating the processes and avoid waste and redundancy in a residential hot water solutions provider company.

### 15.1.1 Robotics and Automation for Supporting Industry 4.0

Among the various applications for robotics and automation towards supporting AI-based industrial innovation (Industry 4.0), Javaid et al. (2021) highlight the following key areas relying on the capabilities of advanced robotic and machine vision coupled with other sensing technologies such as tactile and force sensing:

- Manufacturing industry, with a vast array of applications including automated metal forming processes.
- Agriculture, where the integration of engineering solutions allows to improve energy efficiency and AI-based decision-making can improve crop yield and resource efficiency. Robotic systems have been used to replace tiresome operations such as pruning, weeding and watering.
- Smart homes where an array of appliances and home chores can be automated.
- Healthcare where robotics has been applied to augment the capabilities of surgeons, opening the door for minimally invasive surgery. Combined with imaging techniques, including automated diagnosis from images, robots have provided a plethora of medical devices and procedures that have enhanced medical interventions and reduced morbidity and recovery time.

- Automotive industry, where robotics application has been the most widely implemented and one of the first adopters of robotic solutions, where further innovation is anticipated in human–robot interaction.
- Logistics and warehousing, where robotic systems have also been heavily used for rapid and accurate retrieval and storing tasks.

Furthermore, Patange and Pandya (2023) propose the following areas of application of AI and ML specifically for the Mechanical Engineering discipline:

- Control of building services systems such as heating, ventilation and air conditioning (HVAC), water distribution and predictive maintenance.
- Diagnosis of incidents such as fire events using principles of thermodynamics, ML and quantum mechanics.
- Solution of computational fluid dynamics problems using AO tools.
- Automated guided vehicles, which is a key objective of the automotive industry.
- The wider application of robotics and machine vision in the industry.

### 15.1.2 Achievement of SDGs through Robotics and Automated Systems

Lee et al. (2022) provided valuable insights into the contribution of a green manufacturing industry as part of climate goals and general sustainable development agenda of a nation, and the specific place of robotics in this process. Among their findings, the authors report heterogeneity among the 34 countries studied from the year 1993 to 2019, that industrial robots enable a green manufacturing sector through green research and development (R&D) investment and moderation of environmental regulation, and the stimulating effect of robotics for an Industry 4.0 transformation. Based on the outcomes of the study, increased penetration of robotic systems in industry was recommended in various industries, with government incentives through innovation subsidies, tax relief and special talent subsidies, developing countries should invest in building capacity for R&D and innovation to benefit from the spillover and profit-enhancing effects of industrial robotics application beyond the automotive and electronics industries to transform other sectors.

Hanna et al. (2022) reported on the lack of regulatory and safety standards when it comes to the human–robot interaction which certain workcell configurations require, although Arana-Landín et al. (2023) concluded that Industry 4.0 technologies such as AI, IoT, Robotics, augmented and virtual reality help to reduce occupational health and safety risks. Coronado et al. (2022) reviewed the various metrics used to evaluate the quality of human–machine interface (HMI) as part of an Industry 5.0 (I5.0) framework which focuses on the social and planetary impacts of industrial activities beyond the technical attributes covered by Industry 4.0, aligned to the increasingly need to inculcate environmental, social and governance (ESG) dimensions in sustainability projects over and above mere life cycle costing analysis from an economical perspective. Within this Industry

5.0 framework, the key aspect of human–robot collaboration (HRC) is an emerging area of research (Baratta et al. (2023), Ikumapayi et al. (2023)). Gualtieri et al. (2022) investigated the influence of cognitive ergonomics in the design of human–robot collaborative assembly systems and noted an improvement in the user experience by implementing such guidelines.

Wang et al. (2023) studied the ability of robotics to reduce carbon emissions, a crucial objective of all nations to abate the climate crisis in support for SDG 13: Climate Action. They reported a clear reduction in carbon emissions with robotic application processes, with greater potential for emission reduction in less industrialised regions. Upadhyay et al. (2023) looked into the achievement of the much-coveted circular economy transformation through an Industry 4.0 pathway, with desirable societal benefits, hence making the link between Industry 4.0 and Industry 5.0. This is confirmed by the study of Zhang et al. (2022) with a positive correlation found between robotic integration in industrial processes and green productivity.

The use of AI has been reported by Calabrese et al. (2023) in the investigation stage itself to analyse the data pertaining to the adoption of Industry 4.0 as a means for industrial revolution and sustainability across more than 1,500 sustainability reports using Python's text mining libraries. Robots were among the most often reported technologies, with Asian firms reported to have the highest rate of adoption and their African counterparts, the lowest. Two distinct routes were identified underlying the Industry 4.0 transformation, namely one aiming for operational efficiency with the associated environmental benefits considered as secondary achievements, and another path balancing innovation and environmental goals at the outset. Firms in the east were generally found to follow the first route whereas Western firms the latter. It was remarked that African and South American businesses were at a very early stage in their Industry 4.0 and sustainability journey.

## 15.2 Related Background Theory

A robot is a mechatronics system, which integrates mechanical, electrical and computer engineering concepts to perform processes, broadly classified as robotic manipulators and mobile robotic systems. The precise positioning of the robotic system with respect to the work environment is a crucial component of the system design, where closed-loop control is applied using encoders at joints of robotic manipulators and visual information gathered from cameras mounted on the robot itself or externally. The configuration of the robotic manipulator links and joints provides a mathematical transformation that governs the kinematics of the robot end effector with respect to a base coordinate system, providing an effective model for open-loop control. A similar theoretical mathematical transformation is possible for mobile robotic system, although wheel slippage renders open-loop control complicated.

Therefore, the use of image processing and analysis methods in the field of robotics is common to provide visual inputs for augmenting their capabilities, in addition to other sensing modalities such as tactile and force responsiveness. AI consists of different techniques for reasoning, learning and problem-solving from a non-natural entity, such as a computer, and typically derives intelligence from past data or by repeatedly performing a task and learning from the outcome in what is referred to as reinforcement learning. Given the valuable contribution of sensor data for optimising robotic tasks and the unique optimisation possibilities offered by AI algorithms for data-driven processes, it is clear why the integration of robotics with AI has become widespread across various sectors of the industry, and is a good candidate to support an Industry 4.0 transformation.

This chapter will look in more detail the industrial progress and problems experienced with Industry 4.0 in the Mauritius context. Even though this chapter deals with problems experienced in Mauritius, similar issues are to be dealt with in other low-income or third world countries.

## 15.3 Industrial Context of Mauritius and Barriers to Industry 4.0

Mauritius has systematically diversified from sugarcane production since the 1980s and presently has an economy based on manufacturing, agriculture, financial services and tourism as well as a growing information and communication technology (ICT) sector accounting for over 5% of gross domestic product (GDP). In the year 2021, the imports were valued at around Rs 215 billion while exports were around Rs 82 billion. The manufacturing sector represents over 10% of the GDP and employs over 55,000 staff. The agriculture sector has a labour force of over 8,000 with a 3.3% contribution to the GDP.[2] In the aftermath of the COVID-19 lockdowns, a strong focus has been laid on the tourism sector as a pillar for economic recovery targeting 1 million tourist arrivals. The sector contributed to 23.9% of GDP prior to the pandemic.

Digitalisation has been a key strategy for the government, including in the delivery of services and operations to the citizens as well as policies to transform the insurance and banking sectors together with the necessary legal framework for cybersecurity. The digitalisation objectives of the nation bode well for supporting an Industry 4.0 transformation.

### 15.3.1 Robotics and Automated Systems for Industry 4.0 Transformation in Mauritius

In light of the literature findings reported in the earlier sections of this chapter, and given the distribution of the economic sectors, with growing ICT and financial sectors, where robotic process automation can contribute massively by improving organisational and business operations, the manufacturing and agricultural sectors have known downward trends in the past decades. The pandemic has been an acid test for all countries around the world with regard to their self-sufficiency and resilience and the heavy dependence of Mauritius on imports

---

[2]https://statsmauritius.govmu.org/SitePages/Index.aspx

for supply of its raw materials and food and on the tourism sector was clear observations of the fragility of the economy. On the other hand, advances made in the ICT sector served as great support to maintain services across various sector, including healthcare through remote consultation, in education through online classes and in general through the work from home modality.

A strategic goal of government is to embrace circular economy (CE) principles to improve the resilience of the country in key areas such as energy, materials and water. Clearly, adoption of robotic and automation solutions across these sectors, including the challenging manufacturing and agricultural sectors, are areas of high potential to address the systemic challenges faced over time in the form of reduced competitive advantage with respect to regional and international countries. The wide spectrum of application areas reported in literature provide a strong basis for the Industry 4.0 transformation of Mauritius, where the technical and human resource barriers currently exist, and hence need to be addressed through capacity building, R&D and partnership among local, regional and global institutions to bring about the essential ecosystem of partnerships needed to surmount these challenges. The availability of robotic farming system commercially, referred to as 'farmbots', is a promising area for integrating technology in the agricultural sector to attract our younger generation to enter this essential sector to develop food resilience. Along the same line, a range of automated solutions has been witnessed over the past years to regulate the nutrient supply in hydroponics systems in sheltered greenhouse farming that offers protection against weather vagaries and pests, where IoT solutions are used to monitor and modulate the interior environmental conditions to optimise plant growth. The developmental pathways of developing and developed countries and the associated frameworks used to develop the bespoke route for the country needs to be developed.

As a small island developing state (SIDS), Mauritius is particularly exposed to the effect of climate change with potentially disastrous consequences for the tourism sector, and Industry 4.0 can serve as a means for both developing resilience for a sustainable development of the economy and for technological innovation. Robotics and automation have a clear role to play in this process. Although automation can be considered to be integrated in industry across production and manufacturing industries as well as robotic process automation in business, the area of robotics is currently applied to a limited extent to have the desired impact at national level. Robotic solutions have been reported in the textile and food production sectors where automated systems are used for conveyance and sorting of end products as well as automated diagnostics of quality of production. Therefore, strategies and associated policies need to be evolved at national level to increase the penetration of robotics in industries across all sectors, including manufacturing, agriculture and tourism through capacity building and innovation to develop customised robotic application solutions. By embracing an Industry 4.0 paradigm, the data-driven, scientific approach it entails will usher the country into a new era of technological innovation for optimising our processes while supporting our sustainability goals in the form of the SDGs as well as providing a powerful basis to building disaster risk management capabilities.

## 15.4 Discussion and Conclusion

Based on the key literature findings reviewed, this chapter has clearly established the appeal for developing countries to embrace an AI-based developmental pathway for taking the next step in their economic growth to overcome systemic barriers, well encapsulated by the Industry 4.0 framework. The application of AI techniques, which have matured over the last decade and readily available in the public domain through shared source distributions, is an essential enabler, as the data-driven dimension allows to continuously base important decisions about the process or equipment control to be made judiciously. The existence of proven, robust technological solutions, established framework to model and predict the influence of factors important for a successful transformation and documentation of success story pathways are vital resources that need to be applied in this process.

The favourable economic returns coupled with the proven support for the sustainability and a circular economy, allowing to promote green productivity and reduction of carbon emissions, are vital levers for adopting robotics and automated solutions across the economy. To nurture the necessary ecosystem for this process to unveil, it is essential that adequate human resources are developed in the associated areas, both at general level through undergraduate degrees, specialised courses at master level as well as professional courses. Research funding should be provided to study and recommend the appropriate developmental pathway for Mauritius, with a balanced consideration for economic growth and sustainable development. The contribution of robotic solutions in vital sectors such as agriculture, manufacturing and tourism for Mauritius and similar developing countries can attract our younger generation to embark in these professions as opposed to just white collar jobs, provided an Industry 4.0 paradigm is adopted so that cutting-edge technologies are applied to align to the aspirations of this e-generation.

## References

Arana-Landín, G., Laskurain-Iturbe, I., Iturrate, M., & Landeta-Manzano, B. (2023). Assessing the influence of Industry 4.0 technologies on occupational health and safety. *Heliyon*, e13720. https://doi.org/10.1016/j.heliyon.2023.e13720

Azamfirei, V., Granlund, A., & Lagrosen, Y. (2023). Lessons from adopting robotic in-line quality inspection in the Swedish manufacturing industry. *Procedia Computer Science, 217*, 386–394. https://doi.org/10.1016/j.procs.2022.12.234

Baratta, A., Cimino, A., Gnoni, M. G., & Longo, F. (2023). Human robot collaboration in Industry 4.0: A literature review. *Procedia Computer Science, 217*, 1887–1895. https://doi.org/10.1016/j.procs.2022.12.389

Benahmed, B. D., Jeffali, F., El Barkany, A., & Bakdid, A. (2023). Design and realization of an aeronautical cleaning robot for aircraft maintenance 4.0 based on artificial intelligence. *Materials Today: Proceedings, 72*(Part 7), 3521–3526. https://doi.org/10.1016/j.matpr.2022.08.254

Bhagwan, N., & Evans, M. (2023). A review of industry 4.0 technologies used in the production of energy in China, Germany, and South Africa. *Renewable and Sustainable Energy Reviews, 173*, 113075. https://doi.org/10.1016/j.rser.2022.113075

Bianco, D., Bueno, A., Filho, M. G., Latan, H., Ganga, G. M. D., Frank, A. G., & Jabbour, C. J. C. (2023). The role of Industry 4.0 in developing resilience for manufacturing companies during COVID-19. *International Journal of Production Economics, 256*, 108728. https://doi.org/10.1016/j.ijpe.2022.108728

Bilgen, H. (2021). A global comparison methodology to determine critical requirements for achieving industry 4.0. *Technological Forecasting and Social Change, 172*, 121036. https://doi.org/10.1016/j.techfore.2021.121036

Calabrese, A., Costa, R., Tiburzi, L., & Brem, A. (2023). Merging two revolutions: A human-artificial intelligence method to study how sustainability and Industry 4.0 are intertwined. *Technological Forecasting and Social Change, 188*, 122265. https://doi.org/10.1016/j.techfore.2022.122265

Cheng, X., Zhou, J., Zhou, Z., Zhao, X., Gao, J., & Qiao, T. (2023). An improved RRT-connect path planning algorithm of robotic arm for automatic sampling of exhaust emission detection in industry 4.0. *Journal of Industrial Information Integration, 33*, 100436. ISSN 2452-414X. https://doi.org/10.1016/j.jii.2023.100436

Coronado, E., Kiyokawa, T., Ricardez, G. A. G., Ramirez-Alpizar, I. G., Venture, G., & Yamanobe, N. (2022). Evaluating quality in human-robot interaction: A systematic search and classification of performance and human-centered factors, measures and metrics towards an industry 5.0. *Journal of Manufacturing Systems, 63*, 392–410. https://doi.org/10.1016/j.jmsy.2022.04.007

D'Avella, S., Avizzano, C. A., & Tripicchio, P. (2023). ROS-Industrial based robotic cell for Industry 4.0: Eye-in-hand stereo camera and visual servoing for flexible, fast, and accurate picking and hooking in the production line. *Robotics and Computer-Integrated Manufacturing, 80*, 102453. https://doi.org/10.1016/j.rcim.2022.102453

Emma-Ikata, D., & Doyle-Kent, M. (2022). Industry 5.0 readiness – "Optimization of the relationship between humans and robots in manufacturing companies in Southeast of Ireland". *IFAC-PapersOnLine, 55*(39), 419–424. https://doi.org/10.1016/j.ifacol.2022.12.071

Escobar-Naranjo, J., Caiza, G., Garcia, C. A., Ayala, P., & Garcia, M. V. (2023). Applications of Artificial Intelligence Techniques for trajectories optimization in robotics mobile platforms. *Procedia Computer Science, 217*, 543–551. https://doi.org/10.1016/j.procs.2022.12.250

Garg, C. P., Görçün, Ö. F., Kundu, P., & Küçükönder, H. (2023). An integrated fuzzy MCDM approach based on Bonferroni functions for selection and evaluation of industrial robots for the automobile manufacturing industry. *Expert Systems with Applications, 213*(Part A), 118863. https://doi.org/10.1016/j.eswa.2022.118863

Ghosh, A., Alonso Paredes Soto, D., Veres, S. M., & Rossiter, A. (2020). Human robot interaction for future remote manipulations in industry 4.0∗. In R. Findeisen, S. Hirche, K. Janschek, & M. Mönnigmann (Eds.), *IFAC-PapersOnLine. 21st IFAC World congress*, 11–17. July 2020 (pp. 10223–10228). Berlin: International Federation of Automatic Control (IFAC). https://doi.org/10.1016/j.ifacol.2020.12.2752

Gradim, B., & Teixeira, L. (2022). Robotic process automation as an enabler of Industry 4.0 to eliminate the eighth waste: A study on better usage of human talent. *Procedia Computer Science, 204*, 643–651. https://doi.org/10.1016/j.procs.2022.08.078

Gualtieri, L., Fraboni, F., De Marchi, M., & Rauch, E. (2022). Development and evaluation of design guidelines for cognitive ergonomics in human-robot collaborative assembly systems. *Applied Ergonomics, 104*, 103807. https://doi.org/10.1016/j.apergo.2022.103807

Hanna, A., Larsson, S., Götvall, P., & Bengtsson, K. (2022). Deliberative safety for industrial intelligent human–robot collaboration: Regulatory challenges and solutions for taking the next step towards industry 4.0. *Robotics and Computer-Integrated Manufacturing, 78*, 102386. https://doi.org/10.1016/j.rcim.2022.102386

Hassoun, A., Prieto, M. A., Carpena, M., Bouzembrak, Y., Marvin, H. J. P., Pallarés, N., Barba, F. J., Bangar, S. P., Chaudhary, V., Ibrahim, S., & Bono, G. (2022). Exploring the role of green and Industry 4.0 technologies in achieving sustainable development goals in food sectors. *Food Research International, 162*(Part B). 112068. https://doi.org/10.1016/j.foodres.2022.112068

Ikumapayi, O. M., Afolalu, S. A., Ogedengbe, T. S., Kazeem, R. A., & Akinlabi, E. T. (2023). Human-robot Co-working Improvement via revolutionary automation and robotic technologies – An overview. *Procedia Computer Science, 217*, 1345–1353. https://doi.org/10.1016/j.procs.2022.12.332

Javaid, M., Haleem, A., Singh, R. P., & Suman, R. (2021). Substantial capabilities of robotics in enhancing industry 4.0 implementation. *Cognitive Robotics, 1*, 58–75. https://doi.org/10.1016/j.cogr.2021.06.001

Lee, C., Qin, S., & Li, Y. (2022). Does industrial robot application promote green technology innovation in the manufacturing industry? *Technological Forecasting and Social Change, 183*, 121893. https://doi.org/10.1016/j.techfore.2022.121893

Mazumder, A., Sahed, M. F., Tasneem, Z., Das, P., Badal, F. R., Ali, M. F., Ahamed, M. H., Abhi, S. H., Sarker, S. K., Das, S. K., Hasan, M. M., Islam, M. M., & Islam, M. R. (2023). Towards next generation digital twin in robotics: Trends, scopes, challenges, and future. *Heliyon, 9*(2), e13359. https://doi.org/10.1016/j.heliyon.2023.e13359

Molinaro, M., & Orzes, G. (2022). From forest to finished products: The contribution of Industry 4.0 technologies to the wood sector. *Computers in Industry, 138*, 103637. https://doi.org/10.1016/j.compind.2022.103637

Patange, G. S., & Pandya, A. B. (2023). How artificial intelligence and machine learning assist in industry 4.0 for mechanical engineers. *Materials Today: Proceedings, 72*(Part 3), 622–625. https://doi.org/10.1016/j.matpr.2022.08.201

Raval, M. B., & Joshi, H. (2022). Categorical framework for implementation of industry 4.0 techniques in medium-scale bearing manufacturing industries. *Materials Today: Proceedings, 65*(Part 8), 3531–3537. https://doi.org/10.1016/j.matpr.2022.06.090

Ribeiro, J., Lima, R., Eckhardt, T., & Paiva, S. (2021). Robotic process automation and artificial Intelligence in Industry 4.0 – A literature review. *Procedia Computer Science, 181*, 51–58. https://doi.org/10.1016/j.procs.2021.01.104

Stopforth, R., Davrajh, S., & Ferrein, A. (2016). *"South African robotics entity for a collaboration initiative,"* 2016 Pattern Recognition Association of South Africa and Robotics and Mechatronics International Conference (pp. 1–6). PRASA-RobMech. https://doi.10.1109/RoboMech.2016.7813144

Upadhyay, A., Balodi, K. C., Naz, F., Di Nardo, M., & Jraisat, L. (2023). Implementing industry 4.0 in the manufacturing sector: Circular economy as a societal solution. *Computers & Industrial Engineering, 177*, 109072. https://doi.org/10.1016/j.cie.2023.109072

Vaisi, B. (2022). A review of optimization models and applications in robotic manufacturing systems: Industry 4.0 and beyond. *Decision Analytics Journal, 2*, 100031. https://doi.org/10.1016/j.dajour.2022.100031

Vlădăreanu, L., Gal, A. I., Melinte, O. D., Vlădăreanu, V., Iliescu, M., Bruja, A., Feng, Y., & Ciocîrlan, A. (2020). Robot digital twin towards Industry 4.0. *IFAC-PapersOnLine, 53*(Issue 2), 10867–10872. https://doi.org/10.1016/j.ifacol.2020.12.2815

Wang, J., Wang, W., Liu, Y., & Wu, H. (2023). Can industrial robots reduce carbon emissions? Based on the perspective of energy rebound effect and labor factor flow in China. *Technology in Society, 72*, 102208. https://doi.org/10.1016/j.techsoc.2023.102208

Zhang, Q., Zhang, F., & Mai, Q. (2022). Robot adoption and green productivity: Curse or Boon. *Sustainable Production and Consumption, 34*, 1–11. https://doi.org/10.1016/j.spc.2022.08.025

Chapter 16

# Potential Beneficial Impact of AI-Driven Atmospheric Corrosion Prediction on the UN Sustainable Development Goals (SDGs)

*Yashwantraj Seechurn*

University of Mauritius, Mauritius

## Abstract

The complexity of atmospheric corrosion, further compounded by the effects of climate change, makes existing models inappropriate for corrosion prediction. The commonly used kinetic model and dose-response functions are restricted in their capacity to represent the non-linear behaviour of corrosion phenomena. The application of artificial intelligence (AI)-driven machine learning algorithms to corrosion data can better represent the corrosion mechanism by considering the dynamic behaviour due to changing climatic conditions. Effective use of materials, coating systems and maintenance strategies can then be made with such a corrosivity model. Accurate corrosion prediction will help to improve climate change resilience of the social, economic and energy infrastructure in line with the UN Sustainable Development Goals (SDGs) 7 (Affordable and Clean Energy), 9 (Industry, Innovation and Infrastructure) and 13 (Climate Action). This chapter discusses atmospheric corrosion prediction in relation to the SDGs and the influence of AI in overcoming the challenges.

*Keywords*: Corrosion phenomena; atmospheric aerosols; infrastructure degradation; neural network model; climate resilience; failure prediction

## 16.1 Corrosion Impacts and the Influencing Factors

Infrastructure systems are vulnerable to atmospheric corrosion, leading to major issues worldwide. All forms of physical infrastructure are impacted. Maintenance

*Artificial Intelligence, Engineering Systems and Sustainable Development*, 207–218
Copyright © 2024 Yashwantraj Seechurn
Published under exclusive licence by Emerald Publishing Limited
doi:10.1108/978-1-83753-540-820241016

costs rise, product lifespans decrease and end-of-life management becomes more important. Corrosion has a high societal cost. Replacement, protection and inhibition costs are examples of direct corrosion expenses, while losses due to fire/ spills, equipment downtime, product contamination, environmental damage and overdesigned components are all indirect costs. According to estimates, corrosion is responsible for 5% of a country's gross domestic product (GDP) in direct costs, with atmospheric corrosion costs representing 30%–50% of the total amount (Ríos Rojas et al., 2015).

Atmospheric corrosion is a natural phenomenon that results in material degradation due to reactions involving the material and various chemicals, with multiplex ties in the surrounding environment. Corrosion kinetics is a function of environmental/climatic variables, with a geospatial variation that complicates corrosion control. The shift in weather patterns, due to climate change, adds another layer to this puzzle. An assessment of the future impacts of corrosion on the built infrastructure necessitates a review of the key factors influencing atmospheric corrosion.

### 16.1.1 Relative Humidity (RH)

The formation of a thin surface film of water brought about by rainwater/mist or cyclic condensation (from atmospheric water vapour) is usually the onset of an atmospheric corrosion process, which is fundamentally of electrochemical nature. A wet or alternately wet and dry surface is conducive to the rapid progression of corrosion. The surface water content is influenced by several factors, including surface type and composition, RH, temperature and precipitation. Changes in RH and temperature result in recurrent cycles of wetting and drying, which affect the corrosion rate (Soares et al., 2014). The nature, frequency and duration of these wet and dry intervals govern the formation of the corrosion layer structure and its composition.

In low-salinity and non-polluted areas, RH can be the key factor in increasing the corrosion rate (Seechurn, Wharton, et al., 2022). In chloride-rich environments, condensation on metal surfaces occurs at a RH lower than 100% due to the salinity of the water (Landolt, 2007). Condensation has also been observed to occur on porous surfaces at relative humidities lower than those at which it would occur on flat surfaces. Furthermore, changes in the temperature-humidity complex may lead to a high frequency of the wet/dry cycles, thereby accelerating corrosion. Time-of-Wetness (TOW) is ametric that can be used for RH and is a measure of atmospheric corrosivity. TOW is simply the duration when RH is above 80%, which typically causes surfaces to get damp. The concentration of aggressive species in the electrolyte would likely grow with a larger TOW; however, in some circumstances, a bulkier electrolyte may slow the rate of reactants, migration to the metal surface.

### 16.1.2 Marine Aerosols

Changes in extreme weather events, expected with climate change, such as more frequent and intense storms/cyclones, will result in increased ocean salt deposition. This will cause the thickening of the electrolyte forming on the surface, which is usually associated with the deliquescence of salt particles. Marine salts stimulate electrochemical activity with an increase in corrosion current and can settle on surfaces in two ways: by being dissolved into precipitation or fog droplets, or by falling to the ground undiluted. Back surfaces, which are not washed by rain, have a higher concentration of such contaminants (Sabir & Ibrahim, 2017). Therefore, chlorides that emerge from the evaporation of seawater are either droplets or crystals when they come into touch with metal surfaces. Salt-induced corrosion occurs on a wet surface (Alcántara et al., 2017). When a metal is exposed to water or moisture, it causes a thin film to form, which traps water in specific areas, resulting in a thick electrolyte when surface marine salts dissolve in the liquid. The electrolyte's conductivity is consequently enhanced, which can cause the breakdown of any protective layer (Alcántara et al., 2017; Sabir & Ibrahim, 2017). The severity of the damage increases with a rise in chloride ($Cl^-$) concentration.

Wind velocity and direction influence the salt deposition rate (Seechurn, Surnam, et al., 2022; Vera et al., 2018). It should be noted that the existence of crashing waves in marine areas leads to the production of larger sizes of salt particles in the atmosphere. However, small particles are more easily carried by the wind and tend to predominate further inland from the coast. Nevertheless, aerosol salinity *vs.* distance shows a non-linear relationship due to the effects of barriers and surface washing by rain (Corvo et al., 2008).

### 16.1.3 Gaseous Pollutants

Human activities that generate sulphur dioxide ($SO_2$) contribute significantly to atmospheric corrosion. Combustion of fossil fuels (gas and oil) in industries like power generation and transportation are major contributors to $SO_2$ emissions. The concentration of $SO_2$ in the atmosphere changes mostly with the distance from the emission source and the direction of the wind. An unpolluted atmosphere would have an $SO_2$ content of less than 10 g m$^{-3}$, whereas a polluted one would have a concentration of 10–100 g m$^{-3}$ (Landolt, 2007).

In addition to $SO_2$, the group of nitrogen oxides known as $NO_x$ also has a role in promoting corrosion but to a considerably smaller extent. $NO_x$ can be corrosive when it forms nitric acid in the air (Kreislova & Knotkova, 2017). Sources of $NO_x$ are mainly, but are not limited to, emissions from motor vehicles (high-temperature combustion systems). Furthermore, hostile airborne particles, excluding sea salts, may be deposited as sulphur-adsorbing soot, which results from incomplete combustion when fuel is burned in power stations, incinerators, diesel engines, etc. A high amount of rainfall is known to be highly effective in washing off pollutants deposited on metal surfaces, thereby decreasing the corrosion rate. However, at least 600 mm of rainfall is required for this to occur

(Vera et al., 2018), otherwise rainfall is more likely to speed up corrosion with the increased presence of an electrolyte.

Corrosion can have a significant impact on developing nations, which rely heavily on coal and heavy-oil power generation. Pollution from power industries emitting $SO_2$ is largely unregulated because countries often lack the policy framework to restrict emissions from electricity production. Large industries with extensive engineering infrastructure often support the overarching drive for economic growth. Although these sectors are vital to the country's economic development, the rapid increase in industrial output coupled with the ageing of the underlying infrastructure has led to an increase in the destructive impacts of corrosion. This puts extra strain on already overburdened essential infrastructures. Long-term AI-based modelling of atmospheric corrosion would greatly contribute to extending the useful life of civil infrastructures, with minimal upkeep.

## 16.2 Conventional Methods of Corrosion Prediction

The kinetic model, as a power function, has been extensively used in predictions of the atmospheric corrosion of metals (Alcántara et al., 2017). There is wide acceptance that corrosion damage ($D$) vs. exposure duration ($t$) follows a power law as shown by Eq. (16.1).

$$D = At^n \tag{16.1}$$

where constants $A$ and $n$ indicate the atmosphere's corrosivity and the corrosion layer's protectiveness.

Typically, the power function shown by Eq. (16.2), which involves the logarithmic conversion of $D$ and $t$, is used to fit the corrosion data (Alcántara et al., 2017).

$$\log D = \log A + n \log t \tag{16.2}$$

Interpretation of the two constants ($A$ and $n$) provides valuable insight such that corrosion results could be extrapolated to obtain corresponding values for at least 20 years using 4-year exposure data (De La Fuente et al., 2016). For plain carbon steel, typical exponent $n$ values fall between 0.26 and 0.76 in non-marine atmospheres and between 0.37 and 0.98 in marine atmospheres, with a trend towards attaining higher values in the latter (Alcántara et al., 2017). A recent study on marine atmospheric corrosion of S235 structural carbon steel in Port-Louis (Mauritius) has shown that the coastal locations, of characteristically low airborne salinity, have values of $n$ less than or slightly higher than 0.5 (Seechurn, Wharton, et al., 2022). To calculate the extent of corrosion during any given period, it is necessary to acquire $A$ and $n$, particular to each material and its related environment, through field tests of at least 1-year duration and then insert these values into Eq. (16.1).

The value of the exponent $n$ also indicates the physicochemical characteristics of the surface layer, providing insight into the atmospheric conditions, the effect of weather parameters such as TOW and the other environmental factors of major influence. Eq. (16.1) is a mass-balance equation that demonstrates how the diffusion process is rate-determining, and this rate depends on the diffusive properties of the corrosion layer acting as a barrier between the substrate and the other reactants (Benarie & Lipfert, 1986). The progression of corrosion product development can be inferred from the value of $n$. When $n$ is between 0.5 and 1.0, the corrosion layer's protective efficacy is poor due to an accentuation of the diffusion process. In contrast, $n$ less than 0.5 suggests corrosion product build-up is in accordance with a parabolic function, thereby successfully preventing hostile species from reaching the underlying metal surface (Castaño et al., 2010). Changes in the corrosion layer with a more compact structure, recrystallisation and clustering of particles lead to a reduction in the overall diffusive power. In a perfect diffusion-controlled mechanism, where all corrosion products remain on the metal surface, the rate of corrosion will follow an exponential law with $n$ close to 0.5 (Benarie & Lipfert, 1986). This appears to be the case in inland atmospheres of characteristically mild pollution. Since $n$ equal to 1 is the theoretical upper bound for unrestricted diffusion, $n$ greater than 1 would imply the complete absence of any layer or a highly pervious one. This occurs in extreme marine atmospheres where corrosion layers are most likely to be detached as flakes due to exfoliation, cracking, erosion or simply dissolution. A value of $n$ more than 1 indicates a coastal region regardless of the $Cl^-$ content (Benarie & Lipfert, 1986). Nonetheless, long-duration field tests have not been performed in various marine regions, resulting in a scarcity of corrosion data (Alcántara et al., 2017). Mathematical models may not be eventually validated with recorded data of corrosion rates, to be used for determining the corrosion rates for longer periods. Therefore, $n$ has limited predictive capacity, given that the application of a kinetic model obtained for a particular atmosphere to other regions may be inadequate.

Large-scale worldwide cooperative research programmes, such as ISO-CORRAG and MICAT, have made considerable strides in developing 'damage functions' in globally coordinated initiatives on atmospheric corrosion (Almeida et al., 2000; Knotkova et al., 2010). Damage functions relate corrosion rate to environmental variables, thus enabling the estimation of corrosion at specific locations without the need for lengthy and costly field experiments. Attempts were made to use these functions (also known as 'dose-response' equations) under the conditions prevalent in the Czech Republic to see if they are accurate or if adjustments need to be made (Kreislova & Knotkova, 2017). It was revealed that the $SO_2$ level used in these calculations was measured over a certain duration, and the gaseous pollutant concentration had changed over time. Years with extremely high levels of $SO_2$ had not been included in the data used to create these models, resulting in a disparity between expected and actual corrosion loss for sites exposed to $SO_2$ concentrations above 90 mg m$^{-2}$ d$^{-1}$.

A detailed understanding of the wind regime could be sufficient to predict corrosion in a purely saline atmosphere, given that corrosion would be expected to completely depend on the deposition of $Cl^-$ on the surfaces driven by the wind action. This would avoid carrying out long-time exposures in the atmosphere.

However, deterministic models representing Cl⁻ level as a function of environmental factors, which have been developed from previous experimental work, are
only accurate when applied to the region studied, due to subtly different conditions existing elsewhere (Meira et al., 2008).

## 16.3 Machine Learning Techniques Used in Corrosion Prediction

Forecasts of atmospheric corrosion and implementation of anti-corrosion designs
can be enhanced with the aid of data mining and modelling techniques. Atmospheric corrosion is a non-linear physiochemical phenomenon with complex
chemical kinetics complicating corrosion prediction, thus requiring the use of
analytical and numerical models. High dimensional data are involved, and multiple variables are associated with the atmospheric corrosion process. Regression
algorithms have proven to be inadequate in the analysis of atmospheric corrosion
data, with the dose-response functions often over-estimating corrosion categories
(Castañeda et al., 2016; Díaz & López, 2007). The use of artificial intelligence (AI)
in managing corrosion risks can benefit society in many ways e.g. by facilitating
damage detection/prediction on infrastructures such as bridges, transmission
towers, steel pipelines and port facilities (Nash et al., 2018). Branches of AI such
as machine learning (ML) and genetic programming have been deemed very
accurate and reliable in the estimation of corrosion rate, with the prediction
accuracy usually evaluated from the R-squared statistical measure (Diao et al.,
2021; Mythreyi et al., 2021; Seechurn & Chuttoo, 2022; Thanush et al., 2022).

ML models are particularly useful when multiple variables are involved. The
application of ML algorithm to data from marine atmospheric corrosion studies
has resulted in better mapping of predictive relationships (Yan et al., 2020). One
of the most promising ML techniques in atmospheric corrosion research is Deep
Neural Network (DNN), an improved version of Artificial Neural Network
(ANN), which is a computing system made up of a network of neurons inspired
by the human brain (Coelho et al., 2022; Nash et al., 2018). In atmospheric
corrosion modelling, a neural network typically consists of a first layer of neurons,
each representing a meteorological/pollution parameter with the sole purpose of
receiving and relaying entering data, an output layer which is usually made up of
a single neuron representing corrosion rate, mass loss or penetration depth and
one or more intermediate/hidden layers with neurons which are non-linear
transfer functions. The latter contributes to the learning process with the aim of
establishing relations between the independent and dependent parameters.
DNNs, with multiple hidden layers compared to a single hidden layer for ANNs,
could be more effective in complex atmospheric corrosion situations as encoun-
tered in microclimates whereby the mechanism of interaction between various
environment factors has not been well established.

The efficiency of an ANN is highly affected by the topology, defined by the
number and type of connections between neurons, which makes up a well-designed
network called a multi-layer perceptron. The network can learn more complex
scenarios if it has more neurons in its hidden layer (Díaz & López, 2007). Fig. 16.1

Input layer     Hidden layer     Output layer

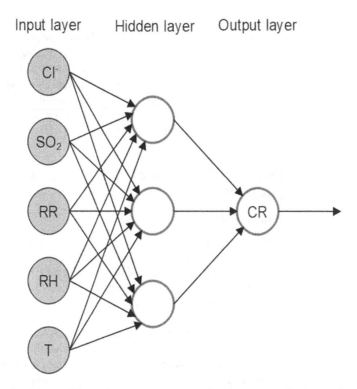

Fig. 16.1.   Three-Layer Perceptron for Atmospheric Corrosion
Prediction With 5 Input Parameters ($Cl^-$ – Chloride, $SO_2$ – Sulphur Dioxide,
RR – Rainfall, RH – Relative Humidity and T – Temperature) and 1 Output
Parameter (CR – Corrosion Rate).

shows a neural network as applied to atmospheric corrosion prediction. Such a
three-layer perceptron is known to give accurate results in function approximation
tasks (Pintos et al., 2000). ANN atmospheric corrosion models must be designed
using experimental data of the influencing environmental factors at each test site
and the observed corrosion rates. The results are improved with a proper network
designed/built from interconnected neurons across multiple hidden layers, forming
a DNN, and large experimental data sets to train the model using relevant
software.

The links connecting one neuron to another across layers are called synapses,
and these carry weights that define the strength of the inter-neuron ties. The data
transmitted to each neuron in the first hidden layer are the summation of the
product of the inputs and corresponding synaptic weights, which are then
modulated via a transfer function. The resulting value is carried to the next layer
again as a weighted average and so on, behaving as a feedforward type network.

The backpropagation training algorithm allows revision of the synaptic connection weights in a reverse direction to reduce the errors observed when comparing the predicted and measured values until an acceptable threshold of error is met. The performance is assessed by the mean square error and residual distribution (Pintos et al., 2000). An adequate knowledge of corrosion processes is required to select the input parameters and consequently interpret the collected data. The use of DNNs can lead to useful numerical models for the assessment of useful life, the costs associated with degradation and corrosion kinetics.

## 16.4 Impact of Corrosion Prediction on the UN Sustainable Development Goals (SDGs)

### 16.4.1 SDG 13 – Climate Action

For the implementation of adequate corrosion management and protection measures, long-term atmospheric corrosion forecasting should consider the impact of environmental factors in the wake of climate change. Temperature, humidity and rainfall play a key part in this intricate process and ongoing changes in such environmental factors could affect corrosion rates. For example, rainfall is expected to become more intense and less frequent in the future (Nguyen et al., 2013), implying less washing-off of pollutants, and the production of marine aerosols may be influenced by shifts in wind patterns. Power generation from coal or heavy oil can further affect local climate conditions since sulphate aerosol and acid rain are both influenced by humidity levels in the atmosphere (Cole & Paterson, 2010). It has been observed that corrosion kinetics in some inland locations are mostly affected by the 24-hour day/night RH cycle (Trivedi et al., 2014). However, rising global temperatures caused by global warming will diminish RH in the years to come. Thus, there will be a lower corrosion rate at these locations due to reduced nighttime condensation, given RH induces condensation, especially at night.

### 16.4.2 SDG 9 – Industry, Innovation and Infrastructure

Building infrastructure in the face of the climate issue is a complex problem. The effects of climate change are both dynamic and geographical; however, the majority of the current models of infrastructure performance assume constant weather conditions (Stewart & Deng, 2015). Building and restoring human infrastructure uses a lot of resources, which have an environmental cost of their own in the form of the materials being used. This is due in large part to concerns about the long-term viability of the materials used in construction, particularly related to corrosion, which hastens the deterioration of structures and poses a special problem for the emerging economies of the world. Over time, corrosion can cause damage to buildings and critical infrastructure, which is not only costly to fix but also harmful to the environment because of metal run-off. The need to advance our knowledge of sustainable procedures and materials for construction has never been greater than it is now, given the world's limited resources and changing climatic trends.

### 16.4.3 SDG 7 – Affordable and Clean Energy

Facilities set up in renewable energy industries are susceptible to atmospheric corrosion, especially in harsh marine/industrial environments. Wind and solar farms with various equipment (wind generators, heat exchangers, etc.) and fittings are mainly metal structures and components. It is common for metallic components forming part of the supporting structure for photovoltaics in the solar energy sector, installed in coastal regions, to start corroding after only 1 year in service (Bender et al., 2022). Low energy output and high maintenance costs can result from a system plagued by frequent component failures. This has a consequence in terms of energy costs to the end users. Therefore, forecasting corrosion behaviour is vital for the proper design of energy equipment to meet safety and reliability standards at a reasonable cost.

Marine renewable energy devices such as wave energy converters, offshore wind turbines and tidal stream generators are among those which have to be considered for the development of robust corrosion protection systems (Musabikha et al., 2017). Corrosion-resistant alloys or cathodic protection techniques have been widely employed in such cases. However, these would still require frequent inspection and monitoring. The application of AI in extracting valuable information in the form of images or data from the marine structures to be then processed using a suitable algorithm would go a long way into extending the maintenance intervals and provide opportunities for in-time remedial actions with a better prediction of failures.

## 16.5 Conclusion

The future of cities/towns and energy infrastructure depends on our ability to find solutions on how to control material corrosion and slow down corrosion rates. Corrosion modelling of a specific metal, based on environmental characteristics, for forecasting, is an essential field of study that needs to be prioritised. With an AI-based model, we can better understand how the changing climate will affect the pace at which metals corrode in the atmosphere. In the pursuit of a more sustainable future, it would help to achieve the goal of lowering the costs associated with any corrosion damage that may occur and pave the way for more environmentally friendly infrastructures.

The purpose is to back innovative approaches to industrial policy in developing nations so that they can promote economic growth without compromising climate and sustainability targets. This move to greener construction is also a challenge for low and middle-income countries that must balance the requirement for economic growth with SDGs.

# References

Alcántara, J., de la Fuente, D., Chico, B., Simancas, J., Díaz, I., & Morcillo, M. (2017). Marine atmospheric corrosion of carbon steel: A review. *Materials, 10*(4). https://doi.org/10.3390/ma10040406

Almeida, E., Morcillo, M., & Rosales, B. (2000). Atmospheric corrosion of mild steel Part II – Marine atmospheres. *Materials and Corrosion – Werkstoffe Und Korrosion, 51*(12), 865–874. https://doi.org/10.1002/1521-4176(200012)51:12<865::AID-MACO865>3.0.CO;2-S

Benarie, M., & Lipfert, F. L. (1986). A general corrosion function in terms of atmospheric pollutant concentrations and rain pH. *Atmospheric Environment (1967)*. https://doi.org/10.1016/0004-6981(86)90336-7

Bender, R., Féron, D., Mills, D., Ritter, S., Bäßler, R., Bettge, D., De Graeve, I., Dugstad, A., Grassini, S., Hack, T., Halama, M., Han, E. H., Harder, T., Hinds, G., Kittel, J., Krieg, R., Leygraf, C., Martinelli, L., Mol, A., . . . Zheludkevich, M. (2022). Corrosion challenges towards a sustainable society. *Materials and Corrosion, 73*(11), 1730–1751. https://doi.org/10.1002/maco.202213140

Castañeda, A., Corvo, F., Fernández, D., & Valdés, C. (2016). Outdoor-indoor atmospheric corrosion in a coastal wind farm located in a tropical Island. *Engineering Journal, 21*(2), 43–62. https://doi.org/10.4186/ej.2017.21.2.43

Castaño, J. G., Botero, C. A., Restrepo, A. H., Agudelo, E. A., Correa, E., & Echeverría, F. (2010). Atmospheric corrosion of carbon steel in Colombia. *Corrosion Science, 52*(1), 216–223. https://doi.org/10.1016/j.corsci.2009.09.006

Coelho, L. B., Zhang, D., Van Ingelgem, Y., Steckelmacher, D., Nowé, A., & Terryn, H. (2022). Reviewing machine learning of corrosion prediction in a data-oriented perspective. *Npj Materials Degradation, 6*(1). https://doi.org/10.1038/s41529-022-00218-4

Cole, I. S., & Paterson, D. A. (2010). Possible effects of climate change on atmospheric corrosion in Australia. *Corrosion Engineering, Science and Technology, 45*(1), 19–26. https://doi.org/10.1179/147842209X12579401586483

Corvo, F., Perez, T., Dzib, L. R., Martin, Y., Castañeda, A., Gonzalez, E., & Perez, J. (2008). Outdoor-indoor corrosion of metals in tropical coastal atmospheres. *Corrosion Science, 50*(1), 220–230. https://doi.org/10.1016/j.corsci.2007.06.011

De La Fuente, D., Díaz, I., Alcántara, J., Chico, B., Simancas, J., Llorente, I., García-Delgado, A., Jiménez, J. A., Adeva, P., & Morcillo, M. (2016). Corrosion mechanisms of mild steel in chloride-rich atmospheres. *Materials and Corrosion, 67*(3), 227–238. https://doi.org/10.1002/maco.201508488

Diao, Y., Yan, L., & Gao, K. (2021). Improvement of the machine learning-based corrosion rate prediction model through the optimization of input features. *Materials and Design, 198*, 109326. https://doi.org/10.1016/j.matdes.2020.109326

Díaz, V., & López, C. (2007). Discovering key meteorological variables in atmospheric corrosion through an artificial neural network model. *Corrosion Science, 49*(3), 949–962. https://doi.org/10.1016/j.corsci.2006.06.023

Knotkova, D., Kreislova, K., & Dean, S. W. J. (2010). *International atmospheric exposure program: Summary of results*. ASTM International.

Kreislova, K., & Knotkova, D. (2017). The results of 45 years of atmospheric corrosion study in the Czech Republic. *Materials, 10*(4). https://doi.org/10.3390/ma10040394

Landolt, D. (2007). *Corrosion and surface chemistry metals*. EPFL Press.

Meira, G. R., Andrade, C., Alonso, C., Padaratz, I. J., & Borba, J. C. (2008). Modelling sea-salt transport and deposition in marine atmosphere zone – A tool for corrosion studies. *Corrosion Science, 50*(9), 2724–2731. https://doi.org/10.1016/j.corsci.2008.06.028

Musabikha, S., Utama, I. K. A. P., & Mukhtasor, M. (2017). Corrosion in the marine renewable energy: A review. *International Journal of Environmental Research & Clean Energy, 7*(1), 1–9.

Mythreyi, O. V., Srinivaas, M. R., Amit Kumar, T., & Jayaganthan, R. (2021). Machine-learning-based prediction of corrosion behavior in additively manufactured Inconel 718. *Data, 6*(8). https://doi.org/10.3390/data6080080

Nash, W., Drummond, T., & Birbilis, N. (2018, October). A review of deep learning in the study of materials degradation. *Npj Materials Degradation*, 1–12. https://doi.org/10.1038/s41529-018-0058-x

Nguyen, M. N., Wang, X., & Leicester, R. H. (2013). An assessment of climate change effects on atmospheric corrosion rates of steel structures. *Corrosion Engineering, Science and Technology, 48*(5), 359–369. https://doi.org/10.1179/1743278213Y.0000000087

Pintos, S., Queipo, N. V., Troconis De Rincón, O., Rincón, A., & Morcillo, M. (2000). Artificial neural network modeling of atmospheric corrosion in the MICAT project. *Corrosion Science, 42*(1), 35–52. https://doi.org/10.1016/S0010-938X(99)00054-2

Ríos Rojas, J. F., Escobar Ocampo, D., Hernández García, E. A., & Arroyave Posada, C. E. (2015). Atmospheric corrosivity in Bogota as a very high-altitude metropolis questions international standards. *Dyna, 82*(190), 128–137. https://doi.org/10.15446/dyna.v82n190.46256

Sabir, S., & Ibrahim, A. A. (2017). Influence of atmospheric pollution on corrosion of materials in Saudi Arabia. *Corrosion Engineering, Science and Technology, 52*(4), 276–282. https://doi.org/10.1080/1478422X.2016.1274839

Seechurn, Y., & Chuttoo, L. S. (2022). Corrosion of carbon steel in Mauritian water bodies. *Revista Materia, 27*(2). https://doi.org/10.1590/S1517-707620220002.1366

Seechurn, Y., Surnam, B. Y. R., & Wharton, J. A. (2022). Marine atmospheric corrosion of carbon steel in the tropical microclimate of Port Louis. *Materials and Corrosion*. October 2021. https://doi.org/10.1002/maco.202112871

Seechurn, Y., Wharton, J. A., & Surnam, B. Y. R. (2022). Mechanistic modelling of atmospheric corrosion of carbon steel in Port-Louis by electrochemical characterisation of rust layers. *Materials Chemistry and Physics, 291*(April), 126694. https://doi.org/10.1016/j.matchemphys.2022.126694

Soares, C. G., Garbatov, Y., Zayed, A., & Wang, G. (2014). Influence of environmental factors on corrosion of ship structures in marine atmosphere. *Corrosion Science, 51*(9), 2014–2026. https://doi.org/10.1016/j.corsci.2009.05.028

Stewart, M. G., & Deng, X. (2015). Climate impact risks and climate adaptation engineering for built infrastructure. *ASCE-ASME Journal of Risk and Uncertainty in Engineering Systems, Part A: Civil Engineering, 1*(1), 1–12. https://doi.org/10.1061/AJRUA6.0000809

Thanush, A. A., Chitra, P., Kasinath, J., & Surya Prakash, R. (2022). Atmospheric corrosion rate prediction of low-alloy steel using machine learning models. *IOP*

Conference Series: Materials Science and Engineering, *1248*(1), 012050. https://doi.org/10.1088/1757-899x/1248/1/012050

Trivedi, N. S., Venkatraman, M. S., Chu, C., & Cole, I. S. (2014). Effect of climate change on corrosion rates of structures in Australia. *Climatic Change, 124*(1–2), 133–146. https://doi.org/10.1007/s10584-014-1099-y

Vera, R., de Rincón, O. T., Bagnara, M., Romero, N., Araya, R., & Ossandón, S. (2018). Tropical/non-tropical marine environments impact on the behaviour of carbon steel and galvanised steel. *Materials and Corrosion, 69*(5), 614–625. https://doi.org/10.1002/maco.201709873

Yan, L., Diao, Y., Lang, Z., & Gao, K. (2020). Corrosion rate prediction and influencing factors evaluation of low-alloy steels in marine atmosphere using machine learning approach. *Science and Technology of Advanced Materials, 21*(1), 359–370. https://doi.org/10.1080/14686996.2020.1746196

Chapter 17

# In Situ Durability Assessment of Natural Composite Structures by Considering Artificial Neural Network (ANN) Modelling

*Ramful Raviduth*

University of Mauritius, Mauritius

## Abstract

The consideration of alternative sources of material for construction is imperative to reduce the environmental impacts as two-fifths of the carbon footprint of materials is attributed to the construction industry. One alternative material with improved biodegradable attributes which can contribute to carbon offset is bamboo. The commercialisation of bamboo in modern infrastructures has significant potential to address few of the Sustainable Development Goals (SDGs) itemised by the United Nations, namely SDG 9 about industry, innovation and infrastructure. Other SDGs covering sustainable cities and communities, responsible consumption and production and climate action are also indirectly addressed when utilising sustainable construction materials. Being a natural material however, the full commercialisation of materials such as bamboo is constrained by a lack of durability. Besides fracture mechanisms arising from load-induced cracks and thermal modification, the durability of bamboo material is greatly impaired by biotic and abiotic factors, which equally affect its natural rate of degradation, hence fracture behaviour. In first instance, this chapter outlines the various factors leading to the durability limitations in bamboo material due to load-induced cracks and natural degradation based on recent findings in this field from the author's own work and from past literature. Secondly, part of this chapter is devoted to a new approach of processing the surge of information about the varied aspects of bamboo durability by considering the powerful technique of artificial intelligence (AI), specifically the artificial neural network (ANN) for prediction modelling. Further use of AI-enabled technologies could have an impactful outcome on the life cycle

Artificial Intelligence, Engineering Systems and Sustainable Development, 219–230
Copyright © 2024 Ramful Raviduth
Published under exclusive licence by Emerald Publishing Limited
doi:10.1108/978-1-83753-540-820241017

assessment of bamboo-based structures to address the growing challenges outlined by the United Nations.

*Keywords*: Bamboo; sustainable development goals (SDG); durability; artificial intelligence (AI); artificial neural network (ANN); prediction modelling

## 17.1 Introduction

Among the numerous challenges faced in our modern society, mass urbanization and improper construction practice has led to irreversible environmental and ecological damage. To curb this ongoing issue, the need to develop resilient and sustainable infrastructure is calling for innovative solutions in the construction industry including the utilization of sustainable materials. Adoption of such an approach will also align with SDG 9 about industry, innovation and infrastructure. Despite having been widely utilised in construction building for more than 1000 years, there is still growing interest in the use of natural materials such as bamboo in modern construction housing and advanced architecture, given their numerous benefits to the well-being of humans. Besides, bamboo provides excellent sustainable traits by being present in abundance in most tropical countries around the world. In addition to having a high growth rate, they are cost effective and have immense potential to be scaled up into engineered products.

The consideration of natural materials in construction also addresses SDG 11 about sustainable cities and communities with the goal to provide safe and resilient settlements for people in developing countries. Being a sustainable material, which is readily available in many developing countries located in the tropical regions, bamboo could be considered for erecting temporary shelter following natural disasters. It could be easily used to create safe, inclusive and durable housing for long-term use, if proper treatment is applied. New innovations, to address their dimensional variations and durability by considering new treatment methodology, are indispensable to expand the use of bamboo culms in present-day building structures.

Moreover, SDG 12 about responsible consumption and production calls for conscientious planning from utilisation of available resources to the waste disposal stage. The consideration of sustainable alternatives for conventional construction materials should address part of the unsustainable consumption and production patterns which are contributing to climate change, biodiversity loss and pollution. Natural materials like bamboo are excellent alternatives to conventional building materials, given their sustainability trait. Such materials can contribute to reducing the overall environmental impact of construction developments while maintaining a direct connection between mankind and nature. New research and development about the use of non-chemical-based treatment methodologies should also contribute to a smooth degradation at the waste disposal stage in symbiosis with the environment.

The use of natural material in building construction also overlaps with SDG 13 about climate action as their overall contribution to greenhouse gas emissions is significantly lower. Given their relatively lower embodied energy in comparison to conventional building materials, natural materials display a much lower carbon footprint as their production involves a less energy-intensive process. Besides, the use of sustainable natural materials which can regenerate at a faster pace will ease the current strain pose on primeval forests remaining in the world. This will also add to carbon offset, thereby addressing the global concern of climate change in line with SDG 13.

## 17.2 Factors Affecting Bamboo Durability

The overall concept of sustainability in general is further enhanced by making most of the material in actual service condition. To achieve the greatest performance over their service lifetime, both durability and strength are some of the fundamental aspects which should be considered when manipulating natural construction materials such as bamboo. The term durability in this context, which can have several meanings in material science, specifically refers to the ability of natural materials to withstand failure due to natural degradation and load-induced cracks. Being a natural material, bamboo is prone to premature degradation and bears a relatively short life span ranging between 1 and 3 years if utilised in sheltered conditions.

Durability limitation via natural degradation comprises of both biotic and abiotic factors. Biotic factors such as insects, marine borers and fungi can all lead to the degradation of natural bamboo if left untreated. To address the challenges posed by biotic factors, natural bamboo can thus be treated against specific types of insects, marine borers and fungi, namely termites, Limnoria and white rot fungi, respectively. On the other hand, natural degradation caused by abiotic factors mainly originates from physical factors emerging from the environment such as UV rays, rain, humidity and temperature. To maximise the durability of natural materials in such environmental conditions, adequate treatment measures and specification for use must be prescribed.

In addition to natural degradation, load-induced cracks also have significant implications on the durability performance of natural-based materials. Load-induced cracks can originate from internal loading due to self-weight as well as from external loading modes resulting from wind and snow. In brittle and hard material like bamboo, the forces resulting from these two modes of loadings, namely compressive, bending, shear and torsion, can lead to premature failure once the yield strength threshold is exceeded (Ramful & Sakuma, 2020). Besides the exhaustive list of factors contributing to the natural degradation and load-induced cracks in bamboo, other noteworthy considerations, namely the harvest practice and construction practice were found to have an equally strong influence in that respect.

Being a natural material of inhomogeneous nature, the propensity of materials like bamboo to premature failure by fracture largely depends on a combination of notable factors involving the species characteristics, morphological and micro-structural features among others. Approximately 1,000 types of bamboo species have been reported to exist around the world which are mostly distributed in countries located in the tropical regions. The distinct variations observed in the inherent features and characteristics among various bamboo species occur as a result of their location and natural environment. Some common aspects of bamboo material which vary with species type are their morphological features such as node interspacing, culm diameter and wall thickness (Ghavami, 2016). Moreover, given their orthotropic nature, the interaction of bamboo culms with environmental factors or due to applied treatment modifications often results in a non-uniform structural behaviour which vary in accordance with the three principal material directions.

The modification of natural materials by specific treatment methodologies over the years was found to significantly limit their rate of natural degradation while enhancing other aspects of their physical and mechanical characteristics. Several proven treatment methodologies, which are broadly classified under the traditional and conventional chemical methods, have shown positive results when applied to natural material like bamboo. One distinctive means of treatment under the traditional approach involves smoke treatment which is a type of thermal modification applied in either a conventional or accelerated manner (Ramful & Sakuma, 2021). On the other hand, short-term chemical treatment involves dipping and spraying methods, while long-term chemical treatment involves more advanced techniques such as the modified Boucherie treatment (Kumar et al., 1994).

The diverse methodologies observed in the treatment modification of natural materials, which vary in terms of applied medium, duration of treatment and their intensity, can have considerable impact on their inherent characteristics. For instance, smoke treatment was found to provide both improved dimensional stability and resistance to fungi and termites (Kaur et al., 2016; Liese, 2018) at the expense of a reduction in ductility and toughness. Similarly, the mentioned chemical treatment methodologies can have significant influence at countering biotic factors to the detriment of physical and mechanical traits such as moisture content and modulus of elasticity respectively. Additionally, the rate of water absorption and penetration within bamboo structure was found to depend on the applied medium and intensity of treatment modification, which in turn had an influence on the fibre saturation point (FSP) inside the plant cell walls. The increase in moisture content below the FSP had a corresponding implication on the mechanical properties of bamboo material as its strength and ductility were found to be impacted and enhanced respectively (Jiang et al., 2012; Ota, 1953; Xu et al., 2014).

From the above findings, the use of untreated bamboo in construction is restricted as it is found to be susceptible to natural degradation by numerous factors present in its operating environment. Moreover, bamboo material subjected to treatment modification was found to have enhanced attributes in some aspects of durability at the cost of reduced physical or mechanical characteristics. It is imperative to conduct a qualitative assessment in order to obtain an optimum balance between durability and structural performance in bamboo-based materials for specific application requirements. To achieve the optimum durability-performance, both the desired physical and mechanical characteristics have to be compared along with the forecasted durability of the material in-service.

## 17.3 Alternative Means for Assessment and Prediction of Durability

To augment the use of natural materials in modern structures, it is essential to maximise their service lifetime through accurate prediction techniques in a time- and cost-effective manner. The advanced prediction technique would take into account the extensive number of factors affecting the durability of bamboo material and their corresponding effects on the physical and mechanical characteristics. The conventional prediction methodology about the durability of natural materials is not entirely accurate due to the unavailability of key information, simplified assumptions and lack of suitable analytical methods. With the surge in real-time data and analysis in the construction sector which is expected to take place with the upcoming Fourth Industrial Revolution or industry 4.0, having the right platform and tool for efficient data processing will be decisive (Taffese & Sistonen, 2017).

One capable tool for analyzing and processing big data, which would otherwise be too complex to be dealt with by traditional data-processing technique, is via the Artificial Intelligence (AI) approach. The use of AI technology in building and construction 4.0 was found to provide substantial benefits to the construction industry in general. It can be used as an assessment tool to evaluate the service-life of conventionally constructed buildings in terms of their durability prediction and life-cycle analysis (Baduge et al., 2022). Machine learning has also been applied to assess the durability and service-life assessment of conventional concrete structures, given their aptness at predicting with high level of accuracy the deterioration mechanism. The deterioration mechanism, which is based on complex and physical processes, could be successfully predicted following the collection of large amounts of in-service datasets via wireless sensors (Taffese & Sistonen, 2017).

AI technology encompasses major sub-fields ranging from machine learning to neural networks which are implemented for advanced analysis and logic-based processing to interpret events, support processes and automate decisions. In this chapter, the biological-inspired technique of artificial neural network (ANN) will be considered for prospects of implementation as an advanced prediction model for durability assessment of bamboo-based structures.

### 17.3.1 Artificial Neural Network (ANN)

ANNs are broadly classified under machine learning and are commonly referred to as neural networks or simulated neural networks (SNN). ANN model possesses the learning ability of the human brain by replicating the network model of biological neurons via a computational framework consisting of an inter-connected group of nodes (Sridhar et al., 2023). The nodes or artificial neurons operate similar to biological neurons by connecting and sending signals to one another. Data from one node to the next are transmitted once the output has reached above a specified threshold value. ANN model bears numerous benefits and operates in a dynamic way by constantly improving in accuracy by relying on training data also referred to as datasets. Once the ANN model has been sufficiently trained via extensive datasets fed through the input layers, the fine-tuned learning algorithm model can be used to classify and cluster surge in data for improved decision-making at a swift pace.

The powerful ability of ANN to process large datasets means it has high potential to be considered and implemented as an analytical tool in many applications. ANNs are, therefore, classified into different types and selected in accordance with their usage. The common types of ANN include multilayer perceptrons (MLPs), convolutional neural networks (CNNs) and recurrent neural networks (RNNs). The ANN model's structure requires both a specific system design and well-defined system parameter for logical operation and work initialisation, respectively (Sridhar et al., 2023). In the system design, the input neurons, output neurons, hidden layers as well as neurons in each hidden layer must be considered (Sridhar et al., 2023). In general, the ANN architecture consists of nodes in hidden layers which are operated via activation functions (Özşahin, 2012). ANN model also incorporates network training functions and performance functions in its algorithm (Özşahin, 2012). In previous studies, the traingdm has been employed as the network training function while the mean square error was selected as performance function (Özşahin, 2012).

## 17.4 Application of ANN Model for Durability Assessment

As described earlier, AI has high potential to be implemented in numerous fields outside the Engineering sphere, given its capabilities at processing large data sets in a smart and expedite manner. As reported in recent studies from literature, the application of AI technology, in particular the ANN model, to predict and assess the durability of principally natural-based structures will be covered in the forthcoming sections of this chapter.

### 17.4.1 Utilisation of ANN Model to Evaluate Durability of Natural Bamboo

From literature review, the application of AI technology in conventional building and construction is still at its infancy stage while its consideration in the durability assessment of non-conventional and natural materials is sparsely available. Moreover, the use of AI technology as an analytical tool to assess and predict the durability behaviour of natural bamboo material based on their physical and mechanical properties is highly limited in literature. Among the few reported studies, ANN model was used to determine the change in colorimetric parameters and the change in mass loss of small clear bamboo specimens by considering input datasets such as heat-treatment duration and temperature (Gürgen et al., 2019).

ANN model was found to be a better predictive model than the conventional multiple linear regression model, given the low percentage error obtained between the predicted and actual results (Gürgen et al., 2019).

In contrast to durability assessment, AI technology was implemented in one study to investigate other aspects of bamboo materials, namely in the optimisation of their manufacturing process. The processing of bamboo requires specific consideration, given their orthotropic nature as well as their inherent geometrical features such as existence of nodes, tapered culm section and varying wall thickness (Sakhale et al., 2014).

### 17.4.2 Utilisation of ANN Model to Evaluate Durability of Bamboo-Based Composites

Conversely, numerous research studies involving the application of AI technology to monitor the changes in the physical characteristics of bamboo-based composites have been conducted in recent past (Ighalo et al., 2021; Majumdar, 2011; You et al., 2022). For instance, alternative methods to evaluate the mechanical characteristics of bamboo-wood composites (BWC), namely their modulus of elasticity (MOE), have been developed by considering a non-destructive approach based on ANN (You et al., 2022). The predictive ANN models were designed to predict the modulus of elasticity by processing both physical and mechanical material data such as density and dynamic MOE, respectively (You et al., 2022). The dynamic MOE was computed by considering bending vibration test data measured from both the longitudinal and transverse directions (You et al., 2022).

ANN has also been applied to the development of engineered bamboo products such as bamboo fibre composites (BFC) to model their water absorption behaviour (Ighalo et al., 2021). Result findings indicated that the ANN model was able to predict the water absorption behaviour in BFC to a high level of accuracy (Ighalo et al., 2021). Such prediction models with high fidelity are assumed to help both design and maintenance engineers in their daily tasks of building design and in the setting of appropriate maintenance regimes, respectively (Ighalo et al., 2021). Given its noteworthy accuracy and consistency as a predictive model, the application of ANN models to estimate the physical and mechanical properties of bamboo-based materials has shown commendable results. For instance, the thermal conductivity of knitted fabrics made out of cotton–bamboo yarns was predicted with a high level of accuracy by using the ANN model (Majumdar, 2011).

### 17.4.3 Utilisation of ANN Model to Evaluate Durability of Bamboo-Reinforced Concrete Beams

One specific type of bamboo composite material drawing huge interest among researchers is the bamboo-reinforced concrete beams which has the potential for consideration as a better sustainable alternative material in the construction industry (Gunasti et al., 2020; Mishra et al., 2019; Sridhar et al., 2023). AI technology, in particular the ANN model, was considered to estimate the mechanical properties of such natural-fibre-reinforced material (Gunasti et al., 2020; Mishra et al., 2019; Sridhar et al., 2023).

The ANN model developed was found to estimate the mechanical properties of bamboo-fibre-reinforced concrete, namely its compressive, split tensile and flexural strengths, at a high level of accuracy (Sridhar et al., 2023). The input layers in the adopted network architecture of the proposed model consisted of seven neurons based on the content of the composite material such as bamboo fibre content, cement content, aggregate content and water content accuracy (Sridhar et al., 2023). The neural network-Leven Berg-Marquardt (NN-LM) and the neural network gradient descent (NN-GD) were considered as the optimisation algorithms to train the neural network model accuracy (Sridhar et al., 2023). In accordance with regression test results ($R > 0.90$), both the NN-LM and NN-GD were found to be optimum ANN models for trustworthy and accurate network performance, following systematic training, testing and validation stages accuracy (Sridhar et al., 2023).

As further application, ANN was considered to predict the structural behaviour of bamboo-reinforced concrete beams (Mishra et al., 2019). For accurate estimation of the beam's deflection, the relationship among the applied load, tensile strength of reinforcement material as well as the percentage amount of reinforcement were selected as the key parameters forming part of the input layers (Mishra et al., 2019). Moreover, the input data were processed via the Levenberg-Marquardt backpropagation algorithm which was selected as the network training function in the hidden layer of the ANN architecture model (Mishra et al., 2019).

Moreover, the application of ANN model to predict the mechanical properties of bamboo-based materials was found to yield results with an error prediction of less than 1% (Gunasti et al., 2020). In this study, the ANN model was implemented to diagnose the shape and distribution of the load-displacement curves of the bamboo-reinforced concrete beam material (Gunasti et al., 2020). The ANN model would determine the predicted results via neural network training functions until an acceptable variation of error is reached (Gunasti et al., 2020). The use of the ANN model in this study, specifically to validate experimental investigations, was found to be beneficial as it was assumed to overcome common errors caused by humans, equipment calibration and test method (Gunasti et al., 2020).

### 17.4.4 Durability Evaluation of Other Natural Composites by the ANN Model

The susceptibility to degradation of natural-based materials such as wood and natural fibre composites due to environmental conditions still poses a major concern for architects and design engineers. One of the common forms of degradation experienced by such materials when exposed to a moist environment condition is water absorption and swelling (Ighalo et al., 2021; Özşahin, 2012; Pujari et al., 2017). The implementation of AI technology to predict and model the change in the behaviour of other natural composite materials in general due to varying environmental conditions has shown accurate and conclusive results as reported in several studies (Özşahin, 2012; Pujari et al., 2017).

For instance, ANN models were developed and implemented to obtain accurate prediction about the complex behaviour of natural materials to environmental conditions such as water absorption behaviour (Özşahin, 2012). The multilayer-developed ANN model was found to be a reliable tool to estimate the moisture absorption and thickness swelling in oriented strand board with high level of accuracy (Özşahin, 2012). Dataset for the input layers based on treatment variables such as relative humidity, layup type, resin type, wax content and resin content were processed via the multilayer ANN model which consisted of two hidden layers comprised of 10 neurons each (Özşahin, 2012). Similar to the observation made by Gürgen et al. (2019), the ANN model was found to yield more accurate results than regression analysis to predict the water absorption of jute and banana fibres reinforced epoxy composites (Pujari et al., 2017).

## 17.5 Discussion and Direction for Future Work

In light of the above findings, there is high potential for consideration of a new approach to process the surge of information about the varied aspects of bamboo durability. Similar research methodology based on AI, which has been applied to the durability assessment of concrete structures sensors (Taffese & Sistonen, 2017) including bamboo-reinforced concrete beams (Gunasti et al., 2020; Mishra et al., 2019; Sridhar et al., 2023), could be adapted for the durability assessment of bamboo-based structures.

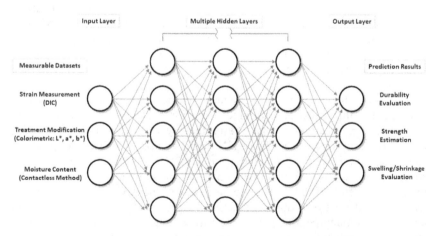

Fig. 17.1.   The Proposed Network Architecture of the ANN Model for the Assessment and Durability Prediction of Bamboo-Based Structures.

### *17.5.1 Proposed ANN Model for Durability Prediction of Bamboo-Based Structures*

The proposed network architecture of the ANN model for future use in the assessment and durability prediction of bamboo-based structures is shown in Fig. 17.1. The architecture of the ANN model consists of the input layer, multiple hidden layers and the output layer. As part of the input layers, measurable datasets in terms of strain measurement, moisture content and colour change due to treatment modification could be obtained via the digital image correlation (DIC) technique, digital moisture metre and colorimetric parameters L*, a* and b*, respectively.

The datasets will be decisive for accurate training and modelling of the ANN model. The ANN model will be trained via the network training functions in its hidden layers until an acceptable variation of error is reached. Once sufficiently trained, the refined ANN model could be used to interpret large datasets and predict the desired output parameters with a high degree of precision. The specificity and accuracy of the datasets has direct influence on the output layers of the proposed ANN model for improved reliability in the prediction of durability, strength and shrinkage or swelling behaviour.

## 17.6 Conclusion

The conception of this chapter was to establish a novel approach to efficiently assess the durability of natural-based structures by considering AI technology for improved sustainability and resilience in actual service condition. Based on the findings gathered from literature data, the application and usage of AI technology to assess and predict the durability behaviour of natural structures in general has been highly limited. The sparsely reported studies involving the application of AI technology to assess natural materials were mainly focused on the prediction of the durability-performance of natural-based composites such as bamboo-reinforced concrete beams in terms of their mechanical and physical attributes.

The aim of this chapter was to provide a holistic overview of numerous factors affecting the durability of natural construction material like bamboo, while proposing a novel approach via AI technology to analyse and predict their durability status in real time. The ANN model was considered as the specific AI technology in this chapter to predict the durability-performance of natural-based structures in line with input datasets ranging from strain measurement to colorimetric parameters. The training and modelling of the ANN model with specific datasets via the network training functions is forecasted to predict specific traits about the durability-performance of the natural material such as their durability, strength and shrinkage or swelling behaviour with high accuracy. The conception of such a prediction model is believed to have the ability to process large datasets and predict the durability-performance of natural-based structures efficiently in real time.

# References

Baduge, S. K., Thilakarathna, S., Perera, J. S., Arashpour, M., Sharafi, P., Teodosio, B., Shringi, A., & Mendis, P. (2022). Artificial intelligence and smart vision for building and construction 4.0: Machine and deep learning methods and applications. *Automation in Construction, 141,* 104440.

Ghavami, K. (2016). Introduction to nonconventional materials and an historic retrospective of the field. In *Nonconventional and vernacular construction materials* (pp. 37–61). Woodhead Publishing.

Gunasti, A., Dewi, I. C., Dasuki, M., Ariyani, S., Mahmudi, I., Abadi, T., Rahman, M., Hidayatullah, S., Nilogiri, A., Desta Galuh, S., & Eko Wardoyo, A. (2020). The prediction of stiffness of bamboo-reinforced concrete beams using experiment data and Artificial Neural Networks (ANNs). *Crystals, 10*(9), 757.

Gürgen, A., Topaloğlu, E., Ustaömer, D., Yıldız, S., & Ay, N. (2019). Prediction of the colorimetric parameters and mass loss of heat-treated bamboo: Comparison of multiple linear regression and artificial neural network method. *Color Research & Application, 44*(5), 824–833.

Ighalo, J. O., Igwegbe, C. A., Adeniyi, A. G., & Abdulkareem, S. A. (2021). Artificial neural network modeling of the water absorption behavior of plantain peel and bamboo fibers reinforced polystyrene composites. *Journal of Macromolecular Science, Part B, 60*(7), 472–484.

Jiang, Z., Wang, H., Tian, G., & Yu, Y. (2012). Sensitivity of several selected mechanical properties of moso bamboo to moisture content change under the fibre saturation point. *BioResources, 7*(4), 5048–5058.

Kaur, P. J., Satya, S., Pant, K. K., & Naik, S. N. (2016). Eco-friendly preservation of bamboo species: Traditional to modern techniques. *Bioresources, 11*(4), 10604–10624.

Kumar, S., Shukla, K. S., Dev, I., & Dobriyal, P. B. (1994). *Bamboo preservation techniques: A review.* INBAR and ICFRE.

Liese, W. (2018). Protection of bamboo in service. *World Bamboo and Rattan, 1*(1), 29–33.

Majumdar, A. (2011). Modelling of thermal conductivity of knitted fabrics made of cotton-bamboo yarns using artificial neural network. *Journal of the Textile Institute, 102*(9), 752–762.

Mishra, M., Agarwal, A., & Maity, D. (2019). Neural-network-based approach to predict the deflection of plain, steel-reinforced, and bamboo-reinforced concrete beams from experimental data. *SN Applied Sciences, 1,* 1–11.

Ota, M. (1953). Studies on the properties of bamboo stem (part 9). On the relation between compressive strength parallel to grain and moisture content of bamboo splint. *Bulletin of Kyushu University of Forestry, 22,* 87–108.

Özşahin, Ş. (2012). The use of an artificial neural network for modeling the moisture absorption and thickness swelling of oriented strand board. *BioResources, 7*(1), 1053–1067.

Pujari, S., Ramakrishna, A., & Padal, K. B. (2017). Prediction of swelling behaviour of jute and banana fiber composites by using ANN and regression analysis. *Materials Today: Proceedings, 4*(8), 8548–8557.

Ramful, R., & Sakuma, A. (2020). Investigation of the effect of inhomogeneous material on the fracture mechanisms of bamboo by finite element method. *Materials, 13*(21), 5039.

Ramful, R., & Sakuma, A. (2021). Effect of smoke treatment on flexural strength of bamboo hierarchical structure. *BioResources, 16*(1), 387–402.

Sakhale, C. N., Waghmare, S. N., Undirwade, S. K., Sonde, V. M., & Singh, M. P. (2014). Formulation and comparison of experimental based mathematical model with artificial neural network simulation and RSM (response surface methodology) model for optimal performance of sliver cutting operation of bamboo. *Procedia materials science, 6*, 877–891.

Sridhar, J., Gobinath, R., & Kırgız, M. S. (2023). Evaluation of artificial neural network predicted mechanical properties of jute and bamboo fiber reinforced concrete along with silica fume. *Journal of Natural Fibers, 20*(1), 2162186.

Taffese, W. Z., & Sistonen, E. (2017). Machine learning for durability and service-life assessment of reinforced concrete structures: Recent advances and future directions. *Automation in Construction, 77*, 1–14.

Xu, Q., Harries, K., Li, X., Liu, Q., & Gottron, J. (2014). Mechanical properties of structural bamboo following immersion in water. *Engineering Structures, 81*, 230–239.

You, G., Wang, B., Li, J., Chen, A., & Sun, J. (2022). The prediction of MOE of bamboo-wood composites by ANN models based on the non-destructive vibration testing. *Journal of Building Engineering, 59*, 105078.

Part 5

# Impact of AI-Enabled Sustainability and Enterprise Development on UN SDGs

# Chapter 18

# The Manufacturing Sector in Mauritius: Building Supply Chain Resilience and Business Value With Artificial Intelligence

*Satyadev Rosunee and Roshan Unmar*

University of Mauritius, Mauritius

## Abstract

Manufacturing in Mauritius is mostly export-oriented. Any supply chain (SC) failure or resilience deficit may result in cancellation of orders and loss of customers, market share and revenue and reduce capability to compete globally. Addressing this challenge is complex, although digital technologies and artificial intelligence (AI) models can improve resilience by assisting decision-making and mitigate risks, thus infusing greater predictability across the SC.

Supply chains are facing increasing disruptions and uncertainties owing to extreme weather events, the war in Ukraine, market volatility and the ongoing COVID-19 pandemic, among other factors. Manufacturing industries and their supply chains essentially create thousands of jobs that enable economic growth and sustain export capability. In addition, they need to maintain or increase both productivity and efficiency and recover quickly from unforeseen or unexpected challenges – that is they need to be resilient. Transformation initiatives, whether in production or supply chain management (SCM), are never easy. Process changes not supported by data or hurried human decisions can sometimes have unintended consequences, mainly adverse. However, in times of greater uncertainty (war and pandemic), setbacks can have greater consequences on the business. Manufacturers are already apprehensive and report slowing exports as recession concerns have caused consumers and businesses to pull back on spending. There is therefore a need to reduce uncertainty and augment resilience by unlocking and synthesising insights that emanate from the power of data analytics, AI and machine learning to improve the resilience efficiency balance.

Artificial Intelligence, Engineering Systems and Sustainable Development, 233–244

Copyright © 2024 Satyadev Rosunee and Roshan Unmar

Published under exclusive licence by Emerald Publishing Limited

doi:10.1108/978-1-83753-540-820241018

This chapter will discuss the opportunities arising from the adoption and implementation of digital technologies and AI in SCM, leading to better value creation, less greenhouse gas emissions and resilience. The hurdles that enterprises are facing to integrate AI in their logistics and SCs will also be highlighted. This work comments on initiatives that uphold the objectives of SDG 8 – decent work and economic growth, SDG 9 – industry, innovation & infrastructure and SDG 13 – climate action.

*Keywords*: Mauritius; manufacturing; supply chain management; Internet of Things; artificial intelligence

## 18.1 Introduction

Artificial intelligence (AI) generally drives the development of tools for transforming large datasets into resilience-building initiatives. The field of AI is broad-based and rapidly evolving. It is producing technologies that will have impactful socio-economic implications (Abbany, 2018; Schwab, 2016; WEF, 2016). Therefore, the convergence of many digital technologies and AI has the potential to transform manufacturing industry in line with United Nations Sustainable Development Goals (UN SDGs) 8 and 9.

The 17 UN SDGs are central to the regeneration and sustained well-being of the planet. Nevertheless, SDGs should translate into reasonable life's comforts for the global population: access to first-necessity products and services, quality education, clean water and sanitation, renewable energy and quality health services. Digital technologies and AI can render these so-called comforts more accessible and cost-effective with largely positive socio-economic impacts.

The COVID-19 pandemic highlighted major weaknesses in global supply chains (SCs), threatening the resilience of major industries. The pandemic shook to the core the industrial base of many countries, both developing and developed, paralysing their SCs. Manufacturers faced raw materials shortages and longer lead times while demand evaporated in some sectors and skyrocketed in others. Countries need to be prepared for the next pandemic by resolving structural weaknesses in their SCs. SC challenges and their spill-over effects extend far beyond manufacturing and industry. They present an even graver threat to the food security of a country. This could lead to disastrous consequences such as inflationary pressures on food prices and widespread hunger or in a worst-case scenario, famine.

Mangan and Lalwani (2016) state that the aim of supply chain management (SCM) is to get all of the following right at least cost: product, quantity, quality and place and time of delivery. SCM is becoming increasingly challenging owing to intrinsic complexities, greater economic uncertainty, supply and demand volatility and rapid changes in technology (Christopher & Holweg, 2011; Fore et al., 2017). SCs are evolving in such a way that in the near future they might become autonomous and have smart predictive capabilities as reported by major service providers (DHL, 2016; IBM, 2015; WEF, 2017). Internet of Things (IoT) will be a key cornerstone of the SCM of the future. IoT sensors will generate and collect huge quantities of data across SCs. The resulting data patterns and the labels associated with those patterns could be continuously fed to the AI model to improve it, to improve its accuracy, comprehensiveness and robustness (Lee et al., 2018).

Manufacturing firms should deploy AI systems that analyse information in real time, promptly adjust initiatives and targets, monitor operations, make predictions with minimum error rate and take actions to adjust to rapidly changing external environments, in other words build resilience (DHL, 2016). Such SCs will require minimum human intervention (Calatayud, 2017), have predictive capabilities that underpin better risk management and forward planning and reduced carbon emissions.

Once AI has been deployed, enterprises can run the analysis in a systematic manner and at low cost using their own data. The enterprise should also hire people with the right expertise to make the AI model fit for purpose. Enterprises can thus monitor progress in real time and predict bottlenecks and problems so they can keep their initiatives on track. The outputs also provide companies a clearer picture for smarter planning, risk mitigation and possible losses.

Supply chain integration (SCI) is a key enabler. Integration means that the service providers or receivers along the chain are communicating, negotiating and transacting with each other well. Digital technologies and web connectivity are bound to catalyse integration across the SC generating data that can shape an AI model. Enhanced information connectivity and visibility confer the following advantages to SCs: better inventory control, faster product design and development and order validation, shorter lead times, better understanding of customer needs and preferences, enhanced capacity to plan and implement logistics, greater logistics flexibility and punctual delivery and better return on logistics assets and flexibility to manage risks. The barriers to enhanced information connectivity have been lowered considerably as high-performance computer systems are available at low cost.

On the other hand, generative AI's capabilities as demonstrated by ChatGPT and Bard are urging firms around the world to develop and deploy AI strategies. The outcomes of these strategies should hopefully not interfere with the SDGs such as SDG 4 – Quality Education and SDG 10 – Reduced Inequalities, among others. Kai-Fu Lee (2018) has predicted that an AI revolution 'will disrupt the structure of our economic and political systems'. What would happen if such a prediction is vindicated? In the context of industry, it may result in AI-driven massive job losses, hardships and inequalities. Generative AI is here to stay and will possibly influence a number of socio-economic activities in the short to medium term. Without over-emphasising or diluting the challenges posed by generative AI to humankind, in order to promote a happy, industrious society: science, technology viz. AI, ethics and human well-being and the profit motive of industry should co-exist harmoniously. AI has the potential to create more wealth. Equitably distributed wealth can cure a number of societal ills, including poverty, therefore addressing SDG 1 – No poverty.

## 18.2 Digital Transformation, IoT and SCM

As mentioned earlier, digital transformation and IoT have a critical role to play in SCM. A sensor is attached to a consignment to help track its location and status along the SC. IoT has three tech-driven components for: (i) data collection, (ii) data transmission and (iii) data analysis (Dweekat et al., 2017; Lu, 2017). Yan (2017) has suggested that the IoT is 'an internet-based intelligent network which is capable of transferring real-time information, as well as identifying, tracking and managing products through advanced technologies such as radio frequency identification (RFID), infrared sensor, global positioning system and laser scanner'. Ben-Daya et al. (2017) have summarised the expected impact of IoT on SCM as follows: IoT is 'a network of physical objects that are digitally connected to sense, monitor and interact within a company and between the company and its supply chain enabling agility, visibility, tracking and information sharing to facilitate timely planning, control and coordination of the supply chain processes'.

One of the key enablers of IoT is radio frequency identification (RFID) technology (Zhang et al., 2013). SCM has integrated RFID technology in its operations for some years now (Sarac et al., 2010; Zhu et al., 2012). RFID is a wireless communication technology. It can identify specific targets and read and capture relevant data without any form of physical contact (Yan et al., 2017). The technology is based on an integrated circuit fitted with a tag that can store data. These tags are usually attached to packages along the SC and their intrinsic data retrieved through readers wirelessly (Lee & Ozer, 2007). In general, tag information retrieval by readers is contactless.

SC visibility effectively removes technological barriers between SC actors enabling more fluid management of processes (Golicic et al., 2002). Indeed, visibility entails the sharing of real-time and unbiased data. This latter feature is very important for frictionless processes throughout the entire SC (Nooraie & Parast, 2016; Somapa et al., 2018). Data as mentioned earlier is central to building performant AI models for the SCM of the future.

In addition, higher visibility leads to enhanced SCI which significantly reduces risks and increases resilience (Brusset, 2016; Gonul et al., 2017). SCI is defined as 'the coordination of operational, logistical, and planning data to improve production planning, inventory management, and distribution' (Li et al., 2009). As stated by Sanders et al. (2011), 'the very foundations of the supply chain integration concept rest upon the assumption that collaboration takes place between supply chain partners, which is only possible through bidirectional flows of communication, operations data and planning data'.

## 18.3 SCM and AI

There is tremendous pressure on SC actors to decarbonise their operations – SDG 13, and to do it at scale. Tangible decarbonisation is only possible if all SC actors work together, while making necessary adjustments for variances between them, and the proverbial 'limited resources' (CIEL group, 2023). An AI system would help to share learning and plug in decisional and operational gaps.

Calatayud (2017) has suggested that novel algorithms need to be developed to gather data as to how the SC is performing, enable analysis of the data, flag potential risks and their nature and trigger initiatives to eliminate the root causes for the smooth running of the chain. DHL (2016) is piloting a project where analytical and simulation models would process IoT data, infusing the SC with prediction capabilities, minimising errors and take corrective actions to minimise any deviation from the norm. In the context of decarbonisation, at management level, there is enormous support for SC actors to adopt IoT and AI technologies to enhance agility, autonomy, transparency and predictive capabilities (CIEL group, 2023; IBM, 2015; WEF, 2017). There is significant scope in Mauritius for further research in the area of SCM and AI to address SDGs 8, 9 and 13.

## 18.4 AI and Prediction Capability

Demand forecasts provide visibility to SC managers. They give manufacturing firms enough time to prepare the groundwork for future orders. Any SC professional will confirm that any error in demand forecasting can have catastrophic financial consequences for the business – denoted as the bullwhip effect. Thus, the importance of AI as a forecasting tool cannot be over-emphasised. Much work is engaged in evaluating the 'fitness-for-purpose' and effectiveness of different AI algorithms in demand forecasting. Similarly, substantial research is ongoing to refine AI algorithms that perform under data constraints, thereby mimicking real world situations (Singh & Challa, 2016; Slimani et al., 2016). All in all, prediction capability is still limited as illustrated by the global shortage of semiconductors in 2021/22 that paralysed a number of manufacturing industries.

Nayak and Padhye (2018) have reported the use of a multitude of AI systems in apparel SCs. The premier objective is to address common operational challenges faced by the global textile and apparel (T&A) industry, including the Mauritian T&A industry. The Mauritian industry is significantly remote from its main markets (the United Kingdom, the European Union and the United States) and almost all the raw materials that are transformed into T&A are imported. Demand forecasting becomes all the more important as it has to address challenges like just-in-time availability of raw materials supported by responsive logistics at competitive prices, variable production volumes, high demand volatility and shipment deadlines of finished goods. The structural weaknesses that were amplified during the COVID-19 pandemic are being gradually addressed.

Another challenging sector is the perishable goods SC that is highly sensitive to demand fluctuations and strict shipment exigencies, mostly for sanitary reasons. Lu and Wang (2017) and Fikar (2018) have proposed AI-based tools to holistically address major challenges in the perishable goods SC. Traceability and quality control are mandatory requirements in the cold chain industry. IoT supported by AI technologies are being used to give transparency to both requirements. As both load and route planning represent complex logistics in the cold chain industry, Lu and Wang (2017) recommended AI-based solutions. The Tesco supermarket chain in the United Kingdom has been very innovative in managing the supply of cold chain dependent products. It feeds daily weather data into its predictive analysis system. Predictive analysis based on historical sales and weather data and sound inventory management has helped Tesco to capture more revenue (Patil, 2018).

## 18.5 Applying AI Tools to Supply Chain Optimisation Problems

SCM optimisation problems are generally complex owing to the wide array of parameters and variables that need to be factored in. The application of traditional mathematical methods is not always practical when feasible solutions are being sought for complex optimisation problems (Dounias & Vassiliadis, 2015). AI algorithms may help to solve complex optimisation problems in SCM. Nature-inspired algorithms are commonly applied to SC optimisation problems (Vassiliadis & Dounias, 2009). Genetic algorithms are comparatively mathematically simpler and most frequently used to solve SC problems (Icarte, 2016). They can more easily process functions and constraints that are common in SC contexts. The applications of nature-inspired algorithms are indeed numerous: distribution management, vehicle routing, inventory location, planning and cost minimisation, as well as supplier selection (Dounias & Vassiliadis, 2015).

The Mauritian manufacturing sector has duly recognised the value of data and datasets. There are initiatives to have a digital copy of each and every operation carried out in the company. In general, data availability will continue to grow. Large flows of SC data allied with high-performance computing and AI tools are likely to have an enormous beneficial impact on SCM in the coming years.

## 18.6 Advantages of AI in SCM

Fig. 18.1 depicts how SCM is being empowered by AI (BIC, 2018). The key advantages are streamlining of processes, smarter planning, sharper market intelligence and quicker responses. Each advantage is illustrated with the help of one example. Other valid examples may be sought from the literature. AI will be really helpful in SC activities if it is able to maximise the advantages and reduce the metrics that cause delays, disruptions and adverse environmental impacts.

## 18.7 Contrasting Traditional and Digital SCs

With the inclusion of AI, the traditional (linear) SC (plan-source-make-deliver) has metamorphosed into a rather dense network, Fig. 18.2. Data from a number of sources is seamlessly integrated, eliminating reliance on a few or limited number of data sources. There is also a more pronounced integration between networks, increasing frequency of constructive interactions. In the networked model, for instance, communication is multi-directional, and all stakeholders can assist each other to boost their respective efficiencies and business interests. This multi-directional exchange of data is gradually becoming the norm across global SCs.

## Advantages of AI in Supply Chain Management

| Process streamlining | Smart Planning | Sharper Market Intelligence | Quicker Responses |
|---|---|---|---|
| Using real-time and multisource data, starting from demand trends to inventory, AI can help to streamline every process with minimum human input, saving time and reducing errors.<br><br>**Example:** A Chatbot can be used to communicate with potential customers about product specifications, delivery schedules, payment methods. | For planning purposes, large amount of data can be analyzed and insights obtained thereby reducing risks & uncertainties and enhance supply chain security, etc.<br><br>**Example:** Just-in-time manufacturing, cost optimization, better resource productivity and profitability. | Customer data allied with prediction capabilities, exceed customer expectations, better design & enhanced product features. Less vulnerable to SC disruptions.<br><br>**Example:** Convergence of AI & Blockchain; better customer-client relationship, enhanced transparency & network security. | AI can catalyze transport and logistics & dispel procurement & delivery anxieties. Decrease lead times & potentially reduce costs.<br><br>**Example:** Autonomous vehicles likely to empower logistics and transportation with higher return on investment. |

Fig. 18.1.    Advantages of Artificial Intelligence (AI) in Supply Chain
Management (SCM).

## 18.8 Why AI Has Given Mixed Results up to Now?

AI has given mixed results up to now as technological infrastructure and capabilities of SC actors vary widely across the SC. For AI and SCM to complement each other without major hurdles, some pre-requisites have to be satisfied. Overlooking some of these pre-requisites will at best generate subpar outcomes (BIC, 2018).

The list of pre-requisites are as follows:

- adequate tools to capture real-time and multi-source data,
- be consumer-centric or human-centric,
- keep in mind the costs when effecting change,
- focus on a system that is self-learning,
- encourage team-based decision-making,
- secure user feedback when interacting with AI,
- consolidate the AI base supported by adequate funding.

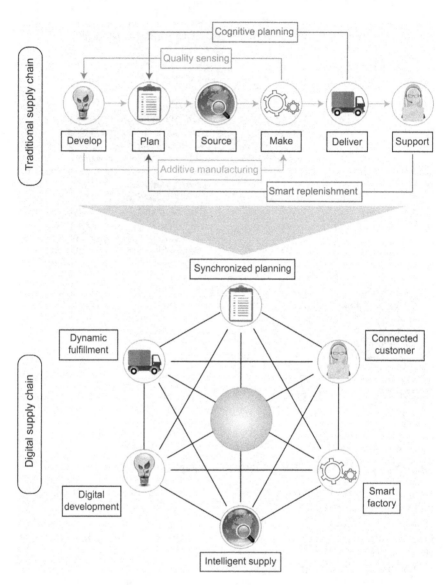

Fig. 18.2.    Contrasting Traditional and Digital Supply Chains.

Accenture (2018) has reported that 85% of companies that have invested in AI struggle to secure a reasonable return on the investment. In some cases, enterprises that are willing to go ahead with AI lack human expertise to extract value. For AI to work, an enabling ecosystem needs to be put in place. Individual businesses would benefit from AI if they are capable to tap value within the wider network, viz. multiple suppliers, sub-contractors, etc. Consequently, AI integration should avoid a fairly narrow objective like cost reduction only. The transition from linear to networked SCM requires an enterprise to be agile and dynamic and eager to leave behind the old ways of doing and thinking.

The common pitfalls faced by enterprises are:

• unsure about appropriateness of AI technology,
• shortage of funds and trained people to implement the technologies,
• change management is difficult to sustain after introduction of new AI tool,
• difficult to evaluate the customer experience.

It is well-known that investments that do not manage to change the customer experience or service level will not lead to growth.

## 18.9 Case Study: Toyota's Logistics and SC Success Story

Toyota has been exploring the use of AI in its logistics operations to improve efficiency and reduce costs. Toyota has developed a number of AI-based technologies that are being used or tested in its logistics operations, including:

• Autonomous vehicles: Toyota is developing a range of autonomous vehicles, including trucks and delivery robots, which are designed to operate without the need for a human driver. These vehicles are fitted with sensors and other technologies that allow them to be road-worthy, safely and efficiently.
• Predictive maintenance: Toyota is using AI to analyse data from its logistics fleet to predict when maintenance will be needed, which can help to reduce downtime and improve efficiency.
• Inventory management: Toyota is using AI-based algorithms to optimise its inventory management, including forecasting demand and identifying opportunities for cost savings.
• SC optimisation: Toyota is using AI to analyse data from its SC to identify opportunities for optimisation and efficiency improvements.

Overall, Toyota is exploring a range of AI-based technologies to improve the efficiency of its logistics operations, empower supply chain optimization and reduce costs.

## 18.10 Conclusion

Prior to the pandemic, the Mauritian manufacturing sector was already at the cross-roads owing to marginal gains in productivity over the past decade, rising costs of production and loss of competitiveness compared to regional manufacturers with similar profiles. The pandemic made the situation worse and worrisome and deeply stressed SCs on both the demand and supply side. By global standards, the Mauritian manufacturing sector is fairly small but it has built a reputation where ethics, trust, quality and dependability are entrenched in the system. The integration of AI can be a game changer in a multitude of ways: frequent constructive interactions leading to value creation, higher productivity, reduced unit service costs, enhanced agility and better prediction capabilities. The analytical capability of AI must help the manufacturing sector to become more responsive, flexible and customer-centric, add to its inherent strengths while helping to discard weak points. The Government of Mauritius published the 'Mauritius AI Strategy' in November 2018. The AI strategy is highly supportive of the integration of AI in manufacturing and underscores the urgency of making the great leap from the traditional to AI-driven.

An AI-driven consolidation and diversification of the industrial base will be salutary as goods exports are yet to cross pre-pandemic levels. Sustainability initiatives are well-entrenched in the manufacturing sector, generating satisfactory outcomes to support the three pillars: people, planet and profit. However, there is still room for improvement.

# References

Abbany, Z. (2018, May 16). What good is AI for UN development goals? *DW*. https://p.dw.com/p/2xllV

Accenture-insights.be. (2018). Digital supply chain: How to unlock the real value of digital. https://www.accenture-insights.be/en-us/articles/digital-supply-chain-how-to-unlock-the-real-value-of-digital-1

Ben-Daya, M., Hassini, E., & Bahroun, Z. (2017). Internet of things and supply chain management: A literature review. *International Journal of Production Research*. https://doi.org/10.1080/00207543.2017.1402140

BIC. (2018). Future supply chains with artificial intelligence. https://www.biginnovationcentre.com/wp-content/uploads/2019/07/BIC_FUTURE-SUPPLY-CHAINS-WITH-ARTIFICIAL-INTELLIGENCE_28.04.2018.pdf

Brusset, X. (2016). Does supply chain visibility enhance agility? *International Journal of Production Economics, 171*, 46–59.

Calatayud, A. (2017). *The connected supply chain: Enhancing risk management in a changing world*. Discussion Paper No. 508. Washington, D.C.: Inter-American Development Bank.

Christopher, M., & Holweg, M. (2011). Supply chain 2.0: Managing supply chains in the era of turbulence. *International Journal of Physical Distribution and Logistics Management, 41*(1), 63–82.

CIEL group. (2023). Personal communication with CIEL's 'Industry 4.0 Team', 03 March 2023, Mauritius.

DHL. (2016). Logistics trend radar. http://www.dhl.com/content/dam/downloads/g0/about_us/logistics_insights/dhl_logistics_trend_radar_2016.pdf

Dounias, G., & Vassiliadis, V. (2015). Algorithms and methods inspired from nature for solving supply chain and logistics optimization problems: A survey. *Research Methods: Concepts, Methodologies, Tools, and Applications*, 245–276.

Dweekat, A., Hwang, G., & Park, J. (2017). A supply chain performance measurement approach using the internet of things: Toward more practical SCPMS. *Industrial Management & Data Systems, 117*(2), 267–286.

Fikar, C. (2018). A decision support system to investigate food losses in e-grocery deliveries. *Computers and Industrial Engineering, 117,* 282–290.

Fore, V., Khanna, A., Tomar, R., & Mishra, A. (2017). Intelligent supply management system. In *Proceedings of the 3rd International Conference on Advances in Computing, Communication and Engineering* (pp. 296–302). Durban.

Golicic, S., Davis, D., McCarthy, T., & Mentzer, J. (2002). The impact of e-commerce on supply chain relationships. *International Journal of Physical Distribution & Logistics Management, 32,* 851–871.

Gonul, C., Nowicki, D. R., Sauser, B., & Randall, W. S. (2017). Impact of cloud-based information sharing on hospital supply chain performance: A system dynamics framework. *International Journal of Production Economics.* https://doi.org/10.1016/j.ijpe.2017.10.008

IBM. (2015). The smarter supply chain of the future. http://www03.ibm.com/innovation/us/smarterplanet/assets/smarterBusiness/supply_chain/GBE03215USEN.PDF

Icarte, G. (2016). Applications of artificial intelligence in supply chain process: A systematic review. *Ingeniare, 24*(4), 663–679.

Lee, K.-F. (2018, September 4). The human promise of the AI revolution. *The Wall Street Journal.* https://www.wsj.com/articles/the-human-promise-of-the-ai-revolution-1536935115

Lee, J., Davari, H., Singh, J., & Pandhare, V. (2018). Industrial Artificial Intelligence for industry 4.0-based manufacturing systems. *Manufacturing Letters, 18,* 20–23.

Lee, H., & Ozer, O. (2007). Unlocking the value of RFID. *Production and Operations Management, 16*(1), 40–64.

Li, G., Yang, H., Sun, L., & Sohal, A. (2009). The impact of IT implementation on supply chain integration and performance. *International Journal of Production Economics, 120*(1), 125–138.

Lu, S., & Wang, X. (2017). Toward an intelligent solution for perishable food cold chain management. In *Proceedings of the IEEE International Conference on Software Engineering and Service Sciences* (pp. 852–856). Beijing.

Lu, Y. (2017). Industry 4.0: A survey on technologies, applications and open research issues. *Journal of Industrial Information Integration, 6,* 1–10.

Mangan, J., & Lalwani, C. (2016). *Global logistics and supply chain management* (3rd ed.). Wiley.

Nayak, R., & Padhye, R. (2018). Artificial intelligence and its application in the apparel industry. In *Automation in garment manufacturing* (pp. 109–138). https://doi.org/10.1016/B978-0-08-101211-6.00005-7

Nooraie, S. V., & Parast, M. (2016). A multi-objective approach to supply chain risk management: Integrating visibility with supply and demand risk. *International Journal of Production Economics, 161,* 192–200.

Patil, R. (2018). Supermarket Tesco pioneers big data. *Dataconomy.* http://dataconomy.com/2014/02/tesco-pioneers-big-data/

Sanders, C., Autry, D., & Gligor, M. (2011). The impact of buyer firm information connectivity: Enablers on supplier firm performance. *International Journal of Logistics Management, 22,* 179–201.

Sarac, A., Absi, N., & Dauzere-Peres, S. (2010). A literature review on the impact of RFID technologies on supply chain management. *International Journal of Production Economics, 128,* 77–95.

Schwab, K. (2016). *The 4th industrial revolution*. World Economic Forum.

Singh, L. P., & Challa, R. T. (2016). Integrated forecasting using the discrete wavelet theory and artificial intelligence techniques to reduce the bullwhip effect in a supply chain. *Global Journal of Flexible Systems Management, 17*(2), 157–169.

Slimani, I., Farissi, I. E., & Al-Qualsadi, S. A. (2016). Configuration of daily demand predicting system based on neural networks. In *Proceedings of the 3rd IEEE International Conference on Logistics Operations Management* (pp. 1–5, art. no. 7731709). Fez.

Somapa, S., Cools, M., & Dullaert, W. (2018). Characterizing supply chain visibility – A literature review. *International Journal of Logistics Management*. https://doi.org/10.1108/IJLM-06-2016-0150

Vassiliadis, V., & Dounias, G. (2009). Nature-inspired intelligence: A review of selected methods and applications. *The International Journal on Artificial Intelligence Tools, 18*(4), 487–516.

World Economic Forum. Artificial intelligence and robots. https://toplink.weforum.org/knowledge/insight/a1Gb0000000pTDREA2/explore/summary

World Economic Forum. (2017). Impact of the fourth industrial revolution on supply chains. http://www3.weforum.org/docs/WEF_Impact_of_the_Fourth_Industrial_Revolution_on_Supply_Chains_.pdf

Yan, R. (2017). Optimization approach for increasing revenue of perishable product supply chain with the Internet of Things. *Industrial Management & Data Systems, 117*(4), 729–741.

Yan, B., Jin, Z., Liu, L., & Liu, S. (2017). Factors influencing the adoption of the internet of things in supply chains. *Journal of Evolutionary Economics*. https://doi.org/10.1007/s00191-017-0527-3

Zhang, F. Z., He, H. X., & Xiao, W. J. (2013). Application analysis of Internet of Things on the management of supply chain and intelligent logistics. *Applied Mechanics and Materials, 411–414*, 2655–2661.

Zhu, X., Mukhopadhyay, S., & Kurata, H. (2012). A review of RFID technology and its managerial applications in different industries. *Journal of Engineering and Technology Management, 29*(1), 152–167.

Chapter 19

# AI for Social Good: Opportunities for Inclusive and Sustainable Development

*Satyadev Rosunee and Roshan Unmar*

University of Mauritius, Mauritius

## Abstract

The age of artificial intelligence (AI) is already upon us. The rapid development of AI tools is facilitating sustainable development and its corollary social good. For AI dedicated to social good to be impactful, it has to be human-centred, striving to achieve inclusiveness, sustainable livelihoods and community well-being. In short, it offers major opportunities to holistically enhance peoples' lives in diverse areas: education, health care, food security, disaster reduction, smart cities, etc. However, ethical, unbiased and 'secure-by-design' algorithms that power AI are crucial to building trust in this technology. Civil society's engagement can hopefully drive the features and values that should be embedded in AI.

This chapter focuses on the societal benefits that AI can deliver. Our initiatives and decisions of today will fashion the 'Social Good' AI applications of tomorrow. Sustainable Development Goals (SDGs) being addressed are 2–4 and 10–11.

*Keywords*: Social good; democracy; food security; health care; education; habitats; disaster response

## 19.1 Introduction

The term artificial intelligence (AI) may be used to describe the overall objective of enabling computers to simulate human intelligence, especially intelligent software that can think, apply judgement and act like a human being, when presented with a problem or query (Cellan-Jones, 2017; Olley, 2019; McCarthy et al., 1955; Russel & Norvig, 2014; Searle, 1980).

Artificial Intelligence, Engineering Systems and Sustainable Development, 245–256
Copyright © 2024 Satyadev Rosunee and Roshan Unmar
Published under exclusive licence by Emerald Publishing Limited
doi:10.1108/978-1-83753-540-820241019

A core application of AI therefore consists of 'automating' tasks that require human intelligence by integrating software and computers. Social good is predominantly human-centric. The fundamental requirements for an AI system to deliver social good are:

   i. It has to be human-centred;
  ii. Seamless interaction between the gamut of AI systems and human activities;
 iii. Effortless collaboration between humans and the AI system;
  iv. AI system that learns and delivers in the most trying circumstances; viz. tsunami, earthquake, flash flood, etc. with ability to self-learn.

As humans, we are collectively responsible for the betterment of society. AI can advance knowledge in a diversity of fields to promote social good and harmony.

The first industrial revolution was powered by machines that essentially acted as multipliers of physical strength. AI machines would essentially amplify our cognitive strength that could potentially accelerate economic growth and social good. Significant research is ongoing that explore AI and societal good (Bostrom, 2018; Cowls & Floridi, 2018).

AI systems for instance can potentially help to design materials that are highly efficient in converting solar energy to electrical energy, manage sensors for monitoring air quality and leakages in water pipes, monitor traffic flow, etc. AI can help us design nanomaterials that can absorb carbon dioxide and mitigate the impact of global warming. The innovations mentioned above are possible owing to the growth of computing power at relatively low cost. Investment in the right AI technologies can go a long way to improve humanity's lot in line with the 17 United Nations Sustainable Development Goals (SDGs) (UN, 2015). Over 30 UN agencies have integrated AI within their mission and objectives (UN, 2019).

Currently there are significant concerns on the ethical, trustworthiness and legal implications of AI applications. Major concerns are potential loss of jobs, privacy intrusions, causing unintended harm, misuse and reaching 'the singularity'. Singularity means the point at which a machine can self-learn without any human intervention (EU, 2019; OECD, 2019; Tegmark, 2017; Walsh, 2018). How we manage all this by striking a robust balance between ethical, legal and moral values will decide whether AI can steer society towards greater social good and enable people to lead healthy and happy lives.

## 19.2 Democracy, Human Rights and SDGs

Democracy is a global common good. Past and contemporary history is a witness that democracy as a political system is the best hope for the survival of the human race and the protection of the planet. As such, academia and civil society play an important role in promoting and cultivating democratic interests throughout the world. Although there is no one-size-fits-all model of democracy, just as there is no one-size-fits-all model for capitalism, there are basic principles that all authentic democracies share, namely: the protection of human rights. AI can be used to monitor and detect human rights violations, such as forced labour and gender-based violence, and help organisations respond to and prevent these abuses.

Achieving the SDGs (UN, 2015) will depend, in large measure, on strengthening democratic institutions around the world. Unlike other forms of political governance, democracies generally self-correct in that they are designed to respond to changes in society and to the will of the people. To ensure that no one is left behind, the United Nations has always stressed the interconnectedness of the SDGs. Yet, it may happen that an initiative yielding positive outcomes with one SDG negates or weakens outcomes with respect to another SDG and its targets. Awareness of this interconnectedness should be the locus of fair and inclusive AI for social good. Future AI applications should target a net positive effect on the maximum number of SDGs, without compromising the benefits of other SDGs. AI for social good applications typically target five areas namely: people, planet, prosperity, peace and partnerships. With a balanced approach, AI for social good researchers should objectively measure the impacts, both positive and negative, of their work.

Higher education, as creator of knowledge, and civil society, as a community of non-governmental and non-business actors, have a responsibility to promote the common good. In this regard, higher education has a key role to play by democratising access to quality education, stimulate awareness of the global SDGs among faculty and students and engaging with community and stakeholders to achieve the goals. Universities are indeed well placed to deal with challenges associated with SDGs through inter/transdisciplinary research and serve as a bridge between scientists and policymakers. With each advance, all stakeholders need to reassess the transformational potential of AI within the parameters of human safety and privacy.

## 19.3 Food Security

The world population will increase by about two billion in 2050. In contrast, land under food cultivation will increase by 4% only, which potentially will not suffice to feed the global population. Tackling this critical global problem would entail the modernisation of 'old school' agricultural techniques. AI technology could be deployed as follows: crop harvesting, drone imagery, remote sensing, proximity sensing, pest and weed control, etc. In the Indian state of Andhra Pradesh, Microsoft is providing advisory services to 175 farmers regarding sowing seeds, usage of fertiliser, remote sensing, etc. (Bagchi, 2019). This initiative has led to an average of 30% higher yield per hectare. Harvest Croo Robotics (2022) has developed an AI-driven strawberry picking machine that emulates human cognition.

Prospera (2023), based in Israel, has developed a cloud-based solution to address the biggest challenges in agriculture. Its indigenous technology collects, digitises and analyses vast amounts of data to help farmers manage their crops and growing systems. Examples abound where AI tools have rendered farming smarter, improving the lives of farming communities. However, AI-driven farming still faces lack of funding and stakeholder validation. The agricultural sector is a prime target for innovative practices, provided hurdles are removed.

## 19.4 Health Care

A rapidly ageing world population will require smart health care that is both affordable and reliable. This is an area where AI can usher in transformational innovations. AI algorithms can help to 'search' the medical research literature, analyse huge datasets and images generated during patient examination. Clinical decision support systems, aided by AI tools, will support medical practitioners with regard to their diagnosis and therapeutic prescriptions (Topol, 2019).

In developing countries where resources are scarce and limited, AI could be used to analyse medical images for faster diagnoses and treatment options. AI and the internet can therefore promote telemedicine for low-risk chronic illnesses and help doctors diagnose and treat patients more effectively (Gray, 2018). The advantages of disseminating new medical knowledge are numerous. Natural language processing can be used to review the literature, with a specific aim, e.g. predict outbreaks of infectious diseases.

The overarching goal is to improve the interpretation of observations and measurements, leading to sound diagnosis, improve treatment accuracy, effectiveness and accessibility (Gray, 2018). Such a goal can only be attained through careful system design, taking into account how physician and AI can reliably complement each other, notwithstanding contextual differences. AI systems could process huge datasets about people's behaviours; say, diet, physical exercise, leisure activities, illness, leading to better public health planning.

Potential impacts of AI on health care:

- drug discovery;
- mining of public data to assist early diagnosis and timely medical treatments;
- render health care more affordable by optimising hospital/clinical costs;
- improved health and well-being of the population;
- focus on prevention;
- just-in-time information for patient care.

Based on these metrics, how can AI technologies be used to enhance patient care?

- Internet of Things: real-time data collection and analysis for diagnosis and treatment purposes;
- An AI system would compile a patient's health data and help the medical practitioner to make treatment decisions;
- The system could act as a 'health assistant' and give targeted health advice;
- In the context of disaster relief, an AI system could connect patients with unaffected hospitals;

- A smart AI system that would render hospital visits less frequent and less necessary, relieving stress on the health care system.

AI could trace alternative pathways for medical research fields that have stalled for decades: new drugs for depression and Alzheimer's disease. The complex interactions of so many proteins in the body are beyond human understanding. An AI system that could generate solutions by 'combining the causal reasoning of human beings with the sheer computation of computers. That would be revolutionary'.

### *19.4.1 Success Stories*

Carrying out surveys to tap public health data is costly, time consuming and biased towards people availing of medical services. An alternative approach is to perform social media analytics to gauge the population's health at little cost. Natural language processing has progressed significantly. It can accurately identify social media posts that hint towards a particular disease outbreak. Sadilek et al. (2016) have reported the use of the Nemesis AI system that can help sanitary authorities to locate food outlets serving contaminated food. A similar method could be used to track influenza or predict drug abuse among particular social media users.

The symptoms of many chronic diseases vary widely across the population, which makes treatment that exactly suit the patient more difficult to pin down. An AI system that can empower treatment decisions from a large dataset is a valuable area of research (Murphy, 2003).

It is widely acknowledged that the health care sector has to adopt an AI system that is perpetually self-learning. The AI system would crunch all the available data about a person (school, hospital health insurance, social services), build appropriate models, and help make the right decisions. It would enable the patient to get dedicated care when needed. The AI system should automatically capture the new data and learn from it.

## 19.5 Education

Education is an area where human-centred AI systems can usher in immense benefits for both learners and teachers. Lakkaraju et al. (2015) have reported the development of a machine learning (ML) framework that can identify learners who require help to graduate or unlikely to apply to college or unenthusiastic about college or fail to embark on a career path following graduation. Over the past several years, some school–university partnerships in the United States have endeavoured to develop AI-based systems to help them identify learners who are at risk of dropping out of high school prematurely. In addition, school records and social network-engaged feeds could be used to identify learners that are at risk of poor performance. Prompt corrective action can, therefore, be taken to remedy the situation.

## 19.6 AI for Sustainability

Sustainability promotes the well-being of environmental, economic and social systems (three pillars of sustainability) that are critical to human societies. The three pillars must be well balanced in order to obtain meaningful outcomes. AI in sustainability therefore requires a 'systems approach', although it is recognised that current AI technologies cannot operate at this scale yet.

For example, when siting a new dam, a comprehensive socio-eco-environmental impact assessment is required. Humans would tend to focus on the obvious benefits to farming, food security and a durable solution to water scarcity. Potential loss of livelihoods, flooding of important cultural and religious sites, loss of wildlife habitats (including endangered species) and changed sedimentation patterns would raise red flags. To better understand the dynamics and intrinsic complexities of such a system, AI tools powered by unbiased data would help. Wildlife is key to sustaining biodiversity on planet earth. AI can be used to monitor wildlife and track changes in the environment, helping conservationists to protect endangered species and preserve natural habitats.

Building and deploying sensor networks is the most common method to capture data relevant to ecosystems. The Trans-Africa HyrdoMeteorological Observatory (TAHMO) project has rolled out a network of 20,000 weather stations to capture weather-related data (van de Giesen et al., 2014). Elephant poachers are an existential risk to wild elephants, mercilessly and illegally killing them for their ivory tusks. Video camera-enabled drones are being used to track elephants and other large animals. The goal of the PAWS Project is to use predictive AI algorithms to prevent poaching events, maximise the deterrence value of patrols while minimising costs (Fang et al., 2016; Nguyen et al., 2016; Yang et al., 2014).

'AI for Earth' is a programme produced by Microsoft (2023). Its aim is to open access to AI tools and educational resources that can stimulate innovation for tackling global environmental challenges. Following an extreme weather event (hurricane), the AI for Earth programme funded a research project in Puerto Rico to study the impact of the hurricane on the El Yunque National Forest. By using AI and data science, the research team analysed the disruptive impact of the hurricane on the trees. Without AI, such a study would not have been possible.

How do forests change, after the passage of hurricanes, can help authorities concerned to take appropriate measures to combat climate change (CC) (springboard.com)?

### 19.6.1 Species Habitats Modelling

SDGs 14 and 15 are concerned with 'life under water' and 'life on land', respectively, acknowledging the fact that biodiversity and its preservation are crucial for the overall wellbeing of the planet. The adverse effects of CC on biodiversity have been extensively documented. Data collected on species can be analysed by well-established techniques such as data mining, statistics and ML to build realistic models. The basic procedure is to do a headcount to estimate population size and to determine their distribution over a given region. One important precaution is to avoid double head counting of a given species across time and space. Given the inexorable advance of CC, it is important to determine which climate variables would affect species in their respective habitats.

A long-term planning priority for a small island developing state like Mauritius is sea-level rise owing to CC. The degree of sea-level rise is fraught with uncertainty. An adaptive management approach that feeds on data updates and accordingly activates model revisions would help to protect costal assets, such as tourist resorts. Nicol et al. (2015) have worked towards the conservation of coastal habitat for migrating birds endangered by sea level rise. Flooding will encroach on the habitat of these migrating birds unless remedial habitat is identified for them.

## 19.7 Social Issues AI Can Help to Address

### 19.7.1 Waste Collection

Waste bins are fitted with global positioning system (GPS) sensors (Internet of Things [IoT]). The sensors send information when they should be emptied. The sensor network enables the municipality to determine the routing of garbage trucks more efficiently, directing them to full bins only. These IoT-enabled waste bins have slashed the number of crews and some routes resulting in substantial financial benefits resulting from savings in labour, operation time and transport costs. This technology has an added advantage of generating less pollution and less congestion.

### 19.7.2 Disaster Response

Floods are a debilitating natural hazard, affecting large and small communities alike. Damage caused is estimated to cost billions of dollars every year. AI can help to build more focused, precise, environmental modelling to address natural hazards. AI systems supported by large datasets and ML could facilitate forecasting, mitigation and response processes. Such benefits could be extended to agriculture also (Chien, n.d.).

AI can be used to scan satellite imagery and social media posts to identify and respond to natural disasters, such as earthquakes and extreme weather events.

### 19.7.3 Poverty Reduction

AI can be used to improve agricultural produce supply chain management, reduce food waste and optimise the distribution of resources to those in need. In this way, AI directly contributes to SDG 2, 'end hunger, achieve food security and improved nutrition and promote sustainable agriculture'.

### 19.7.4 Accessibility

SDGs 10 and 11, 'reduced inequalities' and 'sustainable cities and communities' both require the support of technology. AI can be used to develop assistive technologies, such as speech-to-text software, to make information and services more accessible to people with disabilities.

## 19.8 AI Technology to Improve Mobility

AI is poised to transform mobility and transportation infrastructure. Technology exists that can greatly assist mobility at lower costs increase traffic fluidity and reduce average commuting time. Autonomous vehicles have intrinsic technology to reduce $CO_2$ emissions owing to fewer acceleration and braking patterns. Higher peoples' mobility will improve the vibrancy and congeniality of urban areas, resulting in more fruitful leisure and socio-economic interactions.

Ubiquitous connectivity and instrumentation have enabled the capture of data that were previously lost. Data analytics tools are processing these data into sophisticated models. Thus, in the near future, AI will enable the shift from 'data to decision'.

Traffic congestion is a major cause of stress. Poorly timed traffic signals are known to cause congestion. Most traffic signals operate on preset timings, optimised for average traffic flow conditions. Actual traffic flows are seldom close to the average conditions, and over time congestion becomes inevitable. Smith (2016) has applied AI techniques to manage traffic lights in real time, based on current traffic patterns.

Combining user data from a mass public transit system and other mobility data can help to assess the movement of people and evaluate the mobility gaps of commuters. Data-enabled simulation analysis may be used to drive policy changes for stressless mobility (Zhu et al., 2016).

## 19.9 AI for Public Welfare

The overall end goal of public welfare and safety is to enhance the wellbeing and safety of all citizens. The windfall is increased equity, improved effectiveness and efficiency of public services. AI can impactfully enhance public welfare and safety.

Actions that ought to be taken to create new knowledge are:

- Build data libraries related to priority areas;
- Smarter integration of data sources currently being used in a fractured manner;
- Build models and prediction algorithms of individual behaviours;
- Assessment of existing policies and understand implications if AI is introduced as an enabling tool.

Can AI identify and flag individuals who may commit a crime and eventually get a criminal conviction? Can we pre-empt such misdemeanours and develop appropriate interventions? Predictive policing AI technology may identify police officers at risk of being aggressive towards the public and match them with appropriate duties (Perry et al., 2013). West and Allen (2018) have reported that ML has enhanced the ability to predict crime-prone locations, the likely perpetrators and engage in preventive actions.

Video surveillance can analyse crime patterns and predicts areas at high risk of crime, helping law enforcement to prevent and solve crimes. Street cameras are ubiquitous features of most cities today. They are more helpful in solving crimes rather than preventing them (Arikuma & Mochizuki, 2016; NPR, 2013). One major hurdle is the lack of manpower to visualise large quantities of video footage. AI in this area is improving with its ability to classify incidents with a high degree of accuracy that may lead to prosecution and hopefully deter crime. However, these advances could translate into wider video surveillance. The security of large facilities such as seaports, airports, coastlines, waterways and industrial complexes is being monitored by drones, albeit raising concerns about privacy. Smart city operations use sensors to measure air quality; digital cameras to identify licence plates to facilitate tracking of drivers who commit traffic-related offences.

Responding promptly to emergency calls reinforces public safety. Who, when and how to dispatch to attend to emergency calls is tricky. The public body has to ensure availability of resources and delivery of services without overspending. Predictive algorithms could be used to better deploy emergency responders and save lives by building a reliable dataset on their location and activities.

## 19.10 AI for Equitable and Ethical Policymaking

How does a city council allocate resources to the families, homes, neighbourhoods and communities that are most in need? What metrics do we rely on to mount capacity building programmes that are in line with future human resource requirements and better employability?

AI for social good is driven by data collected on people. Societal and ethical factors dictate that privacy, transparency and traceability of data collection must be maintained. Data bias and uncertainty might impinge on the fairness of a policy decision. When building a 'social good' decision framework, it is important to understand the impact of a decision on the individual as well as understanding the nuances of individual preferences. Secondly, it is important to define the problem within the relevant social context.

The following research methodology could be adopted:

(1) Robust data-enabled and ML models that address bias, incomplete data and data from heterogeneous sources;
(2) Engineer models with predictive capabilities and flexible to 'refresh' – when additional data becomes available;
(3) Advanced models that factor in social contexts and resource constraints for decision-making and planning;
(4) Dependable and cost-effective.

Computer science innovations are key to addressing these core AI problems. Durable and scalable progress in 'AI for Social Good' will depend largely on strict privacy preserving methods, irrespective of the source of information. Additionally, a user-centred design approach will facilitate adoption.

## 19.11 Threats

While the opportunities are numerous, it is important to exert control over potential social harms that misuse of AI can induce in society. Professor Michael Wooldridge, AI researcher at the University of Oxford, in his book 'The road to conscious machines: The story of AI' cautions about a possible fracture to society that is likely to occur in future generations if individuals inhabit their own, AI-powered digital universe promoted by social media. This virtual individualistic world is created by AI tools which find the likes of people and bring it to them while hiding that which they do not like. Such exposure would inevitably disrupt the common values and principles of society by alienating individuals and isolating them in their own social media bubble. Likewise, there is growing concern about 'DeepFakes', which are photos or videos altered by a neural network to include people who were not present in the original, and often used to propagate fake news. These threats have given rise to the need for regulatory frameworks for ethical AI. One of the most influential frameworks is the Asilomar principles, which is a set of 23 principles formulated in 2017 by a group of AI scientists. The first Asilomar principle is that the goal of AI should be to create beneficial intelligence.

## 19.12 Conclusion

'AI for Social Good' research should be approached via cross-sector, interdisciplinary and systems-based approaches. The challenge is to balance the effectiveness of the AI tool with its potential for misuse. Appropriate checks and balances need to be put in place. Indeed, AI could bring numerous benefits to mankind, viz. sustainable development, health care, education, scientific research and discovery, productivity, business innovation and wealth creation. However, some negative impacts – on jobs, social inequality, democracy and possibly national security, are possible threats. AI, as seen, is highly diverse and evolving rapidly. It is becoming increasingly obvious that new modes of anticipating and controlling the unintended consequences of AI need to be deployed.

## References

Arikuma, T., & Mochizuki, Y. (2016). Intelligent multimedia surveillance system for safer cities. *APSIPA Transactions on Signal and Information Processing, 5*, 1–8.
Bagchi, A. (2019). *Artificial intelligence in agriculture.* Mindtree.
Bostrom, N. (2018). *The vulnerable world hypothesis.* The Future of Humanity Institute. https://nickbostrom.com/papers/vulnerable.pdf

Cellan-Jones, R. (2017, October 16). Artificial intelligence – Hype, hope and fear. *BBC News*, 3. http://www.bbc.co.uk/news/technology-41634316

Chien, S. (n.d.). *Senior research scientist and head of the artificial intelligence group at the California*. Institute of Technology's Jet Propulsion Laboratory.

Cowls, J., & Floridi, L. (2018). White paper on an ethical framework for a good AI society. *SSRN Electronic Journal*. https://doi.org/10.2139/ssrn.3198732

Fang, F., Nguyen, T. H., Pickles, R., Lam, W. Y., Clements, G. R., An, B., Singh, A., Tambe, M., & Lemieux, A. (2016). Deploying PAWS: Field optimization of the protection assistant for wildlife security. In *Proceedings of the Twenty Eighth Innovative Applications of Artificial Intelligence Conference* (pp. 3966–3973). AAAI. https://www.cais.usc.edu/wp-content/uploads/2017/07/Fang-et-al-IAAI16_PAWS-1.pdf

Gray, A. (2018, September 20). *7 amazing ways artificial intelligence is used in healthcare*. World Economic Forum. https://www.weforum.org/agenda/2018/09/7-amazing-ways-artificialintelligence-is-used-in-healthcare/

Harvest Croo. https://www.harvestcroorobotics.com/

High-level expert group on artificial intelligence. *Ethics Guidelines for Trustworthy AI*, (2019), 34. https://ec.europa.eu/newsroom/dae/document.cfm?doc_id=60419

https://www.microsoft.com/en-us/ai/ai-for-earth

https://www.springboard.com/blog/data-science/ai-for-good/. Accessed on February 14, 2023.

Lakkaraju, H., Aguiar, E., Shan, C., Miller, D., Bhanpuri, N., Ghani, R., & Addison, K. (2015). A machine learning framework to identify students at risk of adverse academic outcomes. In *Proceedings of the 21th ACM SIGKDD International Conference on Knowledge Discovery and Data Mining*. http://d-miller.github.io/assets/LakkarajuEtAl2015.pdf

McCarthy, J., Minsky, M. L., Rochester, N., & Shannon, C. E. (1955). A proposal for the dartmouth summer research project on artificial intelligence. http://raysolomonoff.com/dartmouth/boxa/dart564props.pdf

Murphy, S. A. (2003). Optimal dynamic treatment regimes. *Journal of the Royal Statistical Society: Series B*, *65*(2), 331–355.

Nguyen, T. H., Sinha, A., Gholami, S., Plumptre, A. J., Joppa, L., Tambe, M., Driciru, M., Wanyama, F., Rwetsiba, A., Critchlow, R., & Beale, C. (2016). Capture: A new predictive anti-poaching tool for wildlife protection. In *Proceedings of the 15th International Conference on Autonomous Agents and Multiagent Systems (AAMAS)* (pp. 767–775). Singapore.

Nicol, S., Fuller, R. A., Iwamura, T., & Chadès, I. (2015). Adapting environmental management to uncertain but inevitable change. *Proceedings Royal Society B*, *282*(1808), 20142984. http://doi.org/10.1098/rspb.2014.2984

NPR. (2013, April 22). Big Op-Ed: Shifting opinions on surveillance cameras. *Talk of the Nation*. http://www.npr.org/2013/04/22/178436355/big-op-ed-shiftingopinions-on-surveillance-cameras

OECD. (2019). *Artificial intelligence in society*. OECD Publishing. https://doi.org/10.1787/eedfee77-en

Olley, D. (2019). *Elsevier – Artificial intelligence: How knowledge is created, transferred, and used* (p. 4). https://www.elsevier.com/?a=827872

Perry, W. L., McInnis, B., Price, C. C., Smith, S., & Hollywood, J. S. (2013). *The role of crime forecasting in law enforcement operations* (Vol. 233). Rand Corporation Report.

Prospera. https://prospera.ag/

Russel, S., & Norvig, P. (2014). *Artificial intelligence: A modern approach* (3rd ed.). Pearson Education Limited.

Sadilek, A., Kautz, H., DiPrete, L., Labus, B., Portman, E., Teitel, J., & Silenzio, V. (2016). Deploying nEmesis: Preventing foodborne illness by data mining social media. *Association for the Advancement of Artificial Intelligence*, *38*(1), 37–48.

Searle, J. R. (1980). Minds, brains, and programs. *Behavioral and Brain Sciences*, *3*(3), 417–457. https://doi.org/10.1017/S0140525X00005756

Smith, S. F. (2016). Smart infrastructure for urban mobility. *Slides from the AI for Social Good Workshop*. http://cra.org/ccc/wp-content/uploads/sites/2/2016/06/Stephen-Smith-AIslides.pdf

Tegmark, M. (2017). *Life 3.0: Being human in the age of artificial intelligence*. Knopf.

Topol, E. (2019). High-performance medicine: The convergence of human and artificial intelligence. *Nature Medicine*, *24*, 44–56. https://doi.org/10.1038/s41591-018-0300-7

van de Giesen, N., Hut, R., & Selker, J. (2014). The trans-African hydro-meteorological observatory (TAHMO). *WIREs Water*, *1*, 341–348. https://doi.org/10.1002/wat2.1034

UN Report. (2019). https://www.itu.int/dms_pub/itu-s/opb/gen/S-GEN-UNACT-2019-1-PDF-E.pdf

UN Sustainable Development Goals. (2015). https://sustainabledevelopment.un.org/

Walsh, T. (2018). *Machines that think*. Prometheus Books.

West, D., & Allen, J. (2018). *How artificial intelligence is transforming the world*. The Brooking Institute. www.brookings.edu/research/how-artificial-intelligence-istransforming-the-world/

Yang, R., Ford, B., Tambe, M., & Lemieux, A. (2014, May). Adaptive resource allocation for wildlife protection against illegal poachers. In *Proceedings of the Thirteenth International Conference on Autonomous Agents and Multiagent Systems (AAMAS)*. Paris.

Zhu, F., Li, Z., Chen, S., & Xiong, G. (2016). Parallel transportation management and control system and its applications in building smart cities. *IEEE Transactions on Intelligent Transportation Systems*, *17*(6), 1576–1585. https://doi.org/10.1109/TITS.2015.2506156

# Chapter 20

# The Applications of Artificial Intelligence in the Textile Industry

*Naraindra Kistamah*

University of Mauritius, Mauritius

## Abstract

This chapter offers an overview of the applications of artificial intelligence (AI) in the textile industry and in particular, the textile colouration and finishing industry. The advent of new technologies such as AI and the Internet of Things (IoT) has changed many businesses and one area AI is seeing growth in is the textile industry. It is estimated that the AI software market shall reach a new high of over US$60 billion by 2022, and the largest increase is projected to be in the area of machine learning (ML). This is the area of AI where machines process and analyse vast amount of data they collect to perform tasks and processes. In the textile manufacturing industry, AI is applied to various areas such as colour matching, colour recipe formulation, pattern recognition, garment manufacture, process optimisation, quality control and supply chain management for enhanced productivity, product quality and competitiveness, reduced environmental impact and overall improved customer experience. The importance and success of AI is set to grow as ML algorithms become more sophisticated and smarter, and computing power increases.

*Keywords*: Artificial intelligence; textile industry; colour matching; quality control; manufacturing processes; smart textiles

## 20.1 Introduction

The textile industry is one of the oldest and most important global industry in the world. It deals with the design, development, production, manufacturing and distribution of textile goods such as fibres, yarns, fabrics and garments. Historically, the textile industry has had its landmarks. In the 18th century, textile production grew significantly out of the industrial revolution as the production of yarn and fabric

Artificial Intelligence, Engineering Systems and Sustainable Development, 257–269

Copyright © 2024 Naraindra Kistamah

Published under exclusive licence by Emerald Publishing Limited

doi:10.1108/978-1-83753-540-820241020

became a mainstream industry. A century later, the industry continued to benefit from technological innovations such as the steam engine, textile machinery innovations and computers. During the 20th century, with the advancement of computer technology and logistics, the textile industry became more global. Other technological advancements such as the introduction of new fibres and fabrics, as well as innovative manufacturing processes, have also influenced the advancement of the industry (Wikipedia, 2023). It is now estimated that the industry is worth US$1.30 trillion and employs over 60 million people in the world (IndexBox, 2022). It is predicted that the industry will grow at an astounding rate of over 10% annually to reach US$ 2.25 trillion by 2025 (Partida, 2022).

The textile industry constantly evolves thanks to new trends, a dynamic market and innovative machinery and technologies. Over the last two decades, the industry has received a new impetus with the continuing development in computer technology and research in artificial intelligence (AI). The applications of AI in the textile industry dates back to early 1990s, but its expansion has been relatively slow. One of the reasons could be that the industry is too conservative in its gainful exploitation, by AI tools, of the large amount of data which are produced by textile processes. The textile industry is global and diversified and there is a need for global laws to protect the manufacturer's data. AI systems transform large amounts of quantitative data into intelligible classification, by spotting trends and patterns (Welamo & Sanpeng, 2021). Many textile industrialists and researchers are actively investigating the potential and applications of AI in various aspects of the textile supply chain. AI is increasingly finding a home with textile manufacturers as the demand for high quality, quick-response and high-tech textile products increases (Shamey & Hussain, 2003; Wong, 2019).

On the technical aspects of textile processes such as spinning, weaving and colouration, there are numerous, known and unknown, variable inputs with a complex interdependence between them. It is very difficult and time consuming to develop an exact mathematical model to predict outputs with high accuracy and precision. Statistical and mechanistic models have their limitations to solve complex problems. Thus, they are not quite reliable as decision-making tools. Mechanistic models, for example, generally simplify the problems and make equations more solvable at the cost of accuracy. By using AI, it is possible to identify, classify, measure and predict textile properties with greater accuracy than when using conventional systems alone (Tehran & Maleki, 2011).

## 20.2 AI in Textile Manufacturing

There are numerous publications on neural network applications addressing a wide variety of textile-related issues such as visual identification of defects, online monitoring of processes, textile property prediction and modelling for designing and prototyping.

Neural networks have been used, over the last two decades, to identify textile defects since there are some problems associated with human inspection (Kuo & Lee, 2003). The process is slow, and is subject to subjective factors and human fatigue which often lead to low productivity and high rejection rates. These problems influence production output and inspection accuracy. Neural networks have emerged as a very useful technique for fault detection due to their ability to be trained to recognise faults robustly and accurately. In fault detection, neural network is often combined with digital image analysis using various image processing methods. A key challenge in many neural network applications is to determine the appropriate input features to be used for modelling. Researchers extract useful information from images and feed them as input features to neural network system (Kumar, 2003). Many researchers employed multi-layer feed forward backpropagation neural network which can be used for learning and classifying distinct defects, thus identifying faults and monitoring quality online (Tehran & Maleki, 2011). For suitable image capture of the textile specimen, for effective image processing by a neural network system, a camera, scanner or other image capturing devices and/or proper illumination condition are required (Bahlmann et al., 1999). For textile property prediction and modelling, the physical and mechanical properties of textile fibres and yarns are used as input variables for the neural network system.

### 20.2.1 AI in Yarn Manufacturing

The quality of a yarn is an important factor that influences the property and quality of a fabric and hence a garment. It is recognised that yarn spinning is a complex manufacturing process, which involves a number of variables such as raw materials, processing methodologies and equipment parameters. Yarn physical properties such as strength, elongation, evenness and bending rigidity are important parameters, which affect the quality and performance of products such as fabrics and garments. More and more yarn production parameters are now determined and predicted by AI-based control system of the yarn manufacturing machinery for enhanced production efficiency and quality (El-Geiheini et al., 2020; Sikka et al., 2022).

In the field of yarn quality control, AI has found wide applications since it is much better than human inspectors at detecting yarn defects, analysing failure rates, adjusting control settings to maximise yarn production process and maintaining yarn quality. AI powered systems analyse programmable quality attributes of yarn such as hairiness, unevenness and tenacity of different types of yarn using digital image analysis (Pereira et al., 2023; Sikka et al., 2022). As the quantity of available data increases, the system continues to optimise the AI recognition process and allows training results to be transferred to production lines (Solomon, 2023). The technology has also reduced yarn grading mistakes to as much as 60%, leading to better yarn grading (Sahu, 2021).

A number of synthetic polymer processing companies such as Oerlikon has digitalised its 'From Melt to Yarn, Fibres and Nonwovens' process chain. The company offers information technology solutions via online applications on smart phones and tablets to monitor yarn production processes (Indian Textile Magazine, 2019).

In the area of yarn modelling, traditional methods are very tedious and models are simplistic, regular and not realistic enough in appearance. Researchers from Cornell have developed an AI algorithm which can model the fibre and yarn properties automatically and realistically. The images of single strands of yarn are scanned using a Computed Tomography (CT) scanner and an AI algorithm is used to convert data from the scan into a 3D fibre-yarn model. The research work may be very useful when designing and prototyping fabrics for many industries such as the automotive and apparel industry (Bharadwaj, 2019).

An adaptive neuro-fuzzy inference system (ANFIS) was developed for the prediction of yarn properties such as tenacity and unevenness. It was based on a set of key input cotton fibre properties such as fibre strength, fibre length, fibre fineness and short fibre content. It was found that the ANFIS model could effectively predict the yarn properties while treating fibre properties as the input variables (Das & Chakraborty, 2021).

### 20.2.2 AI in Fabric Manufacturing

Fabric inspection is still largely carried out by human operators who are prone to making mistakes. Increasingly, many researchers use artificially intelligent system combined with image analysis to automatically identify defects in fabrics. The smart system detects and evaluates fabric defects, and analyses data to generate improved fabric grading system. The system's output is fast and suited for continuous online fabric monitoring. A fabric classification accuracy ranging from 75% to 85% depending on the nature of the defects may be expected. The use of automated fabric fault detection systems would invariably influence positively the production and quality of apparel (Das & Chakraborty, 2021). Fig. 20.1 shows a schematic representation of the computer vision system used for detecting and classifying fabric faults in combination with Artificial Neural Network (ANN) (Eldessouki, 2018). The combined system finds application also in pattern recognition when designing, developing and producing woven and knitted fabrics. Cognex ViDi is an example of an AI technology, developed by Cognex Corp. as a very useful quality control tool that can automatically examine fabric patterning, identify pattern faults with high degree of accuracy (Sahu, 2021). It is a camera-based inspection technology that is developing rapidly to find wider applications in the fabric manufacturing and printing industry (Bharadwaj, 2019; Kumah et al., 2020; Sahu, 2021).

Another AI-powered automated and online fabric fault detection system is WiseEye. A high-powered light emitting diode (LED) light bar is used to illuminate the fabric and a high-resolution camera moves along a rail to capture images of the full width of the fabric during weaving process. The images captured are fed into an AI-based machine vision algorithm to detect and alert for fabric defects. The system may be applied to most types of woven fabrics with different structures in solid colours. The research team plans to develop the fault detection system for fabrics with complicated patterns, such as stripes and checked patterns (The Hong-Kong Polytechnic University, 2022).

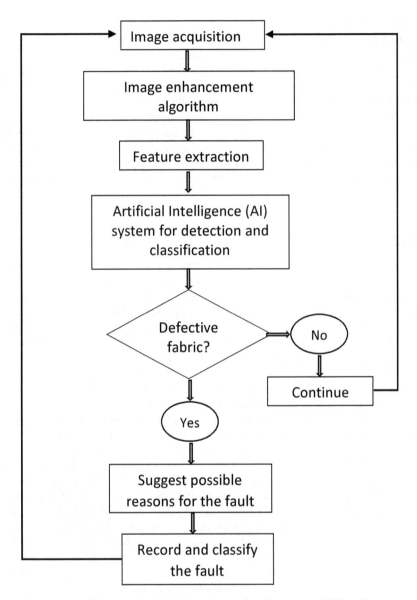

Fig. 20.1.  Schematic Representation of a Computer Vision System Combined With Artificial Neural Network (ANN) for the Detection and Classification of Fabric Faults (Eldessouki, 2018).

In the field of fabric physical and mechanical property prediction, researchers have evaluated the tactile properties of fabrics using backpropagation (BP) neural networks and fuzzy neural network prediction methods to express fabric handle using total hand values. The fabric properties such as weight, thickness, elongation, strength, shear and surface roughness were assessed objectively and conventionally by the Kawabata Evaluation System for fabric (KES-FB) and subjectively by an expert panel. It was found that the AI system agrees better with the subjective test results than that of the KES-FB (Park et al., 2000).

Besides fabric handle, AI systems based on feed-forward BP ANN may be used to evaluate another subjective fabric property such as comfort. The system uses inputs such as weave, thread density, yarn count, area density and thickness to predict the thermal property of fabrics. The technology helps to predict the thermal insulation property of woven textile fabrics based on the input parameters before they are manufactured (Kothari & Bhattacharjee, 2011).

## 20.3 AI in the Colouration and Finishing Industry

Another area where AI is being used in the textile industry is in colour management of dyed and printed textiles. In the textile colouration business, matching the right colour has always been very challenging given the number of variables involved in the colouration of textile materials. Before the advent of computers and automation, formulating a dye recipe to match a specific colour would be based on human experience. Thus, the process of generating a dye recipe would usually need a few colour trials in order to get close to the right or reference colour. Dye mixtures were prepared, applied to textile substrates and the dyed materials were inspected for closeness of colour match and dyeing faults or irregularities. These human operations often lead to colour matching problems which influence production output. Gradually, soft computing has replaced human-driven procedures and became known as computer colour matching or colourant formulation. The theory of computer colour matching or colour match prediction is largely based on tristimulus values which are related to reflectance and which, in turn, are related to concentration of the dyes via the Kubelka-Munk equation. The colourants are characterised by their absorption and scattering coefficients, K and S, respectively. By varying the concentration of the dyes, it is possible to influence the spectral reflectance, as measured by a reflectance spectrophotometer, and hence the tristimulus (XYZ) values of the dyed substrate. The K-M model is extensively used because of its simplicity and ease of determining K and S coefficients for both dyes and pigments and they are used to predict the dye or pigment recipes for colour matching (Mc Donald, 1997).

Fig. 20.2 is a flow chart showing the basis of most traditional computer colour match-prediction systems. The approaches to recipe formulation depended on equations which are approximations of the relationship between reflected light of the textile substrate and colourant concentration. Besides, the relationship between dyes, dyeing parameters, substrate and reflectance is very complex and it is very unlikely to have accurate analytical solutions using approximated mathematical equations. This often resulted in inaccuracies in recipe formulation. Several other approaches based on K-M theory have been developed for colour

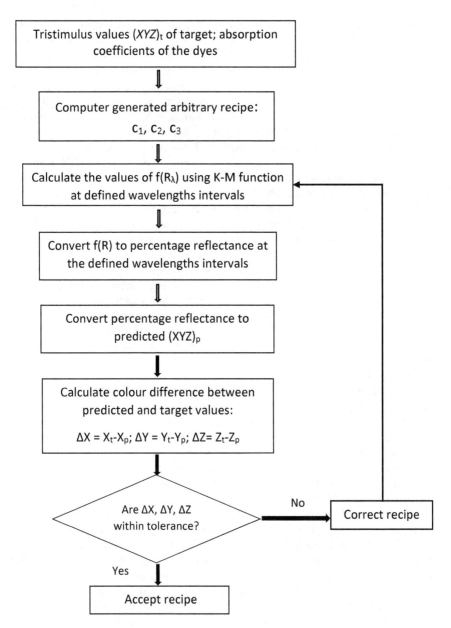

Fig. 20.2.    Flow Chart Showing the Basis of Most Traditional
Computer Colour Match-Prediction Systems.

recipe prediction but with little success. Other AI methods such as neural network, genetic algorithm and colony algorithm have also been reported. Westland et al. (2002) showed that ANNs can learn to map colourant concentrations and spectral reflectance in theory quite well although they struggle to beat the K-M model in reality. However, a hybrid model, based on ANN and K-M models, may out-perform the K-M model. With improved versions of AI, reliable and accurate dye formulations, colour matching and fault detection are possible without human involvement (Westland et al., 2002).

Colour management companies such as Datacolor and X-Rite use machine learning (ML) algorithms to formulate dye recipes. Smartmatch is a ML software from Datacolor, that stores and uses past experiences to produce a colour match with lower colour difference values in fewer attempts, between reference and batch colours, than would have been possible without the software. The software searches through the database to find similar colours on the same material, and then gives a prediction based upon how the dyes would interact. This helps to minimise colour correction steps and makes the process of colour recipe formulation more efficient, less wasteful, more environmentally friendly and less costly (Pelc, 2022).

Currently used ML models are not very effective in instances when the dyeing problem is very complex. One such instance is the dyeing of textile substrates with natural dyes. The latter are gaining increasing attention mainly due to the environmental and health problems which may be associated with the application of synthetic dyes. Shade reproducibility is still a challenge when applying natural dyes onto textile substrates. More recently, ANN and fuzzy logic models were used to predict the colour strength (K/S values) of naturally dyed polyester fabric. Genetic algorithm (GA) was implemented to optimise the models' accuracy. It was observed that AI models can predict K/S and other colourimetric values, such as L\*, a\* and b\*, with mean percentage error values significantly less than those obtained with conventional colour prediction models (Haji & Vadood, 2021). It was also possible, using the AI model, to select colourimetric values randomly to determine the corresponding dyeing parameters. A comparison between the actual and obtained dyeing parameters showed the high accuracy of the model (Vadood & Haji, 2022).

The process of generating colour match recipes for coloured fibre blends, as in mélange yarn, is much more complex than for solid shades and therefore very difficult to automate with high accuracy and precision by conventional colour match prediction ML model. The colour of mélange yarn is mainly affected by the colour matching of the dyed fibres, their ratio and the spinning parameters of the yarn rather than by the dyeing process. Some colour matching tools developed specifically for mélange yarns by Datacolor or X-Rite cannot be used to calculate the recipe for the coloured yarn directly. Thus, colour matching work still relies on experienced colourists. Some researchers developed a spectrophotometric colour matching algorithm based on the BP neural network. The recipe prediction results showed that the colour difference values between the reference and its corresponding batch samples were well within the acceptable limit of 1.0 unit, based on CMC (2:1) colour difference equation, for trained samples. The result was better than those obtained using modified Kubelka–Munk model such as the Stearns–

Noechel and the Friele model for colour match prediction of mélange yarn, with an average colour difference of 1.50 and 2.32 CMC (2:1) units respectively. The greater the value of CMC (2:1) unit, the larger is the colour difference between reference and batch samples. This indicates the capability and practicality of accurate prediction of colour matching for mélange yarn by this method (Shen & Zhou, 2017).

Another attempt by researchers to develop a colour match prediction system based on a model other than the K-M colour model was made by Almodarresi et al. (2019). A neural network-based scanner was developed for colour matching of dyed cotton. More accurate colour formulation prediction was obtained using the neural network and scanner as compared with the combination of neural network and spectrophotometric matching using K-M colour model. Almost 80% of the testing data had a colour difference value of less than 1.5 units as measured using CMC (2:1) colour difference equation (Almodarresi et al., 2019). Chen et al. (2021) proposed an automatic colour matching prediction model, CMR-colour, by incorporating three neural network models including a Convolutional Neural Network (CNN), which is a deep learning algorithm, and two ANN models. They were used to improve the capability of extracting high-dimensional features from spectral reflectance data of dyed textile substrates. It selects the dyes required and respective concentration values of each component in the recipe. The results showed that the CMR-colour model achieved very good performance and this supports its potential and confirm its effectiveness in colour matching prediction for dyeing and printing of textile materials (Chen et al., 2021).

Another problem with conventional tri-stimulus or colorimetric matching system is that there is spectral information loss in the process of spectral reflectance data conversion to tri-stimulus values. The system deals with the overall matching appearance of a colour and not matching individual wavelength. It is understood that when two samples match, their tristimulus values are identical. Tri-stimulus or colorimetric matching model is useful when the colourants available for making the match are not similar to those of the target or reference. However, this may produce metameric matching. The less common but more precise algorithm for dyeing recipe prediction is based on spectrophotometric curve matching. It consists of measuring the reflectance spectra of reference and batch samples then adjusting the reflectance spectrum of the batch sample to match that of the reference sample within allowable error tolerance. The spectrophotometric matching is a viable alternative when the same or quite similar colourants are used on the same substrate. Another limitation of both the tri-stimulus and spectrophotometric curve matching system is that the spectral information of a textile sample obtained by colour measurement instrument such as Datacolor 650 is within a certain band and averaged in a limited region of the sample. If a sample is slightly unevenly dyed, the spectra acquired by the instrument may be limited, and the predicted dyeing recipe will be inaccurate (Zhang et al., 2021).

In recent years, with the development of digital imaging technology, spectral imaging technology such as hyperspectral imaging system (HIS) has been used as an alternative technique for colour measuring and matching. The system combines both spectral and imaging technology to inspect the surface characteristics of samples. It collects and processes colour information from across the spectrum and obtains data for each pixel in the image. However, the large amount of data collected by HIS is difficult to process to achieve good results in spectral matching when using conventional spectral matching algorithm. With the rapid development of deep learning technology, more effective data-processing techniques have been proposed. Zhang et al. (2021) used a deep learning model to predict dyeing recipes with slightly uneven dyeing, using the full spectra as model input. The deep learning model can deal effectively with the full spectral data and extract the correct spectral reflectance of an unevenly dyed fabric sample as it selects those pixels in a specific region whose reflectance is closest to the targeted colour. Compared with the results predicted by Datacolor software, the proposed model displays a better predictive performance, especially for slightly unevenly dyed fabrics or multi-colour measurements of printed fabrics (Zhang et al., 2021).

In printing as compared to dyeing, there are fewer investigations of the application of ANN for colour match predictions. Golob et al. (2008) created an ANN-based system to select ink combinations for printing. They successfully demonstrated the ability to use counter-propagation neural networks to predict ink combinations in textile printing.

In digital transfer textile printing (DTTP), a colour matching algorithm was developed to solve colour mismatch problems between the colour on the designer's display monitor and its corresponding colour when transferred onto the fabric. In digital transfer fabric printing, the colours of the design are first approved on the monitor of the designer, printed on transfer paper and then transferred to the fabric by the application of heat and pressure. However, a colour printed on the fabric usually looks different from how it appears on the designer's display monitor. This is because the same colour may appear differently depending on the characteristics of the display device, illumination, observer and fabric surface property. To match the colours between the display on the print monitor and printed fabric, standard red, blue, green (sRBG) and International Commission on Illumination (CIE) colour systems were used. The sRGB colour system is a neutral and versatile colour system that does not require colour transformation from device to device. The sRGB values of the printed fabric were extracted using a scanner and referred to as the actual or input values and those from the display monitor of the printer were considered as the target or output values. The study was carried out on 100% polyester fabric using disperse dyes. sRGB values of the scanned printed fabric and that of the monitor display were used to train ANN to establish the relationship between target and actual colours. Colour samples printed with corrected sRGB values showed a good correlation with the target colours and both correction methods were proven to be effective (Hwang et al., 2015).

In recent years, digital printing software has evolved with AI. Adobe AI-enhanced software allows for impressive creative expressions and accelerates tasks performance and efficiency. AI brings new perspectives to and has great impact on the digital printing and creative industries (Angerer, 2022).

## 20.4 Conclusion

The textile industry is technologically dynamic owing to its competitive nature. In this information technology (IT) age, it is interesting to see many researchers investigating the applications of AI in the textile supply chain, although, it appears that real AI applications in the textile industry are still at an early stage. Interest is growing fast since it is believed that AI could solve problems such as those associated with human interventions, the variability of textile material as input, the complex interplay of process parameters on quality of product output, machine and human productivity, capability and efficiency.

There are emerging areas where AI is finding new applications, besides the manufacturing sector, such as the fashion and retail sector. This will further help the textile industry to speed up and enhance product development through machine-assisted design, lower costs, improve marketing of textile products, manufacture smart textile products of high quality and value, identify and target potential customers and their preferences, promote products and increase sales. It is clear that the potential of AI in the textile industry is enormous and that it has the capacity to revolutionise the way textile products are designed, marketed, manufactured, delivered and sold.

## References

Almodarresi, E. S. Y., Mokhtari, J., Almodarresi, S. M. T., Nouri, M., & Nateri, A. S. (2019). A scanner based neural network technique for color matching of dyed cotton with reactive dye. *Fibers and Polymers, 14*(7), 1196–1202.

Angerer, S. (2022). Artificial intelligence in digital printing. https://www.fespa.com/en/news-media/features/artificial-intelligence-in-digital-printing. Accessed on October, 2022.

Bahlmann, C., Heidemann, G., & Ritter, H. (1999). Artificial neural networks for automated quality control of textile seams. *Pattern Recognition, 32*(6), 1049–1060.

Bharadwaj, R. (2019). Artificial intelligence in the textile industry – Current and future applications. https://emerj.com/ai-sector-overviews/artificial-intelligence-in-the-textile-industry-current-and-future-applications/. Accessed on November, 2022.

Chen, M., Tsang, H. S., Tsang, K. T., & Hao, T. (2021). A hybrid model CMR-color of automatic color matching prediction for textiles dyeing and printing. In *Neural Computing for Advanced Applications. NCAA 2021. Communications in Computer and Information Artificial Intelligence Science* (Vol. 1449). Springer.

Das, P. P., & Chakraborty, S. (2021). Adaptive neuro-fuzzy inference system-based modelling of cotton yarn properties. *Journal of Industrial Engineering India Series E.* https://doi.org/10.1007/s40034-021-00217-1

Eldessouki, M. (2018). Computer vision and its application in detecting fabric defects. In *Applications of computer vison in fashion and textiles.* The Textile Institute Book Series (pp. 61–101). Woodhead Publishing.

El-Geiheini, A., El-Kateb, S., & Abd-Elhamied, M. R. (2020). Yarn tensile properties modeling using artificial intelligence. *Alexandria Engineering Journal, 59*, 4435–4440.

Golob, D., Osterman, D. P., & Zupan, J. (2008). Determination of pigment combinations for textile printing using artificial neural network. *Fibres and Textiles in Eastern Europe, 16*(3), 68.

Haji, A., & Vadood, M. (2021). Environmentally benign dyeing of polyester fabric with madder: Modelling by artificial neural network and fuzzy logic optimized by genetic algorithm. *Fibers and Polymers, 22*(12), 3351–3357.

Hwang, J. P., Kim, S., & Park, C. K. (2015). Development of a color matching algorithm for digital transfer textile printing using an artificial neural network and multiple regression. *Textile Research Journal, 85*(10), 1076–1082.

IndexBox. (2022).World textile industry-trends, technology, and forecast. https://www.indexbox.io/blog/World-Textile-Industry-Trends-Technology-and-Forecast/. Accessed on May, 2022.

Indian Textile Magazine. (2019). https://www.indiantextilemagazine.in/artificial-intelligence-ai-creating-the-digital-yarn-factory/. Accessed on December, 2022.

Kothari, V. K., & Bhattacharjee, D. (2011). Artificial neural network modelling for prediction of thermal transmission properties of woven fabrics. In *Soft computing in textile engineering* (pp. 403–423). Woodhead Publishing Limited.

Kumah, C., Raji, R. K., & Pan, R. (2020). Review of printed fabric pattern segmentation analysis and application. *Autex Research Journal, 20*, 530–538.

Kumar, A. (2003). Neural network based detection of local textile defects. *Pattern Recognition, 36*, 1645–1659.

Kuo, C. F. J., & Lee, C. J. (2003). A back-propagation neural network for recognizing fabric defects. *Textile Research Journal, 73*(2), 147–151.

Mc Donald, R. (1997). Recipe prediction for textiles. In R. Mc Donald (Ed.), *Colour physics for industry* (2nd ed., pp. 209–291). Society of Dyers and Colourists.

Park, S.-W., Hwang, Y.-G., Kang, B.-C., & Yeo, S.-W. (2000). Applying fuzzy logic and neural networks to total hand evaluation of knitted fabrics. *Textile Research Journal, 70*(8), 675–681.

Partida, D. (2022). How artificial intelligence applies to apparel manufacturing. *AI & Machine Learning.* https://technologymagazine.com/ai-and-machine-learning/how-artificial-intelligence-applies-to-apparel-manufacturing. Accessed on December, 2022.

Pelc, C. (2022). The impact of AI on the textile industry. *AATCC Newsletter.* https://www.aatcc.org/news2022-03a/. Accessed on December, 2022.

Pereira, F., Macedo, A., Pinto, L., Soares, F., Vasconcelos, R., Machado, J., & Carvalho, V. (2023). Intelligent computer vision system for analysis and characterization of yarn quality. *MDPI Open Access Journals, 12*(1), 236.

Sahu, M. (2021). AI in the textile industry – Applications and impact: Cognex – Fabric pattern inspection. https://www.analyticssteps.com/blogs/ai-textile-industry-applications-and-impact. Accessed on November, 2022.

Shamey, R., & Hussain, T. (2003). Artificial intelligence in the colour and textile industry. *Review of Progress in Coloration, 33*, 33–45.

Shen, J., & Zhou, X. (2017). Spectrophotometric colour matching algorithm for top-dyed melange yarn based on an artificial neural network. *Coloration Technology, Society of Dyers and Colourists, 133*, 341–346.

Sikka, M. P., Sarkar, A., & Garg, S. (2022). Artificial intelligence (AI) in textile industry operational modernization. *Research Journal of Textile and Apparel.* https://www.emerald.com/insight/1560-6074.htm

Solomon. (2023). Vision with intelligence. Automated visual inspection of yarn. https://www.solomon-3d.com/automated-visual-inspection-of-yarn/. Accessed on January, 2023.

Tehran, M. A., & Maleki, M. (2011). Artificial neural network prosperities in textile applications. In K. Suzuki (Ed.), *Artificial neural networks.* https://www. intechopen.com/chapters/1472. Accessed on November, 2022.

The Hong-Kong Polytechnic University. (2022). PolyU milestones. Technology and innovation. https://www.polyu.edu.hk/cpa/milestones/en/201903/technology_ innovation/technology/ai_powered_wiseeye_automates_fabric_fault_detectio/ index.html. Accessed on December, 2022.

Vadood, M., & Haji, A. (2022). A hybrid artificial intelligence model to predict the color coordinates of polyester fabric dyed with madder natural dye. *Expert Systems with Applications: An International Journal, 193*(C), 116514.

Welamo, T., & Sanpeng, D. (2021). Application of artificial intelligence in textile industry. *Journal of Emerging Technologies and Innovative Research, 8*(10).

Westland, S., Lovine, L., & Bishop, J. M. (2002). Kubelka-munk or neural networks for computer colorant formulation. In *Congress of the International Color Association, Proceedings of SPIE* (Vol. 4421, pp. 745–748). https://doi.org/10.1117/12. 464656

Wikipedia. (2023). https://en.wikipedia.org/wiki/Textile_industry. Accessed on January, 2023.

Wong, W. K. (2019). 2nd Artificial intelligence on fashion and textile international conference 2019. *AATCC Journal of Research, 8*(Special Issue 1).

Zhang, J., Zhang, X., Wu, J., & Xiao, C. (2021). Dyeing recipe prediction of cotton fabric based on hyperspectral colour measurement and an improved recurrent neural network. *Coloration Technology, 137*(2), 166–180.

# Index

Printed in the USA
CPSIA information can be obtained
at www.ICGtesting.com
JSHW011436030624
64243JS00004B/148

9 781837 535415